643.7   Decker, Phillip J.
D   Renovating brick houses : for yourself or
         for investment / Phillip J. Decker, T. Newell
         Decker. -- Pownal, Vt. : Storey
         Communications, c1990.

            247 p. : ill.

            "A Garden Way Publishing book."
            ISBN 0-88266-592-8(pbk.) : 16.95

15253

            1. Brick houses--Maintenance and repair.
         2. Architecture, Victorian.   I. Decker, T.
         Newell.   II. Title.

14

RENOVATING
BRICK HOUSES

RENOVATING BRICK HOUSES

For Yourself or for Investment

Phillip J. Decker

&

T. Newell Decker

A Garden Way Publishing Book

STOREY COMMUNICATIONS, INC.
Pownal, Vermont 05261

*The authors and publisher gratefully acknowledge Peter Acsay for contributing the
section of cornices in Chapter 12 of this book.*

Cover design by Wanda Harper
Text design by Mallory Lake
Cover Photographs by Nicholas Whitman
Illustrations by Brigita Fuhrmann
Edited by Benjamin Watson

Text composition by Accura Type & Design, Barre, Vermont

Printed in the United States by Courier
First Printing, August 1990

Library of Congress Cataloging-in Publication Data

Decker, Phillip J.
    Renovating brick houses : for yourself or for investment / Phillip
J. Decker, T. Newell Decker.
        p.   cm.
    "A Garden Way Publishing book."
    Includes index.
    ISBN 0-88266-593-6 — ISBN 0-88266-592-8 (pbk.)
    1. Brick houses — Maintenance and repair.   2. Architecture.
Victorian.   I. Decker, T. Newell.   II. Title.
TH4818.B7D43   1990
    643'.7 — dc20
                                                            89-46019
                                                            CIP

For our father,
who gave us many skills.

CONTENTS

Preface

The house renovation movement has grown enormously in the past decade. The 1980s saw many developers who never thought of doing rehabs doing just that, because their customers wanted solid old structures and because people wanted to live in the city. The Tax Reform Act of 1986 slowed rehabilitation of older buildings somewhat, but it has made rehabilitation an individual adventure for the home owner or small developer.

We expect rehabbing to continue in the nineties at the current pace. What may be different is the individuality of the effort. Individual home owners, carpenters, and developers will rehab buildings — many without extensive experience or the skills required for the undertaking. This is why we wrote this book. We intend it to be a resource for those who are undertaking a first or second rehab.

As long as Victorian buildings can be purchased for a fraction of their rehabilitated cost, people will tackle rehabbing. To find two-by-fours that are really 2 inches by 4 inches and a house with oak floors, high ceilings, and real marble is many a home owner's dream. Banks and other lending institutions are now eager to loan for rehabilitation and home improvement, often in creative ways. The drawback is that few people know how to rehab properly. Rehabbing is not new construction, especially rehabbing that requires a fair amount of restoration. This book is full of information about planning, obtaining the necessary permits, evaluating what you have in order to decide whether to replace or renovate, how-to hints, and information about buying materials and working with subcontractors. We hope that it will prove indispensable, whether you act as general contractor, carpenter, or do-it-yourselfer.

Rehabbing is not for everyone. It takes a lot of time — in most cases years — to rehab a house by yourself. It is hard and sometimes frustrating work. It never proceeds as quickly or smoothly as you originally thought it would. If you live in the house while you work, it is immeasurably worse. But finished rehabs are very valuable, and few things can compare to the satisfaction you derive from completing a magnificent rehab by yourself (and maybe with a few subcontractors).

This book is not about restoration, though we discuss restoration processes throughout. The philosophy of the book is rehabilitation — to return the house to a habitable condition. This may require restoration, remodeling, a complete gutting of the building, or any combination of those processes. We are not averse to "gut rehabbing" — removing most of the interior of the structure and building a new house within the brick shell. We believe that each building requires complete analysis to determine the rehabilitation process, and if restoration is indicated, it should be done. But you cannot spend more on a building than it will be worth when it is done. That is our guiding principle.

Neither of us has vested interest in pushing the reader in a particular direction. Whether you want to do it yourself or hire a general contractor, our advice is the same. Whether you are an advocate of restoration or gut rehabbing, this book should be useful.

This book would not have been possible without the help of several individuals. The authors wish to acknowledge Mike Curren and David Kruel, both developers; John Kohlhoff, carpenter; Ben Kurdi, Crown Manufacturing; Al Brown, Southwest Lumber; Mr. Fellenz of Fellenz Antiques, who has forgotten more about Victorian trim and hardware than most of us will ever know; Gene Beaver, Beaver Plumbing, who along with our father taught us plumbing; Lyn Minnis and Tom Scatizzi, Central West End Savings and Loan; Bob Gorsuch, Kitchen Wholesaler; Joan and Gary Burger; Suzanne Goodman, Washington University Medical Center Redevelopment Corporation; and *all* of St. Louis, who knowingly and unknowingly taught us many aspects of this business. Phil also depended greatly on his secretaries, Michelle Wethington and Teresa Speth. Newell wishes to thank his family for their profound patience. We are both indebted to our friend and master cornice builder Peter Acsay for contributing the section on cornices and reviewing the entire text.

Chapter 1

AN INTRODUCTION TO RENOVATING

There are a number of reasons why a person would want to buy a brick house and renovate it. Probably the greatest is need, which usually stems from a desire to fix something, to take something old and unusable and transform it into something usable. But need also comes from lack of money. If the only way you can buy a house in a district in which you wish to live is to buy the worst property on the street and fix it up, that is need. We believe that most people get into rehabbing and restoration because of the satisfaction it gives them. A lot of satisfaction comes from turning an ugly duckling into a beautiful swan or helping a city grow and rejuvenate. We have also found that many professional people have a need to do things that provide immediate feedback. Carpentry and rehabbing do that.

Regardless of the reason you wish to rehab a brick building, we welcome you to the adventure. We will outline the process and guide you through it. We will explain how to get started, how to find materials, and how to get people to help. We will give you hints and some secrets of rehabbing, especially the rehabilitation of brick buildings. We will concentrate, to a large extent, on Victorian structures. Probably 50 percent of the available rehabable buildings in this country, particularly in large cities, are from the Victorian era.

TERMINOLOGY

Before we start this adventure, we need to get some terminology straight. First, *renovation* is the process of taking a structure that is uninhabitable and turning it into something that is habitable or useful for some other purpose, such as a commercial office building. You may totally gut the building, restore what is existing, or use some combination of the two. The term *rehabilitation* is often used synonymously with renovation. We will use it as well, because the term *rehabbing* is so common in this business.

Restoration is the process of returning something to its original condition. Sometimes you will see the term *historical restoration*, which means returning something to its original condition with particular attention to the details of its first construction. Any structure that was built in 1880 has probably been remodeled or rehabbed two or three times. Restoration may simply be the process of returning it to its last remodeling or rehabilitation. Historical restoration is restoring that building to its condition as built in 1880.

Let's stop here and look at an example. Phillip bought a small, working class house that was built in 1897. It had been remodeled in the 1920s, at which time bathrooms were installed, steam heat was added, and the kitchen was renovated. The house was destroyed in a 1927 tornado and rebuilt. In the 1940s, it was turned into two apartments, one up and one down. Restoration would return it to its state in 1942, but historical restoration would return it to an 1890s single-family residence. After evaluating the property, we decided that it wasn't worth restoring. The apartment units were not large enough to generate the income needed to pay for restoration. It also wasn't worth historical restoration. Therefore, we gutted it, retaining only the exterior walls.

The point of this example is that you must look at a structure and decide whether to rehab it or restore it. Let the house "talk" to you. It will reveal its charm and restorable qualities if you study it. Your decision may involve a complex cost-benefit analysis that relies on many factors that are difficult to quantify.

We reserve the term *remodeling* to mean patching something up or making other cosmetic changes such as rehabbing one room at a time. If you buy a house in which everything is fine except the kitchen, which needs to be updated, and you decide to replace the cabinets and floor, we would call the resulting activity remodeling. This book is not really about remodeling; it is about rehabilitation, which is guided by the state of your building and the amount of money available. It might include restoration, rehabbing, or remodeling, and it might require gutting the building to start.

Gutting means to remove most of the internal parts of a brick house. A total gut is the removal of all trim, stairs, plaster, and lath; the electrical, plumbing, and mechanical systems; and the windows and nonbearing walls. You end up with the exterior brick walls, interior bearing walls (which may be altered), possibly the windows, and the floors. Partial guts include saving windows, nonbearing walls, stairs, and so on. In some cases, you may wish to restore the first floor of a house (though usually not the kitchen) and gut the remainder. Gut rehabbing is often easier than restoration. It is easier to install new material than deal with old, but the end result is a modern house. Gutting also may require more money.

WHY BUY A BRICK HOUSE?

This question is easy to answer. The majority of buildings available for rehab in your geographic location are probably brick, though that depends upon where you live. If you live in the plains states, San Francisco, or much of the Northeast, wood frame buildings may predominate. But if you live in the Midwest or in any large city, it is more likely that the Victorian-era buildings are brick. The

reason is that many of the major cities had devastating fires in the late 1800s and passed legislation banning everything but brick buildings. Cities such as Chicago, St. Louis, Denver, New York, Cincinnati, and Louisville have many rehabable brick buildings. Since most rehabbing books have been written for the wood structures of New England, this book is written for people who face the formidable task of rehabbing a brick structure.

Regardless of what is available, brick buildings are beautiful and solid. Most people are convinced that they need to buy a brick building because of how it looks on the outside, not because of how it looks on the inside. Those brick walls will last a long time if they are maintained properly. They also provide an extremely sound structure. If a Victorian brick building is standing today and it has no structural faults, it probably will stand for another hundred years if it is maintained properly. Brick buildings are beautiful, sound, readily available in cities, and sometimes inexpensive.

Do not ignore the possibility of finding an old brick warehouse and building a beautiful loft apartment in it. You get all the advantages of open space in an inexpensive structure. A warehouse often can be converted into a beautiful house with big windows and lofty ceilings.

THE PHILOSOPHIES OF THIS BOOK

This book is written with three basic philosophies in mind: (1) you can do all the work yourself if you wish; (2) you need imagination to rehab; and (3) you need to investigate every step before you attempt it. The following sections discuss these issues in more detail.

DOING IT YOURSELF VERSUS BEING THE GENERAL CONTRACTOR

In deciding whether you will do all the work yourself or simply act as a general contractor, you must address four issues: (1) whether you have the time to do the work or are allowed by law to do it; (2) whether you have the skill to do it; (3) whether you have the desire to do all the work; and (4) whether you can afford to hire subcontractors. If you do not have the time or skills to do this project yourself, you will have to hire other people for some aspects of it. Even if you plan to do it all yourself, you probably will end up contracting out things such as heating and air-conditioning because there is simply no need to do them yourself. You can usually get a furnace and an air conditioner installed for very close to their retail purchase price because the heating ventilation and air-conditioning (HVAC) people get better wholesale prices than you can. It is also likely that you will choose to have your plumbing done for you. Gluing plastic pipe is not very difficult (though soldering may be), but it is time-consuming to do plumbing, and you have to understand the complex plumbing codes. Furthermore, plumbing inspectors are much harder on home owners than on plumbing contractors. In some cities, you are required to hire a licensed plumber or plumbing contractor and/or electrician. If you are working on a multiunit building, you will have to hire licensed professionals to do the plumbing and electrical work. Other areas such as finishing drywall and painting also may be better hired out to a subcontractor.

Very few people will do every single bit of the work themselves. It takes a long time to do a rehab when you have to do it all yourself, and you encounter a great deal of frustration. Our advice is to get some contractors to do part of the work. The real question may be whether you have the money to hire subcontractors.

Another thing to keep in mind is that you may start out planning to do it all yourself, then mess up and have to hire a subcontractor to fix your mistakes. This will cost a little more, because the contractor has to correct what you did and then do it the right way. Don't be afraid to do this, however. It's okay to try something and then, if it doesn't work out, hire a subcontractor. You have lost only a few materials. It costs a little more money, but the cost is offset by the experience you gain and the money you save when you do succeed in doing

something yourself.

Regardless of how you start out, you will end up being a general contractor to some extent. We highly recommend Carl Heldmann's book *Manage Your Own Home Renovation* (Garden Way Publishing, 1987) about being a general contractor. Chapter 9 of this book also deals with subcontractors. It is important to understand that the decision to subcontract does not have to be made at the outset.

Using Your Imagination

Imagination is an important element in rehabbing. You must be able to visualize the finished product before you get started. Practice using your imagination. Picture tearing out walls and rearranging a house in several different ways. Most importantly, when you walk into a building, do two things. First, figure out where the bearing walls are and visualize the building totally gutted except for those walls. That is the available space for rehabbing. The difference between a bearing wall, a partially bearing wall, and a nonbearing wall is discussed in chapters 13 and 15. Second, go to the basement and look at the pipes, wiring, and furnace. Imagine what you will have to replace and what you can live with. See the finished product, as well as what you have to do to create that product.

Imagination is even more important in building condos or apartments. You must be able to see different living spaces in a building. For instance, without using your imagination, you would probably buy a duplex (either up and down or side by side) and put two living spaces in it. But we have bought duplexes and put in three spaces: a condo down, a condo up, and a condo across the back, up and down. You will not always want an architect to determine these kinds of things for you, and you will not get one to do it on the spot while you are inspecting a building. So, you must rely on your own imagination.

Using Your Research Skills

Besides the willingness to try any rehab task and the ability to imagine different outcomes and possibilities in a building, you need to be willing to do research. Note that we said "willing to" not "able to." Research takes time, energy, and persistence. It does not necessarily take skill. You simply need the motivation to find the best price, the highest quality material, or the most knowledgeable contractor or supplier. Investigation is critical to getting the best price and finding the information you need.

KEY PEOPLE IN REHABBING

You must deal with some key people in any rehab project. It is likely that an architect will be involved at some point. An architect is not always necessary, depending on how much a building is changed structurally. An inspection engineer is necessary, however. Few people are trained to look at a building and find the hidden faults, but an inspection engineer is trained to do just that. Although architects and developers do inspections, we recommend hiring an engineer. It is more important to look for structural faults than for wiring or plumbing problems, especially if the building is going to be gutted anyway.

Several craftspeople also may be required. The first will probably be a carpenter. In fact, you may need two carpenters, a framing and a finish carpenter. (We highly recommend splitting these areas of responsibility, because a good framing carpenter does not usually make a good finish carpenter.) You may also need someone to do your heating and air-conditioning, a plumber, an electrician, someone to do drywall (both put it up and finish it), a carpet layer, and a painter. You may need a mason, either to fix masonry problems or to retuck-point the building. How many of these people you become involved with depends on how much of this project you do yourself and how much you subcontract. Regardless of whether you do the job yourself or subcontract it out, you will probably want to talk to these craftspeople to find out some of the tricks of the trade and how to buy materials.

References

OLD

Cyclopedia of Architecture, Carpentry and Building: A General Reference Work. Chicago: American Technological Society, 1909.

Ellery, Nathaniel. *Permanency in Building Construction: 61 Reasons Why the Owner Should Demand Brick and Steel.* San Francisco: Brick Building Bureau, 1913.

NEW

Basic Carpentry Illustrated. Menlo Park, California: Lane Publishing Company, 1984.

Bracken, John. *Restoring the Victorian House and Other Turn-of-the-Century Structures.* San Francisco: Chronicle Books, 1981.

Brooks, Hugh. *Illustrated Encyclopedia of Building and Construction Terms.* Englewood Cliffs, New Jersey: Prentice-Hall, 1976.

Bruns, R.M. *How to Buy and Fix up an Old House: A Guide to House Renovation.* Bethesda, Maryland: Home-Tech Publications, 1976.

Camesasca, Ettore. *History of the House.* New York: Putnam, 1971.

Jackson, Frank W. *Practical Housebuilding for Practically Everyone.* New York: McGraw-Hill, 1985.

Jones, Jack Payne. *Handbook of Construction Contracting.* Carlsbad, California: Craftsman Book Company, 1986.

McGuerty, Dave. *The Complete Guide to Contracting Your Home: A Step-by-Step Method for Managing Home Construction.* White Hall, Virginia: Betterway Publications, 1986.

Nash, George. *Old Houses: A Rebuilder's Manual.* Englewood Cliffs, New Jersey: Prentice-Hall, 1980.

The Old House Journal: A New Compendium. Garden City, New York: Dolphin Books/Doubleday & Company, 1983.

Chapter 2

FINDING THE RIGHT BUILDING

Before anyone invests in a rehab project, it makes sense to ensure that it is the right house. This is particularly true of a rehab where you do the work alone. In this chapter, we discuss different architectural styles and some of the history of building in the United States, and then we define what we think a rehabable structure is and how to find one. The architectural style and age of a building may be a factor in choosing a building.

ARCHITECTURAL STYLES

Keep in mind that this book is about rehabilitation of a house and is not limited to restoration. This is not meant to be a discussion of great architectural styles or great houses in the United States but simply a discussion of the different styles of houses you may encounter. We urge you to examine more specific sources if you wish to investigate a particular style.

Every house is likely to have unique features, but it will typically belong to an architectural style and have several structural or ornamental similarities with other houses in that style. Architectural styles reflect changing modes of living, social customs, economic conditions, technological improvements in construction, and to some extent geographical differences. Some of the differences within a style are subtle, and some are glaring, although houses designed in the same architectural style usually have similar proportions and overall shapes. The arrangement of windows, dormers, and chimneys usually conforms to a recognizable pattern. The type of roof, the construction materials, porches, embellishments, moldings, and other components provide further clues to the architectural style. Knowing the architectural style is essential before proceeding with any renovation work in a rehabable house. It may not be that important in a rehab where little or no restoration will occur, but to avoid misguided alterations that do not conform to the architectural style you must identify that style and use it as a guide.

Assigning specific dates to an architectural style is very difficult and, for the most part, arbitrary. A style usually evolves and falls out of favor gradually. Although the elements of the Greek Revival style originated as early as 1790, this style did not reach maturity until 1820, and by the 1840s and 1850s it was falling out of favor, particularly in the East. In other areas of the country, it evolved up until the Civil War, persisting in California until the 1870s. Through most of the eighteenth and nineteenth centuries, architectural styles moved from east to west. But by the late nineteenth century and early twentieth century, some architects and builders in the Midwest and West began creating unique styles or variations that traveled eastward.

Victorian houses are those built during the reign of Queen Victoria of Britain (1837-1901), though Victorian styles persisted until well after World War I. More homes of the Victorian era than of any other period have survived, and many different styles were popular.

Remember that homes built in the Victorian era fall into two categories: large homes built for the wealthy and working-class houses. The majority of Victorian homes and the majority of homes available for renovation, particularly in cities, are working-class dwellings: row houses, company houses, and the homes of bureaucrats, bankers, and shopkeepers. The Victorian period saw a staggering amount of home construction because the American population grew from 17 million to 50 million people, and 12 states were admitted to the union.

Georgian

The first style of brick house in America was the Georgian style, which went through two cycles: the early Georgian from 1700 to 1750, and the late Georgian from 1750 to 1780. Georgian houses were based on early English prototypes that were in turn influenced by sixteenth-century Italian architecture. These were classically correct houses

Early Georgian

Late Georgian

and were almost always located in urban areas. Late Georgian houses are more elaborate and imposing than early Georgian houses, and most Georgian houses appear in New England, Philadelphia, and Baltimore.

Federal

The Federal style began to appear in the late 1780s and persisted until approximately 1830. In some respects, the Federal style was the United States' first national style, although it was still influenced

Federal

by British architecture. The major differences between Georgian and Federal are in their proportion, scale, and ornamentation. The Federal house is usually rather plain. It is a rectangular cube topped by a low-pitched gable roof and has tall chimneys that are symmetrically arranged. Many Federal houses also have shutters.

Greek Revival

American architects, seeking a uniquely American style, began to build Greek Revival houses in the 1820s. They used the Greek temple as the basis for their architecture. These houses incorporate Grecian columns in their porches and porticoes. The first Greek Revival buildings were built in Philadelphia, but the style became very popular in Baltimore and the Mid-Atlantic states and extended to Pennsylvania and western New York. In the 1850s, people moving to the Midwest brought this style with them, and some of the most imposing Greek Revival houses are found in the South, where this style continued long after the Civil War. By 1860, however, the United States was ready for a change, and critics had begun to challenge the temple style of architecture for residences, arguing that it should be reserved only for public buildings.

Greek Revival

Gothic Revival

Gothic Revival was popular at the same time as Greek Revival, from about 1820 to 1860. Gothic Revival houses are very fanciful and flamboyant, with pointed arches, window tracery, casement windows with diamond panes, cloverleaf patterns, and Gothic crosses.

Gothic Revival

Italianate Mansion

Vernacular Italianate

Italianate

One of the more popular styles both before and after the Civil War was Italianate. Houses were built in this style between 1845 and 1880, and they tend to be very classical and reserved. Italianate houses were built out of a variety of materials, including brick, wood, stucco, stone, and brownstone.

Mansard or Second Empire

A predominant style during the Victorian era was the Mansard design. This is a very confident, imposing, and stately style that was popular

Mansard (or Second Empire)

between 1860 and 1880. It is also known as Second Empire or French Academic and was a revival of a French seventeenth-century style of architecture. In fact, it is named after a French architect of that period. The roof line is its distinguishing characteristic. The house has an entire story above its eaves and gutters. Mansard houses may or may not have extensive cornices at the eaves. In France, the style came about because houses were taxed by the number of stories they had. The attic area was exempt, so the Mansard style afforded a way of adding a story of living space tax free. Similarly, many Federal houses in the United States have a third story of half windows because, in this country, houses were taxed by the number of windows and half windows were not taxed.

Mansard houses are more expensive to rehab than other styles because they usually entail significantly more work to retain the unique architectural style and to repair the roof and cornices. Also, these houses often have stone fronts, which can be very expensive to repair. The Mansard style spread rapidly across the United States and was prevalent in most eastern and midwestern cities. Many Mansard houses are large mansions, but some are of moderate size. You also can find one-story cottages and town houses in the Mansard style.

Romanesque

The styles that predominated after the Civil War were Romanesque and Queen Anne. We are most familiar with the Romanesque style because of

the large number of these buildings in St. Louis. Romanesque houses are robust, and they tend to have round arch openings and large features. Most are moderate-sized, well-built, single-family houses or row houses, although in the Midwest

Romanesque

large mansions were built in this style, which appeared between 1875 and 1900. Romanesque homes were frequently built of stone, and in areas of the country where heavy stone was not available, Romanesque designs were used only for public buildings.

Queen Anne

The Queen Anne style appeared in the United States in 1876 and persisted until the turn of the cen-

Queen Anne

tury. This style originated in Britain and represents almost every known material, architectural characteristic, and embellishment. The name is misleading because it does not refer to the architectural features of houses built during the reign of Queen Anne (1702–1714) but to the workmanship of that era. Queen Anne houses tend to have steep gables, dormers, turrets, wings, lots of balconies, large porches, and many different styles of windows. Queen Anne houses appear everywhere in the United States and were very popular in the West.

Shingle

The Shingle style appeared in 1880. Shingle houses were big, homey, and rambling; they were unpretentious and had few embellishments. These houses can be found all over New England, and a variation called the First Bay Tradition was popular in San Francisco. This style flourished along the West Coast until the end of the nineteenth century. Houses in this style are most often wood framed, but many were built of stone, particularly the first story.

Craftsman and Bungalow

The early twentieth century saw revivals of the Georgian and Federal styles, as well as many hybrid styles. The most popular was the Craftsman house, usually constructed of wood. The Bungalow style was a mass-produced version of the Craftsman house with a low-pitched roof, broad gable porch, and wide overhanging eaves. It was usually only one and a half stories high.

Styles Considered in This Book

For the most part, the styles that we deal with in this book are the Georgian, Federal, Greek, Gothic, Italianate, Mansard, and Romanesque styles. Most Queen Anne, Shingle, and Craftsman houses were built of wood, not brick. For more information about architectural styles, we suggest that you consult Rusk's *Renovating the Victorian House* (101 Productions, 1982) and Hanson and Hubby's *Preserving and Maintaining the Older Home* (McGraw-Hill, 1983). A trip to your local library or to the library of a university with a school of architecture might be productive. You also might consider visiting your local American Institute of Architects office.

WHAT IS A REHABABLE STRUCTURE?

A structure that is a candidate for renovation is one that is not now suitable for habitation. Such structures are inexpensive, but they go fast in areas being renovated and often require substantial work. Since most buildings are suitable for habitation at some level, you must look for characteristics that make it uninhabitable for most potential buyers. For instance, you might find candidates for renovation in an area where older homes have been turned into rooming houses or apartments and the area is returning to single-family ownership and occupation. Or you might find such houses in an area of large Victorian homes that are not being kept up because it is too expensive to do so. Remember that the early pioneers get the bargains but also take the risks. Even old warehouses are capable of being turned into condos or loft apartments.

One of the things you must decide early is what kind of housing you want to end up with. Ask yourself, "Am I looking for a single-family residence of a certain Victorian style?" "Am I looking for a large house or a smaller building, such as a small working-class or row house?" "Do I want to live in a condo?" It is possible to rehab a larger building and turn it into two or three condos or to rent part of a large house that has one or more apartments. Some people also don't mind living in an ex-warehouse loft apartment or condo over a business space. The options are unlimited, and the choice you make depends on your and your architect's creativity in designing space and choosing the structure.

Old houses and buildings can be a deal. Even perfectly habitable older homes sell for 30 percent less than new homes. In fact, more people buy older homes than new ones. But not every old house is a bargain.

Many things can affect the price:
· Historical significance can add to the perceived value, even if the home is a wreck. The significance can be architectural or as a result of past events that took place in or around the house.

- The neighborhood can carry a premium. Historic, safe, and stable neighborhoods add to the price of a home.
- Location can push the price up or down. Nearness to highways and commercial areas, for instance, or location in a particular school district or town can have positive or negative values. Many old houses are not considered historic and will not command premium prices.

Look for these features in a bargain home:
- Part of it is livable. That cuts lodging costs.
- Its utilities are operable, making it possible to upgrade them gradually.
- You can make the home appealing without destroying the character that comes from Victorian housing's woodworking details and quality materials.
- The house will give you a chance to putter, without demanding a great deal of attention just to make it habitable.
- The exterior is beautiful, but the interior needs to be gutted.

Regardless of the situation, a rehabable structure has certain characteristics. First and foremost, it should be a sound building on the exterior. It costs one to two dollars per square foot to tuck-point a building. It is also extremely expensive to replace sandstone sills or other fancy work on the front of Victorian buildings. We suggest avoiding buildings of the Mansard architectural style if they are in poor condition because of the expense involved in replacing mansard roofs and cornices, even though we will tell you how to do it. A rule of thumb is to avoid a building in which you may have to invest $25,000 to $40,000 in the exterior before you can even start thinking about the interior. If the building needs no tuck-pointing in the near future, has a sound roof, and needs minimal work on the exterior, the expense of renovating the structure may be cut in half. This kind of rehab project is also the easiest to do.

A rehabable structure should always have a sound foundation that has no evidence of recent movement. In Chapter 4, you will see a heavy emphasis on examining the foundation, basement, and outside of the structure.

A rehabable structure should have a sound roof.

That is not to say that the shingles need to be in perfect condition (they can be replaced), but the roof itself and its support must be sound. The roof should not sag or contain any rotten framing timbers or boards, especially if it is a mansard roof. If it has a cornice, that should be in excellent condition. If an extensive cornice or dormer system is not in excellent shape, be very careful in your analysis of costs versus resale value. If the house has a flat roof, it will probably be replaced completely in the rehab. If the house has a composition shingle roof, age will determine replacement. If it is over ten years old, plan to replace it. Do not let replacement of tar or asphalt roofing material be a deterrent to purchase, as this will not be a large expense. If the house has a slate or tile roof, however, it should be sound because replacement will be expensive.

A structure worth restoring or rehabbing has level floors or floors that can be easily leveled. If you plan to keep the plaster, the floors cannot be moved too much. Furthermore, the bearing structure of the building should be sound or easily repairable. Shoring up bearing walls, jacking structures level, and replacing beams or joists are all heavy, difficult, and potentially dangerous jobs. Each is discussed in more detail in Chapter 13. Remember that the structural integrity of bearing walls and floors will greatly affect the cost of rehabbing a structure and the time needed to do it.

As far as rehab work is concerned, age probably does not matter. We would be more likely to buy a structure that is 75 to 90 years old than one that is 25 years old, although you can find restorable or rehabable structures anywhere from 20 to 200 years old.

The condition of the interior of the building dictates whether it is a candidate for restoration or rehab. We usually restore some of the building and rehab some of it. Sometimes the best buys are the ones that become gut rehabs.

Other things to look for are rotten material, termite damage, and water damage. None of these are determining factors in a rehab. It is not unusual to see damage from termites or rot because of leaking toilets, bathroom fixtures, or kitchen fixtures. What is important is the extent of this damage. Structural damage done in previous rehabs of the building also is common. When previous rehabbers put plumbing or steam heat in a building, they often cut through joists or caps of bearing walls to install the pipes. That kind of work probably resulted in some structural damage to the house, such as sagging floors or crushed posts under beams. Sometimes you can see joists cracked in the basement from the extra stress placed on them. Such damage will have to be fixed, and that can get expensive when you have to start jacking up or rejoisting floors. If you must change the living space radically, as in a gut rehab, such problems are easier to fix.

HOW TO FIND A BUILDING

Location is the major consideration in looking for a building. You can decide to go to an area that has been heavily rehabbed, such as a redevelopment district, an area that other individuals have already started working on without state or city incentives, or an area where the city is offering incentives to encourage rehabilitation. In these areas, your investment is relatively safe. However, you could put a lot of money into a building in an area that has not completely swung toward rehabilitation and not be able to resell it. If the prices of rehabable structures have been driven up significantly because of the amount of rehabbing that is going on in an area or because all the structures available are owned by one redevelopment corporation, you must be very careful about the cost-effectiveness of buying in the area. Is it worth doing the work yourself, or would it be better to buy one of the buildings that has already been redone? Investigation is the key.

Another issue of concern when you are looking into a district where a lot of rehabbing has been done is that some buildings might be only half done. Beware of this kind of situation when you inspect a building, as you might have to tear out the work that's been done and start over again. You cannot afford to pay for the previous owners' mistakes or their investment. In our experience, most partially rehabbed buildings cost more to renovate than those where you start from scratch.

In some hot rehab areas, the good deals often go to the developers or real estate agents, so an indi-

vidual might have trouble breaking into the district. Sometimes you have to move fast and cannot wait a month or two while you do your homework. At other times, you may be the only one who is willing to invest the time and money needed to rehab a building.

Where do you search for possible rehab projects? You can go to real estate agents, a historic district office, a redevelopment corporation office, or savings and loan organizations in neighborhoods that are being rehabbed. You also can find such places in the want ads or by knocking on doors.

Many real estate agents do not care about rehabilitation, but their commercial divisions may have a number of potential rehabs available. An agent may not know of structures that are suitable for rehabbing, but he or she should know rehab developers and the areas in which they are working. Be aware of two things when dealing with real estate agents: (1) They are paid a 6 to 8 percent commission for their efforts, which will increase the price you pay for a building, and (2) many agents buy and rehab buildings themselves. If you rely on real estate agents, we think that you will be the third (and last) person at the trough. You see the property only after the developer and agent examine it.

If you want to find a rehab in an area that is either a historic district or a redevelopment area, talk to the people in charge. Historic districts have many rules governing what you can and cannot do to the exterior of your building. Redevelopment corporations limit the number of apartments or condos you can put on a given street and limit or suggest what you can do to the outside of your building. In both cases, the historic district or redevelopment corporation will often help you buy a building if those in charge think you will do a good job of restoring or rehabbing it. They also will help you meet the requirements for tax abatement. Tax abatement is an obvious benefit of going into a redevelopment corporation area (see Chapter 7). The important point is that the redevelopment corporation or historic district office will know which buildings are available, even if they are not yet on the market. They may even tell you of buildings they are acquiring through eminent domain.

It is also likely that redevelopment corporation personnel can point out buildings that they would like to see rehabbed but whose owners are uncooperative. The owners might be willing to sell to you before the redevelopment corporation takes them to court in order to force them to comply with the corporation's regulations.

Also watch for signs on rehabs indicating which bank or savings and loan is providing the financing. These institutions may provide leads on houses, or they may have a building that they had to repossess and will be willing to sell to you. Ask to speak to the bank officer specializing in the area of town in which you are interested.

One of the best ways to look for property is to be a want ad watcher. Keep in mind, though, that everyone else is seeing the same ads. It may be advertised by a real estate agent and have been on the market for some time. But many people place ads in an effort to sell before going to a real estate agent.

Probably the best way to find property is to go to the area of town you're interested in and start knocking on doors. Look for properties that have not been rehabbed. Find the people who have gutted a building but never got started again or discovered that they could not afford it. Find the people who own property they simply do not want or who own apartment or rooming houses that have exhausted their tax depreciation. Ask the tenants who owns the building or check the tax records at the courthouse.

Our advice is not to follow only the conventional methods of locating a building. Everyone looks in the newspaper and goes to a real estate agent. Be willing to knock on doors and talk to people who know the area. That is how you find the good buildings before anyone else does.

Regardless of which method you choose, you must be willing to invest some time in the search. You also should plan your search around a schedule. If you plan to subcontract the work out, you should find a building in the summer for an October or November sale. Gutting, carpentry, and mechanical work can all be done in the dead of winter. Most developers and contractors are not as busy in the winter, so you can always find subcontractors who will work for less money at that time. If you plan to do it yourself, you should find a building sometime in October, November,

December, or January so that you can purchase it no later than March or April. You can spend most of the spring gutting the building and the summer doing structural and carpentry work. You will then be ready for your subcontractors in late fall and through the winter.

Here are some other issues to consider when looking at buildings:

· Look at the neighborhood. Find out about fire insurance rates, zoning, property taxes, and the basic security of the neighborhood. Ask yourself whether you want to live there and what your neighbors will be like. You probably will have to talk to prospective neighbors to determine some of these things.

· Look at the houses. See if the basements are barred or if they have glass blocks instead of windows. Are there bars on all the windows on the first floor and even on the second floor?

· Look in a newspaper, ask around, and see what the crime rate is in that area. If the neighborhood is a moderately high crime area, it may increase your expense by having to bar windows and install a burglar alarm.

Check the city's zoning ordinances, especially if you want to rehab a single-family dwelling into a multiunit building. You also may need to look at deed restrictions. A real estate broker, title insurance company, or attorney can determine deed restrictions. Zoning and deeds are discussed in Chapter 7.

Do not attempt to rehab without fire insurance. Some areas are considered worse fire risks than others, particularly in the inner city. Fire insurance rates should not differ so much that they will prevent you from doing a rehab if you really want to, but you might want to check to see if you can even get fire insurance while you are rehabbing the building. Insurance is discussed in Chapter 6.

Taxes may escalate dramatically in a neighborhood that is being improved through rehabbing. In a redevelopment corporation or historic area, however, you might be able to get a tax abatement for 10 to 25 years for rehabbing a building. This possibility is discussed in Chapter 7.

Look at a building several times before you buy. Look during the day and in the evening. What is parking like in the evening? What is traffic like during rush hours? Look at the building when school lets out and see how many children live in the neighborhood. Also look at the building during a rainstorm if possible. You can get a good feel for whether it has a wet basement or not.

Never buy the house for yourself; always buy it for the next owner. If you rehab a house when you are middle-aged, you will probably sell it. Always look for resale appeal—not only where the house is situated but also how it looks on the outside and how the inside will look when it's finished. This concept is magnified in the rehabilitation of condos.

INSPECTING THE PROPERTY

Have a structural engineer, particularly a foundation engineer, inspect the building. You should be able to learn enough about heating, plumbing, electrical systems, roofs, and the like to be able to inspect a building yourself and determine how much it will cost to rehab it. You do not need a building inspector to tell you these things. Instead, hire an engineer who can look at a building and tell you if there are any structural problems. The best way to find one is to ask developers, other rehabbers, or historic or rehab districts who inspects their houses for them. You can also look in the phone book under engineers, foundation engineers, building engineers, or inspection engineers.

The engineer will inspect a number of items and guarantee in writing the condition of each one. Some inspections can even be backed by an insurance policy. The $75 to $300 that you will pay an inspection engineer is a good investment. He or she will check the foundation for cracks, water prob-lems, heaving, and so on. He or she also will check the first-floor framing (sills, beams, plates, and joists) for rotting, insect damage, and settling; the exterior walls, roof, doors, and windows for rotting, cracking, or deterioration; and the well and/or septic tank if those are present. We guarantee that you won't regret hiring an engineer to check these things for you.

References

OLD

Munby, Alan Edward. *Introduction to the Chemistry and Physics of Building Materials.* London: A. Constable & Company, 1909.

Weiss, Howard Frederick. *The Preservation of Structural Timber.* New York: McGraw-Hill, 1915.

NEW

Camesasca, Ettore. *History of the House.* New York: Putnam, 1971.

Cantacuzino, Sherban. *New Uses for Old Buildings.* New York: Watson-Guptill Publications, 1975.

Fagg, Christopher. *How They Built Long Ago.* New York: Warwick Press, 1981.

Fairbridge, Kingsley C. *Loft Living: Recycling Warehouse Space for Residential Use.* New York: Saturday Review Press/E. P. Dutton, 1976.

Hanson, Shirley. *Preserving and Maintaining the Older Home.* New York: McGraw-Hill, 1983.

Sherwood, Gerald E. *How to Select and Renovate an Older House.* New York: Dover Publications, 1976.
_____. *New Life for Old Dwellings.* New York: Drake Publishers, 1977.

Chapter 3

ARE YOU A RENOVATOR?

In this chapter, we tell you the reasons *not* to take on a renovation project. We don't want to dissuade you from proceeding on your project but to give you some realistic expectations about the scope of the project and its effect on other aspects of your life. We want to help you determine whether you are a renovator, talk about attitudes toward renovation, and discuss health hazards in rehabbing.

HOW TO DETERMINE WHETHER YOU ARE A RENOVATOR

You are about to embark on a project that will take at least a year, and probably two to three years, especially if you can work only on weekends. Even if you work full-time and hire most of the work out, you will not be able to do a complete rehab on a large building in less than six months. No matter how well you plan, things will go wrong. You will start gutting the house, and the more you remove, the more you will find that needs to be removed. Plaster is a good example. When you start removing loose plaster, you will soon find yourself with an entire room *without* plaster. You will be frustrated as you learn how to do various tasks that are new to you. You will be frustrated when you cannot keep to your timetable. You will need patience and persistence.

Rehabbing takes a lot of money. You have to understand how to accumulate capital through financing for this kind of project. We will give you hints on raising money, but we cannot teach you how to handle money. If you are a poor bookkeeper, you should read a book on accounting.

Rehabbing is hard work. If you are overweight, have not exercised in several years, or have a bad heart, you probably shouldn't try to rehab yourself. This doesn't mean, however, that you can't be your own general contractor. Rehabbing also takes somebody who can work long hours. Many readers may plan to rehab at night and on weekends after a full day at work. If you are doing research now because you want to start a rehab in six months, start exercising now.

You may think that you need to have carpentry, plumbing, and electrical skills. We do not believe that you need these skills, but you do need some other basic skills that we will discuss as we proceed through the book. Most importantly, you have to be the type of person who is willing to try anything once. If you are willing to try, you will probably be able to figure it out. You will undoubtedly find some things that you may not want to do yourself. These are things that you *can* do but that will end up costing you more money and time to do yourself than by hiring a professional to do them for you. An example is finishing drywall. Sure, you can do it, but you will probably spend hours fixing your mess. You might think that you are doing a great job finishing the drywall yourself, but after you get it painted, you will see every little imperfection. If you hire a professional, he or she will finish it so that it will look perfect when it is painted.

Some basic skills that you will need are knowing how to hammer a nail, how to use a saw, and how to solder plumbing fittings. If you do not have these skills, you can probably learn them at the local community college or high school or by helping an experienced person do a project. Even just hanging around allows you to watch and learn.

One of the important traits needed in rehabbing is a sense of wonder about buildings. When you go into an old house, do you look at it and wonder about the craftsmen who built it, what is behind the walls, or what is in the attic? Do you feel the need to go into the basement and see how the building was put together? When you look at an old dilapidated structure, do you picture what it looked like when it was originally built? We believe that one of the primary skills in rehabbing is being curious about architecture.

A good rehabber also needs a profit motive. You have to look at rehabbing as you would look at any other business. You are there to do something efficiently and to make money; it's as simple as that.

We feel strongly that a rehabber has to have some research skills. You must want and be able to investigate things. This is extremely important when it comes to buying materials. Sometimes it is best to buy everything at one place, get a discount, have it delivered, and be done with it. But sometimes a little research can save you thousands of dollars. For instance, let's say you are renovating a large Victorian home and you have to replace most of the 40 to 50 existing windows. The difference between $400 windows at retail and $200 windows at wholesale is $8,000 to $10,000. That is where investigatory skills are important. You need to find out who makes those windows and how you can buy them wholesale. You cannot afford to buy retail, even with a 10 to 15 percent volume discount, when you can buy wholesale. We always approach these projects as scientists, and we continue to learn how to do it better and for less money.

Another thing that is important is not to try to reinvent the wheel. Everything that you are going to do in any rehab has been done by someone else. Why should you have to start from scratch? This book is part of your investigation, but it is only a start. Read the books listed in the references at the end of each chapter and write to manufacturers for more product information. Also, you should con-

sider subscribing to one or more of the following journals or book clubs:

Remodeler (free to professionals)★
P.O. Box 1067
Skokie, IL 60076
(publishes annual supplier guide)

Old House Journal (for restorers)★
69A Seventh Avenue
Brooklyn, NY 11217

Custom Builder (free to professionals)
P.O. Box 985
Farmingdale, NY 11737
(publishes annual product guide)

Fine Homebuilding (very expensive)★
63 South Main Street, Box 355
Newtown, CT 06470

The Journal of Light Construction
RR 2, Box 146
Richmond, VT 05477

Practical Homeowner
P.O. Box 50421
Boulder, CO 80321-0421

House Beautiful
1700 Broadway
New York, NY 10019
(publishes annual product guide)

Renovator's Supply (catalog of hardware)★
Millers Falls, MA 01349

The Spec Guide
P.O. Box 470
Peterborough, NH 03458
(to compare product cost and capabilities)

How-to Book Club
Blue Ridge Summit, PA 17294-0800

Popular Science Book Club
P.O. Box 1763
Danbury, CT 06816

Time/Life Home Improvement Series★
Box C 32066
Richmond, VA 23261-2066

★ *Highly recommended*

Investigation also involves asking people in the business questions. These professionals know where and how to buy quality items. If someone in your neighborhood is rehabbing, talk to him or her. Also talk to sales representatives for various companies. If your community has an association of rehabbers, join it.

APPROACHES TO REHABILITATION

There are many different approaches to a rehab. The approach you take will depend to a large extent on your reservoir of time and of money. It also may depend on the building that you purchase. If you must work a 40-hour week, it is unlikely that you will take on a total gut rehab. You will probably buy an older house and fix it up or restore it. There are, however, people who buy houses that need to be totally gutted, and they gut them one room at a time over a period of several years.

We recommend not living in a rehab if at all possible. It is always there facing you unfinished, and tension tends to run high. Sometimes you can compromise by living in your current home until one space in the new building is rehabbed. Then you can move into that space while you work on the rest of the building. If you do this, we recommend that you start from the top and work down. Dust and dirt fall. The last thing you want to do is finish the first floor and then carry everything you work on from then on through it. We also recommend rehabbing floor by floor rather than room by room. We make these recommendations primarily because of the dirt and mess, but it is also more efficient to gut the entire building at one time.

One of the best projects is a duplex. You can live in one unit while you rehab the other. When the first unit is done, you can move into it and then finish the second unit. One variant is to buy a large house and design the rehab as a two-family structure with an apartment on the third floor and maybe some of the second floor. Rehab the apartment first and move into it while you rehab the rest of the house.

ATTITUDE PROBLEMS

A total rehabilitation of a house is an all-encompassing endeavor. You will spend a tremendous amount of time and energy investigating and learning about the building trades. Every time you go out, you will be drawn to hardware stores. You will be on the lookout for parts suppliers. You will slow up at garage sales to see what you can buy for the project. You will be thinking about where curtains will hang, where bookshelves will go, where walls will be. As the day ends, you will lie awake picturing your project. After a while, the house occupies your every waking thought and most of your dreams.

This obsession can cause severe family problems, as it will exacerbate any tension that already exists. Before beginning a rehab, both partners in a relationship or all members of a family must be motivated to do the project. Everyone must want this project, and their participation in it should not be assumed. This is particularly true with teenagers. Sit down with your spouse and talk about the situation. Make sure that what is required of each family member is stated very clearly.

Keep in mind that constant vigilance will be required to keep yourself from falling into bad habits, including feelings of self-righteousness and ignoring other family members' needs. Do not bottle up frustrations and let them brew. Keep talking about things, and recognize the danger signals before serious problems develop.

HEALTH HAZARDS

Several things can cause health problems in rehabbing. Today most people don't know about "painter's colic," which disappeared among professional painters a generation ago with the banning of lead paint. With the resurgence of rehabilitation of older homes, however, amateur rehabbers have begun to notice flu-like symptoms such as stomachaches, headaches, and disorientation. These symptoms can hang on for weeks and even get worse. Often when you question a person rehabbing a house about these symptoms, he or she cannot think of anything out of the ordinary that might be causing them. But it finally comes down to the fact that they have been sanding their walls for weeks and the house is loaded with lead paint. If you strip paint, refinish furniture, demolish walls, or paint in the basement, you are often working in a dangerous environment. You might expose yourself not only to lead but also to asbestos and benzene, which have been connected to cancer.

A number of toxic chemicals are used in construction, but there has been almost no research directed specifically at home improvement buffs who use these substances. The most common problems are nonfatal poisonings and chronic allergic reactions, and the most difficult to define are those that are caused by long-term exposure to products such as paint, solvents, paint strippers, lead, and asbestos. Some toxic exposure is apparent almost immediately. For instance, the fumes from most construction adhesives are very toxic, and if they are used in a closed space, they will cause chest pains. The worker knows immediately that he or she must ventilate the area or stop working in it.

A class of chemicals known as organic hydrocarbons causes many short-term effects. Methylene chloride, an ingredient in many paint strippers, has been associated with chronic bronchitis, allergies, asthma, and emphysema. Benzene, methylal, toluene, and turpentine result in similar problems. Other seemingly innocuous materials such as plaster dust and sawdust also can cause these problems. Being around these chemicals does not always cause new diseases to develop, but it will exacerbate already existing conditions.

Short-term effects from a single exposure to a paint stripper might seem to fade away quickly because the body breaks down the chemical and excretes it. But if you spend months stripping your woodwork on weekends, you could see a cumulative effect, since your body does not have time to get rid of it between work sessions. The potential long-term effects are much more frightening and less well defined, but paint strippers have been found to cause cancer in laboratory animals.

Dust may not kill you, but it can cause severe reactions in people with existing respiratory problems. We have found this to be true particularly in sanding drywall. Also, sawdust from red woods can be toxic to people who are allergic to other substances. If you start sneezing or have some other allergic reaction whenever you start cutting redwood, cedar, or red oak, a chemical in the wood is causing this. You should wear a dust mask while you are working with that wood. You also should be careful when sawing treated lumber for decks or other outside structures. This wood is treated with arsenic and is very toxic. Wear a dust mask and dispose of the sawdust immediately. Do not burn the scrap wood in your fireplace.

Other kinds of dust also can be toxic. Demolition of old heating and plumbing systems in which asbestos was used as insulation can release large quantities of deadly dust into the air and thus into your lungs. We suggest that you do not try to remove asbestos yourself. You should hire a licensed asbestos firm or other demolition company to do it for you. If you have a choice, it is better to live with it than to remove it because you can cover it with other things to keep the asbestos dust out of the air.

There are a number of strategies for dealing with toxic materials around your rehab. For example, instead of using a chemical stripper to remove wallpaper, use a wallpaper steamer. Use water-based paints instead of oil-based paints. Always ventilate when using paints or adhesives.

Carpal tunnels are channels in the wrist bones through which nerves, tendons, and blood vessels pass on their way to your fingers. Many carpenters and rehabbers have learned about their carpal tunnels the hard way. Numbness and pain begin in the middle finger or the outside two fingers and sometimes progress up the arm. This problem is called *carpal tunnel syndrome*, and it occurs when swelling from irritation or fluid buildup of the carpal ligament puts pressure on the median nerve. Jobs that require repetitive and stressful wrist motion bring on the syndrome. Driving nail after nail into two-by-fours will do it. About the only way to avoid this is to avoid hammering, buy a framing hammer (because it is heavier), hire a carpenter, or use a nail gun.

SOME FINAL TIPS

The following are some final tips and suggestions for the potential rehabber. They are taken from Jones, Cury, and Cury's *Restore Your Future: A Profit Guide to Renovation* (Cury Jones Publishers, 1980).

1. Do not become involved in a rehabbing project unless everyone concerned is enthusiastic from the beginning. You will need all the cooperation, patience, and optimism you can get.

2. Do not take on more than you can afford to renovate. A 30-room Georgian mansion may be the house of your dreams, but do you have the time and the capital to make it livable? Remember to consider heating and cooling costs in any kind of structure on which you are working.

3. Do the rehab in a logical order. Do not start painting or hanging wallpaper in a house that has a poor roof. Do the rehab in the order of the chapters of this book. Gut the house, roof it and install windows, clean it, frame it, then install plumbing, wiring, HVAC, insulation, and drywall, paint it, trim it, and then put down flooring and cabinets.

4. Use professional help when it is economical. There is nothing wrong with being a do-it-yourselfer, but in some areas doing it yourself will cost more money.

5. If you have to, you can learn to do anything. Just because you do not know carpentry, electricity, or plumbing now does not mean you cannot learn. Plumbing and electrical work are among the easiest things in the world to do. You do not pay plumbers and electricians for what they do; you pay them for what they know.

6. Get your priorities straight. Are you rehabbing this house for sale or to live in? If it is for you and you are on a limited budget, you can probably live with outdated bathroom fixtures or a 1950s kitchen. But if you are going to sell the house, cutting corners in these areas is not appropriate.

7. Do not go out and buy costly tools for the reno-vation process. If you are going to rehab a large house to live in the rest of your life, it may be important to acquire some tools, such as ladders and saws. But if you are doing only one rehab, it is a good idea to rent or borrow the molder and table saw you need.

8. Do the outside first. Fix the roof and the exterior walls, and clean up the yard as soon as possible. Be aware of your neighbors.

9. Before you pick up a hammer, decide what you are going to renovate and what you will restore. Restoration is a much more expensive proposition than rehabilitation.

10. Search for advice, especially free advice. Do your homework. We emphasize throughout this book that it is extremely important for you to spend at least a year doing research before you attempt a rehab. Do not be shy about asking questions. Do not be shy about asking for publications. Go out and buy books. Do not be shy about asking for discounts on products. You will learn in Chapter 8 the tricks of getting products at discount. Do not be afraid to hire subcontractors for short periods of time so that you can work with them and ask them questions. You will learn from them and then be able to do the job yourself. You can save time and money if you do all this investigation before you start your renovation.

11. Develop a schedule. Most rehabbers, even if they have done several houses, come to a point when everything seems to be half done. No room is finished, and everything appears to be bogged down in 20 different projects. The secret to avoiding this is to have a plan and a budget before you start. Know exactly when each step is going to occur and how much it is going to cost.

12. Do not become emotionally involved in buying the house, rehabbing it, or selling it. This is a work project: it has to be done, you do it, and you go on.

13. Always be mindful of safety, especially when you are working by yourself. Wear safety glasses, proper shoes, gloves, a mask, and anything else that is required for safety. Cutting corners to save a few dollars is not worth putting out an eye or sawing off a finger.

JOB OVERVIEW

Following is a brief overview of the tasks you may encounter in a renovation project. With some annotation, this list is grouped by difficulty and is provided for the average worker who has the skills to do a passable job (not a person who has mastered each of these skills or professions). This list should give you an idea of which jobs might be good candidates for subcontracting.

Beginner

Demolition (if you stay away from taking out bearing walls)
Interior painting
Exterior painting
Stripping paint inside and out
Wallpapering (This can be tricky, and wall preparation is critical.)

Intermediate

Hanging drywall (not difficult once you get the system down)
Paneling or installing plywood
Patching or repairing walls
Insulating (as long as you are fastidious about insulating everything)
Weather-stripping
Hanging storm windows, awnings, or shutters
Doing small masonry jobs
Tuck-pointing
Drywall installation and taping (takes practice)

Intermediate to Difficult

Framing (as long as it is not structural)
Subflooring
Flooring (except for laying carpet and hardwood floors)
Plastering (It takes a long time to learn this skill.)
Finishing walls with materials such as ceramic tile
Refinishing floors
Installing prebuilt cabinets or vanities
Interior trim work
Exterior trim and siding
Roofing
Installing fireplaces or woodstoves
Furnace duct work (This can be tricky in tight places.)
Plumbing with plastic or copper pipe
Electrical wiring (except for the circuit breaker box)

Expert

Rebuilding cornices, mansards, or dormers
Removing or replacing bearing walls
Framing and finishing stairs
Masonry work (especially brick work)
Installing furnaces and air-conditioning equipment (Jeopardizing expensive equipment by using an unskilled installer is not a good idea.)
Hanging windows and some doors
Building your own cabinets from scratch
Inspecting the work

References

OLD

Lafever, Minard. *The Modern Builder's Guide.* New York: Daniel Burgess & Company, 1846.

Munby, Alan Edward. *Introduction to the Chemistry and Physics of Building Materials.* London: A. Constable & Company, 1909.

NEW

Craycroft, Robert Clarke. *Residential Reuse: A Manual of Design and Construction Methods and Techniques.* St. Louis: St. Louis Community Development Agency, 1977.

Fagg, Christopher. *How They Built Long Ago.* New York: Warwick Press, 1981.

Hanson, Shirley. *Preserving and Maintaining the Older Home.* New York: McGraw-Hill, 1983.

Johnson, Edwin. *Old House Woodwork Restoration.* Englewood Cliffs, NJ: Prentice-Hall, 1983.

Reiner, Laurence E. *How to Recycle Buildings.* New York: McGraw-Hill, 1979.

Sherwood, Gerald E. *How to Select and Renovate an Older House.* New York: Dover Publications, 1976.
_____. *New Life for Old Dwellings.* New York: Drake Publishers, 1977.

Chapter 4

INSPECTING OLD HOUSES

Unlike most material objects, a well-built house that is properly maintained does not wear out, at least over a period of several hundred years. It may become outdated and lack certain conveniences and comforts, but it rarely wears out. Tests conducted on timbers from Japanese temples 3 to 13 centuries old indicate that the wood did not deteriorate and that only shock resistance is reduced after several centuries. All other structural properties of the wood were maintained. Brick buildings are no different if they are properly maintained and tuck-pointed.

Despite this permanence, many older houses are razed or abandoned. Some houses deteriorate to a point where rehabilitation is impractical, but many can be restored to a sound condition and updated in convenience and comfort at a fairly low cost. Whether or not a house is worth rehabilitating can be determined only by a systematic inspection and evaluation. In essence, this is a two-step process. First, you find out what is wrong with the house and what it will take to put the house back in a livable condition, and second, you determine the utility of it, or the cost-benefit ratio of doing that work. Will you have invested more money in the house than it could conceivably be worth when you are finished?

A house will tell you a lot if you look at it closely. You can see structural defects and determine the things that require repair. You also must look beyond the surface, because much of the surface can be replaced. Obviously, if a house has major structural problems, such as bulging walls, large cracks in the foundation, or severe spalling of the brick, you should pass it up and purchase another. Before making a decision about an obviously sound house, you have to go inside and systematically gather information. This chapter discusses the items examined in such an inspection.

You should read this entire book before inspecting a house, because the points covered in this chapter and summarized in the House Inspection Checklist (Table 4-1) will not cover everything. This chapter and the following two chapters on cost estimating and financing are designed to tell you whether a house is a feasible rehab. An inspection engineer can tell you whether it is structurally sound (see Chapter 3).

When inspecting a house, wear old clothes and carry a flashlight and rule. Also take along a camera and binoculars. This may save you later trips back to the property.

THE FOUNDATION

The most important component of a house is the foundation. It supports the entire house, and problems with it can have far-reaching effects. Check for general deterioration that will allow water or moisture to enter the basement. This will require expensive repairs. More importantly, check for uneven settlement, which will distort the house and even begin to pull it apart, particularly in a brick structure. Look for cracks at the corners and door frames out of plumb. Some localized settling, particularly if it is minor, can be corrected by releveling beams or floor joists and is not a sufficient reason to reject a house. Only if the settling is so severe that it has damaged the exterior brick should the house be rejected.

TABLE 4-1
HOUSE INSPECTION CHECKLIST

Attic
    any signs of leaks? _____
    structural damage? _____
    adequate ventilation_____
    _____
    insulation _____

Cornice, Mansard, and Soffits
    type _____
    repairs needed or replacement _____
    _____
          (take a picture)

Exterior Walls
    plumb _____
    cracks_____
    bulges _____
    window flashing _____
    tuck-pointing _____
    stonework_____
    painted _____
    color and type of mortar_____
    _____
    windowsills _____
    needed repairs _____

Foundation
    type _____
    cracks_____
    water _____
    mortar _____
    no. of water spigots and location _____
    steps _____
        (evidence of insects/termites)
    does ground slope away? _____
    repairs needed _____

Roof (Go up there or use binoculars)
    type _____
    age _____
    evidence of repairs _____
    ridge line _____
    repairs needed or replacement _____
    _____
    flashing _____
    chimneys _____
    gutters: type _____
      needed repairs _____
      gutter board _____
    if flat roof, covering on top of walls _____

Fireplaces
    number and size _____
    flue lining _____
    damper _____
    airflow/draw _____
    repairs needed _____

Porches and Decks
    type of construction _____
    _____
    plumb _____
    paint and repairs needed _____
    _____
    wood contacting the ground? _____
    _____

Basement
    foundation _____
    structural framing _____
    windows _____
    joists _____
    furnace _____
    wiring _____
    plumbing: supply _____
                      waste _____
    floor _____
    evidence of water _____
    insects or termites _____
    electrical service: _____ amps: _____
    repairs _____
    _____

Framing
    size and condition, _____
    sagging/needing jacking _____
    stair openings _____
    squeaky stairs _____
    springy floors or stairs _____
    damage from added plumbing, etc. _____
    _____
    insulation _____
    repairs needed _____
    _____

Windows, Doors, and Floors
    windows: size and number _____
    _____
    type _____
    replace or repair needed _____
    _____
    exterior doors: size and number _____
    repair/replace _____
    _____
    number and type of interior doors _____

floors: type _____

condition _____

repairs needed or replace_____

sags? (jump up & down on floors) _____

_____

Walls and Ceilings

type _____

cracks/problems _____

_____

damp plaster? _____

trim _____

paint/wallpaper_____

Kitchen

cabinets _____

plumbing _____

fixtures _____

floor _____

walls and ceiling _____

replace or repairs needed_____

_____

_____

_____

Mechanical Systems

HVAC _____

_____

_____

plumbing _____

_____

_____

electrical _____

_____

_____

water heater _____

burglar alarm, TV cable, smoke alarm, telephone _____

_____

_____

_____

water pressure _____

electrical service _____

_____

outside lateral waste line _____

replacement or repairs needed _____

General Considerations

structure _____

_____

lot _____

_____

yard _____

_____

neighborhood _____

Check the grading of the ground and determine whether water will run away from the foundation. If you have a stone foundation, pay particular attention to the mortar between the stones. You might even use a screwdriver or ice pick to check if it is crumbling. If the foundation or walls are painted, pay particular attention to whether something is tuck-pointed or caulked. People often use caulking to cover up problems and then paint over it. Brick buildings are often painted to avoid the expense of tuck-pointing. Go inside the basement and check for dampness, water damage, and any indication that water is coming in through the foundation.

THE ROOF

Look at the general appearance of the roof. Is it shingle or tile? Are there any mismatched shingles or splotches of roofing cement that indicate sloppy repairs? How many layers of roofing are there? If there are many layers of asphalt roof, you will have to strip them off before reroofing. A roof with several layers often looks lumpy, and it is very susceptible to wind damage. Are the roof ridges straight? If there is a pronounced sagging or any erratic lines along the ridge, the underlying structure may be damaged.

If the ridge line is not straight and the roof does not appear to be in a uniform plane, some repair is necessary. It may sag due to improper support, inadequate ties, or even sagging rafters. Inspect the attic for sagging rafters or inadequate support down to the bearing walls. Rafters often sag because the dimensions of the wood are too small or because they are spaced too far apart. Determine whether you can jack up the roof or whether it will have to be replaced. Does sagging carry all the way down through the house? If so, you may want to reject this house because it takes a lot of work to fix settlement down through several floors.

While you're in the attic, look for insulation, particularly between the rafters or attic joists. If there is no insulation there, there is probably no insulation anywhere else in the house. Most houses built before World War II had no insulation, so it is not unusual to see that. If insulation was added, ask for

verification from the owner. Also check around windows and electrical boxes, to see if you can feel cold air coming through.

What kind of roof is there, and what is its condition? Asphalt roofs last between 20 and 25 years. If any of the shingles are wearing, curled, ripped, or cracked, you will probably have to replace the roof. Flat roofs (tarred roofs) have a life span of 15 years maximum. Look very closely for wear around flashing, skylights, and chimneys, as well as cracking or blistering. You can patch small areas, but a new roof will have to be installed by professionals. Wood shingles are good for 30 to 40 years. Look for rot in them. Slate can last 100 years if it is installed correctly. Things that destroy slate roofs are structural shifting, falling tree limbs, and rusty nails. If the slate has been patched with roofing cement or it is badly spalled, you will probably have to replace it. Metal roofing will last a very long time, but look for rust and poor patching.

Regardless of what kind of roof the house has, check the flashing around chimneys, in valleys, and around stacks. While examining the roof, look at the chimneys, cornices, attic ventilation, and gutters. Look at the mortar joints and the caps on chimneys. Chimneys require a careful inspection because they often need work. If the house has cornices or a gable roof, inspect these carefully because they are extremely expensive to repair or replace. Look for rot and for weak structural members. Also look at attic ventilation. There may be severe water damage around the eaves from ice buildup or a hot attic. The easiest ventilation is a natural airflow through the soffits exiting at some high point, usually a gable end or a ridge vent or fan. Finally, look at the gutters: What kind of material are they made of? Are they rusted? Do they have holes in them? Are they clogged? Are they securely attached to the house? Examine the gutter board (the one-by-six or one-by-eight behind the gutters) for rot. If you can't tell what kind of material the gutters are made of, use a magnet to check.

THE EXTERIOR WALLS

The exterior walls should be plumb and free from

any bowing or bulging. It is very important to put your face up against every wall and look up it for bulges and bows, particularly above and below windows. To a certain degree, most walls are out of true, and this should be expected in an old house. But excessive bulging usually means there is an undermined foundation problem or severe water damage inside the walls where the exterior veneer of brick is pulling free from the wall. If you are examining a house with a flat roof, when you go up on the roof, take a ball of string and a weight or plumb bob and drop the string down the side of the house to look for bulges. It is always easier to look down from the top than to look up from the ground.

Look for cracks in the brick. Be more concerned about horizontal cracks than vertical ones. You will often find vertical cracks or mortar separation between first- and second-floor windows caused by water getting into the higher frame. This is easily corrected with tuck-pointing, installing new windows, or applying some caulk. But horizontal cracking indicates settling of a house.

Also look at the mortar. The mortar should be soft in a pre-1900 building. Also look for the use of portland cement in masonry repairs. This should not be used because it spalls the brick. Pay attention to the color of the mortar, as patch work might have been done in a different color. When we stripped the paint on one house, we discovered that there were three different colors of mortar, with entire walls done in different colors. Eventually we found out that the house had been almost totally demolished in a tornado and had been rebuilt.

It is very important to prevent water from entering a masonry wall, so pay attention to the tuck-pointing on a building. We have rejected many buildings simply because of the cost of having to repoint the entire building. The same goes for houses with extensive cornice work. If a house has an extensive cornice and it is all rotten, the cost to repair it is going to be extremely high.

If the mortar in a wall is crumbling, the wall will have to be raked, cleaned, and repointed. The expense is considerable. Keep in mind that masonry that has been painted will have to be repainted every five or six years. If the paint looks new, suspect a cover-up. You also should think twice about strip-ping paint from an old building. The painting was probably done originally because the owner did not want to repoint or to cover flaws such as different-colored mortar. Chemical stripping is very expensive and messy if you do it yourself. Sandblasting to remove the paint will remove the fired face of the brick and leave the soft interior, which will then deteriorate much faster.

OTHER EXTERIOR ITEMS

The trim should be in good condition and meet the siding or brick without gaps. If there are gaps, are they caulkable? How much of the trim is rotted? Are the window frames rotted? Check particularly the exterior frame; sash and brick mold are fairly easy to fix, but fixing the frame is more difficult. Are the soffits and cornice rotted? That will almost always be the case if the roof leaks. Is the paint peeling and falling off? If so, it probably has moisture behind it. Are windows and doors plumb and free from binding or jamming? Is there flashing above all doors and window caps, and does it fit snugly?

Siding should fit tightly with the trim. If the house has stucco, look for cracks or bulges. Push on the bulges to see if they are springy. If they are, the stucco has probably come loose and will have to be redone. Be sure you check all the sills very carefully. If the house has wood sills, see if they are spongy and deteriorated. If a wood structure has been added to the brick, look for insect damage and rot. If there are any wood piers, check those very carefully.

CHIMNEYS AND FIREPLACES

The most obvious defects to look for in chimneys are cracks in the masonry and loose mortar, particularly at the top of the chimney. Make sure that the chimney is lined. Many chimneys in Victorian buildings are not. Any cracks or loose mortar can be a severe hazard if the chimney is not lined. If this is the case, you must either calculate the cost of a flue liner or decide not to use the fireplaces. All chimneys should be supported on their own footings. While you are in the attic, make sure no framing is less than an inch away from the chimney flue. Make sure the fireplace has an opening damper. If it does not, you will have a severe heat loss and will have to add a damper or put an insert into the fireplace, both of which are expensive. One of the best things to do to check a chimney is to roll up a few sheets of newspaper, light them, and see how well the fireplace draws. A fireplace in good working order will draw well after a minute or so. If you are thinking about putting an insert into a fireplace, make sure that you have room to do that. The old coal inserts used in Victorian buildings do not have the required depth to use new fireplace inserts in their place. Also, only a 6-inch flue liner will usually fit in older chimneys, but most newer inserts require an 8-inch flue.

PORCHES AND DECKS

Porches and decks are very vulnerable to decay and deterioration. Sometimes wood steps are placed directly on the ground, which is a poor practice unless treated wood is used. Check all parts of a wood porch or deck for decay; check to see whether the stairs touch the dirt or are sitting on a cement or stone foundation. Check to see what kind of wood was used to construct the porch or deck. Pay particular attention to the base of old posts or where any two members meet. Keep in mind that you might have to spend several thousand dollars to replace an extensive front porch or a two-story back deck.

THE BASEMENT

One of the most important parts of the inspection is going down in the basement. You need to be thorough in this inspection because this substructure supports everything around it and most of the major systems in the house start here.

Start by looking at the foundation from the inside. Look for cracks, water seepage, settling, bowing in walls, and gaps between sills. Most importantly, make sure the basement is dry. Does it feel dry? Does it smell dry? Do you see any evidence of mildew, rust, or mud? Is the bottom of the furnace (or any other stationary equipment) rusted? Look inside the furnace. Look at the electrical box to find out what kind of electrical service the house has. Has it been updated, or does it still have an old 60-amp box? Look at the wiring. Has any rewiring been done? Have many new circuits been added? Has the box been bridged? Is there either knob-and-tube or Romex wiring? If so, you may have to totally rewire the house. Also look at the plumbing. Is it cast iron? Have any new plastic drain pipes been added? Look at the supply pipe. Is it at least a 1-inch or larger pipe? See if the pipe has been replaced or if it is the original lead pipe. Is it all iron, or is there new copper? If there is copper mixed with iron, check the places where the copper joins the iron. There should be a *dialectic union* with a plastic insert between its two halves, which is designed to prevent the dissimilar metals from touching and corroding.

Now look at the floor. Are there many cracks? See if the house is pulling apart. Stamp your foot on the floor and see if it has a solid feel. In other words, do you have 4 inches of concrete under your foot or 1½ inches? This may be important if you have to start digging up the floor to replace the plumbing. Finally, look at the plumbing stacks where they go into the floor. Do they look solid? Is there any evidence of leaking?

Look over your head at the rafters. Picture the structural support of the house. Where are the bearing walls? Are there beams under the bearing walls? Do you have two-by-eights or two-by-tens? Is there any sagging? Are there any temporary supports? Has any shoring been done? Does the structure look solid and plumb, or does it look as though it has sagged and the joists have been crushed by the weight placed on them? Also, see if any joists have been cut through for plumbing and other such changes.

THE FRAMING

Even in a brick house, most of the structure inside

is wood, and this structure is an adequate indicator of insect damage, water damage, and structural movement. Do not be deterred by the dank confines of a crawl space or attic. Wear old clothes and take a flashlight when you inspect these areas.

Joists and girders should be horizontal, but they rarely are in an old building. If the joists slant gently toward the foundation or the center of the building and they look sound, you probably don't need to worry about them. But if the joists sag in midspan or there is severe bow toward the center of the house, there may be a problem. These joists may need to be blocked, or they may be undersized and not able to carry the load of a modern house. Springy floors suggest undersized joists.

Any wood posts should be supported on pedestals or footings that go through the floor. Make sure that you examine the base of all wood posts for decay and the top of the posts for evidence of crushing from excess weight. Check steel posts for rust and proper footings.

A point of particular concern is the framing of the floor joists around the stair openings. Probably half of the houses built have inadequate framing around stairs, which results in severe sagging. Check the floors around the openings for levelness, cracks in the plaster, or drywall coming loose from the corners of stair openings. When you're walking through a house, always look for squeaky stairs, squeaky and springy floors, and shaky rails around stairs. Some people even carry a marble or ballbearing in their pockets to roll across floors. Another trick is to jump up and down in the middle of a room to see how springy the joists are. Try to determine whether they will carry the weight that you have planned for that room. If you don't have a good eye for levelness, you might want to carry a plumb bob or a small level to check door casings and that sort of thing. Look for cracks in walls around door casings; they are an indication that there is weak framing around the door.

WINDOWS, DOORS, AND FLOORS

Windows and exterior doors usually present one of the more difficult and costly problems in old houses. If they are loose, rotted, or damaged in any way, they will be a major source of drafts and cost a fair amount of money to repair. Check for tightness of fit. Particularly check for rotting in the sash and sill. Be very careful about checking the frames of windows. If replacement of windows is planned, make sure to check whether the windows are a standard size. In cold climates, windows should be double glazed, or the house should have storm windows. If you are inspecting several houses, count the windows and get a feel for their size. This will be a major issue when figuring cost.

Exterior doors should fit well without sticking. They should be weather-stripped and have adequate locks and knobs. Storm doors, if they are necessary, should be present and operable. If the exterior door frame is out of square due to foundation settlement or other racking of the house, the opening will have to be reframed. This is a very difficult job. The lower parts of exterior doors and door frames are most susceptible to decay and rot and should be checked carefully. Also look at the threshold. Interior doors should be checked for squareness. Record the type of door on your checklist. Count the doors and record their sizes to help you figure the cost of the rehab. Also determine the door material and construction. If you have painted paneled doors that are made of oak, they are probably worth stripping and retaining. If they are pine or fir, you may want to replace them. In checking the size of the doors, also make sure to check the width of the wall because frame width will be an issue in the cost of replacement doors.

The most important thing to look for in floors is the levelness and smoothness of the existing floor, especially if you plan to carpet or tile over it. The thickness of the floor is an issue. Make sure that the flooring is at least 7/8 inch thick. If there are hardwood floors, try to determine whether they have been sanded once already. It is preferable to buy a house where the floors have not been sanded previously. A hardwood floor may be 3/4 inch thick or only a 3/8-inch covering over a subfloor. In many houses, 3/8-inch hardwood flooring was added later. This is called "Depression hardwood" and can be sanded only once. If it has already been sanded, be prepared to remove it or lay carpet. If the existing floor is tile, linoleum, or carpet, you probably will want to replace it.

Look for buckling or cupping of the floorboards, which results from high moisture content or from the floor getting wet. Also notice whether the boards are separated due to shrinkage. Floorboards are very difficult to replace because they are tongue-and-grooved. If the floor is softwood, be particularly careful about determining whether it has been sanded. Some softwood flooring without a subfloor cannot be sanded more than once.

WALLS AND CEILINGS

Interior wall covering in old houses is usually plaster but it may be gypsum board. Gypsum board is found in more recently built homes or where there have been previous rehabbing activities. Wood paneling also may have been used to cover damaged walls. Plaster almost always has some hairline cracks, even when it is in good condition. Minor cracks and holes can be patched easily, but beware of very large cracks, which may be an indication of movement of the foundation in the past few years. They also are very difficult to repair.

If you wish to retain the existing plaster, you should know that it will be very difficult to replumb and rewire. In addition, the cost of those activities will increase significantly because you will have to snake the new wires and pipes through the walls. You may have to break through some of the plaster and then patch those areas.

If the walls have been papered, make sure you check the thickness of the paper. If there are more than two or three layers, you will probably have to remove it before applying new paper. This is a time-consuming task. Paint that is cracked or chipped is a good indication of water and moisture. You should assume that most of the paint in older buildings is lead-based and will have to be covered.

THE KITCHEN

In almost all cases, you will have to replace the kitchen. The floor, cabinets, and probably the appliances will all go. You may find a house where the kitchen is the one thing that previous owners have attempted to rehab. In that case, you need to look at the quality of the cabinets and whether they are attached to each other and to the wall properly. Try to move the countertops and the cabinets. Look for chips and other marks in the countertops. Look at the sink, the plumbing underneath the sink, and the wiring and plumbing for the appliances. Check to see if the range hood is vented. Try to get a feel for the layout of the kitchen—whether the sink is under a window and that sort of thing. Can the room be laid out a different way? Look at the traffic pattern between the sink, the stove, and the refrigerator. Is it tight?

Find out how many electrical circuits are in the kitchen. You should have at least three. If all the plugs in the kitchen, including those for the refrigerator and microwave, are on the same circuit, that is a formula for disaster. Assume that you will have to do a fair amount of electrical work. Look for storage space. Is there a pantry or a place to put a pantry? Look at the quality of the flooring. If you find a rehabbed kitchen, assume that the price of the house reflects the work that has been done and that you will lose that money if you redo it.

MECHANICAL SYSTEMS

Because many of the plumbing, heating, and wiring systems in a house are concealed, it may be difficult to determine their adequacy. For the same reason, it is difficult to make major changes without considerable cutting of walls and in some situations even structural members. Thus, it is very important to inspect the plumbing, heating, and wiring before you decide to buy a house. In a very old house, the mechanical systems almost always have to be replaced, and doing so will be a major expense. But there are also bonuses in doing that. Newly installed systems will save energy, as well as space in the basement.

When inspecting the plumbing, water pressure is probably the most important place to start. Check several faucets as high up in the house as you can get to see what kind of water flow the house has. Then go down low in the house and check again. Low pressure can have various causes. The supply line may be too small or the pipes may have deposits of lime or some other material. At least a ¾-inch-diameter service line is required. Most new houses have a 1-inch copper line. Don't be surprised if you find an old lead service pipe, which might be adequate for your needs. Major distribution pipes should be ¾ inch, and most branch lines should be ½ inch. Rarely in an old house will you find copper lines unless they were added in previous rehab attempts. If you have cast-iron and lead lines in a house over 50 years old, you should replace them in a major rehab. Unless you are keeping all the plaster walls intact, replace the old lines with copper and plastic. Check the shutoff valve at the service entrance and make sure it is good. Often you will find a shutoff valve inside the house and a shutoff valve outside by the street. As long as one of them is in working order, you are okay. Be sure to check for leaks in the supply system. Rust or white or greenish crusting of pipes indicates leaks. If you have copper mixed with steel or iron lines, make sure that dialectic unions are in place.

Open up all the faucets in the house and listen for water hammer. This is a severe problem that occurs when you stop the water flowing in the pipe by abruptly closing the faucet. Air chambers are placed in the supply lines at the fixtures to absorb that shock and prevent water hammer. If you have water hammer, the water chambers are either waterlogged or not there. If you have to add them, it means going through the wall where the fixture is. That can be very costly if you are not totally gutting the house.

Keep in mind that the fittings on steel or cast-iron pipes always last much longer than the pipes themselves. Everything may look fine, but the pipe may be extremely thin because of deterioration. There is no easy way to determine the condition of a pipe without sticking a screwdriver through it. You can tap it to see if it dents, but you don't want to put a hole in somebody's pipe while you are inspecting the house.

Scrutinize the waste system carefully for smell and leakage. If the house has a septic tank, ask when it was last emptied and have the owner tell you the exact location of the septic tank cleanout. If the house doesn't have a septic tank, have the owner tell you the exact location of the house vents for the waste line. Every house should have a minimum of one house vent and more if there is a long run to the sewer line. A house vent is a trap with a vent coming up to the surface of the ground. If you were to retain the old line, that is where you would run augers down to clean the line.

Examine the water heater. Assume that you are probably going to replace it, though it is possible that it could be a fairly new one. If you can open a drain valve, do it and see whether the water drains out clear or cloudy and if any scale or rust comes out. Remove the cover of the burner and look for rust scaling.

Examine all the fixtures in the house. They should be firmly mounted and drain quickly. Look for mineral stains, toilet bases that wobble, and water damage to floors. Fill the sinks and let them drain to see if the drain pipes are adequate. In bathrooms, be sure to fill a sink and let it drain totally to see if there is gurgling in the adjacent toilet. If there is, venting is probably inadequate. Upgrading venting in a house is very expensive, but poor ventilation results in septic smells.

When you are inspecting the lateral sewer drainage outside the house, have someone flush every toilet in the house three or four times in a row to send a large volume of water down the sewage line. You can then see if anything backs up. Often you will find that the drainage system outside the house is made of vitreous bell tile, which may have been poorly installed or been broken, allowing tree roots to enter at the breaks or through the joints. These tree roots will clog the line. You can find out if this is a problem by putting a lot of water into the system. These roots can be removed mechanically with augers, but this operation will probably have to be repeated every few years.

It is important to inspect the gas lines in a house. If they look old or abused, have the gas company look at them. Most gas companies offer a free assessment service for lines, but keep in mind that, if they find leaks, they will immediately shut off service and will not restore it without a reinspection. Gas lines should be threaded iron pipe (not galvanized) or copper tubing with flare fittings for short lengths. They should never be plastic, sweated copper, or compression connections.

Try to inspect the heating system. Look at the condition of the chimney. All the mortar should be sound, and there should be a cleanout at the bottom. The chimney should be lined with flue tile but probably will not be in pre-1900 buildings. Ask for the fuel bills for the past few years. If the owner doesn't have them, the fuel company will. Look to see if the furnace has been converted from coal to oil or gas. This type of system is usually wasteful and should be replaced. Regardless of the kind of furnace, check the combustion chamber and look for rust or scaling inside and out. Look for oil stains on the floor. Keep in mind that 30 years or so is the maximum life of most heating systems. Also keep in mind that it is easy to get an expert opinion on the furnace.

There are many different kinds of furnaces. Some old houses have gravity warm air furnaces. These take up a huge amount of space in the basement with their big vent pipes, and the temperature control/heat distribution usually isn't as good as with forced air. Gravity warm air systems are also very dirty. You might find a floor furnace in a small house, especially if it was built between 1900 and 1935. Although this type of furnace may be adequate to heat the house, it can be hard to work on if you don't have a large crawl space underneath the house. In addition, it is sometimes hard to get parts for them.

Steam or hot water systems are very common in Victorian homes because these houses started out with coal inserts or fireplaces and people added hot water or steam heat later. They are extremely simple systems, but there are pipes and radiators everywhere. Small, very efficient boilers are now available for these systems, so the main concern is the quality of the pipes and radiators. We suggest that you get an expert's opinion before deciding to keep or scrap this type of system.

Another kind of heating system that you might encounter is radiant heat from hot water flowing through coils embedded in a concrete floor or plaster ceiling. It is an excellent form of heat but may become air locked, which requires expert attention to restore proper operation. Breaks in coils can be repaired, but that means repairing breaks in floors or ceilings. You also may encounter electric radiant heat, which has no moving parts to wear out but is very costly to operate.

Forced air, if gas, is economical, and you simply need to check the age of the furnace and the condition of the heat exchanger. The choice of electric forced air heat obviously depends on the price of electricity. In most areas, it is a very expensive form of heat. In many areas where the cost of electricity is moderate, you will find heat pumps. The drawback to these is that they pump lukewarm air into the house and therefore run more often than do other types of furnaces. They also run 12 months of the year to either cool or heat the house, and consequently they wear out quickly.

When inspecting a furnace, turn the thermostat up (or on) and see how quickly the furnace starts. Be sure there is no fuel or exhaust smell in the living area when you do that and determine how quickly the house heats up. If you are gutting the house, you will probably replace the old system with a more efficient forced air system, so the basic issues are the age and appearance of the system and the condition of the combustion chamber. Also look at the thermostats. If they are the double setback type, you will want to keep them.

The last mechanical system is the electrical system. The first thing you should look at is the service panel. Many of the electrical appliances that have become common in the past 20 or 30 years overburden the wiring system in old houses. If you are planning to install air-conditioning or other such appliances in the rehab, you will probably have to rewire. Service should be at least 100 amps for an average-size three-bedroom house. Anything larger should probably have 200 amps. Look at the main distribution panel to determine how many amps service and how many circuits the house has. Also look for circuits that have been added; check to see if the panel has been bridged to a second box that has outlets coming from it. The most common service today is 200 amps at 240 volts.

Go over all the exposed wiring to determine whether any armored cable is rusted or any wiring insulation is deteriorated or brittle. When you walk around the house, make sure there is at least one outlet per wall in every room. This is particularly important if you don't plan to gut the building.

Modern building codes call for outlets that are no more than 12 feet apart. Codes also say that kitchen and bathroom circuits should have number 12 wire and that bathrooms should have ground fault circuits. In an older house, that is probably not going to be the case, but you should check. If the wiring has been updated, make sure that the wire size and type of circuit are in accordance with the local codes. If they are not, the new wiring was probably not inspected. If you really want to get fancy, you can check all the outlets in the house to see if they are grounded (there is a tool for doing this). Ceiling lights should have a wall switch; rooms without a ceiling light should have a wall switch for at least one outlet. You really don't need to worry about this if you are going to gut the building.

GENERAL CONSIDERATIONS

An important consideration is whether you plan to buy a total wreck and gut it (the only things you are interested in are the outside walls, the basic bearing framing, and the roof), you are going to save part of it and gut part of it, or you want to save virtually all of it. If you buy a wreck, things such as the furnace, plumbing and electrical systems, plaster, and windows may be irrelevant. The only questions are how much junk needs to be hauled away, the cost of disposal, and how much you can sell. Obviously, the things you are going to look at in such a building are the roof, the exterior walls and structural foundation, the basic layout, and the floors. Whether you go any further than that depends on what you want to do with the building. Always keep in mind the end result while making your inspection, or you could end up inspecting a lot of things you don't need to inspect.

The other general consideration is the current value of the house and what the value will be when you are done. Many factors affect the value. Location is obviously crucial. Layout, appearance, and the unique qualities of the building are important, too, but other things such as privacy, traffic circulation, and room size are equally important and need to be built into the equation. You must look

at the kitchen: its location, size, and plumbing are all significant considerations. Coat closets are always a problem. Most old houses did not have coat closets, and you will need to add one. If you are not gutting the house, where will you put it?

Privacy is also an issue. In old houses, there wasn't much concern for privacy. Today we are more concerned about privacy and the relative locations of bathrooms, bedrooms, and the different living areas (the relaxation area and eating area). Examine the traffic movement between these areas and the degree of privacy in them.

The house's appearance is largely a matter of taste, but simplicity and unity are major considerations. A good period house may be worth preserving, as may any house that is unique in some way. But charm doesn't amount to much and could become much less important after you live with inconvenience, discomfort, and constant repairs. You may save a lot of plaster, old wiring, and old plumbing, but the headaches and hassles later on aren't going to be worth preserving the charm. Most developers use charm to sell the house to somebody else.

The House Inspection Checklist (Table 4-1) will help you remember the things you need to inspect. For a more detailed checklist and discussion of inspecting homes, see Alfred Daniel's *The Home Inspection Manual* (Garden Way Publishing, 1987).

References

OLD

Britton, Thomas Allen. *A Treatise on the Origin, Progress, Prevention, and Cure of Dry Rot in Timber.* London: E. & F.N. Spon, 1875.

Byrne, Austin Thomas. *Inspection of the Materials and Workmanship Employed in Construction.* New York: John Wiley & Sons, 1930.

Richey, Harry Grant. *A Handbook for Superintendents of Construction, Architects, Builders, and Building Inspectors.* New York: John Wiley & Sons, 1905.

NEW

Blackburn, Graham. *The Parts of a House.* New York: R. Marek, 1980.

Brock, D.S., and L. L. Sutcliffe (eds.). *Field Inspec-*

tion Handbook: An On-the-Job Guide for Construction Inspectors, Contractors, Architects, and Engineers. New York: McGraw-Hill, 1986.

Brooks, Hugh. *Encyclopedia of Building and Construction Terms.* Englewood Cliffs, New Jersey: Prentice-Hall, 1983.

Fagg, Christopher. *How They Built Long Ago.* New York: Warwick Press, 1981.

Johnson, Sidney M. *Deterioration, Maintenance, and Repair of Structures.* New York: McGraw-Hill, 1965.

Late Victorian Architectural Details. Watkins Glen, New York: American Life Foundation Study Institute, 1978.

O'Brien, James Jerome. *Construction Inspection Handbook.* New York: Van Nostrand Reinhold, 1983.

Wetherill, Edward B. *Estimating and Analysis for Commercial Renovation.* Kingston, Massachusetts: R.S. Means Company, 1985.

Chapter 5

COST ESTIMATING AND PLANNING

Cost estimating is one of the most important things you will do in a rehab project. Inexperienced rehabbers must be particularly careful in cost estimating and cost-benefit analysis. It is important for anyone inexperienced in any activity to approach it in a systematic fashion. This is especially true when estimating costs.

Cost estimating is not an exact science. No two rehabbers or developers will come up with the same cost on a project. In rehabbing, getting within 5 percent of the actual cost is considered extremely accurate. Lyn Minnis, our friend and savings and loan manager, says that she has never dealt with a first-time rehabber who has not substantially underestimated the cost of at least one project. She encourages people to add up to *30 percent* contingency funds to any project, but people usually resist because it means borrowing more money and making higher monthly payments. Nevertheless, we also encourage it.

Two things happen when you underestimate on a rehab. First, you try to cut costs. The problem with cutting costs is that you usually run out of money at the end of the project when doing the finish work. Your house may have a great electrical system, a great furnace, and outstanding plumbing, but it will look terrible because you economized on the finish work. The second thing that happens is that you have to go back and ask the bank for more money, which is a problem because you will have to pay closing costs again. You may not have to pay some of the initial costs, but you will have to pay others, such as those for getting another appraisal on the house. Thus, it is wise to add 20 to 30 percent for contingency costs to your loan. You can always pay it back to the bank if you do not need it.

In this chapter, we will not discuss prices for items. There are two reasons for this. First, costs vary significantly across the country. The construction costs in San Francisco, New York City, or Los Angeles, for instance, are significantly higher than those in Minneapolis, Denver, Phoenix, or St. Louis, which in turn are significantly higher than those in Atlanta, Nashville, or Louisville. Second, prices change with time. Materials and labor invariably increase in price, so any dollar figures we might give would be quickly out of date. You need to determine what you want to do to a house and then find out how much materials and labor are going to cost in your area.

Here are some hints for cost estimating. Do not simply pull a hardware store or home supply center flier out of your newspaper and estimate costs from that. Every large city has major hardware stores and lumberyards that do a lot of advertising. The advertised prices that you see in newspaper fliers are usually for slightly inferior products or special low prices ("loss leaders") that will not be offered again, particularly when you need them. The best thing to do is to go to a well-established lumberyard with your list of items and ask someone there to give you prices. We discuss purchasing materials and how to buy them wholesale in Chapter 8. Fill in the Cost Estimating Checklist (Table 5-1) to estimate your rehab costs. Make sure to call several subcontractors and several suppliers for each product or subcontracted service. Keep in mind that prices may vary significantly, so shop around.

TABLE 5–1
COST ESTIMATING CHECKLIST

Description	Materials	Labor
Loan closing costs		
Loan P/I during rehab		
Fire insurance		
Inspection fees		
Architect and engineer		
Permit fees		
Utilities during rehab		
Excavation/grading		
Relocating utilities		
Yard/fences/outbuilding		
Footings/foundations		
Shoring		
Replace/repair		
Concrete		
Waterproofing		
Other masonry		
Walls		
Existing chimneys		
Facia		
Porches/decks		
Demolish		
Repair/replace		
Demolition		
Roof		
Interior		
Basement		
Dumpster/hauling		
Initial cleaning		
Windows		
Front		
Other walls		
New Framing (lumber, nails, glue, joist hangers)		
Walls		
Floors		
Ceilings		
Roof		
Additions		
Beams		

Description	**Materials**	**Labor**

Doors
    Exterior
    Interior
    Hardware
Roofing
Skylights
Exterior trim
    Cornices
    Mansards
    Soffits
    Scaffold rental
Exterior siding
Gutters/flashing
Fireplaces/stoves
    Repair/replace
Chimneys/flues
Plumbing
    Supply service
    Interior supply piping
    Waste lateral service
    Interior waste
    Fixtures (tub, sinks, toilets,
      garbage disposal)
    Finish plumbing
    Water heater
    Well and/or septic tank repair
Furnace and air-conditioning
    Repair/replace
    Duct work and grills
    Flue
Electrical
    New service
    Circuit wiring
    TV cable
    Telephone
    Sound system wiring
    Light fixtures
    Built-in vacuum
Insulation
Drywall
    Installation
    Finishing
Plastering
Kitchen cabinets, countertops, and bath vanities

Description	Materials	Labor
Finish carpentry		
Molding		
Bookshelves		
Painting		
Interior		
Exterior		
Wallpapering		
Floor coverings		
Kitchen		
Baths		
Other areas		
Final cleaning		
Landscaping		
Appliances		
Total material + total labor		
Add 20–30% miscellaneous contingency factor	_____	_____
Grand total rehab costs	_____	_____
Add price of house	_____	_____
Ultimate grand total of project	_____	_____
Price to buy a comparable finished	_____	_____
rehab or new house		

You will not develop a complete checklist of costs for most houses that you inspect. You will eliminate some of them because of size, neighborhood, floor plan, or some major structural problem. Eventually, you will narrow the field to two or three houses. At this point, you can either do a complete cost estimate or come up with some ballpark figures. Your choice will probably depend on how much time you have and your experience. With luck, you will find a house that nobody else wants. It is so terrible that you will have plenty of time to purchase it. Sometimes, however, there may be other bids for a piece of property, and you do not have time to complete a detailed checklist. If that is the case, you will have to rely on ballpark figures. You can come up with these figures by reading the following chapters and then estimating the major repair items. A basic rule of thumb is that it will cost about $1.50 to $2.00 a square foot to gut a building, while it will cost $30 to $35 a square foot to restore it. Given those two figures, you can guesstimate what your rehab will cost.

We strongly suggest, however, that those of you who are not experienced do a more complete checklist and figure the total cost based on material and labor costs so that you know fairly precisely what amount of money it will take to do a building and what subcontractors will be needed. This exercise may also help you obtain financing later on. The rest of this chapter is dedicated to helping you make accurate estimates.

Looking at the list of rehab items may be daunting, but all of them can be estimated fairly closely. The principal and interest (P/I) of the loan can be estimated by the bank and depends on the time it will take to do the rehab. If you live in the rehab while you are working on it, this is not really an extra cost. Fire insurance should be carried for the value of the completed building if you can get it. Often you cannot get this much fire insurance until you are close to being done. Insurance typically runs about 50 cents a thousand. Inspection fees are for an inspection engineer and for a pest control service to check for termites (if needed) and should not run more than $200 to $300. Architect and engineer costs depend entirely on the amount of time these professionals are required. If an architect draws complete plans for the building, you may spend several thousand dollars. Permit fees vary widely by locality.

Utilities during the rehab will have to be estimated depending on the cost of utilities in your area. The cost of a portable sanitation unit can be determined by calling a company that supplies such units. The best thing to do when figuring the cost of excavation work and relocating utilities is to get an estimate from subcontractors. Yard work, fences, and removing outbuildings all depend on the individual situation. Estimates for any concrete work can be supplied by the concrete contractor or derived from the cubic yard prices for concrete in your area. Always use professionals for waterproofing, particularly those who guarantee their work, and make sure you get estimates. The cost for masonry varies. Tuck-pointing is usually estimated by the square foot of wall, so that is easy to estimate once you know the square foot price.

Porches and decks will be difficult to estimate because you must determine whether to remove and replace or repair them and then figure out all the lumber costs. Labor costs are even more difficult to estimate if you are going to patch up a porch rather than replace it. The best thing to do for the lumber (interior and exterior) is to get a complete list of the materials and go to the lumberyard for an estimate of total cost.

Demolition will typically cost about $1.00 to $1.50 per square foot depending on the dumping charges in your area. The best thing to do is to mark (with spray paint) the things that will be demolished and ask contractors to give you an estimate.

Cleaning is also a difficult item to estimate. The cleaner you keep the building, the happier your subcontractors will be and the better work you will get. You will need both initial cleaning (even if you do not gut the building) and final cleaning. These can be estimated by calling a cleaning service and asking how much it charges for construction clean-

ing based on the size of the building. The service can usually give you a ballpark figure over the phone.

Windows can be estimated simply by counting the number of windows and knowing their approximate sizes. Most windows are sold by the total perimeter. If you know that dimension and the particulars of the window you wish to purchase, you can get estimates very easily. Doors can be estimated the same way, by knowing the number of doors and their sizes (if standard sizes, simply the width of the door is needed; the height is 6 feet 8 inches).

Roofing is calculated by the square. A square equals 100 square feet of roof area. If you have to remove many old layers of roofing, it is a good idea to get an estimate. But if you know the type of roofing you want and the number of squares required, you can call up a roofer and get a rough estimate. Chimney costs should be estimated by a mason. The cost of skylights can be calculated by their dimensions.

Exterior trim is difficult to estimate. It depends on the extent of repair or replacement needed. If extensive cornice repair is required, it is best to get an estimate from a carpenter who specializes in that kind of work. Peter Acsay, the person who works for us, can stand on the ground, look at a cornice, and pretty much tell you how much it will cost in time and materials. Siding and gutters work pretty much like roofing; if you know how many squares of siding you need or how many linear feet of gutters plus the number of corners, you can get a fairly precise estimate of cost.

For plumbing, heating and air-conditioning, and electrical systems, our advice is to make a complete list of materials that you will need. Go to plumbing and electrical supply houses and ask them to figure the costs, or bring in subcontractors for all three and ask for bids. It is extremely important that you shop for prices. Costs will vary widely, particularly in heating and air-conditioning. When estimating, though, use slightly high bids. This will help you pay for overruns later on. Comparison shopping also will ensure that unusually high bids do not make you reject a building based on those costs.

Insulation can be figured by the square foot, or

you can ask a subcontractor to estimate the cost. You must determine whether you will use R-11, R-13, or R-19 insulation in the walls (use R-30 in the ceilings), then calculate the number of square feet needed and multiply that by the price your suppliers give you.

To estimate drywall costs, call a drywall supplier in your area and get a square foot price, but do not forget all the nails, tape, and other materials that go along with it. Calculate finishing separately. Alternatively, you can ask a drywall contractor to estimate the cost for the entire building on a square foot basis. It may run anywhere from $.50 to $1.00 a square foot, with one-third of that being the drywall and materials, one-third being the hanging, and one-third being the taping. We urge you to bring in a professional to do any kind of plastering and get an estimate for that.

Measure for kitchen cabinets, countertops, bath vanities, finish molding, and floor coverings, then take the list of materials or a diagram to a supplier for prices. Finish carpentry labor can be figured at about the same rate as rough carpentry. Painting materials can be calculated on a square foot basis. It is usually easy to get estimates on painting and wallpapering. Wallpapering labor is usually a set dollar amount per roll.

If you plan to do all or a substantial part of the work yourself, we urge you to go beyond this checklist for cost estimating. List the carpentry supplies. List the electrical items, including wire, light fixtures, plug-ins, and sockets. List the plumbing supplies you need down to the length of pipe and the number of 90-degree elbows. Remember that, when you do something yourself, it is easy to exceed your budget. When you hire contractors on a bid basis, budgeting becomes their problem. They must get the work done within the budget they have determined, or they do not make a profit. You do not have to worry about it. Although this makes life easier, you are paying for peace of mind. Not only are you paying the subcontractor for labor, but you are also paying for his or her profit and a calculated contingency amount. If a subcontractor estimates a large contingency factor that he or she does not use, his or her profits are higher. If you plan to do the whole job yourself, list all the materials and then add in some subcontractor labor costs as a contingency factor.

When the subject of budgeting comes up, rehabbers and remodelers often say that budgeting is for the big guys. They know what their volume is, and their bank account tells them how much money they have. These people fail to realize that budgeting can help them eliminate a lot of errors in judgment due to haste or inexperience. If you are new to this business, it is imperative to practice very strict budgeting. As we mentioned before, probably the biggest reason to do this is to avoid running out of money and skimping on the finish work. In addition, the better prepared you are and the more completely you have documented and estimated this project, the happier the bank will be to lend you money.

Two other books provide useful information about cost estimating. The first is Carl Heldmann's *Manage Your Own Home Renovation* (Garden Way Publishing, 1987). In Chapter 5 of that book, Heldmann discusses cost estimating and gives prices for some types of items on a square foot basis. The second source, if you can find it, is Benjamin Williams's *The Remodeler's Handbook* (Craftsman Book Company, 1977). This book was designed for professionals and discusses estimating construction jobs in detail.

FINAL PLANNING

Often in cost estimating, you must plan the building layout and design before costs can be finalized. If you find a building in which the existing floor plan is acceptable to your living needs, it will be a big plus. But if the building needs to be gutted, changing its floor plan is not a big deal, except for the increased costs of structural and partition framing. Before you start any construction, you need to finalize your design.

Many Victorian houses, especially row houses and buildings with "shotgun" hallways (hallways that run the length of the house), are difficult to redesign. Many row houses have windows only in the front and back. Most often the kitchen ends up in the back and the living room in the front, with an embarrassing amount of unused space in the center of the house. In some projects, we have put the kitchen in the middle of the house and the living room and master bedroom at the opposite ends. These are the kinds of issues that need to be addressed in planning a redesign. A pamphlet titled *Designing Affordable Houses* (November 1983), put together by the U.S. Department of Housing and Urban Development, Office of Policy Development and Research, is available from the U.S. Government Printing Office, Washington, D.C. 20402. This pamphlet is very useful if you are doing preliminary design work.

The rooms and spaces in a house can be broken down into four main categories: living, utility, storage, and circulation. The living room and bedrooms come under the heading *living*. They should have daylight and will take up most of the space in the house. The utility section includes the kitchen, bathroom(s), and utility room, which may or may not have daylight. Where it is impossible for either the kitchen or bath(s) to have a window, most building codes require mechanical ventilation (skylights are also an option). Storage is required in every house, as is circulation space (corridors and stairs). Each of these should be determined by the placement of other spaces, though the existing stairs may be a constraint in a rehab if your finances and/or experience are not up to moving them.

If you are doing basic planning, you need to keep in mind some dimensions. The *minimum* space for a living room should be 150 square feet, with the smallest dimension being 10 feet. The dining room should have a *minimum* of 100 square feet, with the smallest dimension being 8 feet. Kitchens should not be *less than* 60 square feet, and bedrooms should be no *smaller* than 120 square feet, with the smallest dimension being 9 feet. Keep in mind that these are absolute minimums, and in most cases the rooms should be much larger.

Orientation of Rooms

Orientation is the concept of making the best use of the available sunlight and views. For example, although it may be best to have the living room windows facing south for maximum sunlight, there may be a view on the other side of the house to warrant having the living room on that side. In most urban settings, the living room faces the street,

but then people buy heavy drapes to cover up the large windows, thus counteracting the original intention of letting in light. Also keep in mind that a large picture window installed in the front of an older house may destroy the house's appearance.

Orientation also has another meaning. Sometimes in older houses, you need to beam structural walls to increase the space needed for a living room, family room, or kitchen. If this is necessary, remember that beams must be deep enough to take the load required by the span and that they will be visible unless covered by a dropped ceiling. In this case, orientation means that the beam must relate to something in the room. If the beam is properly located, it will be the dividing line between a living and dining area or a living/dining area and kitchen. If the beam is improperly placed it will look awkward. Steel I beams do not take as much space as wood beams and can be concealed by a dropped ceiling so that its placement will not cause an orientation problem.

Zoned Living

When the basic orientation of rooms is being considered, adjacency also is important. We have broken down the various rooms and spaces into four categories (living, utility, storage, and circulation). The category of living space also can be broken down into three functions: living, eating, and sleeping. The sleeping function is typically separated from the others for privacy and quiet. Bedrooms and bathrooms form a self-contained group, typically on the second or third floor. It should not be necessary, for instance, to cross the living room from a bedroom to get to a bathroom. Also, the dining area should not be far from the kitchen. The layout of the house should be zoned to provide the main functional areas. You also should decide in which area you will spend most of your time. If it is in the kitchen and dining area, that may become the most important area in your house.

The relationship among the three zones and any outdoor decks, patios, or entrances is called circulation. The traffic patterns in the hallways and stairways that connect these areas and allow passage between them are important. You need to separate noisy areas from quiet ones by using buffers such as long hallways, closets, utility areas, and stairways. You also need to examine traffic flow — whether you have a circular flow around the house or a straight flow through the house — and what that will do to carpet wear and use of different zones. Do not forget laundry areas and closets, particularly coat closets. It is often easy to put the laundry room in the basement, but if you have extra space in the sleeping area, put it there. Sometimes it is best to have the laundry room closer to where the dirty clothes are. Then you can put the storage area in the basement.

Cost Concerns

Another factor that is extremely important in overall planning is the cost — that is, how your design affects the cost of the project. The most important item here is plumbing. There are three basic rules for reducing plumbing costs: Have as few pipes as possible, keep them as short as possible, and bend them as little as possible. One of the most expensive items in plumbing is the waste stack, or vertical pipe into which all the fixtures discharge. This will rise through the house and out of the roof, thereby venting sewer gases above the house. If bathrooms and kitchens are scattered throughout the house, you will need several stacks. In new construction design, architects and builders always try to put bathrooms and kitchens back to back and stack them in multistory houses so that everything can tie into one stack. This concept also is important in rehabbing, particularly since it is usually more difficult to get the plumbing into the house (keep in mind you may not be replacing the roofing material, and it is not easy to break through slate or tile to accommodate a stack). Kitchens and bathrooms also should be centrally located so that you can put the hot water tank close to them.

This same concept holds true for electrical service (although running wire is not nearly as expensive as running pipe) and for heating and air-conditioning. For instance, you may not want to place the living zone at the far end of the house when the furnace is in the center.

Many new houses are being built with the kitchen, dining room, and entertainment area all in one space. There is also a growing interest in rehabbing old commercial or warehouse space into loft apartments or condos based on an open con-

cept. These layouts may appeal only to people who lead a particular lifestyle, but the idea of opening up space is attractive to many people.

In addition to the removal of walls, interesting space can result from the removal of floors or ceilings, provided that it is structurally feasible to do so. Lowering floors and taking out ceilings tend to be very expensive modifications. These types of changes should be made only with the help of an engineer, and they probably should be made only when it is necessary to rebuild the entire floor structure or ceiling for some other reason.

A double-story space can add an exciting dimension to a house, but in a brick building, it is dangerous because the removal of large areas of structural floor may cause the outer walls of the house to buckle or even collapse. If you are considering taking out a structural floor, you will probably have to put a number of steel rods all the way through the house. These rods may detract from the space you are creating. It is imperative that you have an engineer deal with these issues. One of the problems when dealing with a two-story space in an old house is what to do with the windows. In most cases, people try to make continuous windows, which often destroys the aesthetics of the house's exterior. We tend to discourage this type of design, although opening up wider staircases can produce the same effect.

Planning room by room is discussed in detail in many other books, and, in most cases, you will probably live with the space in your house as it is or at least as it is defined by the bearing walls. If you plan to make extensive changes, you should consult an architect. If you do the planning, you might make the wrong decisions based on inadequate information or costs, and you may not be happy with the end result. See references at the end of this chapter if you wish to design your own space within the basic structure of your building.

HOW TO MEASURE AND DRAW YOUR HOUSE

Many people are put off by the apparent complexity of architectural drawings, but the lines of the house are not that difficult to put on paper. The one drawing that is difficult to do is an elevation, which is a side view of a house. Sometimes it is even hard to get the measurements needed for such a drawing.

Working drawings usually consist of plans, sections, elevations, and details. A *plan* is what you would see by looking directly down on a house if a huge chainsaw cut a horizontal cross section through all the halls and partitions. A *section* is a view of a vertical cross section cut down through a house by the hypothetical saw and is typically a section of a floor, the vertical wall, and half the roof. An *elevation* is a drawing of the outside of the house. A *detail* may include an elevation, but it usually

FIGURE 5-1. **A)** *Sample floor plan drawing*

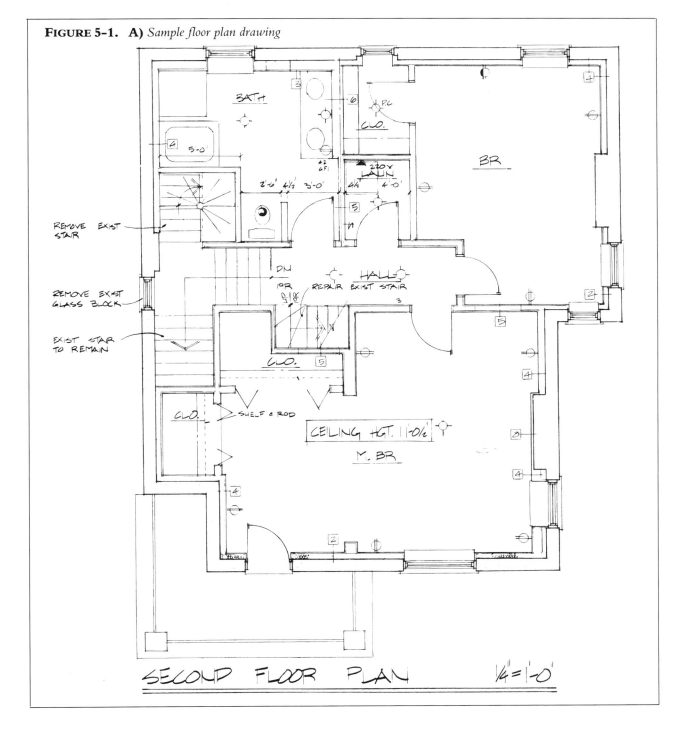

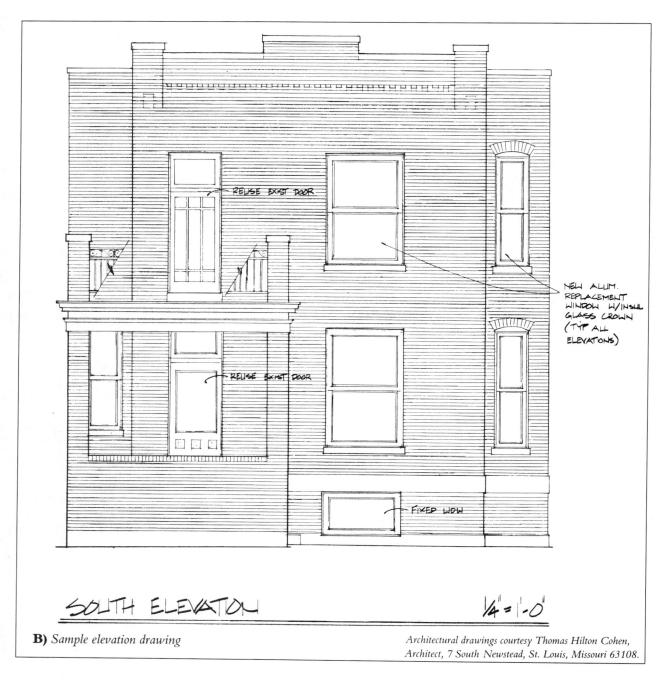

SOUTH ELEVATION   1/4" = 1'-0"

B) *Sample elevation drawing*

Architectural drawings courtesy Thomas Hilton Cohen, Architect, 7 South Newstead, St. Louis, Missouri 63108.

includes special features of the house, such as kitchen cabinets or wiring. Working drawings are drawn to scale and look like the illustrations shown in Figure 5-1.

The basic symbols and elements of architectural drawings are detailed in many texts, and virtually every high school has an architectural drawing class. The first step in drawing working plans is measuring the building. The basic tools for measuring are a 25- to 50-foot measuring tape, a yard-

stick or rigid ruler for measuring heights, a legal pad, and a pencil. Begin with a simple outline sketch of the layout of each floor, then start measuring every dimension. Do not forget to measure the thickness of walls and partitions. No matter how simple you make your basic starting sketch, make sure you show all projections, recesses, windows, doors, and door swings. Use the largest sheet of paper you can conveniently carry around for your drawing. Try to keep everything proportional, as doing so makes understanding the drawing easier later on. Also make sure everything is legible. Some people use graph paper, but if you can draw a straight line you probably don't need it.

For the most part, accuracy needs to be only to the nearest quarter inch. You do need to be more precise when determining multiples of building materials, such as 8-, 10-, or 12-foot lengths of drywall or 16-inch centers in studs. It is also important to understand that all the measurements should be taken to the plaster or drywall, not to baseboards or projecting wood trim. Keep in mind that old

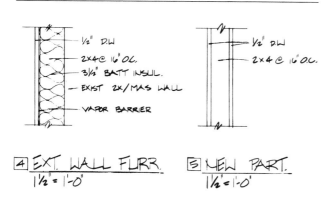

C) *Sample wall section drawing*

buildings are never square, so you may want to measure the diagonals of rooms. Also, measure the width of brick buildings both at the floor and at the ceiling. The measurements will be different.

Sketch stairways in addition to measuring the size or depth and width of the runs. Note the number of treads, the rise (the distance from the top of each tread to the top of the next tread), and the number of risers from floor to floor. If possible, show other elements in the building, such as flues, stacks, and pipes, and be sure to mark bearing walls.

To make your final drawings, you will need a T square, a small drawing board or a square desk top, a 45-degree triangle, a compass, a circle template, and an architect's scale. Do not use an engineer's scale because feet are divided into tenths instead of twelfths.

Armed with this simple equipment, you are ready to make the drawings that you will need for the building commission. The complexity of these

drawings depends on the complexity of your project. As we have discussed, if there are major structural issues, you will probably have to have an architect or engineer stamp the drawings, so it may be best to have an architect or engineer do them from scratch.

It may be feasible to do your own drawings if you keep the existing floor plans of the building; take out the plaster; replace the plumbing, electrical, and heating systems; and redrywall and finish the building with no structural changes or repairs. Ask the local building commission whether the code requires working plans to be professionally drawn and whether any structural elements require engineering analysis. If so, you will have to hire an engineer or an architect to provide these services.

If the building commission does allow you to draw your own plans, determine how detailed they must be and how many copies of the plans you must submit for permit. In general, you should submit the most complete drawings you can produce, including specifications for materials, floor plans, elevations, and cross sections of walls and windows. If you plan to add new windows, the manufacturer will be able to supply cross sections of these. You also may need a site plan (a drawing of how the buildings sits on the lot) or a survey. Specification lists are helpful if you plan to hire a contractor or subcontractors for the job. Step-by-step instructions for developing working drawings is beyond the scope of this book, but many drafting books are available, including *Architectural Drafting and Design* by Donald Hepler and Paul Wallach (McGraw-Hill, 1981).

References

OLD

Arthur, William. *Estimating Building Costs*. 2nd Ed. New York: Scientific Book Co., 1928.

Burrell, Edward J. *Elementary Building Construction and Drawing*. London, N.P., 1911.

Hodgson, Frederick Thomas. *The Builder's Guide and Estimator's Price Book*. New York: Industrial Publication Company, 1890.

Ingraham, George H. *Comparative Cost of Various*

Types of Construction for 3 Houses. N.P.: National Fire Proofing Company, 1911.

Wilson, J. *The Mechanic's and Builder's Price Book*. New York: Appleton, 1859.

NEW

Ball, John E. *Builders Math, Plans, Specifications*. Revised and edited by Tom Philbin. Indianapolis: Bobbs-Merrill, 1983.

Bellis, Herbert F. *Blueprint Reading for the Construction Trades*. New York: McGraw-Hill, 1978.

Clifford, Martin. *Basic Drafting*. Blue Ridge Summit, Pennsylvania: TAB Books, 1980.

Helton, Joseph E. *Simplified Estimating for Builders and Engineers*. Englewood Cliffs, New Jersey: Prentice-Hall, 1985.

Jackson, W.P. *Estimating Home Building Costs*. Carlsbad, California: Craftsman Book Co., 1981.
_____. *Carpentry Estimating*. Carlsbad, California: Craftsman Book Co., 1987.

Lewis, Jack R. *Architectural Draftsman's Reference Handbook*. Englewood Cliffs, New Jersey: Prentice-Hall, 1982.

Muller, Edward John. *Reading Architectural Working Drawings*. Englewood Cliffs, New Jersey: Prentice-Hall, 1981.

Roy, Robert L. *Money-Saving Strategies for the Owner/Builder*. New York: Sterling Publishing Co., 1981.

Traister, John E. *Blueprint Reading for the Building Trades*. Carlsbad, California: Craftsman Book Co., 1985.

Wetherill, Edward B. *Estimating and Analysis for Commercial Renovation*. Kingston, Massachusetts: R.S. Means Co., 1985.

Williams, Benjamin, ed. *Reducing Home Building Costs*. Carlsbad, California: Craftsman Book Co., 1978.

Chapter 6

BUYING, FINANCING, AND INSURING A HOUSE

Four topics are discussed in this chapter: pricing the rehabable structure, making an offer and purchasing the building, financing it, and obtaining insurance for it.

Before we discuss determination of the price to be offered for a rehabable structure, let's discuss the concept of overimprovement. A house is considered to be overimproved if the money spent on the rehab cannot be recovered when the house is sold. Obviously, the concept of overimprovement does not take into account the owner's enjoyment of changes in the house during his or her term of occupancy.

The two key factors governing overimprovement are the sale value of the improvements made and the location of the house. Most people know about cost in relation to location, but it is a common misconception that the cost of a particular home improvement will increase the value of the house by an equal or greater amount. In fact, most home improvements add only 40 to 75 percent of their costs to a home's market value. It is important to manage a rehab so that you can recapture costs when the house is sold.

The value of the house also is influenced by the value of surrounding property and the quality of the neighborhood. We suggest that you look for rehabable structures in historic or redevelopment districts, because the surrounding properties will increase the value of your finished project. But many other areas also are experiencing dramatic increases in property value—some because of location, and others because of charm or uniqueness. It is important to get a feel for the location of the

restorable structure. That is why it is important to live in an area or town for some time before you look for a house to rehab. You should always call the appropriate city offices to learn of planned parks, sidewalks, trees, or freeway projects, rehab loan programs, or any other public works projects in a given area. One of the things that we do is to drive along the back alleys of a neighborhood. You can tell what the neighborhood is really like by looking at the backs of houses.

Regardless of what you do to investigate a rehabable structure, it is extremely important that you understand the concept of overimprovement. You do not want to put so much money into a rehab that your costs are more than you could ever recoup by selling the house.

PRICING THE REHAB

The typical method for determining an offering price for a house is to find out the prices of comparable houses. To a real estate broker, comparables are structures that have been sold in the past six months and are similar in nature, size, and neighborhood to the house in question.

There are several ways of finding comparables. One way is to find a real estate broker, who will have immediate access to previous sales information through the multiple listing service or the registrar of deeds at the local courthouse. Without using a real estate broker (and we suggest that you do not), you can go to the registrar of deeds yourself. Drive through the neighborhood of interest, find the houses that are currently being rehabbed or look as though they have been recently, write down the addresses, go to the registrar of deeds, and look up the date of sale and the selling price. Another way to do this is to ask banks or savings and loans for selling prices of comparable houses. This is also a good way to get to know a loan officer who may be able to help you later with financing.

If a building will be a gut rehab, one of the things you can do is estimate the value of the foundation, outside walls, and roof. Then add that to the value of the land the structure sits on to come up with a comparable price. If all you are getting is a foundation, roof, and walls, then that is all the building is worth. Given that strategy, the only thing you have to do is determine the cost of land in the area.

At this point, you will have a basic estimate of what you think the rehabable structure is worth as is. You also will know how much the rehab will cost. Now you are ready to determine whether the project is viable. Acquiring a rehabable house is vastly different from acquiring a home or personal residence. The purchaser, in determining a fair offer for a home-to-be, considers the prevailing value, comparable houses in the area, the size of the mortgage and monthly payments, and the costs of improvements to be made over a long period. When seeking a house for renovation and resale, however, you are dealing with different issues. Often there are no other houses to which this house can be compared. The rehab may require major alterations in a fairly short time, and you may or may not be considering a speedy resale. The area may be one in which there is a large number of structures in their original condition, or the area may have very few habitable structures. Often the seller is dealing with the same issues.

Do not assume that the only properties you should consider are those that are listed or that a broker shows you. In real estate, everything is for sale for the right price. The issue is what is the right price. What is right for the seller usually is not right for the buyer, but if the seller is desperate to sell, then the two definitions of *right* come closer together. The closer the asking price comes to the offered price, the closer both parties are to the right price.

BUYING THE HOUSE

Once you have begun your search and you have scrutinized all serious prospects, you will start to understand an area. As you keep learning about houses in general and that neighborhood in particular, you will know a true bargain when you see it. You will be less swayed by gimmicks, pressure, and real estate salespeople. The trick to buying a rehabable structure is to remember that you do not have to buy this house. Be dispassionate. The ultimate way to do that is to own or rent a house, live in it, be perfectly happy, and then go out and look for something to rehab that might make you even happier.

Remember, everything is negotiable. Negotiate the little items first; save the price for last. Never be pressured. Never believe it when someone tells you that another person is interested in the same house; that's an old trick. Be very specific about what you will need to fix up the house; use your House Inspection Checklist from Chapter 4 to do this. If you are in doubt about anything, stop talking and think. Keep all discussions businesslike and be polite. Never walk through a house and tell the present owner all the things that you are going to tear out of it. If you do, he or she may not want to sell it to you.

Bidding on a house is an emotional experience, even if you are determined to remain aloof and are an experienced rehabber who has gone through this process several times. By the time you are ready to bid, you will have seen the house several times and begun to identify with it. You have pictured the house as it will be redone. You may even have fallen in love with certain charming aspects of it. You have seen its potential, and the more you think about it, the more difficult it is to let go. But you need to remain detached so you don't make a poor decision.

Keep in mind that you will most likely get a counteroffer unless the seller is truly desperate to sell. Many buyers make their first offer lower than the price they are willing to pay to allow for the probability that the seller will make a counteroffer. Others make only one firm offer. It is generally better to make a lower offer, because most people like to bargain and most prices are established with bargaining in mind. For more information on negotiating to buy a house, read Robert Allen's *Nothing Down* (Simon & Schuster, 1984).

Real estate brokers often do a lot of the things we have just discussed. If you are an inexperienced buyer, a broker's fee may be justified. If you are experienced in buying property, a broker's services may not be needed. Brokers are accustomed to working for the seller, so if you do retain a real estate broker, make sure that that person understands that he or she must represent you. Another important point is that brokers in rehab areas are often in the business of finding, buying, and restoring rehabable structures for themselves or in connection with builders. We strongly suggest that you avoid using brokers in rehab areas for that reason alone. They are not likely to show you the better properties. The best thing to do is to get to know the neighborhood yourself or to go through a historic or redevelopment district office.

If you are interested in rehabbing a building, one of the easiest things that you can do is investigate the neighborhood. You do not need to pay the broker to do that for you, especially since he or she may not show you the things that you are most interested in. Good rehab buildings are typically not advertised for sale. Often the owner is not thinking about selling. If you can find property like that, you will discover two benefits. First, the owners will not put any money into the property in order to sell it. That is money saved because it would go into the asking price. Second, the property price will not have been influenced by a real estate broker.

If you do not use a real estate agent to help with negotiations, it is probably a good idea to consult a lawyer, preferably a real estate attorney. Remember that everything concerning real estate must be in writing, or the agreement is legally unenforceable.

When you reach an agreement with the seller, one of you should draw up a sales agreement. Do not sign it until your lawyer has examined it. It is customary to give a binder (money) to a third party (usually a lawyer or real estate agent) but not to the buyer. Try to make the binder as small as possible. Also, build in as many contingencies as possible (for

example, financing or zoning), to give yourself a way out of the deal. While you investigate financing and other matters pertinent to the status of the building, you should have the building inspected structurally, investigate the zoning regulations for that area, have your lawyer or a title company conduct a title search, investigate property taxes, and find out if you can get financing.

FINANCING

For years, renovation financing was a problem at banks and savings and loans because of the institutions' loan-to-value ratio on older houses. Whereas banks loaned 75 to 90 percent of a new property's appraised value, they would typically loan only 60 to 75 percent of the value of a property that required renovation. To compound that problem, they often used loan disbursement schedules keyed to new construction. That is, they required the rehabber to have the work done much faster (four months) than is possible. Renovation involving substantial demolition actually reduces the value of the property before it increases it; consequently banks have traditionally not favored rehabbing.

The banks' attitude toward renovation has improved substantially in the last few years, because renovation has proven economically viable in many cities and because of community and government pressure on banks to make rehab loans. A bank must comply with the Community Reinvestment Act, which supports rehabbing, or it will lose its charter. Further, GNMA (Ginny Mae) and FAMA (Fanny Mae) have increased the funds available for renovation in the past few years.

Banks have not altered their requirements for prospective buyers, however. A monthly housing payment for mortgage, taxes, and insurance combined still should not exceed 35 percent of the gross monthly income of the applicant (in most areas of the country). The applicant also needs to be gainfully employed. There is a tendency for those who rehab their own houses to feel that, since they are saving so much in "sweat equity," they can put that savings into a larger house and therefore take more than 35 percent of their income to support the house. If a bank will loan at a higher rate, it means you may end up being house poor. We do not think that borrowing against your sweat equity is a good move. It makes little sense to go through all that hard work and then find yourself unable to go out to eat. You might as well have bought the finished product. We suggest that you try to stay within the 35 percent range. Do not use other types of secondary financing to get yourself to the point where your housing costs are extremely high. A well-planned rehab will reduce the likelihood that you will need a second mortgage to finish the project.

For a conventional mortgage, most lending institutions will loan 75 to 85 percent of the price you are paying for the house, conditional on a satisfactory appraisal and your credit history. If you were buying a finished house, the bank would loan up to 80 percent of the house's appraised value. In rehabbing, the present house may be worth only a fraction of what it will be worth at the end of the rehab. Most banks have rehab programs in which they will appraise the property as rehabbed and loan 75 to 80 percent of that amount. The catch is that they can do that only if you give them a complete plan and budget for the rehab. In other words, you must have done your homework before you approach the bank.

Banks offer a wide variety of mortgages. Consult your local lending institutions or a real estate agent for information on different types of mortgages. This is discussed further in Chapter 7.

So far, we have assumed that you do not already own the house. If you do own the house, there are three ways to generate rehab funds: (1) a home improvement loan; (2) a home equity loan; and (3) refinancing of the original deed of trust. The bank will evaluate your ability to repay and will appraise the house as in every other case. Keep in mind that the interest rate is almost always higher for home improvement loans and that it is usually higher for loans under $15,000. With the rapid appreciation in real estate values in many parts of the country, home equity loans and second deeds of trust are excellent ways to obtain funds for rehabs. You are basically borrowing against the home's increase in value since you purchased it.

Another source of funds may be subsidized city rehab loans. These loans tend to be used primarily for the correction of code violations, but they can pay for other work as well. For information on these programs, contact your city or state department of community development. Forty percent of the Community Development Block Grant disbursements are used for residential rehab programs. Metropolitan areas with more than 50,000 residents receive federal block grant funds directly; in smaller areas, these funds are handled by the state.

You might also be able to tap three other sources of funds. First, if your employer has a credit union, inquire about home equity loans or purchase loans. The credit union may or may not fund rehabs, but it is worth checking because the interest rates would be lower than those at most banks. Second, check neighborhood savings and loans in a rehab area. When an area starts being rehabbed and property values begin to increase, a savings and loan might appear on the scene to support further rehabbing. Third, if you are rehabilitating a house for trade or business (a bed-and-breakfast establishment, an office, or rental housing), you may be eligible for federal preservation tax incentives. That topic is discussed in more detail in Chapter 7.

In some instances, the money that you save by rehabbing the house yourself or acting as a general contractor can be used essentially as a down payment. This will depend on how much you are going to save on the overall project and on the bank's policy. Everything involved in asking a bank for rehab money is based on the structure's market value when it is finished. For example, if you buy a 3,000-square-foot building suitable for rehabbing for $40,000 and you calculate that the rehab will cost $30 per square foot, you will need $40,000 for the building and $90,000 for the rehab, amounting to $130,000 total. If the building is appraised at $156,000 or more, and if the bank is willing to loan 80 percent of the appraised value, then it will be willing to loan you the $130,000 for the project. If the appraisal is less than $156,000, the bank will loan only 80 percent of that amount, and you will have to make up the difference out of your own pocket. Assuming that the bank will allow you to get into a rehab with none of your money invested, the above example demonstrates one investing approach. In most cases, however, even if the appraisal comes in higher than $156,000, the bank will insist that you put some of your money into the project. The bank's reasoning is that it is too easy for you to walk away from a project if you have no money in it. Some banks are more flexible if they are very sure that you are going to finish the project. This is another reason for you to be well prepared when you walk into the bank.

Let's stop here and discuss what you need to do *before* you walk into the bank. Before you go to a meeting with a bank officer to discuss a loan, you need to do your homework and prepare yourself thoroughly. You should have a signed sales agreement on the building and have occupancy and building permits. If you are in a historic or redevelopment district, you also should have met any requirements of the district. You should have filled out the Cost Estimating Checklist (see Chapter 5) in detail, including all bids from contractors or subcontractors and price sheets from supply houses where appropriate. One thing that we typically do is write a narrative of what we plan to do to the building and when we plan to do it. Make this as short as possible. You also should contact an insurance agent and line up insurance. Be able to discuss the process of restoration or rehabbing.

When you go to the bank, be totally prepared. Know how much the rehab is going to cost and how long it is going to take. If you plan to do a fair amount of the work yourself, do not be afraid to tell them that you have not had much experience, but detail everything you *have* done. If you have attended any classes or workshops or your father or mother was a skilled craftsperson, tell the bank. If you helped someone else on a project, or if you have watched a professional work on a project in preparation for buying your own rehab, tell the bank. Everything counts. Put it all down on paper. Keep in mind that bankers tend to be finance people. That is how they think and operate, so you should do the same.

In his book *Manage Your Own Home Renovation,* Carl Heldmann points out the very important fact that bankers will be very wary if you want to manage your own project. You should not be defensive about this, however, because bankers are also wary of most professional general contractors. With many lenders, an automatic "no" is a matter of policy in initial talks about rehabbing. You must walk in prepared and assertive, because only you will be able to persuade the bank that you are capable of managing your own renovation project.

You will find varying loan rates and requirements. Make sure that you shop around. The requirements for you may be more important than the interest rate. Most large cities have a newsletter that lists the requirements and the mortgage rates for different kinds of loans at all banks and savings and loans. This document is sold to real estate agents. Find the publisher of that newsletter and subscribe.

Be persistent in finding a lender. Don't forget that your job is to persuade the lender to give you money. Don't be surprised at the bank's reluctance to lend money for an unfinished project. If you had $100,000 in your pocket, would you give it to somebody on a promise?

If the loan is approved, the lender will usually give you an advance, which should be enough to purchase the structure and start some of the work, but the remainder of the money will stay in the bank. As you complete a portion of the work, it will be inspected by a disbursing agent or inspector, who will fill out an inspection report and a disbursement schedule. This indicates to the bank or savings and loan that more funds can be disbursed to you. The funds are disbursed through a title company or the bank's own construction program, which may charge 1 percent of the loan to provide this inspection and disbursement service. It should be noted that you will pay interest only on the money that you have received. One way that banks ensure that you contribute some money to the project is to require you to pay the first portion of the renovation costs. You are reimbursed for these when the house is completed. At that time, your money, the purchase money, and the construction loan money is converted into a permanent loan.

Several very important people are involved in any rehab project. You will have control over most of them because you are the one with the money. However, two of them will have control over you. One is the disbursing inspector, the person who inspects your house and determines whether the bank should disburse a portion of the construction funds. The other is the city building inspector (framing, plumbing, and electrical). You need to be nice to these people, but you also must be honest and forthright with them. You do not want to waste their time, try to fool them, or hide things from them. If they catch you, they will never trust you again.

INSURANCE

Insurance coverage is extremely important. In rehabbing, the house changes value as you work on it. It goes down in value before it goes up. Most insurance companies will not offer home owner's insurance on rehab projects or on houses that are appraised at less than $40,000. You will, however, be able to get a policy that covers fire and other basic damage. Shop around for insurance. In most cities, individuals who steal for a living target houses that are being renovated because they know no one is there at night and there are probably going to be valuable tools or supplies in the building. The problem is that you can rarely insure against theft in a rehab, so unless you live in it, you'll have to lock your tools in a very strong box or take them home with you. Also, if the structure was a derelict, the former occupants (vagrants) might try to break into it.

If you *can* find a full home owner's policy for a rehab, take it. If you are buying a run-down wreck to gut, get just a fire policy, but you may have to be very conscientious about guarding the building. If you plan to install a burglar alarm, do so quickly. The reason you usually see new outside doors and windows being installed first in most construction projects is to make the building a bit more secure. This is not only to prevent theft but also to protect against liability claims.

If you live in an earthquake area, you should probably have earthquake insurance, especially if you are rehabbing a brick building that was built prior to the turn of the century. Earthquake insurance is generally carried as a rider on another policy, and prices vary considerably.

All property insurance policies have minimum and maximum coverage stipulations. Replacement cost to insurance companies does not reflect the value of the land; it is concerned solely with the physical structure. Most insurance companies will not insure early Victorian solid brick structures at replacement cost. Instead, they will insure them at fair market value, which is typically less than the replacement value of the structure as it was originally built. Try to obtain insurance for the full amount of your loan at minimum and preferably at the appraised finished value of the house. That may be difficult with some insurance companies. If the insurance policy has a deductible, you can use that to your advantage. Insurance companies are more attracted to a $100,000 policy with a $1,000 deductible than to a $50,000 policy with a $100 deductible.

Many home owner's policies for older homes also stipulate that the insurer will pay for repairing damage only if modern construction materials were used during replacement. This means that you will have to use drywall instead of duplicating the original lath and plaster and wall-to-wall carpeting over a plywood base rather than heart pine or quarter-sawed oak floors. When shopping for insurance, make sure the agents tell you exactly what will be insured so that you can make an informed decision.

You also may want to consider liability insurance. For the next 12 months or so, you are going to be managing a renovation, and several people will be on your property doing dangerous things for which they may or may not be properly insured. Unless you require evidence of workmen's compensation and liability insurance from all your subcontractors, you should carry your own liability insurance. If you can get liability insurance attached to your fire or home owner's policy at a reasonable price, we recommend that you do so. You do not need someone falling off a ladder and suing you because he or she (or an employer) does not have any insurance to cover medical bills.

References

OLD

Graham, Frank Duncan. *Audel's Carpenters and Builders Guide.* New York: T. Audel & Co., 1939.

Nichols, Edward. *Contracts and Specifications.* Chicago: American Technical Society, 1912.

Peker, Charles G. *Hints for Carpenters.* New York: Industrial Book Company, 1909.

Plant, J.C., and A.S. Johnson. *Contracts and Specifications.* Chicago: American School of Correspondence, 1912.

NEW

Alth, Max. *Be Your Own Contractor: The Affordable Way to Home Ownership.* Blue Ridge Summit, Pennsylvania: TAB Books, 1984.

Hamilton, Harper. *How to Prepare Building and Construction Contracts.* Boulder, Colorado: Hamilton Press, 1977.

Heldmann, Carl. *Be Your Own House Contractor: How to Save 25 Percent without Lifting a Hammer.* Pownal, Vermont: Garden Way Publishing, 1981.

Jones, Jack Payne. *Handbook of Construction Contracting.* Carlsbad, California: Craftsman Book Co., 1986.

McGuerty, Dave. *The Complete Guide to Contracting Your Home: A Step-by-Step Method for Managing Home Construction.* White Hall, Virginia: Betterway Publications, 1986.

Rauch, Paul H. *How to Be Your Own Contractor: Remodeling, Additions, Alterations, Building a New Home.* Andover, Massachusetts: Brick House Publishing Co., 1988.

Chapter 7

DEALING WITH CITY HALL

You can avoid a lot of wasted time and money by making your first order of business a search to find information about city and county regulations concerning construction. How you do the work on your house—including specific construction techniques and types and grades of material (even down to the kind and size of nails)—is regulated by your local building codes. Because building codes will have a profound effect on your renovation plans, especially in urban areas, it is imperative that you find out about, and visit, your local building authority well in advance of buying a property and planning the rehab.

It is also important for you to investigate incentives that may be available for rehabbing in your area. There may be city, county, state, or federal money available for rehabs. There also may be tax incentives for rehabbing in your area.

A number of government agencies will have an impact on your project, and it is important that you understand all their regulations. This chapter reviews the different agencies that you might have to deal with. Conduct your own investigation to determine which agencies you *have* to deal with and which ones you *should* be dealing with.

RESTORATION TAX INCENTIVES

Restoration is not the focus of this book, but it is possible that you may find a rehab in a historic district. Even gut rehabs are feasible in most districts as long as the front of the building maintains its original character. Rehabbers working in historic districts do, however, have to deal with more agencies than do rehabbers not in these districts.

In a historic rehab, once you have ascertained the physical condition of the structure and done a cost estimate, you must begin to look for information about its original appearance to develop a program for restoration. It is possible that a historic resource survey, which is an inventory of architecturally significant structures, exists for your project area. If so, that will give you a head start.

Most houses are not eligible for the federal tax incentives granted to encourage rehabbing of income-producing historic buildings. Those tax credits are reserved for industrial, commercial, or residential rental properties. If the house is used for trade or business or is rented for housing, such as a bed and breakfast, then it may earn federal tax advantages. First, the building must be individually listed on the National Register of Historic Places, or it must be located in a registered historic district. The rehab project also must be certified. The basis for making this determination can be found in a document entitled "The Secretary of the Interior Standards for Rehabilitation and Guidelines for Rehabilitating Historic Buildings," which is available from the U.S. Government Printing Office, Washington, DC 20402. To pursue tax incentives, the owner of a historic property must submit a two-part application, usually to the state historic preservation officer.

You must find out what your state historic preservation office requires, but here are some hints:
1. Prepare photos of the property's exterior and interior.

2. Make sure to contact your state historic preservation office or the National Park Service regional office and keep in touch with the people there.

3. The Secretary of the Interior has set ten standards that any completed historic project must meet. Make sure you have a list of those standards and understand them.

4. Expect fairness but not leniency. The National Park Service must verify compliance with standards and guidelines, and the investigators are usually strict.

For more information about the requirements for restoration in historic districts, see William Shopsin's *Restoring Old Buildings for Contemporary Uses* (Whitney Library of Design, 1986) or Prentice and Prentice's *Rehab Right* (Ten Speed Press, 1986).

To determine whether your property qualifies for tax incentives, you must first find out whether it is listed in the National Register of Historic Places. If it is, you qualify immediately. Most large libraries have a copy of the register. You also may write to the U.S. Department of the Interior, Heritage Conservation and Recreation Service, Washington, DC 22043, or to your state historic preservation office. If your property is not listed in the register, you do not qualify for tax incentives. If you believe that your property or the district in which it is located *should* be placed on the national register, you can write to your state historic preservation office and request a review of the property or district.

If your property is listed in the register, you will need the following materials to obtain certification for tax incentives: '
1. The Historic Preservation Certification Application. This is a two-part application; one part pertains to the structure itself, and the other pertains to the rehabilitation work.

2. "The Secretary of the Interior Standards for Rehabilitation."

3. Information sheets entitled "Tax Reform Act Incentives and Disincentives."

4. A brochure entitled "Tax Incentives for Rehabilitating Historic Buildings."

5. Additional information pertaining to the Tax

Reform Act of 1986 and beyond. All this information is available from the U.S. Department of the Interior, Washington, DC 20240. Once you have read the brochures and other information, you can complete the application.

LOCAL CODES

Construction is regulated by zoning and building codes. The principal challenges in the construction process are (1) zoning regulations, (2) building codes, and (3) special ordinances and review processes.

Zoning Regulations

Zoning regulations have been established to determine the use, location, and number of buildings in a particular area. They are based on the interpretation of the quality of the environment produced by a given group of buildings or specific uses and population densities. Since the beginning of the century, the courts have accepted the doctrine that zoning is in the public interest. Zoning bylaws also may regulate the amount of parking required, the amount of building coverage allowed on a given lot, the closeness of the building to any side of the lot, the distance the building may be set back from the property line, the height of the building, the distance between buildings, and other such variables.

The recent trend toward converting former manufacturing and commercial structures to living quarters, lofts, art galleries, restaurants, shops, and so on has blurred many of the basic planning assumptions of most city zoning boards, and new urban residential neighborhoods have blossomed in previously run-down commercial areas. To permit the transformation of commercial property to residential living space, the old ordinances must be modified and a flexible approach taken.

If you are planning to convert a house from a single-family dwelling to a multifamily one or commercial space to living space, you must determine whether such a conversion is allowed in your zone. Approach the zoning review process with a cooperative attitude and a willingness to make compromises. Zoning and land use legislation is enacted at the prerogative of the local government, and the review and approval procedures for zoning changes generally require public hearings. In some areas, zoning changes require the approval of other property owners in the area. You will probably have to apply for a bylaw amendment and make a presentation at a public review board. Do your homework and practice if you are not used to making presentations. The more professional your presentation is, the more effective it will be in securing an approval. Good public relations are also important in this process.

If your zoning application is denied, you can appeal the decision at the county or regional level only if you can prove that the local review commission acted in an arbitrary or capricious manner. Make every effort to avoid this step, as it may involve court action.

Building Codes

Building codes have been established to minimize the possibility of personal or property damage due to structural failure, fire, or other hazards. These codes guarantee conformity to basic engineering, ventilation, sanitation, and fire protection standards. Building codes are constantly evolving as new materials are developed. In almost no case will a building you are considering for rehabilitation meet the current code standards. In some areas of the country, special review procedures have been developed to deal with alternatives for historic buildings. Codes also differ significantly for different types of buildings. Multifamily houses and commercial buildings are subject to more stringent requirements than single-family houses. This is particularly true if you are proposing conversion from commercial to public use, for example, from a warehouse to a restaurant. The number of emergency exits, the amount of ventilation, the width of stairwells, and the load capacity of the floors will all be scrutinized in such a case.

Part of an architect's job is to be familiar with zoning laws and building codes. But the people who are most conversant with every aspect of the building codes typically are the building inspectors. If you do not use an architect in your project, *you* will have to be familiar with the building codes, so it is useful to get to know the building inspectors.

Local codes are based on one of four sets of requirements: the National Building Code of the National Board of Fire Underwriters, the Basic Building Code of the Building Officials and Code Administrators International, the Standard Building Code of the Southern Building Code Congress, and the Uniform Building Code of the International Congress Conference of Building Officials. These codes differ because of variances in custom, climate, and even politics. In addition, if the local government wishes to impose more stringent requirements, it will choose one code over another. Contact your local building commission to find out which code, *and which year or version of that code,* is in effect. You can obtain copies of these codes from your local office of the American Institute of Architects, or you can write to the American Institute of Architects, 1735 New York Avenue NW, Washington, DC 20006.

If you are not going to change the structure of your building significantly (you are simply going to gut it and install new electrical, plumbing, and heating systems), you probably don't need copies of the basic building codes; you only need copies of the electrical and plumbing codes. If you plan to hire subcontractors to do the electrical and plumbing work, you don't need copies of any of these codes. You can rely on your building inspector to tell you what's okay and what isn't. If you have to submit a plan to your building commission, the commission will approve it or not approve it, and you can discuss specific points with the building inspector.

Some buildings cannot be modified to meet the code requirements without destroying important architectural features. This is important because, when you do a rehab, the entire building will have to be brought up to code. Common problems are that stairways are not wide enough, balcony balusters may not be high enough, or there is not enough room around a toilet. To cope with these problems, most building codes have a variance process whereby you may be granted an exemption through a review process. Sometimes inspectors can grant variances on the spot.

Keep in mind that the building commission is probably not the best place to go for information about historic building codes. Most alternative codes are initiated by historic preservation departments. In some areas, these two groups may have very different opinions about how things should be done.

Permits

To do any kind of construction work, you must obtain permits from the building commission in your area. Typically, three permits are issued: the building permit, the plumbing permit, and the electrical permit. What requires a permit and what does not will depend on your local codes. Simply redecorating an interior does not require a permit in most cases. Almost everything else does, particularly if any structural work is done. Virtually any plumbing or electrical work also requires a permit. Many people do not obtain permits for minor jobs that technically require them. It is usually prudent to obtain a permit, or at least to inquire as to whether one is required, for the work that you have in mind.

In hiring contractors, the building permit and inspection process are your insurance that the job will be done correctly. A contractor who is not willing to do the job by the book and submit to inspections will probably do a very poor job. If you do the work yourself without a permit, you stand a very good chance of getting caught. Every inspector, particularly building inspectors, has jurisdiction over a particular territory, and he or she knows what projects are in progress. Inspectors also have a habit of driving the alleys, which is a wonderful way of catching people doing rehabbing work. If the inspector in your area notices people working on your house, materials being delivered, or a dumpster sitting in back of the house, he or she will wonder why a progress inspection has not been requested. In most areas, inspectors have the right to inspect your house at that point. If you are caught, you will probably have to pay penalties and extra permit fees. You may have to remove finish work so that progress inspections can be done on the rough work. You may even have to remove all the work. We guarantee that the inspector will be much stricter in examining future work if you didn't obtain a permit in the beginning. If you live in an area that has occupancy permits, you may not be able to sell the house without proving that the work was done in accordance with code specifica-

tions, and you cannot do that without a building permit.

Application for a building permit is made by the owner of the building or an agent for the owner, usually the architect or a subcontractor. You can obtain the permit by completing a standard application form, paying the required fee, and submitting the necessary drawings for review. Fees vary based on the area and the cost of the construction work. They may be anywhere from $5 to $10 per thousand dollars of construction work.

The building commission will probably require a site plan or a legal survey of the property and several copies of drawings indicating the scope of the work to be done. If you are doing a complete rehab, you may need elevations of the front and sides of the building and a floor plan for every floor. Typically, three to five copies are required, depending on whether your building is in a historic district or not. These drawings are reviewed by an engineer at the building commission for structural adequacy and zoning and building code conformance. If you are just going to knock down the plaster, replace the electrical, plumbing, and heating systems, and redrywall, you may be able to do those drawings yourself. Check with the building commission and *the engineer who reviews the plans* to find out exactly what is required before you spend a lot of money for drawings that may not be required.

Research will save you money. The review process takes time—at least a week or two in most areas. This will depend on the scale of the project and how busy the authorities are at the time of your application. They will be much busier in the spring and summer than in the fall and winter. Never walk into a building commission office at lunchtime. That's when everyone else is there. If your renovation is not extensive and the drawings are clear and correct, you may be able to obtain a building permit on the spot after some discussion with the reviewers.

You may or may not have to apply for the plumbing and electrical permits separately. These permits are usually obtained by the subcontractor doing the work, so don't be surprised if there is resistance to your obtaining these permits. In some areas, only licensed plumbers and electricians can obtain permits and do the work. If that is the case, you have the choice of hiring a professional sub-contractor, doing the work without a permit, or being licensed yourself. Most cities allow licensing of owners who wish to do their own plumbing and electrical work. The tests involved are relatively easy, but you should study the codes before taking them. The aim of the building commission is to make sure that anyone doing plumbing or electrical work knows the code and knows what they are doing. Both of the authors have passed these tests to do their own work.

In most cases, your work will be inspected as specified by the building commission at various stages of completion to ensure that it meets code requirements. In almost all cases, rough work must be inspected before it is covered. Thus, you must have structural framing, rough plumbing, and all electrical systems inspected before installing the drywall. If you do not call for progress inspections, the inspector may insist that you remove the finish work so that he or she can inspect the rough work. A final inspection will be required for all finish work. The building inspector will inspect everything but the plumbing and electrical systems. Plumbing and electrical inspectors will inspect those.

Inspectors usually have some leeway concerning what they can approve or reject in a project. The decision probably will be based on an impression of you and your work. Some inspectors go by the book. That may seem unfair, but remember that they are responsible for what they inspect. You may find that inspectors tend to trust some contractors and not others. That makes them a good source of information about which contractors to hire. Don't be surprised if they are very stringent with a sub-contractor and even more so with you. If you do the work yourself, you will have to prove that you know what you are doing and that you did the job correctly. Once an inspector sees that you are very careful about the work, he or she will probably be less stringent.

If you treat the inspector with respect, you will get the same in return. Also, do neat work. Sloppy work suggests that there may be problems. Always clean the area before an inspection and be present for the inspection. If you are not present, the inspector may not be able to find what you have done and

you will have to pay a reinspection fee. If you are present when the inspector finds violations, you can find out immediately how they should be corrected.

ARCHITECTURAL REVIEW BOARDS, LANDMARK COMMISSIONS, AND REDEVELOPMENT DISTRICTS

Architectural review boards and landmark commissions, whose authority is an extension of the local zoning bylaws, deal with visual and aesthetic matters. Redevelopment districts are similar, except that they are given eminent domain over an area and can condemn property, take it over, and either have it rehabilitated or sell it to a developer who will rehabilitate it.

Most architectural review boards and landmark commissions accept the premise that what was done in the past is their guide for the future. They will approve replacement or duplication of architectural elements fairly routinely, but the introduction of new types of architecture, major additions, or extra stories can be a problem. If there is no precedent for a landmark commission to follow, an architect or owner will have to make a very good case for the design. Consequently, it is important that you determine whether your property is in an architectural review board or landmark commission area or in a redevelopment district. They will all control, to some degree, the extent to which you may change your property inside and out.

Many rehabbers attempt to buy property in a redevelopment district because they know that property values will go up. Also, many cities provide tax abatements for rehabbers in redevelopment districts. The best way to investigate these issues is to visit the city planning department and the city community development office. If your area has an office of community development, it will probably administer rehabilitation assistance programs.

A number of assistance programs are available. They vary greatly, however, so you should check with the office of community development concerning specific programs. You may find loan programs that offer low-interest loans to encourage rehabilitation in declining neighborhoods. You also may find home maintenance improvement programs, which offer below-market interest rates to owner/occupants for rehabilitation, particularly for the correction of code violations. You may find weatherization or self-help paint programs. Weatherization programs offer insulation, caulking, weather stripping, replacement windows, and the like, either free of charge or in a subsidized manner. Self-help paint programs provide free paint and equipment for people who are painting their own homes. Often a short training session is required to qualify for these programs.

Cities also offer urban homesteading programs, in which the city acquires property in run-down areas and homesteaders receive this property for a low down payment plus their promise to rehabilitate the property and to occupy it for a given period of time, usually five years. Vacant buildings may be handled under a separate program. Some cities have programs that provide money to cover closing costs for the purchase of rehab property. Some cities also have similar programs for buying rehabs that will be turned into rental property. Finally, many cities offer tax abatements for rehab property. If you buy a piece of property and then rehab it to certain standards, the city will agree to hold the property taxes at their current value for 10 to 25 years. In some cases, the property taxes revert to one-half the current assessed value after 10 years. You may not find out about these programs unless you do some investigation, particularly if you are not in a historic or redevelopment district.

Many cities also offer workshops on rehabilitation, architectural history, and home repair. Your local library is another source of such information. In addition to books, it may have videos or films about rehabbing that you can check out.

References

OLD

Berg, Louis de Coppet. *Safe Building: A Treatise Giving the Practical & Theoretical Rules & Formulae Used in the Construction of Buildings.* 4th Ed. Boston: Ticknor & Co., 1894.

Fitzpatrick, F.W. *Building Code: A Compilation of Building Regulations Covering Every Phase of Municipal Building Activity with Special Emphasis on Fire Preventive Features.* Chicago: American School of Correspondence, 1913.

Hodgson, Frederick Thomas. *The Builder's Guide and Estimator's Price Book.* New York: Industrial Publication Company, 1890.

Marcotte, Charles. *Building Safe-Guide.* St. Louis: Slawson & Pierrot, Printers, 1879.

NEW

Prentice, H.K., and B. Prentice. *Rehab Right: How to Rehabilitate Your Oakland House without Sacrificing Architectural Assets.* Oakland, California: City of Oakland, 1978.

Chapter 8

TOOLS, MATERIALS, AND SUPPLIERS

There are many frustrations in a renovation project. One of the biggest is having an ill-equipped workshop or toolbox. One of the reasons professionals do good work is that they have the right tools. Whether you rehab one house or more, a good set of tools can be the difference between success and failure.

Many purists suggest that the rehabber have a basic tool collection consisting only of hand tools. Anyone who builds or rehabs houses for a living and any part-time renovator whose time is precious, however, will tell you that power tools are a must. Power tools cost about the same as most fine hand tools, and they tend to be faster, more accurate, and easier to use on heavy jobs. The tool collection presented in this chapter is by no means basic. It contains power tools as well as hand tools. Some are specialized rénovation tools, and some more ordinary tools. We believe, however, that the list presented in Table 8-1 contains the bare minimum for a large renovation project. You can borrow or rent the more specialized and expensive tools as needed.

Our list does not include carpentry tools for cabinetwork or other fine finish work, tools and brushes for painting and wallpapering, tools for working with iron or steel plumbing pipe, or masonry tools. The assumption is that these activities will most likely be subcontracted. Although the safety and apparel section appears near the end of the list, safety equipment is by no means expendable. It only takes one trip to the hospital to lose a day's or a season's worth of work.

There are three very basic rules for tools. First,

buy quality. Avoid the bargain racks and shop for name brands, high quality, and a good warranty. Always look for steel that is tempered and drop-forged. You can, however, be flexible here, especially if you are doing only one rehab. A $40 circular saw may last only one rehab, and that may be fine. The more expensive models are usually built to withstand the abuse of continual use.

Second, maintain quality. Be careful with tools, especially cutting tools. Protect cutting edges, retract blades when not in use, and hang up handsaws. Oil metal parts to prevent rust. Do not throw tools around. Clean up your work area so tools do not sit in debris. Organize your tools in some way Do not just throw them in a box; hang them on a wall. In some cases when we have done houses for ourselves, the first area we rehabbed was a shop in the basement where the tools could be stored and maintained.

Third, think safety. Sharp, high-quality hand tools keep you from using excessive or reckless force on a project. Remember, a dull tool is a dangerous tool. Power tools, which are much faster than hand tools, are potentially more dangerous. Wear safety goggles and do not remove blade guards. Do not use power tools when you are standing in a precarious position on a ladder or scaffold. Keep the work area clean of debris so as not to jeopardize your footing. Another safety tip is to pull the plug after using power tools, especially if there are children or pets in the work area. Always use tools correctly and for the job intended. Do not change bits or blades while a tool is plugged in. Always buy tools that fit you. If you are small, you

TABLE 8-1
TOOLS NEEDED FOR RENOVATION

Abrasives
Finish sander
Sandpaper (various grades)
Steel wool
Bench grinder (optional)
Belt sander (optional)
Paint scraper

Boring Tools
$3/8''$ variable speed drill
Drill bit set
Hole saw (nested or $2^1/8''$)
Spade bits (wood, $1/2''$, $1''$)
Power bit extension
Combination drill and
   countersink
Masonry bits ($1/2''$)
Drum rasp or sander

Chisels
Wood chisel set
Cold chisel/brick chisel
Nail sets
Star drill

Clamps and Vises
C-clamps
Pipe clamps
Vise grips
Bench vise or clamping
   workbench

Cleaning Items
Broom, shovel, dustpan
Desk brush
Vacuum (shop vac)
Wire brush and wire
   brush wheel

Drywall Tools (all optional)
Pan
$6''$ drywall knife
$12''$ drywall knife
Corner knife

Files and Rasps
Surform rasp
Flat file set

Hammers and Nail Guns
Carved-claw hammer

Framing hammer ($16''$, 24 oz.)
Short- and long-handled
   sledgehammers
Nail guns and compressor
   (optional)

Measuring Tools
$3/4'' \times 25'$ tape measure
Combination square
Framing square
T bevel
$3'$ to $4'$ level
Line level
Contour gauge
Plumb bob
Chalk line

Planes
Block plane
Jack plane

Pliers
Slip-joint pliers
Channel-lock pliers
Needle-nose pliers
Side-cutting pliers
Kleins or wire stripper

Pry bars
Flat pry bar
Large wrecking bar
Cat's-paw

Router (optional)
1-horsepower router
Router bit set

Saws
Crosscut handsaw
Backsaw
Hacksaw
Compass/keyhole saw
$7^1/4''$ portable circular saw
20- and 40-tooth carbide
   circular saw blades
Saber saw
Saber saw blade set
Reciprocating saw (sawsall)
$10''$ motorized miter box
   (chop box) [optional] or a
   hand miter box

$10''$ table saw or radial arm saw
   (optional)
$10''$ portable band saw
   (optional)

Screwdrivers
Set of standard tip
Set of Phillips
Spiral-ratchet type or
   commercial screw gun

Soldering Tools
Propane blowtorch kit
Solder gun (optional)
Flux brushes

Wrenches
Pipe wrenches
Socket wrench set
Allen wrench set
Adjustable wrenches
Open or box-end wrenches

**Safety Equipment
and Apparel**
Work gloves
Nail pouch/tool belt
Steel-toed work boots
Dust masks
Safety goggles
First-aid kit
Fire extinguishers

Miscellaneous
Putty knives
Stepladder ($2'$ shorter
   than ceilings)
$40'$ extension ladder (optional)
Electrical circuit tester
Heavy-duty extension cords
Drywall/utility knife
Sawhorses
Droplight or other lights
$8''$ to $10''$ planer/molder
   (optional)
Glass cutter (optional)

may be unable to control industrial-sized power tools, so you should buy handyman tools or hand tools that enhance your strength and leverage.

You can find used tools in newspaper advertisements and at flea markets, used tool stores, pawnshops, and rental agencies. High-quality used hand tools can usually be purchased at a fraction of the cost of new ones. Blades on screwdrivers and edges on chisels should be free of large nicks but can be sharpened. In general, avoid purchasing used power tools. You do not know what kind of wear they have received. This is especially true for rental tools, which usually receive rough use. The one exception to this rule is reconditioned power tools that have been returned on warranty and are offered for sale by local manufacturers, service centers, or department stores (such as Sears). These power tools generally have less than one year's wear, have been completely reconditioned, and carry new warranties. Also note that flea markets have developed a reputation as marketplaces for stolen tools. These sources should be avoided, as costly tools may be identifiable.

The basic tools needed for renovation can be very expensive if you have to buy them all at one time. We assume that most of you have accumulated many or most of these tools over time. If you have not, we suggest that you buy the tools as you need them, but continue to look for bargains and maintain quality standards. If you buy them all at once, the tendency is to buy lower-quality tools to keep the price down. If you do buy all the tools at one time, you will need approximately $2,000 to purchase them. Regardless of what tools you have now and how much money you have to acquire tools, remember that the quality of your tools will determine, to a very large extent, the success of your renovation project.

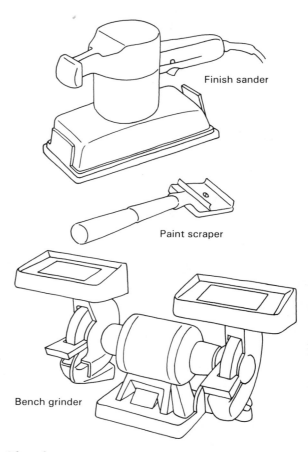

Finish sander

Paint scraper

Bench grinder

TOOLS NEEDED
FOR RENOVATION

Abrasives

Abrasives include sandpaper, steel wool, scrapers, and sanders. To start out, you should buy an

Abrasives

assortment of sandpaper and garnet paper. Buy one or two sheets of emery paper, which is good for polishing. Also buy an assortment of steel wool (fine to coarse grades). If any metal object that is outside needs to be polished, you may want to buy bronze wool. Steel wool particles embed themselves during polishing, which will result in rust streaks later. The bronze wool will not cause this problem.

We recommend buying a finish sander immediately. These are sometimes called orbital sanders. They are used for fine finishing and are usually inexpensive. An optional item, if you are going to do any cabinetwork or refinishing of doors, is a belt sander. Belt sanders are for rough-finishing operations, such as removing paint from a smooth surface. They are much more expensive than finish sanders. Another abrasive tool to consider is a bench grinder, which also is optional. Basically, the bench grinder consists of a motor with a grinding wheel at each end, one coarse and one fine, and is used for metal-fabricating, wrought-iron, or blacksmith work. You also can use it to grind the tips of tools, screwdrivers, and various other things. Bench grinders tend to be extremely useful, so we suggest that you consider buying one of the smaller, less expensive models.

Boring Tools

Boring tools consist of a drill motor and drill bits. We have not suggested that you buy a hand brace or any hand drills because hand drills are typically

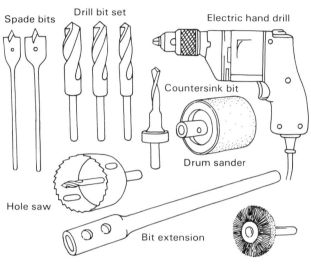

Boring Tools

used for fine woodworking. You should, however, purchase a $3/8$-inch variable-speed reversible drill. We do not suggest a $1/2$-inch drill, but if you expect to do a lot of drilling through beams, buy one. You can buy $1/2$-inch and larger bits with $3/8$-inch shanks, but a problem with $3/8$-inch drills is that they do not have the power to drive a masonry bit through a brick wall or a wood bit through a large beam. That is why many professionals carry $1/2$-inch drills. You will not be required to drill holes through walls or beams very often, and you can usually rent or borrow one when you need it.

You should buy a hole saw and a high-quality drill bit set that includes various size bits. Nested hole saws are best. If you cannot find one of these, at least buy a $2 1/8$-inch hole saw for installing doorknobs. You also should have a spade bit set. These are $1/4$- to $1 1/2$-inch flat drill bits used for drilling in softwood. It may be useful to have a power bit extension. This is a rod, usually 12 inches long,

that extends the drilling depth of straight shank drills. It is very useful for drilling through deep walls or boring holes through more than one stud or beam. When you are putting electrical wires through double or triple beams in the basement, a power bit extension is necessary unless you own a long shank bit in the size required. When purchasing drill bits, be especially conscious of quality. Cheap bits may not last beyond the first hole.

Another item that is very useful is a combination drill and countersink, which will adjust to most common wood screw and drywall screw sizes. This item drills, countersinks, and sometimes counterbores holes all in one operation. You should have a masonry bit set or at least a $1/2$-inch masonry bit. Finally, it is sometimes useful to have a drum rasp or sander that will fit your drill for boring the inside of holes in wood.

Chisels

Your chisel collection should consist of a wood chisel set, a cold or brick chisel, several sizes of nail sets, and a star drill. You will use each of these tools in a brick rehab.

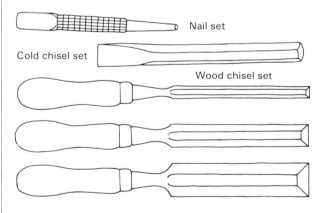

Chisels

Clamps and Vises

You should own several C-clamps and some vise grips. If you plan to do any gluing of large objects, you should have pipe clamps or bar clamps. For quality woodworking, bar clamps are preferable, but they are much more expensive. Finally, you should have either a bench vise or a clamping workbench.

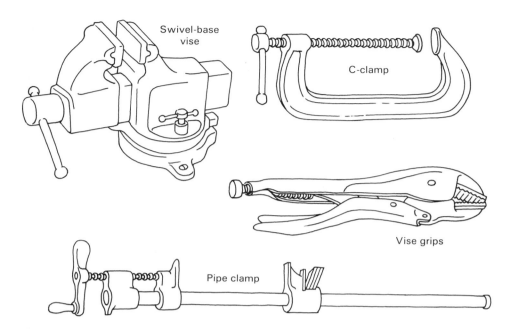

Clamps and Vises

Cleaning Items

You should have a broom, a flat shovel, a dustpan, a dust broom, a wire brush or possibly a wire brush wheel for your drill, and a shop vacuum.

Drywall Tools

You should own a utility knife, a 6-inch and an 11-inch drywall knife, a corner drywall knife, and a drywall pan.

Files and Rasps

You should own a set of flat files and a Surform rasp.

Hammers and Nail Gun

You could do the entire rehab with a curved-claw hammer, but we suggest that if you are going to do the framing, you buy a framing hammer, preferably a 16-inch, 24-ounce one. If you must do any of the gutting of the building, you should also own short- and long-handled sledgehammers.

A nail gun is optional. Very few part-time rehabbers own or use nail guns because they are expensive and dangerous, but a nail gun will cut the time of framing a building in half. A nail gun is a pneumatic tool used with a compressor, so you need the gun, a long air hose, and a compressor. This combination can cost up to $1,000 new but can be pur-

chased for significantly less if you buy a lighter model or purchase these items used. It probably does not make sense for an individual to purchase a nail gun and a compressor to build just one house, but if you plan to do several rehabs, the investment may be worth the time saved. Some nail guns can fire finish nails, roofing nails, and staples as well as common nails.

The advantage of nail guns is that they are very fast. The disadvantages are that they are expensive and can be dangerous. A heavy framing nailer can shoot a 16d nail into a brick wall. Imagine what that would do to your leg. Carpenters who use framing nailers have significantly more accidents than carpenters who stick to hammers. Most of those accidents are caused by overconfidence and carelessness. We assume that an inexperienced rehabber would be much more safety-conscious.

When buying a compressor, you need to be concerned with the cubic feet of air generated at 100 pounds of pressure and the size of the storage tank. These variables determine how fast you can shoot nails. The more portable compressors (pancake and torpedo compressors) are more expensive because they have more complex tanks and are usually rotary rather than piston-driven compressors.

A good air compressor can cost between $300 and $500, but various attachments can be used with day, buying one may be cost-effective if you plan to use it for several different purposes.

Measuring Tools

You should have a tape measure (¾ inch wide by at least 25 feet long), a combination square, a framing square, a T bevel, a 3- or 4- foot level, and a line level. A contour gauge also is extremely helpful. Two tools that are indispensable are a plumb bob and a chalk line.

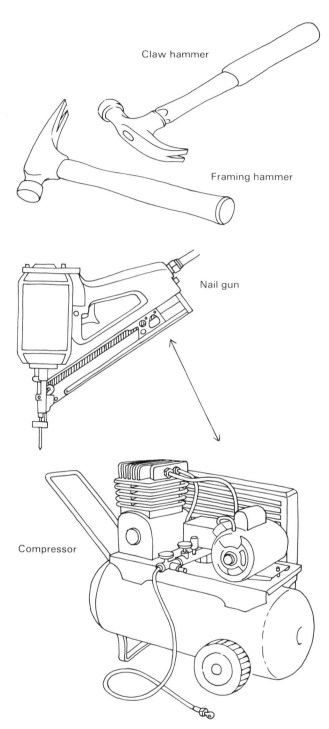

Hammers and Nail Guns

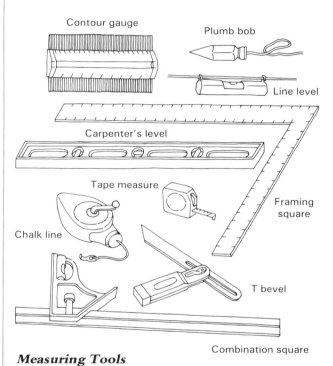

Measuring Tools

Planes

You should have a block plane and a jack plane. One option is to buy a small power plane that is designed for the handyman and is fairly inexpensive. But

it besides a nail gun. These include paint pots, sand-blasting guns and hoppers, and other power tools. A blast of air from a compressor is also good for cleaning tools or blowing sawdust out of corners. Since compressors are very expensive to rent by the

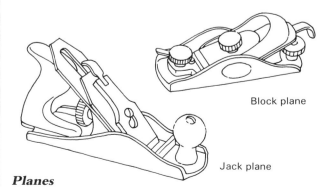

Planes

there are few things that require a plane, especially if you use prehung doors. If you have a large house and plan to reuse the existing doors, a power plane may be useful.

Pliers

You should own at least one pair each of slip-joint pliers, channel-lock pliers, needle-nose pliers, and side-cutting pliers.

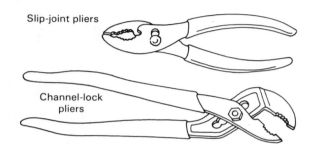

Pliers

Pry Bars

You will need a flat pry bar, a large wrecking bar, and a cat's-paw for pulling nails.

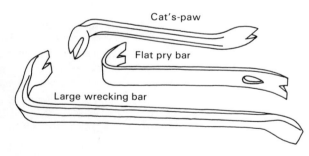

Pry bars

Router

You should own at least a 1-horsepower router and a router bit set. This is not absolutely necessary, but a router comes in very handy in a rehab, particularly if you are doing restoration work. The router itself will not cost very much, but the bit set is expensive. If you have to rent a router, you will still have to buy the bits, so you might as well purchase both items.

Saws

You should own a crosscut handsaw, which is used for cutting across the grain of wood. You will probably use it for 80 percent of your hand cutting. You also should own a backsaw, which is used for making precise cuts in molding. A hacksaw is mandatory for cutting light metal, metal pipe, and polyvinyl chloride (PVC) pipe. Finally, a compass or keyhole saw is needed for cutting small holes, especially in drywall.

We suggest that you purchase a 7½-inch portable straight-drive circular saw. The 7½-inch depth is needed because it is large enough to make miter cuts in 2-inch stock. We also recommend that the saw have 1¾ to 2 horsepower. Most professionals use worm-drive saws because the motor is mounted in line with the blade and the blade does not flex, resulting in an extremely accurate cut. We suggest a straight-drive saw rather than a worm-drive saw for two reasons: It costs less and is easier to use. Use carbide blades with 20 and 40 teeth. If you are careful, one blade of each size may last through one renovation. That will not be true if you buy cheaper hardened-steel blades.

You should purchase a saber saw and a saber saw blade set. Saber saws are used for cutting curves or circles in material and are very handy. We suggest that you spend a little extra money here, as you will use the saber saw over and over again. Another item that we think is mandatory is a reciprocating saw, sometimes called a sawsall. A reciprocating saw is a great investment for renovation work and can often be used in places where a handsaw, circular saw, or hacksaw cannot. A reciprocating saw is expensive, but it is well worth the investment.

We have included three optional items in this list: a 10-inch table saw, a 10-inch portable band saw, and a 10-inch motorized miter box, sometimes called a chop box. You will rarely need a table saw, so you should not buy one just for renovation. If you have one, use it. If you do not have one, you will find ways to get around using it. If you are doing restoration work, table saws sometimes come in handy when you need to match odd-size molding and the like. A portable band saw can be handy, but a saber saw will accomplish most of the same things. If you do not buy a 10-inch motorized miter box, you must buy a hand miter box if

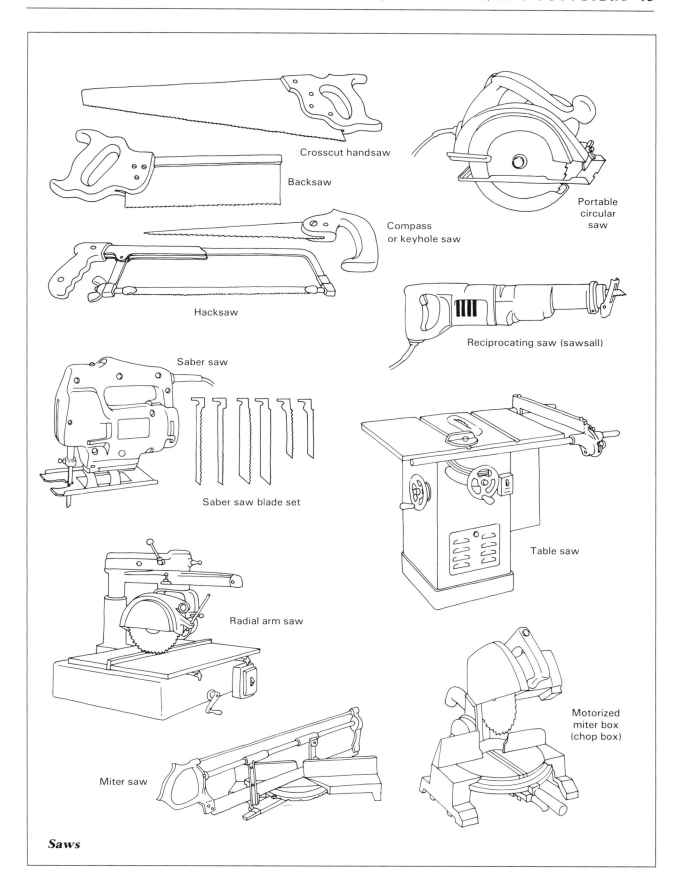

Crosscut handsaw

Backsaw

Compass
or keyhole saw

Portable
circular
saw

Hacksaw

Reciprocating saw (sawsall)

Saber saw

Saber saw blade set

Table saw

Radial arm saw

Motorized
miter box
(chop box)

Miter saw

Saws

you are going to do any finish work. We highly recommend that you buy a chop box. It is light enough to be carried to any work site, yet it is as accurate as a stationary radial arm saw for cutting any kind of molding. If you value your time, a chop box will pay for itself over and over.

Screwdrivers

You should own a set of standard-tip screwdrivers, a set of Phillips screwdrivers, and either a spiral

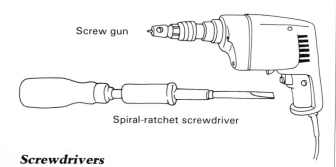

Screw gun

Spiral-ratchet screwdriver

Screwdrivers

ratchet or a Yankee drill. We highly recommend that you purchase a commercial-quality screw gun, as many guns are not powerful enough to drive a 2- or 2½-inch drywall screw into a pine or fir stud. This tool will save you a tremendous amount of time, particularly in doing drywall work and in installing cabinets and countertops.

Soldering Tools

If you have a soldering gun, put it in the toolbox; you will probably use it. If you are installing the plumbing, you will need a propane torch kit, a propane bottle, 50/50 solder, flux, and flux brushes.

Wrenches

You may need pipe wrenches for dismantling pipes, but if you do not want to keep any of the old steel pipes, a sawsall will suffice to cut them out. You may or may not need a socket set. It may come in handy if you have to bolt beams together, dismantle radiators, or perform other similar tasks. We suggest that you have an Allen wrench set; adjustable, or crescent, wrenches; and a set of open- or box-end wrenches.

Safety Equipment and Apparel

You should have the following safety items: work gloves, a nail pouch/tool belt, steel-toed work boots, dust masks, safety goggles, earplugs, a first-aid kit, and one or more fire extinguishers (there may be no water in your building through some of the rehab).

Miscellaneous Tools

You will need the following miscellaneous items: putty knives, a stepladder 2 feet shorter than the ceilings in your building, an electrical circuit tester, several heavy-duty extension cords, at least two sawhorses (we suggest a set of sawhorses for every floor of the house), droplights or other kinds of lights (we recommend very bright lights when you get to the point of finishing drywall), and a good pocketknife.

We also suggest three optional items. The first is a 40-foot extension ladder. If you have to do a lot of work on the exterior of the building or on the roof, the extension ladder is probably mandatory. You can rent ladders and scaffolding, so before you buy, compare the cost of renting versus that of buying. If you plan to live in the house after you are done, you probably should buy an extension ladder because you will need it later. The second optional item is a glass cutter, if you plan to do any window repair or glass replacement. The third optional item is an 8- to 10-inch planer/molder. A number of manufacturers offer small planer/molders for very reasonable prices. If you are doing restoration work, or if you wish to finish your house totally in a hardwood such as oak or walnut, purchasing a small planer/molder may be a very wise investment. Also, if you live in the Midwest, hardwood might be very inexpensive if you buy it at a sawmill. If you want to go to the extra work of producing your own trim from raw lumber, a small planer/molder will be a good investment.

One item that is not on the list but might be useful is an electric airless paint sprayer. Many versions are available to be used for interior and exterior painting. You can rent airless sprayers, but most of these are heavy-duty commercial models that apply the paint too fast for interior use and are very expensive. If you can find a small airless sprayer for a reasonable price and have to do interior painting or have an extensive amount of exterior painting, the cost is justified.

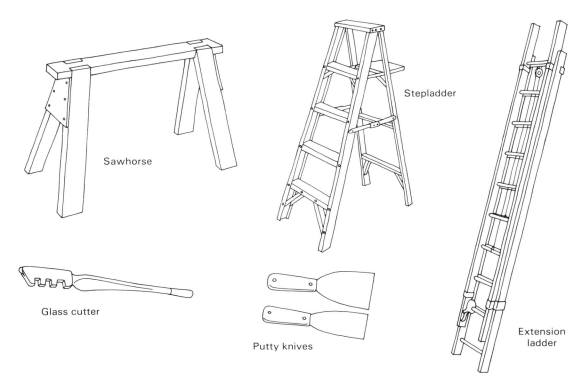

Sawhorse

Stepladder

Glass cutter

Putty knives

Extension
ladder

Miscellaneous Tools

Expendable Items

A number of small items are handy to have around a rehab: razor blades for scrapers and utility knives; some cheap paintbrushes for applying paint stripper, tar, or other sealants; caulking compound in different colors; duct tape; pencils and paper; sheet plastic to cover valuable structures, ceiling holes, and the like; lacquer or paint thinner; oil or some other lubricant; and penetrating oil or some other solvent for loosening stuck parts. Also, save your coffee cans for storing parts and nails, and save all your old sheets, clothes, and towels for rags.

For more information on tools, see Bob Vila's *Guide to Building and Remodeling Materials* (Warner Books, 1986). This is a useful reference for most of the tools and materials that you may need in a renovation project.

BUILDING MATERIALS

In this discussion of building materials, we provide basic information that will help you investigate local sources. Our purpose is not to list all the materials that you may need in a rehab but to give you some tips about types of materials and where to purchase them.

Lumber

During the nineteenth century, lumber was divided into two categories, clear and common. Over the years, other distinctions have been made. Today there are more than 2,000 types and grades of lumber based on quality, strength, milling, seasoning techniques, and finish. For more information on wood types, see the U.S. Department of Agriculture's pamphlet *The Selection and Use of Wood Products for Home and Farm Building* (Superintendent of Documents, U.S. Government Printing Office, Washington, DC 20402). Wood comes in two flavors, hardwood and softwood. Hardwood comes from deciduous trees (trees that lose their leaves every winter), and softwood comes from conifers (trees with needles). Softwoods grow straighter, faster, and taller than hardwoods and therefore are less expensive.

Lumber can be sold by the board foot, the running foot, or the piece. Most lumberyards deal by the piece for do-it-yourselfers. They may deal by the running foot for professional rehabbers, but they will deal in board feet for large orders. A board foot is a piece of wood 1 inch thick, 12 inches wide, and 12 inches long. The actual size may be less than these dimensions, but you pay for the volume of the wood before it is dried and surfaced. For instance, a 1-foot-long one-by-twelve would actually measure ¾ inch thick, 11½ inches wide, and 12 inches long. This is how you figure the board feet of a piece of lumber:

$$\frac{\text{thickness (inches)} \times \text{width (inches)}}{12} \times \text{length (feet)}$$

Thus, the board feet of a piece that is 4 inches thick, 12 inches wide, and 24 feet long is

$$\frac{4 \times 12}{12} \times 24 = 96 \text{ board feet}$$

Construction lumber is usually sold in lengths of 2-foot multiples from 6 to 24 feet. Many types of wood may not be available in even lengths. Some items, such as sheathing and finish flooring, are most commonly sold in random lengths. Longer lengths may be cut only in 1-foot multiples. Studs are sold in specified lengths from 7 to 12 feet and can be two-by-fours or two-by-sixes. All construction lumber is planed, and therefore all dimensions except the length are ¼ to ½ inch less than the stated size. For instance, a two-by-four is actually 1½ by 3½ inches.

Lumber Grades

There are two basic grades of softwood, select and common. Select grades are B and better, C, and D. B and better grade is used for trim, molding, and finish work. C grade has minor defects and can be painted. D grade has minor defects on one side and can be painted on that side, but larger defects on the other side. Common grades are ranked in descending order of quality from number 1 (#1) to number 5 (#5). Number 2 is construction grade, and #3 is standard grade. These are the typical grades you will see in lumberyards. You should order #1 common for heavy structural components and any studs over 10 feet; order #2 for everything else. Make sure the lumberyard does not mix #3 with #2. Home supply centers order their lumber straight from the mill, and they often specify that a portion of #3 be mixed in with bunkers of #2. If you go to a home center that allows customers to pick their own lumber, you will see all that #3 piled up in front of the lumber stack. It's the lumber that people refuse to buy. If you are ordering lumber by the bunker to be delivered to your site, you will get that #3 right along with the bunker of #2. So go to a good lumberyard and make sure that you are getting all #2 or #1 lumber. It is extremely important to order #1 for 10- or 12-foot studs. If you have ceilings that are 10 feet or higher, #2 studs will have too many bows and defects to use them in framing. One option is to use metal studs, but these are more difficult for the do-it-yourselfer to handle.

Hardwoods have a different grading system. The highest grade is termed first, and it is followed by second, select number one common, number two, 3a, and 3b. Today, all mills combine firsts and seconds and call it FAS (firsts and seconds). In FAS, no more than 8⅓ percent can be waste material within certain minimum sizes. Hardwood is sold in random widths and lengths. It may be ⅞ or ¾ inch thick.

A very important element of lumber is the moisture content. For nearly all uses, you will want the moisture content to be less than 25 percent. Dried lumber usually has a moisture content of 12 to 19 percent. It will be stamped S-dry, MC 15, or in some cases KD (kiln-dried). All framing lumber and interior finish lumber must be dry, or it will warp and shrink in place. When you buy dry lumber, it is very important to keep it dry. Storing it in a heated place before installation is a good practice. Keep in mind that in summer, lumber will almost always absorb moisture and expand. When storing your lumber in a heated place, never lay it on an uneven surface.

Most people believe that softwoods such as pine and fir are cheaper than hardwoods, but you should be aware of two important points. First, it is getting harder and harder to get top-grade softwood. Second, most of the oak and walnut in this country comes from the Midwest, particularly Missouri. If you live in the Midwest, it is a good idea to do some investigation into hardwood. Look for finished dimension hardwood in major lumberyards or planing mills, or buy it from a sawmill. You also can buy the rough lumber straight from the sawmill. The lumber should, however, be kilndried. If you buy rough lumber, you must understand grading and sizing of hardwood so that you know what you are purchasing. You can always buy it, transport it to your location, and have it planed and molded there. A local planing mill will be happy to do this, or you can purchase your own planer/molder and do it yourself. If you do only one rehab, you should probably find a planing mill that will sell you what you need finished for a reasonable price. Keep in mind that planing mills will always sell it to you at a cheaper price than a home center or lumberyard. The point here is that it may be possible for you to finish your house in a hardwood such as oak or walnut for the same price as you would pay for finished pine at a lumberyard.

Salvage Lumber

Salvage materials have some advantages and disadvantages. The major trade-off is time and labor versus money. Salvage flooring, molding, and other materials may be the best way to match existing materials, but if you are saving lumber for studs or beams, you will have to pull nails. That is a very time-consuming process. Get a tetanus shot before you start salvaging materials and always wear gloves.

Other Structural Members

You may find that you need trusses and steel or laminated beams. Trusses are fabricated and can be used for beaming or roofing. Using truss plate connectors, you can fashion your own wood trusses out of two-by-fours, but you should seek a structural engineer's help in designing them. The same applies to other structural members, such as laminated wood beams.

Plywood

Plywood is often used for subflooring, roof decking, and sheathing, as well as in other areas. Plywood is made of thin layers of wood glued together. The grain of one layer runs perpendicular to the grain of its neighbors, which is what gives plywood its strength. Common thicknesses are ¼ to 1 inch, and the standard sheet size is 4′x 8′. Plywood grades are N, A, B, C/plugged, C, and D. N has a smooth natural surface, is made from heartwood or sapwood, and is free of defects. A is smooth and paintable, with not more than 18 neatly made repairs. B has a solid surface. C/plugged has an improved C veneer with some repairs permitted. C has tight knots up to 1½ inches and knot holes up to 1 inch. D has knots and knot holes up to 2½ inches. Plywood often has different grades on its two faces (for example, CD). Most plywood today is rated exterior or interior because of the glue that is used in its laminations, but make sure that you use an exterior grade of plywood (for example, CDX). Plywood also is rated by strength using two different numbers. The first number ranges from 1 to 5, with 1 being the strongest. The second number is a fraction indicating the maximum distance the sheet should span on rafters or joists (for example, ³²/₁₆ on rafters spaced 32 inches on center and joists 16 inches on center.)

A minor issue is the amount of formaldehyde outgassing that occurs in plywood. Formaldehyde adhesives are used in some decorative hardwood paneling and some plywoods. These release gases into the house. Some lumberyards carry plywood made with nongassing adhesives, but they are very expensive. High heat combined with humidity induces outgassing, so if you buy your panels ahead of time and store them outdoors in a shelter, much of the formaldehyde will disappear by the time you use them.

Particleboard

Particleboard and other composite-board products are made from wood, but the strength in the materials is engineered by humans. This is the fastest-growing group of building materials, and it is likely to become even more important.

There are basically two types of this material, particleboard and fiberboard. Particleboard is manufactured by chipping or flaking wood, adding glue, and pressing the mixture into sheets. Fiberboard is similar to particleboard, but the wood is pulped into a soupy mixture before the glues are added and the pressure stamping done. The recoil and strength of particleboard has increased significantly since it was introduced in the 1950s. Keep in mind that particleboard is not cross-laminated as is plywood, and it is not as strong, particularly in roofing or structural sheathing applications. However, it can be used in rehabs for applications such as covering old floors and building cabinets. Do not use particleboard for subflooring in bathrooms or kitchens, because it decomposes when it gets wet.

Fasteners

There are many different screws, nails, and glues, and they will all be used in a renovation project. Over 600 pounds of nails are used in building the average 3,000-square-foot frame house. They range in size from ¼ inch to 4 inches. Those under 1 inch are called tacks or brads, and those over 4 inches are called spikes. Nails are traditionally grouped in "penny" sizes—for instance 16d. The d stands for *denarius,* a Roman coin. The number originally referred to the number of denarii it cost to buy 400 nails of a particular size. Box nails are usually ⅛ inch shorter than common nails of the same penny number. A 16d nail is commonly 3½ inches long, and a 10d nail is 3 inches long.

Framing nails can be either common or box, resin-coated or not. Finish nails have small heads and are used in finish work and cabinetwork. Casing nails are similar to finish nails but are hardened with a dull point to allow penetration of trim. Roofing nails are short with wide heads and are often galvanized. They are used to fasten shingles, roofing, and roofing underlay. Drywall nails are usually ring-shanked, as are flooring nails, and are used to attach drywall to studs. The rings help prevent the nail from coming out when the material flexes. Masonry nails are used to attach studs and furring to masonry walls. When cement- or resin-coated nails are driven, the coating melts and quickly resets. Thus, these nails can be driven home with fewer blows and will stay in place. We recommend their use if you are experienced in framing, but, since they are very difficult to remove once they have set, they are not for the novice.

Although screws are more expensive and usually more time-consuming to drive, they provide much better holding power than nails. They are available in steel, brass, copper, and aluminum and in many different types and sizes. Predrilling is recommended for most screws, particularly screws used in metal or hardwood, although self-tapping screws can be purchased for sheet metal. We recommend the use of Phillips-head screws in almost all cases. These prevent the screwdriver from slipping off the screw and causing damage. They are easy to use with a screw gun. Drywall screws are available in various sizes and lengths. We highly recommend stocking drywall screws in 1⅝-, 2-, and 3-inch lengths. They are handy in many rehabbing situations, particularly if you have a screw gun. Keep a bar of soap handy to lubricate the longer drywall screws for ease of driving.

Other fasteners include pop rivets, bolts, washers, nuts, tacks, and brads. All should be purchased specifically for applications as needed. Fasteners made in the United States are by far superior to those made in other countries. The money spent on fasteners adds up, and the more bent nails and screws with heads twisted off, the more money goes down the drain. It is very frustrating to get a drywall screw halfway into the work and have the head twist off. Do not buy fasteners from the local do-it-yourself home center. Go to a lumberyard where the professionals get their supplies.

The final category of fasteners is adhesives. Choosing the right glue can be a bewildering task. If you do not review a book on building materials, it is best to check with a reputable dealer so that you buy the right glue for the job. Currently popular is the hot-melt adhesive used in electric glue guns. This glue is popular because it sets in about a minute, is flexible enough to bind vinyl and fabrics, and also can bind wood, metal, and plaster. It is waterproof and inexpensive, and we recommend using it for many jobs.

A special category is construction adhesives, which are sold in tubes that fit into caulking guns. Construction adhesives are sold in every home center and lumberyard, but they are now made especially for particular jobs: adhering paneling, furring strips, subflooring, foam insulation, and pressure-treated lumber. Investigate the different types of construction adhesives and keep a good stock of such adhesives. One warning about construction adhesives: It is extremely difficult to take things apart once they are glued together. If you are a novice, you may want to use screws rather than glue as much as possible. If you have done renovation work before, you will probably feel confident enough to use construction adhesives everywhere. One big advantage to working with them is that they reduce squeaks later on.

Joist Hangers

The metal pieces that most of us know as joist hangers can be used for many other purposes besides hanging joists. They are used to reinforce the stress of lateral junctures of wood members, eliminating any possible weakness caused by nails pulling out or lumber splitting. They include joist hangers, top plate ties, truss plates, and drywall clips. Your building probably does not need any of these except joist hangers, which will be required by your building codes. Joist hangers are actually a preferred method for hanging joists from headers. The hanger distributes the load over a much wider area than do nails. You can nail the hanger first to the joist and then to the header after the joists are slipped into place, or vice versa. Hangers are available for single and double joists. Framing clips used to attach studs to sill plates and top plates probably are not worth the money. Drywall clips come in handy, as they provide a metal flange backing for drywall, thus eliminating the need for separate nailing blocks in tight places at the end of existing walls. Drywall screws are used to attach drywall to the metal flange.

Miscellaneous Materials

Other materials include roofing materials, paint, insulation, masonry, gutters, exterior siding, door hardware (including garage door openers), disappearing staircases, fencing materials, windows, plumbing materials, electrical materials, flooring materials (including carpeting, hardwood flooring, and ceramic tile), kitchen and bath cabinets, bath vanities, countertops, and faucets. These materials are discussed later in individual chapters.

Resources

One of the best sources of information about tools and materials for renovation is a book by Bob Vila, *Guide to Building and Remodeling Materials* (Warner Books, 1986). Michael Litchfield's *Renovation* (John Wiley & Sons, 1982) also covers tools and suppliers. The best sources of information are manufacturers, retailers, and your public library. Most libraries have a number of books about specific rehabbing activities. Finally, it would be helpful to subscribe to one or more of the magazines listed in Chapter 3, and keep in mind that *Custom Builder* and *Remodeling* have yearly product directories. *Remodeling* also provides a list of suppliers and associations dealing with remodeling and renovation. In addition, *House Beautiful* publishes an annual remodeling product guide.

SUPPLIERS

Shopping for materials and suppliers is like shopping for anything else. The only difference is that you may be spending up to $100,000 for rehab supplies. It is important to shop around because prices and service vary.

You will need several different suppliers. A building supply company or a lumberyard can supply framing lumber, nails, trim, roofing, flooring, paneling, and drywall materials. We recommend that you look for specialty companies for drywall, doors, and windows, however, as their prices may be lower. If they are not, you are probably better off buying everything from one dealer, receiving a discount and possibly enhanced service. We do not like buying from building supply companies that sell a little bit of everything because they often do not have what you need when you need it and the prices are usually higher. If you live in a rural area, though, you may have no choice.

You also will need a plumbing supply store; an electrical and lighting fixture source; a paint store; an insulation supplier; a tile company; a hardware store; a concrete, sand, or gravel company; a brick company; and specialty houses for items such as brass fixtures, staircases, glass, and kitchen cabinets. If you are doing renovation as well, you may need an architectural antique supply store that salvages and resells antique items from houses.

Opening a charge account with a supplier is especially helpful if your renovation work is to be done on construction vouchers from a title company or a savings and loan. In this kind of financial arrangement, you will not be paid for the work until after it is finished; therefore, you need credit so that you minimize use of your own money during the project.

You do not have to be a licensed contractor or a professional developer to have an account at a building supply store or to buy at a builder's discount. Remember, you will be spending $50,000 to $100,000, not $50. Ask the manager if you can open an account and be quoted builder's prices. Once you explain that you are doing a complete renovation and hand him or her your plans or materials list for the project, there should be no problem. The discounts from various suppliers will not be large, but they will add up. One thing to remember is that many building supply houses are cash-and-carry and do not offer discounts to anyone.

It is important for you to understand the procedure that most suppliers follow. Most close their books between the 25th and the last day of each month. They then bill their customers for purchases for the previous 30 days and expect payment by the 10th of the following month. If you pay before the 10th, you often earn an additional 2 percent discount. This may not be stated on invoices, statements, or contracts, and it is not a large amount of money, but, again, it adds up. We know one builder who did not collect his 2 percent discount at a lumber store for several years. When he went into the store with a materials list for a large lake house, he received all the materials free. If you time your purchases so you order just after a supplier closes its books for a particular month, you have anywhere from 30 to 46 days to pay the bill. A May 1 purchase would be due June 10. This gives you time to install the materials, have the job inspected by the title company or savings and loan, receive a construction draw, and pay the supplier's bill from construction loan funds. At the same time, you are getting a 10 to 15 percent discount and probably free delivery.

Most plumbing, electrical, and window suppliers operate the same way. An account at a plumbing, electrical, lighting fixture, or window supplier may be to your benefit if you do not have to pay retail prices for even small amounts of material. If you plan to buy new windows for your entire house,

it is very important to contact the manufacturer's contractor rep to get the price for windows. Do *not* call the retail rep. Windows can be discounted more than 40 percent from retail for developers. In our location, aluminum windows that sell retail for $450 can be purchased for slightly over $150 wholesale.

In today's building market, many suppliers offer special services such as free delivery to a larger customer. Suppliers will also estimate the materials you will need and will develop a *takeoff,* or materials list, from your plans that can save you a lot of time. Sometimes suppliers schedule deliveries of materials to coincide with your construction process. In some cases, the salesperson will even keep an eye on the progress of your construction and make deliveries when new materials are needed.

One trick is to act as though you have a lot of business or have finished several buildings. Open a checking account for your project with a name such as Smith Construction. When you walk into a supplier and demand builder's or wholesale prices, your checkbook may convince them you're a legitimate builder.

Another important point to remember is that every large city has manufacturers that make virtually everything you need for a rehab. In St. Louis, we have paint manufacturers, hardwood manufacturers, kitchen cabinet and counter manufacturers, major hardware suppliers, and so on. Locate those manufacturers in your area. Ask to see the shop foreman, vice president, or builder's rep. Avoid salespeople. Talk your way into wholesale prices. These will be less than a builder's discount from a retail supplier. The problem is that you will probably have to pay cash on delivery, and you may not receive any extra services such as free delivery. At wholesale prices, you will be saving more money than you ever thought possible, and you could probably buy the small truck needed for material pickup with the money saved.

References

OLD

Hasluck, Paul Nooncree. *Woodworkers' Handbook of Manual Instruction.* London: Technical Press, Ltd., 1902.

Hodgson, Frederick Thomas. *The Carpenters' Steel Square and Its Uses.* Philadelphia: Industrial Publication Company, 1906.

Pulver, Harry E. *Materials of Construction.* New York: McGraw-Hill, 1922

Show, Charles Henry. *Wood and Other Organic Structural Materials.* New York: McGraw-Hill, 1917.

NEW

Ball, John E. *Tools, Steel Square, Joinery.* 5th Ed., revised and edited by Tom Philbin. New York: Macmillan, 1986.

Davey, Norman. *A History of Building Materials.* London: Phoenix House, 1961.

Ellison, Donald C. *Building Construction: Materials and Types of Construction.* New York: John Wiley, 1987.

Emerson, Larry. *Builder's and Contractor's Guide to New Methods and Materials in Home Construction.* Englewood Cliffs, New Jersey: Prentice-Hall, 1983.

Litchfield, Michael W. *Salvaged Treasures: Designing & Building with Architectural Salvage.* New York: Van Nostrand Reinhold, 1983.

Russell, James E. *Methods and Materials of Residential Construction.* Englewood Cliffs, New Jersey: Prentice-Hall, 1985.

Williams, Elizabeth. *Building with Salvaged Lumber.* Blue Ridge Summit, Pennsylvania: TAB Books, 1983.

Chapter 9

SUBCONTRACTORS

Different people have different ideas about their involvement in rehabilitating an old house. One person who has many interests elsewhere may want someone else to do all the work. He or she may simply want to walk into the house after it is finished. Another person may insist on doing everything himself or herself. Most renovators fall somewhere in between these two extremes.

A common way of keeping a rehab budget in line with your housing budget is to do the work yourself. While this saves money, it may cost more in time, quality, and general frustration. People often say that remodeling a house can break up your marriage, force you into bankruptcy, drive you to a nervous breakdown, or all three. You must weigh these factors in deciding whether to use professional subcontractors in the rehab.

Consider the following questions when deciding whether to hire someone to work on your house:

1. Which tasks do you like to do? Hiring someone to do the jobs that you do not like will free you to work on projects that you do enjoy.

2. What do you know how to do? If you do not know how to do a certain job, you may not want to experiment on your house. Hire a pro the first time and see how the task is done.

3. How much time do you have? Rehabilitating an old house can be more than a full-time job. If you have only a few hours on weekends to work on your house, you should either expect the project to progress very slowly over a number of years or hire professional help. We emphasize the word professional. You might be able to hire people at lower rates, but you may spend all your time supervising them to make sure they do the job right. Another issue related to time is tools. Subcontractors have specialized equipment that do-it-yourselfers cannot afford and do not really need. This equipment allows them to work faster and more efficiently.

4. How much money do you have? Remodeling can cost up to $100 per square foot. Most people have limited funds to hire someone else to do the job, so they lower the dollar amount per square foot through do-it-yourself "sweat equity." Remember that when the construction industry is slow (around the first of the year), bidding is extremely competitive, and you may be able to hire someone for far less than you could during the summer.

5. Are you in the middle of a rehab and discovering that it is not going as quickly as planned? Does a particular task continue to frustrate you? If so, hiring someone to do some of the work and seeing that segment of the project accomplished will give the entire rehab a shot in the arm.

6. Will hiring a professional be cost-effective? Hiring a pro to do a large project is often cost-effective, but employing one to do a small task is not. For example, if a drywall taper bids on the entire house, he or she will base the bid on square footage. If you have the taper do one room at a time, he or she will probably charge by the hour, which will cost significantly more. The reason for this is simple. The taper has to drive to your house, haul in all the equipment, mix the mud, unpack the

equipment, use it, clean it, and then repack it and haul it all out to his or her truck. All that is lost time on a small project.

It is wise to hire a professional when the job requires technical skills that you do not have and do not wish to learn; when the job requires tools that you do not have, cannot rent, or do not have the money to obtain; when the job needs to be completed in a short time; when your time is worth more than your money; when the building codes baffle you; or when the quality of your workmanship is so poor that you should have someone else do it. Furthermore, the law may require you to hire a licensed contractor for certain jobs, such as plumbing and electrical work.

These considerations aside, there are still many areas in which you can do your own work. You can also choose to be your own general contractor. You can save 15 to 20 percent of the total construction cost by being your own general contractor and even more by doing the work yourself.

Many architects and contractors have virtually no experience in remodeling, renovation, or restoration work. Fewer still are conversant with Victorian houses. You must find out what kind of experience a professional has before you consider hiring him or her. Make sure whoever you hire knows old houses, because renovation poses many problems that new construction does not. Also, many parts of an old house are irreplaceable, and you do not want to trust them to just anyone.

There are several ways to find architects and contractors who know old houses. Check with friends, architects (for contractors), or real estate agents. Visit renovation projects in progress to see who is doing the work. Contact the local branch of the contractors' union or professional group in your area. Check with the historical commission or redevelopment district offices in your area. Finally, talk with building inspectors.

Keep in mind that an architect or contractor will probably send you to view his or her best projects, so what you see is the best that you can expect. Also, do not automatically assume that a prospective contractor has done the work he or she sends you to view until you have verified it. Obtain the license number of the prospective contractor or subcon-

tractor and check it with the licensing authority in your area. This may not be so important when hiring carpenters, but it is very important when hiring plumbers and electricians because of building code requirements.

If you do not want to employ large subcontractors or contractors, do not be afraid to hire a journeyman by the day. Two people can always do something better than one, so you could help the journeyman or hire someone to help you. We believe that it is always best to act as your own contractor and to hire specialists (plumber, electrician, carpenter, and HVAC person) instead of one general contractor.

ARCHITECTS

When considering a major renovation project involving gutting a building and starting over again, you should hire an architect. If you are considering a major restoration project, you also may want to consider using an architect. Architects are important in five areas:

1. Selecting materials. Any architect worth his or her fee should know materials and be able to help you select them.

2. Defining and solving problems involving space. This is where architects are particularly useful. Imagining walls where there are none and no walls where there are walls takes practice. It is a skill that some developers acquire, but it is one that architects are taught as part of their professional training. One of the architect's main jobs is to understand you and the space you need and then design the building that gives you that space. This is why you should consider employing an architect, but only in a project in which you will significantly alter the building.

3. Providing working drawings. It is easier and cheaper in the long run to draw construction details on paper. Also, most building commissions will require working drawings of a project before they issue a permit to start work. An architect, draftsman, or engineer can supply those drawings. If the

building commission will accept only a licensed architect's or engineer's stamp on the drawings, then someone with those credentials will have to do or review the drawings.

4. Satisfying local codes. If a bank or building commission demands the work to be guaranteed by an accredited person, you will have to have the rehab designed by an architect and done by a licensed electrician or plumber, or you will have to be certified yourself.

5. Overseeing job progress. Overseeing work is sometimes difficult if you work during the day. If you hire an architect without hiring a general contractor, the architect might oversee the job and its progress.

Possibly the most important reason for hiring an architect is to design a major renovation or restoration project that entails dealing with significant structural problems. It is mandatory to hire an engineer or architect to solve such problems, so why not take advantage of the architect's design skills as well? Unless you have some major structural problems or special space requirements, you should hire an architect on an hourly basis to provide working drawings. If necessary, you can also hire the architect for design work by the hour. Do not be surprised when the architect spends time or has employees spend time measuring your building. In fact, you should oversee the measuring and make sure that it is done correctly. We have seen more than one situation in which the architect has not measured the building correctly and things did not fit once construction began.

Constructing an addition to an older house is another reason to bring in an architect. He or she can deal with structural considerations such as the proportions of the addition, architectural details, and aesthetics.

FINDING AN ARCHITECT

After deciding to hire an architect, the next step is finding one who is knowledgeable about renovation work. It is important that you investigate and shop for the right one for you and your home. In the long run, finding the right person is well worth the effort. Investigate a number of sources. Consult friends who have hired an architect for renovation work, or look around the neighborhood for residential commercial renovations with fine-quality design and workmanship. Ask the owner for the name of the architect. Get in touch with the local chapter of the American Institute of Architects (AIA). It's always important to know where this office is located because it can be a good source of information, particularly about building codes. Some AIA chapters also have special historic committees. Seek out the local historical society, preservation group, or rehabilitation district office. The landmark commissioner or the municipal historic office will know of architects working in that area. Any university with a school of architecture may offer courses on preservation or renovation.

One developer we know has a unique way of meeting his architectural requirements. He offers a prize for the best rehab design for a particular building by students who are taking an architecture course. He usually gets 30 to 40 different designs from the students, who also receive a grade from their professor and course credit. One or more of them win the prize money. The licensed architect who teaches the class reviews and finishes the plans, then stamps them for the developer. The developer ends up spending significantly less than if he hired an architect to do the entire project.

Find out if the house you are considering is in a designated public renewal area. If so, ask the city whether any agency provides architectural advice to home owners in that district. You also can request information from state or national preservation organizations. Most states have historic preservation offices that maintain lists of architects who are responsible for restoration and renovation projects under the state's supervision.

Architects to avoid are those who view an old house primarily as a blank canvas on which they can showcase their own creativity. This type of architect cannot subordinate his or her ego to the original design of the house. They cannot wait to start tearing things out in order to make "improvements."

On the other hand, there are many architects who understand and respect old buildings and who derive immense satisfaction from restoring their original charm and character. This type of architect knows more about older houses than you may ever be able to learn.

SELECTING AN ARCHITECT

Interview an architect as you would any other subcontractor. Look for technical expertise, design competence, respect for historical integrity, patience, forthrightness, and compatibility with what you envision in your house.

Before contacting any architects, develop a clear description of the house and the work required, even though your plan may change after discussions with the architect. Start out with a realistic view of what you want. After an initial screening of architects, narrow the list to two or three and interview them. Find out whether your job will fit into the architect's schedule and match his or her interests. If you plan to hire an architect by the hour, he or she may not give an initial interview or on-site inspection of the house free of charge. If your plan is to retain the architect for complete design work, these initial interviews should not cost anything.

After each architect understands your project and decides what services you need, ask for a written proposal. These proposals will give you a firm basis for comparing services and fees. For small jobs or producing drawings on a per hour basis, a simple letter of agreement outlining services might be sufficient. Larger projects often require detailed proposals dividing the work into separate phases with separate fees. If the fees differ markedly among architects, check to make sure each architect is offering the same services. Also ask for references. The American Institute of Architects provides a standard form for doing this.

If the architect develops construction drawings, these drawings and specifications will constitute the basis on which subcontractors will bid on jobs. Make sure that these documents are accurate. Remember that the construction documents and the subcontractors' contracts constitute legally binding agreements between you and the builder or subcontractors. If subsequent changes are made, they must be approved by you, the architect, and the builder. You must be prepared for some change orders, but make sure that the work and the additional costs are clearly spelled out. If you plan to use general contractors and architects in this way, we suggest that you visit your local American Institute of Architects chapter or write to the AIA headquarters at 1735 New York Avenue NW, Washington, DC 20006.

In new construction, it is typical for an architect's fee to be based on a fixed percentage (10 to 15 percent) of the total construction cost. This fee is more problematic in renovation and restoration work, because setting a firm construction price is often difficult. Also, renovation work typically requires subcontractors with higher labor costs than those required in new construction. The home owner in this case would pay a proportionally higher fee to the architect. In some cases, the architect will spend more time on research or identification of parts of buildings and preparation of cost estimates than on the actual construction. He or she deserves fair compensation for these services, so most fees are negotiated as a fixed fee plus expenses.

CONTRACTORS AND SUBCONTRACTORS

We believe that you do not need to hire a general contractor. Most home owner rehabs entail many smaller subcontracted jobs and do-it-yourself projects. Without a general contractor, you will have to live with more disarray, the project will probably take longer, and you will assume a greater risk, but you also will save 15 to 20 percent of the total cost of the project.

If you do decide to hire a general contractor, get recommendations from friends, relatives, neighbors, owners of similar houses, building suppliers, subcontractors, and bankers. It is important to get firsthand information about the quality of the contractor's work and to *look* at this work. Make sure that you can talk to the contractor. Your ability to communicate with each other is an important factor. Most contractors have their own way of doing things, which may be contrary to what you have in mind for your building. Check this out.

Reliability in subcontractors is critical. Be certain that your subcontractor has an established business and is a reliable businessperson. If you have to choose between quality and reliability, choose reliability. If a subcontractor does not show up to finish the job, it does not matter whether he or she is the best or the worst in the land. Also keep in mind that fly-by-night operations abound in the home improvement business. Beware of carpenters who work out of the trunks of their cars. A business office, no matter how small, with at least one staff member or a quality answering service are important, and positive, indicators. Remember, though, these things do not constitute proof of skill or quality work, only reliability. Ask the Better Business Bureau if it has received any complaints about the subcontractor. Ask the subcontractor where he or she buys supplies and check to see if his or her bills are paid on time. You also can judge reliability by a contractor's being on time for meetings, the neatness of estimates and proposals, and what other people say about him or her.

Check the subcontractor's license. In some areas, any person contracting for a building job worth more than a given amount as established by state or local authorities must be licensed. The license may be granted when the applicant has passed tests or has a certain level of experience. Ask to see the person's license. You can verify the license status by calling the local licensing authority. Remember, a license alone does not guarantee that the subcontractor will do good work or that he or she is the right person for the job.

Unlicensed people typically charge less and therefore may seem attractive, but if licensing is required for the installation of certain materials, you should not hire unlicensed individuals. This is particularly true for subcontractors such as plumbers and electricians. In fact, we recommend that you never use an unlicensed plumber or electrician. Another important issue is that licensed subcontractors are often required by state law to carry workmen's compensation insurance. If you hire an unlicensed subcontractor, you must carry workmen's compensation to be covered. While most home owner's policies have a workmen's compensation or liability clause, coverage is usually limited to an employee who works no more than 20 hours a week. A home owner's policy can be amended to cover a full-time worker, but be sure to check the coverage and additional cost with your insurance agent.

A licensed subcontractor also may carry property damage or public liability insurance, although this is not typically required by law. The subcontractor may pay several thousand dollars a year in premiums for both workmen's compensation and public liability insurance. This cost will be passed on to you, but the insurances can be of great benefit to you. Licensed subcontractors sometimes carry bonds to guarantee that you will have monetary recourse if they walk off the job before it is completed. Regardless of licensing, find out in advance what kind of insurance and bonds the subcontractor carries.

In most areas of the country, using unlicensed subcontractors for some jobs is fine. We routinely use unlicensed HVAC people and carpenters. We only concern ourselves with licensing for plumbers and electricians, because our building codes require it. Just make sure you understand what your local codes stipulate before you hire any subcontractors.

Just as with an architect and general contractor, you need to evaluate a contractor's experience with houses similar to yours and his or her sensitivity to renovation projects. Find out if the subcontractor has a thorough understanding of the building codes affecting your project. You may be able to find this out through the licensing authority or by asking the subcontractor some simple questions.

Once you have narrowed down the list of subcontractors, get competitive bids in writing based on the same set of written specifications. Also ask them to estimate the time frame for the project. If a subcontractor suggests adding something that is not in your written specifications list, have him or her bid on that separately. Each subcontractor should indicate his or her hourly charge plus the cost of materials. Remember that the lowest bid may not be the best bid. Sometimes it is a good idea to throw out any bids that are excessively high or low and decide among those in the middle.

The most important task in finding good subcontractors is to get and check references. If they take offense, move on. A little investigation now will reduce many problems later on.

SUBCONTRACTOR BIDS

Some subcontractors may want to combine the material and labor costs in their bids, but you should ask them to separate the two. Subcontractors can often buy materials cheaper than you can and will often get superior quality material from their suppliers. But you should still know what you are getting.

When the job is finished, you should hold back 10 percent of the subcontractor's payment until you have inspected the work, compared it to the plans and specifications in the contract, and lived with it for a brief time (typically not more than a week), to be certain that everything functions properly. The contract should specify the percent that will be held back as well as the time before full payment will be made. When you inspect the property, make a list of any problems (this is typically called a punch list) that the subcontractor must correct before receiving the balance due.

Most contracts require proof of workmen's compensation and liability insurance. Some states also have lien laws, and contracts should contain a lien waiver. This document frees you from any financial responsibility if a contractor does not pay his or her subcontractors or suppliers. You should not pay the contractor unless he or she has provided a signed *and notarized* lien waiver. The contract also should state when the work will begin and end.

Scheduling Subcontractors

Subcontractors should be scheduled according to the sequence of the job. More than one subcontractor can work at once, but, for the most part, the demolition contractor must be finished before the carpentry contractor can start, the carpentry contractor must be finished before the plumbing, heating, and electrical contractors can begin, and so on. Electricians and plumbers usually dislike working together, but it is not unusual to see heating contractors working with a plumber or an electrician

at the same time in a building. Insulators usually cannot do their job until the plumbing, heating, and electrical systems have been installed. And, of course, the roofers would come immediately after the carpenter had the roof ready for roofing. Brick masons could work at almost any time. The more reliable your subcontractors are, the smoother the project will go. Their reliability in meeting your schedule will allow you to coordinate work time, so that all of your subcontractors can come and go without being in each other's way.

Don't forget that your most effective control over your subcontractors is how you pay them. Reliable people will always be reliable, but unreliable people will be reliable if they get paid only when they are reliable. No one is ever paid in advance in this business. Pay for work and progress only.

Carpenters are usually paid at each major stage of their work — tearing out, framing, interior trim, and exterior. Plumbers and electricians usually draw 50 to 60 percent of the contract price when their rough-ins are finished and draw the remainder when the project is done. Draws for HVAC contractors vary according to the amount of equipment they must install, though it should not exceed 60 percent unless all the equipment is set, including outside compressors and heat pumps.

Payments to other subcontractors also should be based on work accomplished. *Never* advance a subcontractor money to buy materials. If it is absolutely necessary, buy the materials yourself.

Supervising Subcontractors

Your subcontractors are not working on their own houses, and therefore, they will not necessarily be striving for perfection. You can expect much more than an acceptable job, but it is highly unlikely that you will see a perfect job. If you want perfect, do it yourself.

In most rough-ins, the local building inspector, architect, title company, or bank inspector will decide whether the work is acceptable. You have to spend most of your time inspecting the cosmetics — painting, trim, finish carpentry, flooring, and so on. If something is not done right, do not pay until it is redone. If it is not feasible to redo it, then try to reach a compromise. Compromise is essential in dealing with subcontractors. If they do work that they deem to be acceptable but you do not, they probably would rather compromise on the agreed-upon price and get on with the next job rather than redo something. If you are fighting for them to redo something and they are fighting to move on, try to reach a compromise. They will never fix it the way you want it if you pressure them.

In business circles, the term *trolling* refers to the process of walking through a manufacturing plant to look for problems. In construction, this is called the walk-through. Always walk through your building after each stage of the project and make a common-sense appraisal of what has been done. You do not have to be an architect or inspector to notice that studs, walls, or doors are not plumb. Check to make sure that things operate correctly. Be picky; ask questions; expect cleanliness.

Always ask your subcontractors questions. Most of them are capable of offering sound advice. In most cases, subcontractors are fiercely independent. Do not watch over them constantly while they do their jobs. This does not mean that you cannot demand honest work and withhold money if you do not get it. Just don't be a pest.

Even though contractors, architects, and subcontractors might tell you something to the contrary, there is nothing in a rehab that you cannot do if you want to. It may take you more time, and may cost you more money and material, but don't let anyone tell you that you cannot do it. We think it is best for the rehabber to do the carpentry, drywall, and painting and let masons, plumbers, electricians, and HVAC people do the rest. The reason is that they are fast. An electrical contractor may send two or three people to wire a large house in two days. The same is true for plumbers and heating people. If you do any of those jobs yourself, it may take two weeks for each. The decision of whether or not to hire a subcontractor depends on how much time you have, how much money you have, the scope of your project, whether you live in the building, and a number of other variables. Just remember that, given enough time and money, you can do anything you want.

References

OLD

Graham, Frank Duncan. *Audel's Carpenters and Builders Guide.* New York: I. Audel & Co., 1939.

Nichols, Edward. *Contracts and Specifications.* Chicago: American Technical Society, 1912.

Peker, Charles G. *Hints for Carpenters.* New York: Industrial Book Company, 1909.

NEW

Alth, Max. *Be Your Own Contractor: The Affordable Way to Home Ownership.* Blue Ridge Summit, Pennsylvania: TAB Books, 1984.

Hamilton, Harper. *How to Prepare Building and Construction Contracts.* Boulder, Colorado: Hamilton Press, 1977.

Heldmann, Carl. *Be Your Own House Contractor: How to Save 25 Percent Without Lifting a Hammer.* Pownal, Vermont: Garden Way Publishing, 1981.

Jones, Jack Payne. *Handbook of Construction Contracting.* Carlsbad, California: Craftsman Book Co., 1986.

McGuerty, Dave. *The Complete Guide to Contracting Your Home: A Step-by-Step Method for Managing Home Construction.* White Hall, Virginia: Betterway Publications, 1986.

Rauch, Paul H. *How to Be Your Own Contractor: Remodeling, Additions, Alterations, Building a New Home.* Andover, Massachusetts: Brick House Publishing Co., 1988.

Chapter 10

DEMOLITION

egardless of whether you renovate or restore, you will want to remove some material from the building. It may entail taking out one wall, gutting a kitchen, or even gutting an entire floor. This chapter is about stripping the material from the building to be rehabbed and how to dispose of it or store it. You should know before you enter the building whether your job will involve partial or total demolition. The inspection of the building and your decision to buy the building were based on how much material had to be removed and replaced versus how much could be restored. Some buildings are wonderful because they can be totally gutted and a new building built in the interior. Other buildings are desirable because very little needs to be stripped out of them; they are almost totally intact and can be restored. Other buildings are available where the first floor parlor and living room area is restorable (and quite beautiful), while the rear kitchen and upper bedrooms can be gutted. Regardless of your particular situation, you need to know how to go about demolition, when to remove things, and how to dispose of the material.

DISPOSING OF THE MATERIAL

The material that you remove from the building will typically fall into three categories: plaster, wood, and metal. It can all be disposed of together at the local dump, or it can be handled separately, since the wood and the metal have other uses and can be recycled. (The plaster has no other use and will have to go to the dump.) Within those categories, you have three choices for getting the material to a dump: in a dumpster, in your truck, or by professional haulers. If you take much material out of a building, don't think about hauling it to the dump in your pickup. One square foot of wall will typically generate one cubic foot of debris if you don't save the lumber. If you think about the number of walls to be removed from a building in a typical rehab, that is a tremendous amount of debris. In a complete rehab, you may generate up to 15,000 pounds of debris per 1,000 square feet of building. Contract with a garbage company and have a large dumpster placed at the construction site, or hire a group of individuals who specialize in gutting buildings or at least cleaning up rehab debris and have the equipment to handle a gut rehab. The nicest, cleanest way to do it is to have a dumpster run up against the back of the building and toss everything out the windows and into the dumpster. We have gutted many buildings by simply throwing the material out the back of the house into a huge pile. Then we hire haulers to come by with a Caterpillar and load the debris into semi-trailer trucks for hauling to the dump. This method is obviously very messy and tends to destroy the grass and sometimes even concrete walkways.

If your city puts dumpsters in the alleys for garbage, do not use them for your debris because, if you get caught, you will be fined. It does not cost that much to have material hauled away; you can always find people with dump trucks who are willing to shovel it out of the house and haul it for a fairly reasonable price. The overall price of gutting a house and getting rid of the debris often depends on the fees that the local dump charges.

HIRING SOMEONE TO GUT YOUR HOUSE

We have totally gutted only one house by ourselves, and we will never do it again. For the amount of money it costs to have a house gutted, the back-breaking labor involved is often not worth doing it yourself. The only way that you should consider doing it yourself is if you are rehabbing your house one room or one floor at a time or if you are on a very tight budget. The other thing that you may consider is knocking down all the plaster and pulling down all the lath yourself, then having a crew come in to shovel it out of the house into a dump truck and haul it away. In a large city where a lot of rehab work is done, you will find people who specialize in this kind of work. They salvage lumber, bricks, and metal, from which they make a fair amount of money, so their fees for doing the work are not very high.

If you hire a crew to do the total demolition, be careful that they know what is and is not a bearing wall (see Chapter 13). Some demolition crews start tearing things down without paying attention to such things, so make sure you are there to supervise. Sometimes even you will find a wall that you think is not a bearing wall but really is. If they start tearing it out, the floors may collapse, which may result in injury and major reconstruction costs.

SIFTING THROUGH THE DEBRIS

When removing debris from a building, it is usually worth your while to separate dimension lumber (two-by-fours, two-by-tens, and so on), cabinets, and metal from the lath and plaster. The lath and plaster are worthless, but you can usually find someone who will buy virtually everything else, including doors, windows, sash, old glass, dimension lumber, aluminum storm windows, radiators, old furnaces, and pipes. This material also may be of value to you. For instance, some of the most beautiful rehabs are those in which the old doors have been retained. Even if the doors are fir or pine, they are probably panel doors, which are worth reusing. You can buy a prehung panel door for less than $150, but there is nothing like having a solid, old-style panel door. You can also use old doors on one floor and new doors on other floors.

It is also likely that you will need some of the lumber that comes out of a building. Dimension lumber will come in handy in doubling studs and stringers that are cracked or have holes cut through them for plumbing. Modern lumber doesn't match the dimensions of old lumber. You almost always need two-by-four stud fill-ins or blocking (most old walls did not have blocking). Sometimes you will need to butt a wall up against an existing wall, and old lumber comes in handy for nailers (see Chapter 15). You can save yourself quite a bit of money by using some of the old two-by-fours.

The old pipe, wire, duct work, or radiators have value as salvage material. Steel is worth salvaging only by the ton, though radiators have brass fittings. Wire is usually copper, which is quite valuable. All the sash have value. If you are pulling old storm windows off the house or replacing the windows entirely, they are salvageable. Glass is reusable, and the frames of aluminum storm windows are valuable. Nonferrous metals are a scarce resource and have a high resale price.

Try to keep these materials when you gut a building. If you rehab yourself, keep them for recycling. If you contract with a salvage company for demolition, the company will expect to get the materials, so you will need to work that out. Be sure you keep whatever you think you will need for the rehab and keep it separated so it remains with you. Even if you have dimension lumber left over after the rehab, you can always cut it into firewood or give it away.

In cities, the health department is usually concerned about lead-based paint. If you have a huge pile of debris in your backyard or in an alley and it is full of lumber with lead paint, you may be cited for storing lead-based materials outside. Another thing to be aware of is that some salvagers will not buy copper wire unless you burn off the insulation. That may not be possible in a city with pollution controls, so it may not be worth salvaging. Also, wire is often not worth salvaging because the wires go through studs and they can be very difficult to pull out.

All hardware is worth salvaging. You may want to get it cleaned or clean it yourself and then reuse it. If old hardware has heavy layers of paint on it, soak it in paint stripper. When it is down to bare metal, boil it in vinegar to remove the tarnish and then polish it. Or take it to an architectural salvage operation, where you can either have it cleaned or sell it. We often just sell the old hardware and then purchase cleaned hardware for the rehab.

Hardwood flooring sometimes can be reused if it is taken up carefully. If you leave it down, do not drop plaster walls on it; it is best to put a tarp, an old rug, or linoleum down before you gut the walls. If you will refinish the floor anyway, just make sure it is ¾ inch, and you can sand out any scratches.

Pulling nails out of old lumber is a tedious job, and, unless you have teenage children who are willing to do it, the lumber is not worth salvaging beyond your immediate needs. Do not try to reuse two-by-fours in new framing. The labor spent in pulling nails is not worth the $2 to $3 that a new stud costs.

UTILITIES DURING DEMOLITION

During demolition, you will either remove all the electrical circuits from the building or have the electricity shut off. How, then, do you keep electricity in the building? In a complete gut, turn off the main breaker and cut or disconnect every circuit wire out of the electrical box. Then connect two circuits on loose lines (about 50 feet each) that have junction boxes on the end that can be rolled up. Subcontractors can use these two circuits. If you plan to have more than one subcontractor in the house at one time, run more than two circuits.

If you are gutting a whole building or will eventually rewire the entire building regardless of the extent of gutting, the best thing to do is to run two circuits, one for upstairs and one for downstairs. If you will retain some of the building intact, including the wiring and plumbing, you must figure out which circuits stay and which ones go. It still may be best to run one or two temporary circuits out of the main box, shut off the rest of the box, and then figure things out after you have determined what needs to be gutted. You should probably hire a professional to test the circuits when you start turning them back on.

Plumbing works much the same way. You have to decide what is going to stay and what has to go. If all the plumbing is going to go and you have cast-iron waste stacks, the best thing to do is start from the top and work your way down. It would be nice to break the line in the basement and close up the connection going underground, but the weight of the entire stack is resting on that connection. The stack may come crashing down through the floors if you break it out at the basement. Try to drop as few pieces down it as possible, especially if you are considering saving the lateral waste line that runs to the sewer. Use a sledgehammer, wear goggles, and be careful.

It is probably a good idea to install new sewer lines. This is a considerable expense, but you probably have a clay line, which is very susceptible to problems such as invasive tree roots. Since you will probably put significantly more plumbing load into the house, it is almost mandatory that you put in new waste service.

If the house has a 1-inch lead or galvanized water supply line and you have good water pressure, you may not have to replace it unless you expect to pour concrete or build a deck over the line. In rehabbing a house for resale, we always redo the lateral lines for the waste plumbing, water supply, and gas supply so there is no problem later on. If you do not plan to replace the lateral lines, it is important to have them shut off and plugged so you do not fill them with debris once you start gutting the house. Try to keep some water supply available to you, if possible, while you are doing the rehab.

FLOORS AND BEARING WALLS

A structure must bear several kinds of loads: a roof

load, a floor (or live) load, and, depending on where you live, a snow load. These loads must be transferred to the ground, or the building will collapse. This transfer is done by the bearing walls (see Figure 10-1). It is extremely common in Victorian buildings to find a wall that goes down the center of the house to help carry some of the load. In some narrow row houses, joists may go all the way across the house, but almost always there is a center wall. If there is a shotgun hallway, the inside wall of that hallway is almost always a bearing wall.

The easiest way to find out whether a wall is or is not bearing is to go into the basement and find the direction of the joists. Bearing walls run perpendicular to the floor joists and usually run the length of the long dimension of the building. Find the center beam on which overlapping joists rest. Anything above that beam is bearing, whether it is a wall, a post, or a column. If a post or column is resting directly on a doubled or tripled joist or some kind of blocking, anything above the post is bearing. Bearing walls usually have a base plate (a two-by-four flat on the floor on which the studs rest) and a double cap (a two-by-four on top of the wall), but this is not always the case.

Do not look at the construction technique of a wall to determine bearing walls in Victorian homes. Conceptualize the loads in the house and determine how they are transferred to the foundation. And remember, anytime you cut a stud and the saw binds or removal of studs gets progressively more difficult, beware. You may have a bearing wall. Sometimes there is not a straight stacking of the bearing walls. You may find a beam in the basement, but when you go to the first floor, you find the bearing wall one or two feet to the side of that beam. Then you go to the second floor, and the bearing wall is two feet off the beam in the other direction.

Finding the main bearing walls is not always enough. Most old buildings also have partially bearing walls. A partially bearing wall is a wall on a lower floor that helps support a wall on an upper floor. If there is a wall on the second floor, particularly if it is running in the same direction as the joists, you will find a wall or doubled joists underneath it on the next floor down. If it does not make sense to have a wall on the floor underneath, you

will find that the wall will be resting on a doubled or tripled joist. But, in a situation where it makes sense to have a wall underneath, the upper wall will be supported with just one (maybe two) joist(s) with a partially bearing wall underneath. In the basement, the partially bearing wall will either have one or two posts underneath it or a triple joist supporting it. A wall going across joists will usually be supported by a partially bearing wall. If you must move a partially bearing wall on a lower floor, you will need to support the wall on the upper floor in another manner. You must either add posts or strengthen the underlying joist(s).

Read Chapter 13 before attempting to remove any bearing walls. You must build a wall on each

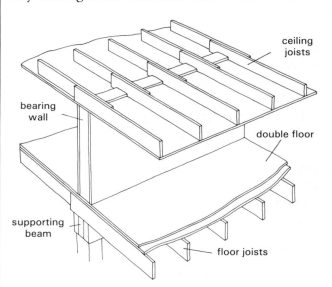

FIGURE 10-1. *A bearing wall.*

side of the bearing wall about two feet away. Build these walls just like a bearing wall, with a double cap and studs on 16-inch centers. When that is done, you can remove the studs of the bearing wall and replace them with a beam or a new bearing wall. Table 10-1 lists the dimension sizes for beams, but check with the city building commission, which will probably require an architect or engineer to sign off on the plans where any bearing members are removed and replaced. Make sure that if you beam an old bearing wall, that the beam is resting on posts that transfer the load to the foundation.

After you have determined the locations of bearing and partially bearing walls, it is important to go into the attic and look for strongbacks (see Figure 10-2). A strongback is a two-by-six or two-by-eight running on top of and perpendicular to the ceiling joists. It is nailed to a flat two-by-four, which is nailed to the ceiling joists. The strongback rests on some kind of a post or wall at each end, so its load goes down through the house to the foundation. The strongback helps hold up the joists, and it is very important that you do not remove it or the support under it. If you remove a wall that has a strongback sitting on it, you will either have to put a post underneath the strongback or replace the wall.

Before you start taking a building apart, look for joists and other bearing members (particularly the caps of bearing walls) that have been cut to accommodate plumbing added later. It is very common to find walls whose caps have been cut through for a 4-inch cast-iron stack. It is also common to find two-by-ten flooring joists that have been cut three-quarters of the way through to accommodate plumbing, especially around toilets. These must be replaced or strengthened.

REMOVING PLASTER, LATH, STUDS, AND WALLS

When removing plaster, the easiest way to do it is to knock the plaster off with a hammer and then pull down the lath. If you knock a hole in the wall or ceiling and stick a two-by-four into the hole in the same direction as the studs or joists, you can then pull down a big part of the ceiling or wall by pulling on the two-by-four. Do not worry about trying to knock down the plaster one piece at a time. Get down the biggest pieces possible, unless you are trying to save some of the plaster or lath, but be careful not to drop the entire ceiling on your head.

When it comes to taking out studs and walls, if you do not want to save the lumber, use a sledge-hammer to beat out one end of each stud (usually the bottom end) and pull it out. Another option is to cut through the middle of the stud and take out the bottom and top in short pieces. Be very careful if you use a power saw. If the saw blade binds

when you start cutting in the middle of the wall, assume that this is a bearing wall and stop cutting. It is also a good idea to stop if studs get progressively harder to beat out. You may be getting more weight on each remaining stud because the wall is bearing. If you knock out studs with a sledgehammer and a cap starts sagging, stop and reappraise the situation.

When we gut a building, we knock down all the plaster and lath, clean up, then start taking out walls. It is a lot easier to see what you are doing when all the plaster is down and out of the building. You can figure out which walls are bearing, which are partially bearing, and which are not bearing. You also can see the floor joists and flooring once the ceiling plaster is down. This method is highly recommended for the do-it-yourselfer.

WINDOWS DURING DEMOLITION

You should save the existing windows intact while you are gutting the building to keep out vandals and the weather. This is important if you are doing the work yourself. You cannot gut a building in two or three days, so you must keep the glass intact. We cut several pieces of plywood the size of the typical or the largest window so that when we are working in a room, we can prop or nail the plywood over the inside of the window frame while we are knocking down the plaster, particularly the ceiling plaster around that window. This also prevents us from putting a two-by-four through the glass. Obviously, if you cover up the windows, you are not going to have any light, so you have to weigh the possibility of breaking window glass against working in less light.

DEALING WITH OTHER SYSTEMS

Radiators have valuable brass fittings, so if you are doing the work yourself, take out those fittings. You can break them off with a good 3- to 10-pound hammer. Keep in mind that if you have a huge radiator and you cannot get it out of the building by yourself, it is easy to lay it on a pile of plaster or a piece of plywood (if you are saving the floors) and take a sledgehammer to it. Radiators are usually made of cast iron and break relatively easily. Another option is to take them apart. Old radiators are typically bolted together with rods at the top and bottom. But the bolts are probably corroded, so taking them apart is not very easy to do. It is easier just to break them up.

The same goes for the cast-iron soil pipe: break it up. You will probably have to saw out the iron supply pipe unless it has cast-iron fittings. You can break cast-iron fittings, but not forged ones. The best saw for that purpose is a sawsall with metal blades.

Cast-iron furnaces can be broken up the same way, but remember that many old furnaces are covered with asbestos. If this is the case, it may be simpler to hire somebody to remove the furnace and dispose of the asbestos. When removing a furnace, always wear a mask to protect against asbestos dust and soot.

Often you will find wires and coal gas supply pipes (³⁄₈-inch steel pipes for coal gas lighting) inside walls. If you are not going to insulate those walls (they are not exterior walls), you do not have to worry about removing these things.

Everything you remove will be full of nails. There are two kinds of nails: nails that fasten lath to studs and joists and larger nails that hold studs and dimension lumber together. The larger nails need to be pulled out, but most of the small nails (the lath nails) can be pounded in. Those nails will not be big enough to stop a drywall nail. You will probably not drywall directly over the old studs and joists anyway because they are not plumb (see Chapter 20). Take care of the nails fairly quickly so that no one gets stuck. If you have taken out old drywall, also remove the drywall nails.

SAVING FINISH MATERIALS

There are two ways to gut a building without removing everything. One is to knock down all the

plaster and leave the lath and finish molding intact, then put drywall over the old lath. If you redo plumbing and wiring in the walls, the easiest thing to do is to cut out the lath between two joists and run all the plumbing and wiring up that 16-inch space, then drywall over it. You can save a tremendous amount of work if you do not have to move all the woodwork, doors, and trim while you remove the plaster, rewire, replumb, and then drywall. If the plaster is very thick, you may have to use double drywall. In some older Victorian buildings, you will find a wide casing on the door and then a piece of trim molding at the edge (see Figure 10-3). Sometimes, you can simply remove the trim molding, knock down the plaster, drywall, and then put the trim molding back on. Even if there is up to a ½-inch space between the new drywall and the molding, the trim molding will hide it. If you have that trim molding, you can sometimes remove it and drywall right over the old plaster with ³⁄₈-inch drywall, then replace the trim. The trouble with redrywalling with ³⁄₈-inch material is that you cannot do it on outside walls because there is nothing to attach the drywall to. You cannot just glue it on or screw through it into the brick, so you will have to replaster exterior walls. You also will pay significantly more for plumbing and electrical work, because the subcontractor will have to cut small holes in the old walls.

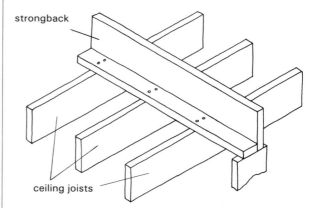

FIGURE 10-2. *A strongback running over ceiling joists.*

The second gutting alternative is to take down all the lath and plaster but leave the trim molding around the doors and windows intact. Make sure you remove the plaster at least ½ to 1 inch behind the molding. You must shim all the studs with one-by-twos or run one-by-twos perpendicular to the studs (you can also use metal J-channel for this), then attach the drywall to these. A table saw is often needed to cut the shims so that the ½- or ⅝-inch drywall fits tight against the backs of the door casing and baseboards. This process tends to be as messy as complete demolition. You end up saving the existing molding, but you inherit the damage you do to the molding in knocking down the plaster. But it does solve some of the problems of replumbing and rewiring.

We do not recommend either method very highly, as both require a lot of work. The first, though, is better than the second. Unless there is something worth restoring, we suggest that you just gut everything. You must, however, consider these alternatives because of the possible savings you can realize by not having to buy supplies such as new doors and trim.

REMOVING FINISH MATERIALS

When removing trim, try to keep the materials intact because you can sell or recycle them. The best thing to do with trim is to pry it out gently with a flat pry bar. You will usually find a nail every 12 to 18 inches. When you pull nails out of trim, use a pair of pliers or flat cutters to grab the nail at the back. Turn the pliers or cutters sideways to pull the nail out of the molding instead of pushing it through the front. That way, you will not chip the wood as you might by pushing the nail through the front.

Most large cities have architectural salvage stores that will buy these materials. Often you can trade your materials for others that have been stripped by the company or you can purchase matching materials there. You will probably have to pay a premium for the stripped materials. You must, however, weigh the value of the trim purchased against the time required to remove it intact.

In taking out doors, it doesn't take much effort to pry the hinge loose or unscrew it so that the hinge stays intact. If the plaster is gutted from the

building, you can sometimes use a sawsall to cut the nails that hold the frame in place and take the frame out in one piece. If your doors are in decent shape, you can leave the frame and door right where they are. The problem is that the door frame will be wider than is needed with drywall because the plaster was thicker than the drywall, so you may have to shim the door casing.

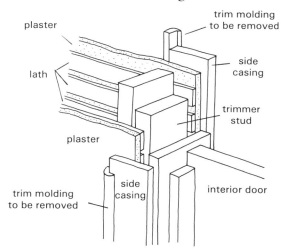

FIGURE 10-3. *It is often possible to temporarily remove old trim molding from around a door in order to replace plaster and lath with drywall, then reattach the molding.*

Any sinks, basins, toilets, and bathtubs that are genuine antiques should be carefully removed and saved. The same goes for cabinets. If you want to save a cabinet, pull it loose (it is usually nailed to the wall in older houses) and keep it intact.

If you think you will use something, save it. Save all hardware, doors, and working toilets. Bathtubs and basins are usually not worth saving unless they are antiques, but toilets may be. Even if you don't plan to use the old kitchen cabinets in the rehabbed kitchen, they may come in handy for a workshop or laundry room in the basement.

STORING MATERIALS

Depending on how much material you are saving, you will need a storage space. One obvious place is the basement. Once you have removed the fur-

TABLE 10-1

MAXIMUM SPANS FOR BUILT-UP BEAMS

Species	Grade	Supported Joist Length (ft.)	Size of built-up beam, inches											
			3-2 x 8		4-2 x 8		3-2 x 10		4-2 x 10		3-2 x 12		4-2 x 12	
			ft.	in.	ft.	in.	ft.	in.	ft.	in.	ft.	in.	ft.	in.
Douglas Fir Western Larch	No. 1	8	8	10	10	6	11	4	13	4	13	9	16	3
		10	7	4	9	4	9	4	11	11	11	5	14	6
		12	6	4	8	0	8	0	10	3	9	9	12	5
		14	5	7	7	0	7	1	9	0	8	8	10	11
		16	5	0	6	4	6	5	8	0	7	10	9	9
	No. 2	8	8	2	9	5	10	5	12	0	12	8	14	8
		10	7	3	8	5	9	4	10	9	11	4	13	1
		12	6	4	7	8	8	0	9	10	9	9	11	11
		14	5	7	7	0	7	1	9	0	8	8	10	11
		16	5	0	6	4	6	5	8	0	7	10	9	9
Pacific Coast Hemlock Amabilis Fir Grand Fir	No. 1	8	7	7	9	1	9	8	11	7	11	9	14	1
		10	6	4	8	0	8	0	10	3	9	9	12	5
		12	5	5	6	10	6	11	8	9	8	6	10	8
		14	4	10	6	1	6	2	7	9	7	6	9	5
		16	4	4	5	5	5	7	6	11	6	10	8	6
	No. 2	8	7	0	8	1	8	11	10	3	10	10	12	6
		10	6	3	7	2	7	11	9	2	9	8	11	2
		12	5	5	6	7	6	11	8	5	8	6	10	2
		14	4	10	6	1	6	2	7	9	7	6	9	5
		16	4	4	5	5	5	7	6	11	6	10	8	6
Pacific Coast Yellow Cedar Tamarack Jack Pine Eastern Hemlock	No. 1	8	8	5	9	9	10	9	12	6	13	1	15	2
		10	7	0	8	9	8	11	11	2	10	10	13	7
		12	6	0	7	7	7	8	9	9	9	4	11	10
		14	5	4	6	8	6	10	8	7	8	3	10	5
		16	4	10	6	0	6	2	7	8	7	6	9	4
	No. 2	8	7	8	8	10	9	9	11	4	11	11	13	9
		10	6	10	7	11	8	9	10	1	10	8	12	4
		12	6	0	7	3	7	8	9	3	9	4	11	3
		14	5	4	6	8	6	10	8	6	8	3	10	5
		16	4	10	6	0	6	2	7	8	7	6	9	4
Balsam Fir Lodgepole Pine Ponderosa Pine Spruces (all species) Alpine Fir Aspen Poplar Large-toothed Aspen Poplar Balsam Poplar	No. 1	8	6	4	8	0	8	0	10	3	9	9	12	6
		10	5	3	6	8	6	9	8	6	8	2	10	4
		12	4	7	5	9	5	10	7	4	7	2	8	11
		14	4	1	5	1	5	3	6	6	6	5	7	11
		16	3	9	4	7	4	9	5	10	5	10	7	2
	No. 2	8	6	4	7	10	8	0	10	0	9	9	12	2
		10	5	3	6	8	6	9	8	6	8	2	10	4
		12	4	7	5	9	5	10	7	4	7	2	8	11
		14	4	1	5	1	5	3	6	6	6	5	7	11
		16	3	9	4	7	4	9	5	10	5	10	7	2
Western Red Cedar Red Pine Western White Pine White Pine	No. 1	8	6	9	8	6	8	7	10	10	10	5	13	2
		10	5	7	7	1	7	2	9	1	8	9	11	0
		12	4	10	6	1	6	3	7	10	7	7	9	6
		14	4	4	5	5	5	7	6	11	6	9	8	5
		16	3	11	4	10	5	1	6	3	6	2	7	7
	No. 2	8	6	7	7	7	8	5	9	9	10	3	11	10
		10	5	7	6	10	7	2	8	8	8	9	10	7
		12	4	10	6	1	6	3	7	10	7	7	9	6
		14	4	4	5	5	5	7	6	11	6	9	8	5
		16	3	11	4	10	5	1	6	3	6	2	7	7

Table adapted from *Canadian Wood-Frame Construction*, with permission of the National Research Council. Ottawa, Canada.

nace, pipes, and duct work, the basement will be fairly clean and may be a good place to store material. If you are planning to rehab the basement, you cannot store materials there. One option is to do all the work upstairs and then do the basement last. If you are redoing the plumbing, you will have to break the concrete floor in the basement and dig trenches to install the new plumbing. That must be done before you can store materials there. Make sure you store materials only in a warm, dry place. Dampness can result in warped molding or warped or cracked panels and doors. If the rehab will last several months and wood is stored in the basement, a dehumidifier may be in order.

When you consider the effort and the expense of storing materials, the time in rehabbing those materials, and the cost of having doors, trim, and molding stripped or stripping them yourself, it may be more cost-effective to buy new materials unless you have very beautiful hardwood trim and doors.

References

OLD

Comstock, W.T. *Victorian Domestic Architectural Plans and Details: 734 Scale Drawings of Doorways, Windows, Staircases, Moldings, Cornices, and Other Elements.* Reprint of 1881 edition. New York: Dover Publications, 1987.

NEW

Abrams, Lawrence F. *Salvaging Old Barns and Houses: Tear It Down and Save the Pieces.* New York: Sterling Publishing Co., 1983.

Colby, Jean Poindexter. *Building Wrecking: The How and Why of a Vital Industry.* New York: Hastings House, 1972.

Horwitz, Elinor Lander. *How to Wreck a Building.* New York: Pantheon Books, 1982.

Johnson, Edwin. *Old House Woodwork Restoration: How to Restore Doors, Windows, Walls, Stairs, and Decorative Trim to Their Original Beauty.* Englewood Cliffs, New Jersey: Prentice-Hall, 1983.

Litchfield, Michael W. *Salvaged Treasures: Designing and Building with Architectural Salvage.* New York: Van Nostrand Reinhold, 1983.

Chapter 11

MASONRY

The term *masonry* refers to materials such as stone, brick, tile, concrete, and some combinations of these. Brick is perhaps the most common type of masonry, since it was the first type to be standardized in shape and produced in large quantities. The building that you are going to rehab is probably made of brick, so a good deal of this chapter is devoted to brick masonry.

In discussing the renovation and repair of masonry, we will need to address two issues. First, your house has a foundation that is made of some type of masonry. You need to inspect both the inside and the outside of the foundation and make any necessary improvements. Second, your house has some type of masonry enclosing the living areas. You may or may not be able to inspect both the inside and the outside of this component. Certainly if you rip out all the inside walls, you will expose the inner side of the brick shell of the house. In most cases, however, any renovations that you make to the masonry walls will be made on the outside only.

Much has been written on the subject of masonry. The U.S. Government Printing Office (Washington, DC 20402) is a good source of information on this topic. For instance, the Department of the Interior (National Park Service, Preservation Assistance Division, Technical Preservation Services) publishes a series of "preservation briefs," which are short, technical discussions of individual issues relevant to the preservation and renovation of historic buildings. Several of these publications have to do with masonry. In addition, periodicals such as *New Shelter, The Family Handyman*, and *Old House Journal* sometimes publish helpful information about masonry. Your local library is a good source for books on this subject; some of the more valuable references are listed at the end of this chapter.

MASONRY TOOLS

We feel that you should subcontract most masonry work, although some chimney repairs and tuckpointing are do-it-yourself projects. Bulging walls, dropped door/window arches, and structural repairs may not be. If you plan to do masonry work, you should have several special tools at your disposal. One of the basic rules of home improvement is that there is a tool for almost every project and if you have that tool the job will be much easier.

Following are the basic tools you will need for masonry work:

Trowel. If you have no other tool in your toolbox, you must have this one. You will use a trowel to mix mortar, cut bricks, scoop mortar, butter the bricks, tap the bricks into place, and fashion the type of joints that you desire.

Mason's hammer. This hammer looks a bit like those used by archaeologists. It has a flat nose for tapping and a long, sharp pick for scoring and breaking.

String level. This is a very small level that can be

hung on a string stretched taut over a course of bricks to help keep them at the same height and level.

Mason's level. This is similar to a standard carpenter's level but is at least 4 feet long. It is used to make sure walls are plumb and level.

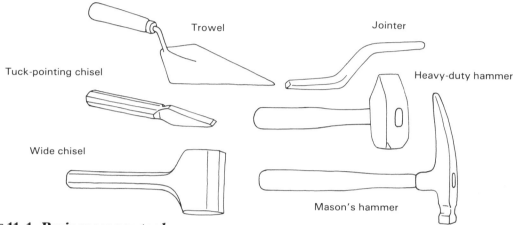

Tuck-pointing chisel

Trowel

Jointer

Heavy-duty hammer

Wide chisel

Mason's hammer

FIGURE 11-1. *Basic masonry tools.*

Tuck-pointing chisel. This chisel is used to clean out old joints before they are repointed.

Jointer. This is used to finish the joints between the masonry.

Wrecking bar. This is useful in separating old bricks and for other jobs requiring brute force.

GENERAL INSPECTION

Before you begin renovating your building, it is useful to walk around and through it making notes of what must be done. Once you have such a list, you will be able to prioritize the masonry items needing repair in order of importance.

Outside Inspection

A careful outside inspection can reveal problems or potential problems inside your home. For example, wet basements or bowed and buckled foundations can be traced to poor water runoff in the yard. Start with an inspection of the gutters and downspouts. Make sure that all these are clear of debris

and that they fit together tightly. You will probably have to take off the downspouts and hold them up to the light to make sure that the bends are not plugged. Be sure to look at the lower bend where the downspout comes to the ground. Sometimes the underside of the pipe will be rusted through. If this or some other problem is preventing the water from being directed out and away from the house, the water may be running down between the ground and the foundation and into the basement.

Next, check the lay of the land. Make sure that the ground around the foundation slopes away from the house on all sides. Especially check in front of basement windows for flat spots or places where rainwater can puddle up. An accepted rule of thumb for slope is that the ground around the foundation should slope away from the house at a rate of about one inch per foot for at least six feet. If you find that this is not the case, then you will have to add dirt to increase the slope.

Inspect the driveway and any patios. Over time, the seam between the foundation and the drive or patio might have begun to widen and leak. This is particularly problematic with driveways where settling may have produced natural diversions of wastewater to these seams. If you find that this is the case, you can use a caulking gun to fill in the seams with a product such as latex cement. Purchase high-quality caulk, or you will find yourself redoing the job each spring.

If you discover that the foundation has suffered serious damage, it would be wise to call in a professional. This is particularly true if you find serious buckling or large cracks in the foundation. You will need the advice of a structural engineer to tell you how serious the damage is and just what you can do about it. Frequently, serious buckling of the foundation calls for the placement of pilasters (steel pipes fitting from floor to ceiling and holding back the bulging wall) or the excavation of the dirt outside the foundation so that you can rebuild the wall. Neither job is difficult, but in some areas the local building codes may require that it be done by licensed professionals.

If you do find serious cracks in the foundation, you can easily tell whether they are active by filling them with plaster of paris and then reexamining them in several weeks. If the cracks are visible at that time, you have an active foundation problem that demands an immediate consultation with an expert.

Keep in mind that the soundness of your rehabilitation is only going to be as good as the soundness of your foundation. You can paint and fix up all you want, but if the foundation is settling, sooner or later the cracked walls, uneven and squeaking floors, sticking doors and windows, and cracked glass will return. Time spent assessing and repairing problems with the foundation is time well spent.

Settling of the foundation is the major threat to the structural integrity of the house. Settling occurs for a variety of reasons but usually results in cracking and bulging in the foundation walls. Keep in mind that the dirt surrounding the foundation can move. When the earth moves, it can exert a tremendous force on the foundation walls. The walls are stiff, and the pressure is relieved by cracking. Filling active cracks makes no sense because, even though it may cover up the problem, it is only a temporary solution. They will open up again and again until the underlying problem is fixed. If the reason for the settlement of the foundation is not apparent to you, consult a structural engineer.

Foundations in most older homes were constructed of brick, stone, and, sometimes, concrete. Foundations built before the turn of the century were usually built of brick or stone, and those built after about 1920 were made of concrete.

Problems associated with brick foundations are a bit more difficult to diagnose than those associated with concrete. The major problem associated with a brick foundation is moisture. Brick and mortar are quite porous, and in frame houses or additions moisture seeps in from the surrounding ground and is taken up through the mortar to the sill plate of the house. Over a number of years, this can lead to dry rot in the sill plate and infestation by termites. It is fairly easy to inspect for dry rot. Take an ice pick into the basement and reach up over the top of the foundation wall to the sill plate. Poke the pick into the sill plate wood. If it goes in easily, you should suspect dry rot. Inspecting for termites should be done by a professional. The second problem associated with brick foundations is the deterioration of the mortar between the bricks. This can be seen as long cracks or as mortar that crumbles and falls out when disturbed.

In concrete foundations, the evidence of settling may be a bit more noticeable, since the concrete wall is even less flexible than a brick or stone wall. With a concrete foundation, you must decide whether the cracks are small enough to be patched or whether they are due to major pressure against the wall. Minor cracks can be repaired by filling them with concrete, but major cracks can be a sign of very serious problems. Large cracks should be examined by a structural engineer.

If you have determined that the foundation is reasonably level and square, then you probably have a foundation that is worth saving, and you can go ahead and make the necessary repairs.

If your inspection does not turn up all the answers to your questions, or if you wish to receive further help, you can consult the Department of Agriculture's Soil Conservation Service or your state extension service for free advice.

Inside Inspection

If you see water standing in your basement or leaking through the foundation wall, do not jump to conclusions and call in a professional without a second look. Sometimes this is simply due to leaking or sweaty water pipes. If you see water coming in during a heavy rainstorm, the chances are that you have a groundwater problem. Look for triangular spots on the basement walls. Do these spots bear any relation to problems that you may have spotted on your outside inspection? Keep in mind that, unless it has been treated, concrete is not waterproof. Moisture will seep through the foundation walls and up through the floor slab. A wide variety of waterproofing paints are available at your local hardware store. Application of these paints will solve most moisture problems, but they will not solve the problem of water coming in through large cracks in the wall or at the junction between the floor and the wall.

You can fix cracks in the wall with quick-dry portland cement. You can even purchase products that will set while the water is still seeping in. Ask your building supplier for advice about these products. Cracks between the floor and the wall also can be repaired with portland cement or other latex cement products. It is a good idea to enlarge this type of crack and to chip a wedge shape into it before filling it with cement, as this gives the cement a better anchorage. Chip the wedge so that the wider portion is on the side of the crack farthest from you. Water that is seeping into a basement is usually under a good deal of pressure, so the cracks need to be repaired as tightly as possible.

If you still find that water is seeping into the basement after you have corrected any outside water runoff problems, it is time to call in a professional. This person will be able to provide you with various options, ranging from drainage tile around the foundation to creating a sump and pumping accumulating water out with a pump. Even if you intend to make these repairs yourself, it is a good idea to get the advice of a professional before starting some project that may turn out not to be the answer.

While you are down in the basement, look above your head at the floor joists and beams. Are any of these split or cracked? Are any of the beams sagging or warped? How do these beams look where they sit on top of the foundation wall? A beam that is split or cracked needs to be repaired with another wood beam bolted onto it, or it can be replaced with a prefabricated steel beam (see Chapter 13). If you do not correct this problem, your floors will sag and squeak, and the walls will continually crack. If you see extensive damage to load-bearing beams, it is a good idea to call in a building engineer for advice on repair or replacement (see Chapters 13 and 24).

Also inspect the area around the chimney. Chimneys are often a source of seeping water. Does the brick look sound? How about the mortar? Is it powdery and loose? The mortar and any loose or missing bricks should be replaced. Notice the way in which the vents from the heating system fit into the chimney. Is the fit tight and the seal complete?

CLOSING WINDOW AND DOOR OPENINGS

Just a note on closing up openings by bricking them in. Some rehabbers need to create new openings, and this technique is discussed in Chapter 14. Most rehabbers, however, tend to close up existing openings, and many do it inappropriately. Under most historic rehab regulations, closing an aperture can only be done if the filler brick is set back 1½ to 2 inches, so that the original shape of the opening and its brick arch are left intact and are discernible. Never close up openings in a brick house by framing the opening and covering it with plywood.

REPAIRING MASONRY

Whether you are repairing a brick foundation or a brick wall, the techniques are basically the same. The art of repairing masonry is covered in a number of other publications and will not be discussed in detail here. Instead, we will describe the types of materials that old homes are made of and the problems that commonly plague them. Some mention will be made of repointing, since this almost always needs to be done. In addition, we will discuss moisture problems, as well as the cleaning of masonry buildings.

Brick and brownstone are by far the most common construction materials in older city homes. Brick is clay that has been fired into a standard shape and size. Brownstone is a reddish sandstone and is very popular as a building material in the East and Midwest, especially in Romanesque architecture. It was often used as a facing material over brick. The use of concrete block is almost always restricted to foundations, but from time to time it can be found as the principal construction material. Terra-cotta is made of clay but is mixed with sand and fired at a high temperature, which usually makes it stronger than brick. Terra-cotta was often molded into a hollow block form (much like today's concrete blocks), then glazed to protect it from the elements.

Cleaning

Whatever the material, you should give some serious consideration to a general cleaning before you begin any other repairs. Cleaning will increase the beauty of your rehab and uncover hidden repair needs. Cleaning methods generally fall into three major categories: water, chemical, and abrasive. Water methods soften the dirt and rinse it from the surface. Chemical cleaners react with the dirt and other deposits and quicken the removal process. (Chemical cleaners are also used for removing paint from brick.) Abrasive methods usually include sandblasting, in which a fine, high-pressure spray of sand is directed against the masonry. This removes the outside layer of the masonry, though, and we do not recommend that you use this type of cleaning.

Water methods include low-pressure wash, moderate- to high-pressure wash, and steam. Stiff bristle brushes are used along with a good deal of elbow grease. Keep in mind that water will penetrate all the cracks in the mortar and also be absorbed to some extent by the masonry. Water also may bring soluble salts out of the masonry, and after drying they will be seen as stains. You should not use any of the water methods if there is a possibility of below-freezing weather, as that could crack the wall. Keep in mind that the wall may take a week or more to dry out. Despite these potential drawbacks, the water methods are by far the simplest to carry out, the safest for the building (and you), and the least expensive.

Most chemical cleaners are water-based, and so they have the same potential problems as the straight water methods. In addition, you have to be aware of the potential environmental and personal health hazards associated with chemical cleaners. Before attempting to use chemical cleaners on a masonry wall, find out what type of masonry is involved. Some chemical cleaners react with certain types of masonry, which could result in damage. For instance, marble and limestone are easily damaged by acidic cleaners. The salts in the mortar may be leached out by chemical cleaners such as hydrochloric acid (muriatic acid), which will result in staining.

Abrasive cleaning can be done with grinding disks, wire wheels, or sandblasters, but all remove the top layer of the masonry. This type of cleaning should never by used on historic buildings where the brick may be soft or there is any ornamental masonry. In addition, when brick and terra-cotta are fired, the hardest part is the outside skin. Once this is gone, they will have no protection against the elements. The tiny pits that are formed by the abrasion actually increase the surface area of the masonry and leave a larger area on which future dirt and grime can settle.

One of the most common problems uncovered by cleaning and inspecting your mortar wall is loose mortar. The chief cause of this is moisture. The source of the unwanted moisture should be carefully investigated and fixed. The problem usually stems from leaking or inefficient gutters and downspouts. Portions of the building may have settled below ground level, and thus water is seeping into the brick as a result of capillary action. Water constantly splashing up on the building's walls also may contribute to these problems. Masonry buildings are inherently porous, and they promote the migration of water through the walls.

Previous owners might have painted the brick to avoid tuck-pointing or to hide the addition of used brick. Since you are probably going to have to repoint the building, it will be necessary to strip off the paint. This can be done with a commercial paint stripper, but the task is best left to a professional, since the chemicals are dangerous to humans as well as to the environment. If you discover that previous repairs have been made with mismatched mortar or used brick, you will probably be better off to leave the paint or add a fresh coat.

Tuck-pointing

Once the source of excessive moisture has been identified and remedied and you have cleaned the brick, you can begin to repair any damage. Repairing loose or missing mortar between bricks is called *repointing*. This is a tedious task requiring much patience and some specialized tools. It ought to be scheduled for a period of relatively warm weather, when the wall temperatures are between 40°F. and 95°F.

The first step in any repointing job is to remove all the old and loose mortar. The best, though slowest, method for doing this is to use a tuck-pointing chisel with a hammer. Cut a square groove in the mortar, keeping the groove about ½ inch deep. Be sure to wear eye protection when you do this. Once the joints have been cut to the correct depth, clean them with a stiff bristle brush, such as a wallpaper brush. It is possible to grind out the old mortar with a wheel on a grinder or circular saw. This procedure can be dangerous, though, and is recommended only if you have experience with these tools.

To reach all the joints along the building's walls, you will have to erect scaffolding. Scaffolding will allow you safe access to an entire wall at one time, and prevent you from having to use a ladder. Scaffolding is available for rent and is easily assembled with a few common tools. The easy access to your work will be well worth the time you spend putting up the scaffolding before beginning the job.

The next step is to mix the mortar. The new mortar must match the original mortar as closely as possible. If you use the wrong type of mortar, the new mortar may chip off the old brickwork as it dries. Mortar that is stronger or harder than the bricks will not give, and the stress will be relieved through cracks or spalling in the brick. It is a good idea to have the original mortar analyzed. Contact a preservation society for recommended mortar analysts. If you cannot get the old mortar analyzed, try to mix what is known as type O mortar. This mixture closely resembles the standard old mortar and is composed of 1 part portland cement, 2 to 4 parts lime, and 7 to 8 parts fine sand. It should be fairly stiff and should keep its shape when you roll it into a ball. Since portland cement is very hard, it should not be used as the only binder in the mortar to be used with the soft bricks commonly found in older homes. The type O mortar described above is soft and porous and changes very little in volume during temperature fluctuations.

You will have to experiment with various coloring agents to match the new mortar to the old. The simplest method is to mix a small sample and allow it to cure. Once it is cured, break it open and compare the inside color with the inside of a broken piece of the original mortar.

Place the new mortar in the cleaned and dampened joints with a joint filler. Press the mortar firmly into the joint. Once the mortar has dried to the point where it will hold an impression of your finger, it can be used to repoint. This is done with the jointer. Most jointers today are shaped to form a concave joint, but close inspection of your wall may reveal that the original pointing was done with some other shape. You may choose to match that shape or use the concave design. After about a week, go back and knock off any large chunks of mortar that may have stuck to the masonry. Clean any residual mortar from the face of the brick with muriatic acid. Then treat the new joints with a waterproofing compound if you wish.

Cutting Brick

Occasionally you will have to cut a piece of brick so that it will fit. This can be accomplished with either a saw equipped with a masonry blade or with a bricklayer's chisel and hammer. The chisel and hammer method is faster. When using the chisel, place the blade on the cutting point of the brick, tilt the handle slightly toward the waste end of the brick, and strike the end sharply. Be sure to wear safety glasses when doing this type of work.

Having taken care of the foundation and the outside walls of your rehab, you can move on to the roof. In the next chapter, we discuss common roof problems and repairs.

References
OLD

Baker, Ira Osborn. *A Treatise on Masonry Construction.* New York: John Wiley & Sons, 1892.

Bancroft, Robert M., and Francis Bancroft. *Tall Chimney Construction.* Manchester, England: J. Calvert, 1885.

Gilbreth, Frank B. *Bricklaying Systems.* New York: M.C. Clark, 1909.

Shaw, Edward. *Practical Masonry.* Boston: B.B. Mussey, 1846.

Ungewitter, Georg G. *Details for Stone and Brick Architecture in Romanesque and Gothic Style.* New York: Hessling & Spielmeyer, 1858.

NEW

Adams, Jeannette T. *The Complete Concrete, Masonry and Brick Handbook.* New York: Van Nostrand Reinhold, 1983.

Advanced Masonry. Alexandria, Virginia: Time-Life Books, 1982.

Dobson, E. *Foundations and Concrete Works.* West Orange, New Jersey: Albert Saifer, 1986.

Kreth, R.T. *Advanced Masonry Skills.* New York: Van Nostrand Reinhold, 1978.

Masonry. Alexandria, Virginia: Time-Life Books, 1976.

McKee, Harley J. *Introduction to Early American Masonry: Stone, Brick, Mortar and Plaster.* Washington, DC: National Trust for Historic Preservation, 1973.

Pennycook, Bob. *Building with Glass Blocks.* Garden City, New York: Doubleday, 1987.

Better Homes and Gardens Step-by-Step Masonry and Concrete. Des Moines, Iowa: Meredith Corp., 1982.

Chapter 12

ROOFS AND CORNICES

A weather-tight roof is a basic ingredient in the preservation of a structure, regardless of its age, size, or design. The roof also imparts much of the building's architectural character. The hipped roofs of Georgian architecture, the turrets of Queen Anne, the mansard, and the graceful slopes of the Shingle and Bungalow styles are examples of the use of roofing as a major design feature.

No matter how decorative the pattern or how compelling the form, the roof is a highly vulnerable element that will inevitably fail. A poor roof will permit the accelerated deterioration of historic building materials (masonry, wood, plaster, and paint) and will cause general disintegration of the basic structure. Repair is desirable as soon as failure is discovered, and temporary patching methods should be chosen carefully to prevent inadvertent damage to sound or historic roofing materials and related features. Before you do any repair work, you should understand the historic value of the materials used on the roof. Then a complete internal and external inspection of the roof should be planned to determine all causes of failure and to identify the alternatives for repair or replacement.

If your home is over 75 years old, it is quite reasonable to assume that the roof has some historic value that ought to be retained. With that assumption in mind, let's examine some of the common types of roofing materials found in historic dwellings.

Clay tile. Clay has been used in America since the early days of European settlement. In some cases, settlers remembered the great fires that swept through London in the late 1600s and so built houses in Boston and other cities with tile roofs as a precaution. Tile comes in a variety of dimensions and shapes, but most tile fits together with an overlapping lug and hole or two holes in which a peg is placed.

Slate. In early America, slate was imported from Wales, although sources of slate were known to exist in America. The problem with American slate was largely one of transportation to coastal cities. Slate was popular because it was fireproof and available in several colors.

Shingles. Wood shingles were popular throughout the country in all periods of building history. The size and shape of the shingles tend to differ according to the local building practices. The availability of specific types of woods in certain locations dictated the material from which the shingles were made.

Metal. Metal roofing in America is a nineteenth-century phenomenon. The most common types of metal used were tin, lead, and copper. Metal was often used in places where the shape or pitch of the roof made it difficult to use wood or tile. Later, metal was corrugated to increase its strength over longer spans. It also was coated with zinc (galvanized) to protect it from rust. Once rolling mills were established, metal roofs became very popular. The material was often embossed with clever designs to imitate wood or tile.

Other materials. Asphalt shingles and roll roofing came into use during the 1890s.

INSPECTING YOUR ROOF

To inspect your roof, go into the attic on a bright,

sunny day so that you can see the sunlight shining through any gaps in the roofing material. If you can see daylight, water can come in through the same holes. Mark the holes so that you can see them from the outside when you start the repair process. While in the attic, look carefully at all the roof timbers. Are any cracked or bowed? Look carefully for stains indicating that water is seeping through the roofing material.

Then go outside and look up at the roof or actually climb up on it and get close to the problem. (Caution: When you go up on the roof, wear rubber-soled shoes and be very careful, especially on slate and tile, which are quite fragile.) If you would rather not climb up on the roof, you can do a good job of inspecting it by looking through a pair of binoculars. Look for damaged or missing tiles or shingles. Notice the state of the flashing around the chimney and other places where pipes come through the roof. Check the flashing around dormers and wherever else the roof joins other parts of the house. Inspect the valleys that exist between wings of the house. These must be in good shape and free from accumulations of debris. Inspect all the drain gutters and the downspouts. Often, if a house has not been well cared for, the downspouts will be plugged, especially at the elbows. You will probably have to remove the elbows to see inside the spouts. Tap on the gutters to see if they are rusted through. If they are badly rusted, you will hear a dull thud rather than a ringing sound. Walk slowly around the house and look up at the fascia on the underside of the roof overhang. Is the wood in good shape, or can you see rotten spots and holes? Holes in this part of the roof are an invitation to birds and squirrels to make their nests in your attic.

If you have a flat roof over all or a portion of the house, and you have no attic from which to examine the underside of it, you will have to climb up and inspect it from the outside. Inspection of a flat roof is much like that of a sloping roof, since you will be looking for obvious patches, tears in the roofing material, cracks, bad flashing, and so on. Some older flat roofs were covered with roll roofing, tar, and then pea gravel. If a good share of the pea gravel is missing and large expanses of the roofing material are exposed, chances are good that

there are leaks. Another thing to look for on a flat roof is places where the roof sags. Water will pool up in these spots during heavy rainstorms.

If you decide that the roof needs to be replaced, it is a good idea to get a second opinion from a roofing expert. Roofers are only too happy to provide you with a free estimate of what they think must be done. If you both agree that the roof needs to be replaced, the next issue is whether all the old roofing material must be stripped off. If the roof is made of tile or slate and most pieces are intact, it is usually not necessary to strip the roof, and repairs can be made by replacing only the damaged tiles. If, however, the roof is made of shingles, the decision will depend on how many layers of old material are already present. Each city has regulations concerning how many layers of roofing material are allowed before it must be stripped down and a new single layer applied. In many cases, the limit is four layers. Check your local codes to determine the limit in your area. Certainly the job of reroofing is much easier and cheaper if the new material can be applied over the old. With each new layer, however, the load on the roof increases dramatically, so considerable thought should go into this decision.

Stripping a roof is a messy job, but you can do it yourself. It is best accomplished quickly and at a time when you can depend on the weather to cooperate. When the last layer of roofing material is gone, you will be left with only the stringers (or roof boards) running at right angles to the roof joists separating you from the attic, so a rainstorm would be disastrous. In most modern construction, the roof is covered with sheathing plywood, which will provide some protection from the elements.

An old flat shovel is the best tool to use in stripping a roof. Start at the ridge and work down to the eaves. It is a good idea not to expose more roof than you can recover in one working day. Have rolls of plastic sheeting available just in case.

ROOFING MATERIALS

Remember that your house may be a historic building, and you may want to retain the architectural integrity of the original roof. If you live in a historic district with covenant agreements, you may have no choice but restoration. Even if it is not a historic structure, you will want to select the roofing material that is best suited to the design of the house. Following are some types of materials that you may want to consider.

Flashing

Flashing is common to all roof types. It is usually made out of thin sheets of metal or some other waterproof material that are overlapped in such a way that water cannot enter the building around protrusions through the roof or in places where the roofing material meets the sides of the house. Because flashing is usually made of metal and metal rusts, the flashing on an old house may be completely gone.

Asphalt Shingles

By far the most popular roofing material is asphalt shingles. They are durable, inexpensive, and easy to use. They come in many styles and colors; some even look convincingly like wood shingles. The most common type of shingle is the three-tab, single-strip type. Each shingle is 36″ x 12″ and has two slots cut into it so that when the shingles are on the roof, they appear to be many smaller shingles rather than large ones. Asphalt shingles are either organic or fiberglass. The organic ones are made of cellulose fiber that is saturated with asphalt. The fiberglass shingles are made from fiberglass and also are saturated with asphalt. The primary advantage of fiberglass shingles is that they will outlast organic shingles by as much as ten years. Asphalt shingles are sold by the square (100 square feet), and each square weighs a different amount depending on the thickness of the shingles. When considering the weight of the shingles, remember that if you are going to do the job yourself, you will have to carry the material up onto the roof. Some suppliers will sell you the shingles with a "delivered to the roof" pricing structure. This can be an advantage.

Roll Roofing

Roll roofing comes in 3-foot-wide rolls and is either smooth surfaced or has a mineral (sand) coating. The smooth-surfaced material is generally used on roofs that are to be covered with tar. Roll roofing

is made from the same materials as shingles but is generally cheaper. The major drawback to this type of material is that it does not look as nice as shingles when the job is done. On flat roofs or a slope of the roof that cannot be seen from the ground, this type of material might be a reasonable alternative to shingles.

Metal Roofing

Roofing made of corrugated or ribbed galvanized steel costs about the same as asphalt shingles but has the advantage of lasting 40 to 50 years. Steel roofing with an enamel finish can be obtained in many colors. Other types of metal also are available, including tin, aluminum, and copper, but they may be more expensive. Ribbed roofing can generally be applied by the home owner, but metal roofing requiring seaming is best left to the pros.

Wood Roofing

Perhaps the most popular wood for roofing is red cedar. Cedar shingles can be purchased in a variety of styles and shapes. Wood shakes (rough-cut shingles) come in various lengths and widths and at least two different thicknesses. A wood roof will last about 15 to 20 years, and if sprayed with a preservative, its life expectancy can be extended another 15 to 20 years. The preservative will have to be reapplied about every five years. For the do-it-yourselfer, replacing a wood roof is a time-consuming task but one that he or she can do successfully, especially if the roof is not too steep.

Slate and Tile Roofing

These are among the most durable roofing materials. They are expensive to install but will last several lifetimes. A major disadvantage for the do-it-yourselfer is the weight of the materials and the problem of moving around with them while up on the roof. Tiles are usually about $3/16$ to $1/2$ inch thick and come in a variety of sizes and shapes. You will find that a square of this type of roofing will weigh in at about 800 pounds. It is probably wise to leave the installation of this type of roofing to the pros. Imitation slate can be purchased in the form of mineral-fiber roofing shingles. (One brand-name is a product called Supra-Slate, which is made up of portland cement, silica, and asbestos.)

They do look like the real thing and weigh somewhat less.

REPAIRING YOUR ROOF

Before taking on the task of redoing a roof, you should be aware that the job is dangerous and strenuous. Should you decide to hire a roofer, make sure that the person comes well recommended and that he or she has adequate insurance against any damage that might occur during the process. Make sure to get a firm estimate in writing. Also make sure that you understand what the roofer will guarantee when the job is finished. If the roof has to be stripped, make sure that you determine who will haul the old roofing material away.

Whether you repair or replace your roof will depend largely on what you saw when you did the inspection. If you choose to replace the roof, you should give some thought to preserving its historical significance. Will your budget permit you to replace the roof with a historically appropriate material? Will the local building codes allow you to do anything less? If you choose not to use a historic material, can you use materials that look like the original? In this section we discuss the repair of several types of roofing material and suggest where you can purchase these materials.

Flashing

Where the roof intersects any walls of the house such as dormers, porches, or other wall structures, flashing must be intact, or there will be leakage. Usually the siding on a dormer will stop about 1 to 2 inches above the level of the roof, and the flashing will extend up under the siding about 4 inches and 4 to 6 inches under the roofing. This will form a waterproof bridge across the intersection of the roof and wall. Flashing should also be used where chimneys come up through the roof and where any pipe such as a drain vent protrudes from the roof. Flashing material is sold in rolls of varying widths. Lip flashing, which is molded, is placed at the corner of the roof to prevent water from running back under the roofing material. Flashing is available from most building supply outlets.

Slate Roofing

Although slate roofing lasts a long time, it does break and pieces will slide off the roof. A common reason for breakage is rusted nails. As the nails rust and iron oxide builds up on them, they increase in diameter and exert pressure on the brittle slate. Slate is a natural material and as such will have varying degrees of durability depending on where it was quarried. Most of the slate that comes from the United States will last 75 to 175 years. Those that come from Welsh quarries have been known to last for more than 1,000 years. Slate is purchased by the square. For smaller restoration jobs, it can be obtained in smaller amounts. Expect to pay $200 to $1,200 per square depending on the quality of the slate and the amount purchased. If you are willing to compromise authenticity, remember Supra-Slate as a less expensive alternative.

When you replace slate, it is a good idea to try and blend it into the existing slate. You may not have been able to match the color exactly, but if you remove some of the existing slate and then replace it by mixing in the new, you probably will not notice the difference. The details of how to replace or repair a slate roof are beyond the scope of this book. We suggest that you read *Slate Roofs*, a 1926 publication of the National Slate Association that is now available as a reprint from Vermont Structural Slate Co., Fair Haven, VT 05743.

Metal Roofing

The most common type of metal roofing is the tin roof. Actually the roof is made of steel plates that have been coated with tin. Usually this roofing material comes in sheets that are 10″ x 14″, 14″ x 20″, or 20″ x 28″. The tin coating develops a film of stannic oxide, which protects the base material from corrosion. Should this thin coating wear off, the base material will begin to rust. Once this happens, the two different metals will come into contact with each other, and the galvanic action that results will increase the speed with which the roof deteriorates.

The methods of repair for metal roofs can range from a simple patch to complete replacement. If the problem is with a joint or nail, it can be fixed by cleaning the area and resoldering the joint or the nail hole. If you are not familiar with tin roofs and how they are put down, read several of the references listed at the end of this chapter. The replacement of a tin roof involves not only special nails and clips but also a rather extensive process of treating and painting.

CORNICES

In this section, we discuss the inspection, repair, and replacement of cornices. Even though we explain how to rebuild a cornice, if your cornice needs replacement, we highly recommend that you hire a subcontractor experienced in cornice repair. We do this for two reasons. First, this type of work requires experience. It is done high up in the air on scaffolding, requires good carpentry skills, and is strenuous. Furthermore, it is not without risk. Cornices are fastened to the house. Fasteners rust and wood rots, so cornice pieces can fall. Second, cornice work takes time. This activity is perfect to assign to someone else while you concentrate on the interior of the house. Think through the pros and cons before you take on cornice (or dormer) work.

A cornice on a masonry building has both practical and aesthetic functions. It serves primarily as a gutter to carry water away from the roof, usually on the primary facade of the building. Unlike a gutter, though, a cornice describes a level line around the building (see Figure 12-1). A preformed

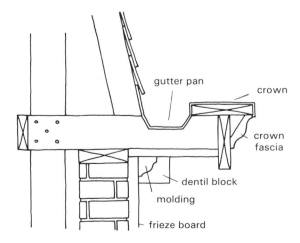

FIGURE 12-1. *Cross-section of a typical cornice attached to a Mansard roof.*

gutter is installed with pitch to allow for drainage. Because the cornice is level, the gutter pan behind the crown molding is slanted to allow the water to drain to the downspout. In fact, the profile of the preformed gutter is derived from that of crown molding.

On the styles of architecture popular in the second half of the nineteenth century, such as Second Empire and Italianate, the cornice evolved into an integral component of the building design. On these cornices, which may not even carry a gutter pan, the crown molding and projecting soffit protect a frieze board (see Figure 12-2). This frieze board, attached to the face of the building, carries various decorative elements, including brackets, dentils, modillions, bed and panel moldings, recessed panels, and cornice blocks, among others. It is the use, design, and combination of these elements that make each building unique and also present special problems in its maintenance and repair.

Normally, the only attention cornices receive is a few coats of paint and a patched gutter pan. When a cornice is repainted, the details are often lost under a monochromatic paint scheme, and many coats of paint tend to hide the original details. The play of shadow and light and the contrast of colors on various elements is as important for a cornice as is its function to protect the structure.

Cornices need repair or replacement for a number of reasons. Often birds or squirrels build nests in the structure, chew through wood, and allow water to enter. Sometimes the gutter pan rusts through, and water leaks into the cornice or dry rot attacks the structural members from the inside. Sometimes the pans are relined until their accumulated weight causes the cornice to sag, which results in puddling and leaks.

It is extremely difficult to assess the condition of a cornice from the ground. Although dripping water and obvious holes can be easily seen, much damage can be hidden. It is sometimes possible to view the gutter pan from dormer windows or the roof, but doing so will not give you a complete picture of the condition of the cornice.

Because of the cornice's height from the ground and projection from the building, the use of ladders and ladder jacks is impractical. The only safe,

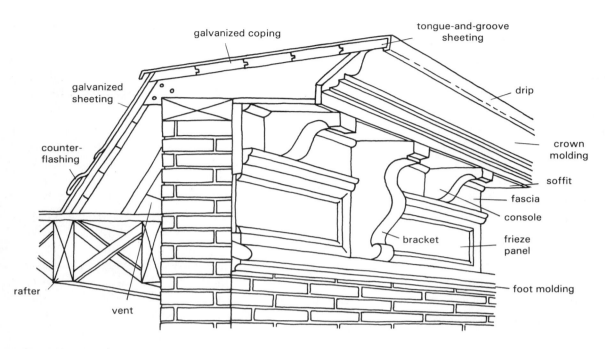

FIGURE 12-2. *Parts of a cornice and associated roofing members on a flat roof.*

practical, and efficient way to work on a cornice is to scaffold it. The run of the cornice can be scaffolded, or towers can be built at the corners and connected with long aluminum stages.

Scaffolding and all its auxiliary components are available for rent, but great care must be taken in erecting and working on scaffolding. High work on 36-inch-wide staging does not appeal to everyone. But rental companies will often erect the scaffolding, and well-built scaffolding is as stable as the ground it rests on. If a worker is careful and uses the available safety devices, there is little danger of accidents.

Once the scaffolding is erected, a thorough examination of the cornice must be made to determine the scope and sequence of the work necessary to repair and replace it. At this point, you can determine whether a complete tear-off, some structural work, or only work on the decorative elements is required. The masonry behind and around the cornice also should be examined and repaired if necessary (see Figure 12-3 for some examples of cornice damage).

The first item that needs to be checked is the condition of the gutter pan. It should have no rust or holes and should not sag, as sagging allows water to collect in it. If the pan is rusted, has holes, or has

been repaired with roofing materials, it needs to be relined. If it sags, some structural work is necessary before the sheet-metal work can be done.

The rest of the cornice should then be thoroughly examined. Gently remove and save all loose pieces. Look for any signs of rot behind the paint and any open seams, miters, or joints. Remove elements that are too damaged to be repaired for replication. If

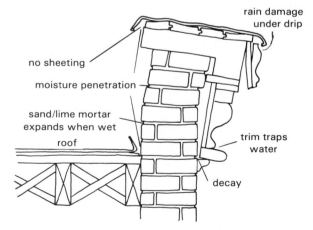

FIGURE 12-3. *Common signs of structural damage in a cornice.*

you are working around accumulated bird droppings, be sure to wear mouth and nose protection. Histoplasmosis, a fungal infection of the throat, lungs, and lymph nodes, can be caused by breathing in dust from these droppings.

Cracks, splits, open miters, and rotten wood should be repaired with a good-quality, sandable two-part epoxy. Caulks, wood fillers, and putties are not suitable for repair of damaged cornice elements. These products do not stick tightly to the wood or expand and contract with the rest of the cornice. Within a short period of time, gaps will be noticeable or the fillers will pop out. Large, flat pieces of wood can be cut out and replaced with suitable primed wood. Galvanized sheet metal can be used to cover curved and flat elements. If the metal is primed and finish painted correctly, it will not be noticeable.

Those elements that cannot be patched or filled with epoxy must be replicated and replaced. Crown moldings and bed and panel moldings are often available with the same outside dimensions and often the same or a similar profile as the original. It can be cheaper to buy and install suitable stock moldings than to try to reproduce original ones.

The cornice brackets, modillions, blocks, dentils, and so on can be reproduced by a planing mill, woodworker, or home shop depending on the complexity. Unless the item is carved or embossed, a band saw, jigsaw, and planer can be used to reproduce these elements. Use the examples saved to make similar patterns. Often the carved or embossed elements can be separated from the rest of the element and affixed to the replacement piece.

If structural work is necessary, access must be gained to the *lookouts*, the structural members that support the cornice. If the old lookouts are structurally sound but sagging, it is possible to scab on new two-by material to the old lookout. Fastening work on a cornice should be done with a screw gun or pneumatic nailer using galvanized fasteners. Plywood gussets also can be screwed, glued, or nailed to the old lookouts to realign the cornice. It may be possible to replace broken lookouts with new two-by material if access to framing members is available. Once the structure is repaired and stabilized, work can begin on the other elements of the cornice.

If a complete tear-off is required, it is extremely important that a detailed, dimensioned plan of the existing cornice be made at this time. Measure all the components and their relationship to one another, noting any unique details such as step-ins, step-outs, and changes in soffit projection. Take some photographs to aid in the rebuilding. Once this is completed, remove the cornice and haul away

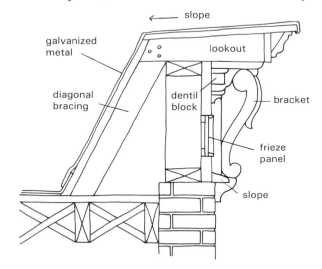

FIGURE 12-4. *The cornice's lookout ties back into diagonal bracing attached to the roof's framing members.*

the debris, keeping examples of representative elements.

With the drawings of the cornice and examples of the elements, plan the replacement cornice in consultation with a planing mill or woodworker. Decide which elements can be stock and which will need to be fabricated. Normally a suitable stock molding or a combination of moldings can be found to match the original. Most planing mills have knives in stock from previous jobs. If these profiles closely match yours, the cost to use them is negligible. Modillions, dentils, brackets, and so forth will have to be fabricated. Most of these pieces are fairly simple. They are built up with layers of wood, bandsawed, and combined. It is difficult to reproduce carvings or embossings. You can reuse old carvings or make a mold of the old carving and have it cast in fiberglass or some other material. These can then be attached to the cornice bracket.

The other items are available from the lumberyard. These are the substrate for the gutter pan (if any), the soffit, the frieze board, and the lookouts. Lookouts are two-by-four to two-by-ten material, such as treated wood. Make sure the wood is not prone to lateral splitting because this can weaken the member at its cutout for a gutter pan.

On old cornices, the frieze board and soffit were usually made of solid wood 7/8 to 1 inch thick and 6 to 20 inches wide. No comparable modern material is available at a reasonable price. Plastic-coated plywood, also known as MDO plywood, is suitable if it is installed properly. This type of plywood is designed for exterior use and is available in 4' x 8' sheets that are ½ or 5/8 inch thick. The veneers of plywood are covered by a smooth plastic sheet that is ready to receive paint. If this material is installed to protect the edge grain from moisture and exposure, it will outlast any other wood. All other types of plywood are unsuitable for cornice work, as the grain shows through the paint and delamination is almost certain. The frieze board and soffit can be ripped to width at the lumberyard or on a table saw in accordance with your drawings. The cornice fascia should be good quality one-by material of the correct width. The gutter pan substrate can be either number 3 common one-by stock or 5/8-inch plywood.

All this material, with the exception of the treated lumber lookouts, should be primed on all sides with an alkyd-based wood primer before installation. This will help the material to resist dry rot and will prolong the life of the cornice.

The framing of the cornice begins with the installation of the lookouts. These tie back into roof framing members or a knee wall (see Figure 12-4). Because the old lookouts were often 1 inch thick, the slot through the masonry must be increased to accept the two-by material.

If the cornice does not have a gutter pan, every lookout will be cut the same. If there is a gutter pan, every lookout will be different (see Figure 12-5). The projection from the building and the width remain the same, but the cutout for the gutter pan must be progressively deeper to allow for the water to drain.

The spacing of the lookouts is determined by the framing members to which they are attached. The gutter needs a fall of ½ inch per foot. The first cutout on the high side of the gutter should be ¾ inch to allow for the substrate. The front and back of the cutout should be at an angle to match the roof

or counterflashing. Avoid making the cutout 90 degrees, as it will be harder to install the gutter pan. Each succeeding lookout is cut to match the ½ inch per foot fall, determined by its spacing to the downspout. Once all the lookouts are cut, fasten the ends.

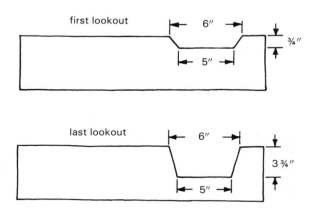

FIGURE 12-5. *A cross-section of the gutter pan depth on the first and last lookouts. Each succeeding lookout is cut to match a fall of ½ inch per foot, to allow for proper drainage.*

With a helper ready to screw or nail the lookout to the framing, plumb the lookout and have it project the correct distance. Then attach the lookout and repeat the procedure at the other end of the cornice. Run a line between the end lookouts, and use it to fasten the rest in their correct positions.

The next step is installing the crown fascia, crown, and gutter pan substrate. The crown fascia is attached to the lookout ends, mitered at the corners, and mitered at the lookout for a splice joint. The crown is then attached over the fascia with the correct reveal and nailed into the lookout ends. The corners and joints should be mitered to ensure a tight fit. The back, bottom, and front of the gutter pan substrate are then attached to the lookouts, with the back and front being ripped at a taper to match the drop in the pan. A piece of plywood or one-by connects the top of the lookout to the crown molding; this will tie together the crown and the lookouts.

When the gutter pan substrate is complete, have a sheet-metal contractor familiar with this type of work line or reline the pan with paint-grip-galvanized or coppered sheet metal of a suitable gauge. All seams, laps, and miters should be soldered securely. Do not use aluminum flashing, asphalt roof products, or silicone sealants on the gutter pan. None of these products will do a proper job, and all will fail fairly quickly. A properly installed pan soldered by a competent contractor will ensure no future maintenance problems.

While the pan is being fabricated, you can install the soffit, frieze board, and decorative elements. Make sure the frieze board is securely fastened to the face of the building and the edge grain of it and the soffit are protected by moldings. Also be sure to hide the butt edges of the soffit and frieze board behind brackets. The modillions, bed moldings, brackets, foot moldings, and so on can now be installed. Be sure all the elements are primed and well fastened, with no open joints to catch water.

When the gutter pan and downspout are installed, prime the pan with suitable paint and add the correct flashing. Be sure that the pan extends over the top flat of the crown molding and has a drip edge. The rest of the cornice can now be caulked and painted with two coats of paint in the planned color scheme.

When completed, a properly constructed and painted cornice will not only crown the house but it will last, with little or no maintenance, for at least 20 to 50 years. *Old House Journal* published some excellent articles about the inspection, repair, and replacement of cornices in its August/September 1985 and November 1985 issues.

References

OLD

Blake, Ernest George. *Roof Coverings.* New York: D. Van Nostrand Co., 1925.

Briggs, Martin S. *A Short History of the Building Crafts.* London: Oxford Press, 1925.

McCawley, James. *Roofing: Estimating, Applying, Repairing.* New York: J. McCawley, 1938.

NEW

Bolt, Steven. *Roofing the Right Way: A Step-by-Step Guide for the Homeowner.* Blue Ridge Summit, Pennsylvania: TAB Books, 1986.

Brumbaugh, James E. *Complete Roofing Handbook: Installation, Maintenance, Repair.* New York: Macmillan, 1986.

Hornung, William J. *Siding & Painting Contractor's Vest Pocket Reference Book.* Englewood Cliffs, New Jersey: Prentice-Hall, 1984.

Install, Donald. *The Care of Old Buildings Today.* London: Architectural Press, 1972.

Labine, R. A. Clem. "Repairing Slate Roofs." *Old House Journal*, December 1975, pp. 6-7.

Lefer, Henry. "A Birds-Eye View." *Progressive Architecture*, March 1977, pp. 88-92.

Peterson, Charles E. "Iron in Early American Roofs." *Smithsonian Journal of History*, no. 3 (1968), pp. 41-76.

Poore, Patricia, "Tile Roofs." *Old House Journal*, September/October 1987, pp. 22-29.

Roofing and Siding. Menlo Park, California: Lane Publishing, 1981.

Chapter 13

STRUCTURAL INTEGRITY

Fixing structural defects can be the most difficult part of a renovation project. If you suspect that a house has structural problems, you should always consult a structural engineer before you buy it. Problems often are much more complicated than they appear on the surface. Also remember that structural renovation will, in most cases, be very costly. This is particularly true for structural problems in the exterior brick walls (see Chapter 11).

Most very serious structural defects can be detected by just looking at the house. Sight along the ridge line of the roof or up and down exterior walls; compare the roof line with those of neighboring buildings or with windows in the same building; compare ceiling lines with the tops of doors; look at the slope of the floors, especially toward the center of the house; look for doors and windows that do not operate properly; look for gaps or buckling in exterior siding. Frame houses have a lot of give; they can be raised, pushed, or pulled back into line. Brick houses do not have much give. If there are bulges in a brick wall and a structural engineer indicates that the wall will be sound with tuck-pointing, it will still look the same after it is repointed. The only way that it can be put back into line is to take it down and rebuild it, which is prohibitively expensive. The interior of a brick building is made out of wood, however, and it can be put back into alignment, particularly if all the plaster and lath have been removed.

Whether you do a particular structural task or hire someone to do it for you depends on the scope of the problem and your personal experience in dealing with structural issues. We suggest that you consult a structural engineer or an established builder to make sure what you are doing is correcting the problem and not intensifying it or creating other problems.

DETERIORATION AND DEFICIENCY

Deterioration refers to structural members that have declined in strength because they have rotted or become bug-infested. *Deficiency* refers to lumber that was or is too light for the load it must carry.

If insects are found, hire an exterminator to get rid of the pests. He or she will suggest ways to keep the bugs from reinfesting the house. Ask the exterminator whether the infested wood must be removed. If possible, old wood should be left in place and bolstered with new wood. Make sure, however, that you do not leave any insect larvae that may be responsible for reinfestation.

If the problem is rot, first take care of the moisture that is causing it. You may have to add vents to a basement or crawl space, cover a basement floor with sheet plastic, or pour a concrete floor. Make sure that all posts are sitting on concrete piers. If rot occurs above the first floor, the problem is probably a leaky roof or improperly flashed windows. Rotten lumber can be left in place and bolstered with new lumber, but you must make sure that the rot does not spread. Scrape out all the soft or saturated wood and saturate what is left with a good preservative. When placing new wood next to rotten wood, it is a good idea to use pressure-treated lumber. Brush the new member with preservative, then place plastic, asphalt, or felt paper between the two pieces. When wood is rotten at major structural junctures, you can reinforce the area with joist hangers or steel angle iron, but it is best to replace those members. A nail gun is perfectly suited to nailing new joists to old joists in confined spaces. If you don't have a nail gun, put a few nails in to hold the member in place and then drill and bolt it. Bolting two members together may be required by your local building code, so check with the building inspector or a structural engineer.

When is the lumber in a house deficient? If the floor is extremely springy or the windows rattle when you walk across the floor, then the joists are not sufficient. Go to the center of the room and jump up and down to test the structure. Keep in mind the load you plan to put in the room. If you have a grand piano, a heavy bookcase, or a large amount of furniture, any give at all with the weight of one or two individuals will mean that the floor is deficient. If the slope of a floor is more than 1/8 inch per foot, it probably should be leveled. The slope of a floor acceptable in new construction is about 1/2 inch per 16 feet.

To correct a deficiency, determine exactly where and why the problem exists. Some deficiencies exist because a bearing wall has not been supported properly on the floor below. Sometimes the joists have been cut into by inept renovators or during early attempts to add plumbing or steam heating to the building. Often the problem stems from the building's design. The walls in many houses built in the late 1800s were not stacked—that is, a wall on the second floor did not have a partially bearing wall or beam supporting it from the first floor. In some situations, bearing walls are so far out of line that the weight of the upper wall bows the floor joists. Sometimes joists beneath pianos or heavy cast-iron bathtubs have been bowed. The easiest solution is to put a bearing beam under the center of the floor rather than replacing all the joists. But remember: bows in joists that were created over many years will not disappear overnight, even with a new supporting beam.

A sloping floor is easy to fix if it is caused by a sagging post. Look for joists that are obviously undersized or girders that are too small. Also look for any previous renovation that may have cut into structural members, particularly in bathrooms. Look for cracks that run perpendicular to the grain of a structural member or start at the lower end of a member and run diagonally across it. These are stress cracks, and they are very serious. Small cracks that run through the grain are called *checking* and are not a problem.

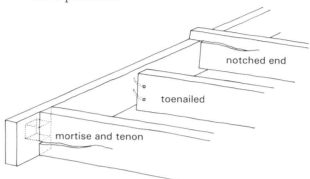

FIGURE 13-1. *Three examples of failed beam connections.*

Cracks often result from failed connections between beams (see Figure 13-1). Since metal was relatively expensive in earlier times, these connections are most likely made with wood. The mortise-and-tenon joint was common. A square peg at the end of one beam was inserted into a square hole of the supporting beam. The tremendous amount of weight concentrated at the end of the beam often split it just below the bottom of the peg. This type of failure is often found at the edge of stair openings, where the weight of several joists sits on one beam. Look for crack patterns around stairs. This type of failure can be dangerous if the connection suddenly collapses.

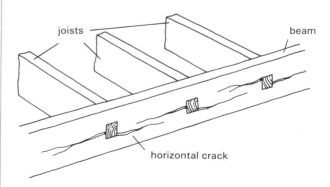

FIGURE 13-2. *A central axis beam crack.*

If a series of square holes were cut in a supporting beam to accommodate joists, another structural problem might result. This is called a central axis beam crack (see Figure 13-2). Basically, it is a crack that goes from one hole to the next in the supporting beam. A central axis beam crack breaks the supporting beam in half lengthwise and leaves two smaller boards, with the lower half supporting the joists.

Problems also exist if nails were substituted for wooden connections. A few toenailed or through-nailed spikes in the end of a joist are not enough to keep it from dropping in the long run (see Figure 13-1). Nails are fine for holding lumber where the forces are pushing the wood together, such as in a stud wall. When the loads are trying to pull the pieces apart or slide them by each other, however, nails are not a very reliable connector. This is why joist hangers are required today.

Too much weight at the end of a beam can cause the area below to fracture. This is common in brick buildings and can be seen by looking at exterior windows with stone lintels and a very small amount bearing on the wall below. A shear crack will run down the wall from the end of the lintel to some-

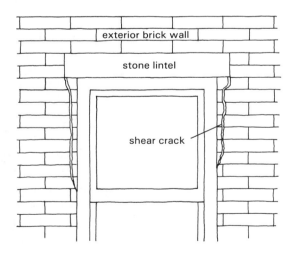

FIGURE 13-3A. *Shear cracks under the concentrated load of a stone lintel.*

place alongside the window (see Figure 13-3). On the interior of the building, a beam carrying several joists or some other excessive weight may crush the brick below its bearing pocket in the wall. The beam itself also may be crushed. You will often

see stepped cracks running down from pocketed beams.

When a beam is too small to carry the load placed on it, it will sag, becoming shorter in length and thus slipping out of its pocket in the brick wall. This also tends to crush the end of the beam. You should start to worry if less than 2 inches of a beam are still resting in a brick pocket or on a brick wall.

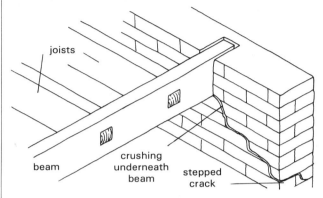

FIGURE 13-3B. *Stepped cracks caused by a bearing failure in a beam pocket.*

Undersized columns supporting everything in the basement also present problems. If there is too much weight for the size of the column, it will bend to one side or be crushed at one end. The bowing of a column is usually easy to spot, especially if it is a brick column. You will see cracking at the mortar joints on the side that is bowing out. Short columns tend to be crushed rather than bend.

Finally, examine all the joists in the house for holes, slots, or other signs that some material has been removed. Always avoid cutting through joists or notching joists yourself. If you have to run a pipe or a wire through a joist, drill a hole. Many renovators in the past simply notched the joists, which reduces the dimension of the piece and can result in stress cracks. If the notches are small, reinforce the joist with steel plates or by adding another joist. Try not to locate any heavy fixtures directly over such junctions.

USING JACKS

Sagging joists or beams in a house need to be repaired, and you will have to support the house while you work on its structural members. Use either a jackscrew or a hydraulic jack to do this. You may also use a jack post, which works like a jackscrew. The nice thing about using a jack post is that you can put it in place and leave it as permanent support. Do not do this, though, unless you build a concrete pier underneath it as a foundation to support the weight. If you do not, the concrete floor under the post will probably crack, and the post will not support the house.

We use hydraulic jacks for most of our work. If you use a hydraulic jack, get one with a capacity of at least 10 tons. You will also need a number of heavy blocks of wood: ends of two-by-twelves, two-by-tens, or two-by-eights. Keep in mind that a hydraulic jack is not designed to sustain a heavy load for a prolonged period of time. It is designed to lift the load only until another support can be found. When lifting a load with a hydraulic jack, always support it immediately by shimming every time you raise the jack. The jack may slip or blow a seal, and if there is no support under the beam, the beam, you, and/or the house might collapse.

If the house has a basement or crawl space with a concrete floor at least 3 to 4 inches thick, set the jack directly on the floor. If the floor is not as thick as that or you have a dirt floor, use large pieces of wood for footings underneath the jack. If you know you are going to use a jack post or some other new permanent post, you can always dig a hole and fill it with concrete to form a footing. Check the concrete floor; never assume that it is 4 inches thick.

We have two hints about using jacks. First, start at the bottom, in the basement, and work up to correct sagging floors or bearing problems. Second, this is best done when there is no plaster in the house—in other words, after the house has been gutted and cleaned. If the plaster in the house is to be saved, raise or jack the house in increments of ¼ inch *or less* and let it sit for 24 to 48 hours or longer. Most experts recommend raising it ¹⁄₁₆ inch a day. Remember that the house may have taken years to settle, so you should take your time jacking it up. Most of the finish surfaces nailed to the structure have become accustomed to the house sag, and jacking the house up too quickly will result in cracks and separations in plaster all over the house.

Clean out your basement before jacking. You will need adequate space and light to see what you are doing. Also remember to jack higher than you need to because, when you release the jack, the structure will compress somewhat. To determine how much you have to jack, put a nail on the side of each end of a joist as low as it will go. Tie a string between the two nails. This string will be straight. Jack the center of the joist up to it.

When jacking a house, you will hear loud cracking and popping noises. This is normal. Remember that the jack is lifting an incredible amount of weight. Beware, however, if you hear loud popping sounds after you have finished raising the house an increment. This is a sure sign that something either has given or is giving. Also, at every increment, check doors and windows to make sure they continue to operate correctly. And, finally, plumb all jacks. Make *very* sure they are level before you start jacking by using cribbing or blocks of wood underneath them. Never try to jack a house with a jack that is not on solid footing and is not absolutely plumb.

FOUNDATIONS, BEAMS, AND POSTS

Foundation failure in brick buildings is rare. Although houses settle, most do so very gradually, and old-time builders were extremely careful about the foundation because of the weight and complexity of the brick wall on top of it. What often fails in the basic foundation of a house is the bearing beams and the posts that hold those beams in the basement. Metal posts rarely require replacement, but wooden ones do because they are susceptible to rot and compression. Beams will be susceptible to cracking, rot, and crushing at their ends.

Replacing a beam is a fairly complex operation. Jack the beam to the place where you want it to be, so that the floor above it is level. Then install a shoring wall on each side of the beam constructed from two-by-fours or four-by-fours. The latter are strong enough to bear almost any load but light enough to move easily. Shoring will consist of vertical posts with plates at the top and bottom. If you have a dirt floor, make sure to support the bottom plate of the shoring wall or pour concrete before this is done. You must have a solid footing for the shoring wall to sit on. Place shoring as close as possible to the member being repaired or replaced. You should be able to get it within a foot of the beam.

When constructing the shoring wall on each side of the beam, make sure that the tolerances are exact and all the lumber fits tightly. The easiest method is to tack the plates to the overhead joist, place the bottom plate, and cut the studs so that they have to be knocked in with a hammer. Another method is to build the shoring wall and then put it in place. Use hardwood shims between the shoring wall top plate and each joist to make it tight. The shim should be held in place with nails. The beam is then taken out and replaced. Jacks are put back underneath the beam to move it up to the joists (shim high joists), the beam ends are shimmed, and the posts are replaced. Then the shoring walls are removed, and the jacks are let down slowly, compressing the joists, the new beam, and the posts.

Problems sometimes result not because a beam or a post fails but because the footing or pad underneath a post fails. In some old houses, wood posts were simply stuck in the ground with rocks underneath them, and the cement floor was poured around them. Thus, there is little footing underneath the posts. When jacking up a beam to replace a post, make sure to check the footing underneath it. If there is none, you may have to pour one. In putting in new wood beams, make sure that they fit tightly. It is best to persuade them into place with a sledgehammer. Future compression and rot can be minimized by putting a square piece of ¼- or ½-inch steel on top of the post. Felt paper or plastic at the bottom of the post prevents moisture from rotting it. Metal columns are probably better than wood posts because they do not compress.

JOISTS

When joists fail, they usually do so because they are undersized, because they have been cut by unwise renovators or plumbers, or because they have rotted. Leave the weakened joist in place and rein-force it with another joist attached to it. The reasons for leaving it in place are that it has flooring nails driven into it, so it is very difficult to remove, and it also has some strength left.

Installing the reinforcing joist is no picnic. Joists sit tightly on something at each end. Also, older joists tend to be a different size than the new material, although most old joists will be larger than the new planed material, which is a help. The problem is that you have to get the new joist into one end pocket and then into the other. In a basement that is fairly open, the new joist sometimes can be pushed over the central beam and then pulled back into the pocket in the brick wall. You will have to break out the brick pocket to accommodate the new joist and remove all bridging. Make sure to cement it all into the wall when finished. When the new joist is in place, jack up the center of the old joist so that it is level with the new joist and then nail and bolt them together. Shim the joist at the central beam. Finally, replace all blocking or bridging between joists that you removed to put in the new joist.

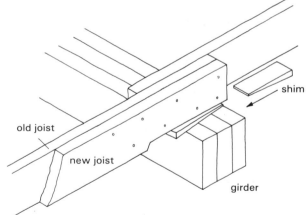

FIGURE 13-4. *Notching and shimming is one common method of adding a new joist to reinforce an existing, weakened joist.*

One common method for installing new joists is the notch and shim method. It is used where both ends sit on sills or girders. As seen in Figure 13-4, the easiest way to get the joist into the limited space is to notch the lower edge of each end and then once the joist is put into place, shim it tight. This method is used where the space is so tight that you cannot put the joist up at an angle and then turn it so that it lies flat with the old joist. In some cases, you may have to notch the top of the joist on a beveled angle so you can slip it up over the beam.

When working with joists, you also have to be concerned about making a fire cut. A fire cut (Figure 13-5) is a diagonal cut that removes a triangle of wood from the top edge of a joist. The angle of the fire cut is steep. Along the top edge of the joist, measure in 4 inches from the corner and make a mark. Then draw a line from this mark to the bottom end corner of the joist and cut along that line. The fire cut is required by law in most areas, particularly in row houses and houses sharing a brick wall. The purpose of the fire cut is to prevent the joist from pulling down the brick partition walls should a fire occur. As joists burn, they typically collapse in the middle of the span. The top corner of a squared end joist would dislodge the bricks above it as it fell or would pull the wall toward the joist. Because a fire-cut joist has no upper corner to restrict the fall, it will leave the surrounding brick intact. Consequently, the brick wall will not fall when the house burns. One nice thing about fire cuts is that they often help you to put a full-length joist into a brick pocket from the bottom.

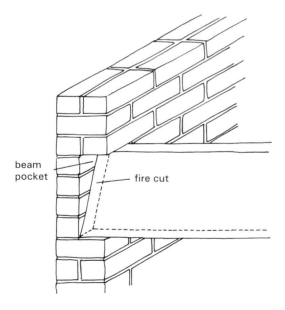

FIGURE 13-5. *A fire cut is a steep diagonal cut that removes a triangle of wood from the top edge of a joist. Its purpose is to prevent the joist from pulling down a brick wall should a fire occur.*

REINFORCING JOISTS AND BEAMS WITH METAL

The most common way to reinforce joists and beams is with joist hangers (see Chapter 8). Although some feature built-in nailing tabs, most connect to the face of pieces being hung with 8d nails and to the supporting members with 16d nails. Angle iron also is used to reinforce joists and beams. The strength of a piece of angle iron is derived from the fact that it has two sides at a right angle and thus it resists twisting in any direction. It is also easy to use in tight places. You can use sections of angle iron to support joists by attaching the angle iron so that one side rides on the bottom of the joist and the other side rides on the side of the joist. Then drill and bolt through both the angle iron and the joist to hold it in place. You may need to place the angle iron against the joist, put a jack or post underneath to jack it up, and then drill bolt holes when it is level or above level.

One use of metal for increasing the strength of both joists and beams is called a *flitch plate*. This is a flat steel plate that is attached to the side of an old joist. The new joist is installed next to the flitch plate, and the entire assembly is bolted together. This may also be done using a plywood core rather than a steel core. The plate remains strong because it is held flat between the two joists. One problem you might encounter with predrilled steel plates is lining up the bolt holes in the two joists and the steel plate.

A steel I beam may be used as a new girder to support the center spans of joists. Steel I beams also are commonly used in place of bearing walls. The size of the I beam should be determined by a structural engineer, since this is a complex calculation depending on the number of stories, the loads on the floors, and several other factors. Any plans calling for the use of steel beams will probably require the stamp of a licensed engineer anyway. In most cases, you will need to increase the pocket size for a steel beam and cement it in when you are done. A word of warning: When you are working on beam pockets in brick walls, be careful not to pop a brick out on the outside of an exterior wall.

When the pockets are done and you are ready to install the I beam, you need the following: (1) lots of friends (an 8-inch I beam weighs about 20 pounds per foot), (2) heavy stepladders to support the weight of the individuals lifting, and (3) at least two jacks to raise the girder section into position under the joists. When the beam is in place, shim the ends tightly and attach the beam to the joists with temporary bracing if necessary and then cement in the pocketed ends. Do not release the jacks or bracing until the pocket repairs have dried thoroughly.

For more information about structural carpentry, particularly in areas we have skipped such as rafter and sill repair, see Litchfield's *Renovation* (John Wiley & Sons, 1982).

REPLACING LOAD-BEARING WALLS

Load-bearing walls transfer loads downward to the foundation and footings. Because removing, replacing, or opening up these walls affects the structural integrity of the house, these are among the most important tasks you will do. Decisions about bearing walls will likely be determined by the local building codes, a structural engineer, or an architect. Hiring a structural engineer to work with bearing walls is always money well spent, especially in figuring the requirements and distances to be spanned.

Have an expert determine the size of the header or beam used to support the load and what the header or beam sits on. Keep in mind that each end of the header should be supported by at least 3 inches of bearing surface. If the beam is holding up a major portion of the house, the minimum requirement in most building codes is 4 inches. Many builders use the following rules of thumb in relation to spans:

· A two-by-six will span 6 feet.
· A two-by-eight will span 8 feet.
· A two-by-ten will span 10 feet.
· A two-by-twelve will span 12 feet.

Always use Number 1 common lumber for beams.

Never use Number 2 lumber for them. You can increase header spanning distances by adding a core of plywood to a double beam or a steel flitch plate to the center of a header "sandwich." One-half-inch plywood is commonly used because it makes the header 3½ inches thick, the same width as a two-by-four. When installing beams, make it a rule to add the plywood, as it not only strengthens the beam but also gives you the correct width. If glued, such beams are stronger than three individual boards.

SAGGING OR SQUEAKING FLOORS

Many old houses have floors that sag, squeak, or slope. These conditions may not be caused by major structural faults. Wood shrinks and swells according to its moisture content and can cause movement. Movement may also result from the failure of fasteners and the separation of flooring and subflooring. In effect, these are all results of old age.

A gutted house without attractive floors will most likely be carpeted in most areas. In that case, find where the floors are squeaky or there are other imperfections and simply renail the flooring to the joists with flooring nails. In many situations, however, a floor that you want to save and leave uncarpeted will have squeaks or other problems. Sometimes squeaks or sags are as simple as one joist having shrunk or settled. This will result in a gap between the top of the joist and the subfloor. If the gap is small, it can be filled with thin wooden shims or construction adhesive. This will eliminate any bounce or squeak in the floor above. If the gap is larger and the joist is otherwise sound, a two-by-four can be nailed to the joist snug up against the floorboards. Doing this should get rid of the noise, especially if you use construction adhesive in the installation of the two-by-four. Two-by-fours also can be used where joists have been damaged by cutting to make room for pipes.

Another common problem is inadequate bridging between joists. If a floor bounces or vibrates excessively, but the joists are neither undersized nor structurally inadequate, it may simply be that the bridging that stiffens the joists is missing. In most old houses, bridging is made of wood approximately the size of a one-by-two or one-by-four, which is angled both ways between the top of a joist and the bottom of its neighbor and toenailed (see Figure 13-6). You also may see solid bridging between two joists. Bridging stiffens a floor by transmitting loads to adjacent joists. It is very hard to install crossed bridging once the floor is in place,

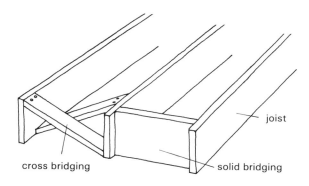

FIGURE 13-6. *Two examples of bridging between joists.*

but you can install solid bridging easily. Sometimes installing extra bridging, particularly with construction adhesive, will eliminate squeaks and vibrations.

If you have springy floors and do not plan to increase the load significantly in a room, one possible solution is to use two-by-four stiffeners with those joists. Nail a two-by-four along the side of each joist on the bottom edge. As long as you do not put a grand piano over the midpoint of these spans, the two-by-fours should be enough to stiffen the joists so that the floor does not deflect. It is even better to bolt a two-by-four like this on both sides of the joist. Whenever cross bridging or two-by-four stiffeners are added for squeaky floors, we suggest the liberal use of construction adhesive. Construction adhesive is great at helping to solve squeaky floors.

Sometimes the addition of a jack post will reduce squeakiness around the beam area. Keep in mind that a number of members are meeting near the beam. Two joists meet on top of the beam plus the flooring; squeaks can be common there. Jacking this up tight may solve the problem, but be careful not to deflect the floor upward so that it separates.

We do not recommend laying a new floor over the old one and leveling it by placing thin wood strips between the old floor and the new. This is a lot of work, requires trial-and-error cutting of shims, and leaves you with a floor that is several inches higher, resulting in doors that must be trimmed and baseboards that have to be moved up. Also, it does not let you look under the floor where the real problem may lie. It is much easier to jack up the house if much of the plaster has been removed (or even with the plaster intact) than it is to build new floors. Jacking also lets you get to know your building well before you start much of the other work.

STAIRS

Stairs will probably require the most complex carpentry and woodworking that a rehabber will do in a house. Stairs also are regulated by strict building codes. The height, the number of carriages, the dimension of the risers and treads, the width of the staircase, and the height of balusters and handrails are all regulated by law (see Figure 13-7). Check your local building codes. Also check to see if

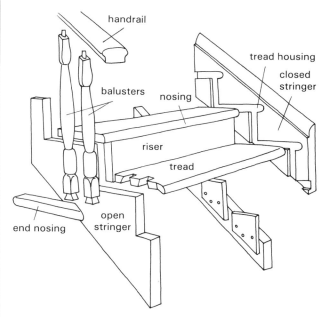

FIGURE 13-7. *An exploded view of a staircase, showing some of the common terms used for its parts.*

owners of single-family or duplex dwellings are entitled to retain original staircases in a rehab without bringing them up to code. This may depend on the extent of the rehab. In most cases, an existing staircase can be retained even though it does not meet current code requirements. If you start changing things, however, you may have to meet current standards.

Whether you renovate or rebuild, make sure that the height of the risers is consistent throughout the flight of stairs. Also try to keep the different stairs in the building consistent. Differences in step height disturb the physical rhythm of climbing stairs and should be avoided. Altering the height is difficult to accomplish in repair work unless you add new flooring or replace a tread with stock that is thicker than the original.

Many of the more obvious ailments of stairs, such as squeaking, groaning, and unstable posts, can be repaired with a small investment of time and probably without having to disturb any major surfaces around them. Quite often, though, minor defects may be the manifestation of major problems. If stairs are to be carpeted, simply find spots where the stairs groan or squeak (by repeatedly walking up and down them) and then renail the treads to the stringers. Since most noises are caused by wood rubbing on wood, the remedy is to tighten the two offending pieces. If the underside of a staircase is exposed, repair can be very easy. If it is not, then the staircase may need to be dismantled.

Most balusters are easy to remove, so you can fix them if they are shaky. Resist the urge to nail them. To get at balusters, free the return molding or end trim at the end of the tread. Remove all the nails, gently knock out the bottom of the baluster, and remove it from the rail. It may be nailed at the top, so pull it slowly. Repair the baluster as needed, then reinstall it, gluing it in place if it is very loose. If the newel post is shaky, you can try to shim the bottom or screw the post down with 3-inch drywall screws. Newels are often hollow with a long, threaded rod running down the inside, and this rod can be tightened at the cap. The rod also may run all the way through the floor and can be tightened underneath in the basement or on the next floor down. You may have to take up the first tread and cut a hole in the flooring to get at the bottom end of the rod.

Sometimes you will have to remove split treads. First remove the balusters from the step, then pry out the tread in one piece. This may be difficult, especially if the other end is housed in a stringer, as will be the case if the staircase is on a brick wall. Getting it out in one piece, however, will facilitate repairing and replacing the tread. If you do get it out in one piece, you can glue it back together with a plywood gusset screwed and glued to the bottom side. If not, have another tread made at a woodworking shop.

Rebuilding a complete staircase or taking a staircase apart and replacing it after a gut rehab is an extremely sophisticated job. If you are game, a number of books can help you: Talbot's *Handbook of Door Making, Window Making and Staircasing* (Sterling Publishing, 1980); Bodzinski's *Stair Layout* (ATP Publications, 1985); or Love's *Stair Builders Handbook* (Craftsman Book Co., 1974). If you hire a contractor or a carpenter to work on your staircase, we suggest that you hire someone who does nothing but stair work. We feel that the construction of stairs is an art better left to the experts. If you have totally gutted your building and have not retained any old stair parts, you can buy a complete staircase or the parts for a staircase. Table 13–1 lists some stair manufacturers.

Repairing a Staircase

For most of us, stairs have a mysterious hidden structure, but once you have taken one staircase apart, they become fairly simple. In most old houses, staircases are often attached to an outside brick wall, with one side facing the interior of the house. Most stairs like this end up tilting down on the inside. This is caused by differential building settlement. The interior wood frame shrinks and settles at a higher rate than the masonry outer wall, which remains fairly stable. Thus, the stair stringer that is attached to the masonry wall stays put, but the inside stringer, which rests on the floor, settles with the floor. Sometimes the wall stringer is pulled away from the masonry wall or the stair treads are pulled out of the stringer. It is also common to find loose balusters or handrails. Sometimes stair problems are due to poor or deteriorated carriages. We have found many stairs in Victorian houses with no center carriage at all.

Sometimes jacking the building up to level the floors will level the stairs, but this will not always solve the problem. The major problem with fixing an old staircase, especially when you have to take it apart, is taking the plaster off the bottom of it. It is not always easy to replace this plaster with drywall, but it is feasible. In old buildings with open staircases, some people put coat closets under the

---

TABLE 13-1

STAIR MAKERS

Arcways, Inc., 1076 Ehlers Rd., Box 763, Neenah, WI 54957

Boston Design Corp., 100 Magazine St., Boston, MA 02119

The Cooper Stair Co., Inc., 1331 Leithton Rd., Mundelein, IL 60060

Goddard Manufacturing, P.O. Box 502, Logan, KS 67646

The Heritage Stair Co., 1200 Trenton Ave. Ext., Uhrichsville, OH 44683

The Iron Shop, P.O. Box 128, 400 Reed Rd., Broomall, PA 19008

Lapeyre Stairs, Bill Way, P.O. Box 50699, New Orleans, LA 70150

Mylen Industries, 650 Washington St., Peekskill, NY 10566

Piedmont Home Products, Inc., 111 E. Church Street, Orange, VA 22960

Prairie Stair Products, Inc., P.O. Box 544, #2 Service Rd. East, White City, Saskatchewan, Canada S0G 5B0

Spiral Stairs of America, 1718 Franklin Ave., Erie, PA 16510

Stairways, Inc., 4166 Pinemont, Houston, TX 77018

Steptoe & Wife Antiques Ltd., 322 Geary Ave., Toronto, Ontario, Canada M6H 2C7

United Stairs Corp., Highway 35, Keyport, NJ 07735

Woodsmiths, 515 Main St., P.O. Box 296, Gunter, TX 75058

York Spiral Stair, Route 32, North Vassalboro, ME 04962

Zepsa Stairs, P.O. Box 7765, Charlotte, NC 28217

---

stairs anyway. This is not always the most aesthetically pleasing solution, but it works when space is tight. It also solves the problem of removing plaster on the bottom of the stairs.

If you do not mind removing the plaster and lath from the bottom of a staircase, you can fix many of its problems. Loose treads, poor stringers, and poor carriages can almost always be fixed in this way. Carriages often have been toenailed to header beams or sit on small nailing strips attached to the header beams, and they may have slipped off of these. This problem can be corrected by installing heavy joist hangers. Before the staircase can be lifted and pushed back into place, all potential obstacles to its movement must be removed. Look for wedges, metal plates, and other earlier repairs that might inhibit movement. You may have to brace the staircase on its outside side. You can then move the stairs back into place, getting them level in all directions, and through the use of joist hangers or other angle iron supports, secure the stairs so they do not move. In all wedging underneath the stairs to fix stair treads, make sure that you use construction adhesive or soak the wedges in white glue.

Regardless of whether you think it is needed or not, install cleats or stepped wood blocking on the center carriage to take the springiness out of each step. Finally, in putting everything back in place, nail the treads into the carriages with 8d finish nails, countersinking the heads, and back-nail the risers to the back of the treads from underneath the stairs with 6d common nails. Replace the balusters and block the underside of the stairs to accept new lath and plaster, drywall, or a combination of both. It is possible to drywall stairs up to a curving ceiling and then switch to plaster.

If you need to replace balusters, you can turn them yourself on a lathe, you can have them made in a woodworking shop or planing mill, or you can try to match them at an architectural antique store. It is best to scour salvage yards for similar balusters or for a matched set with a larger number than you have now.

The *Old House Journal* has published a number of articles about repairing old staircases. It and other sources should be investigated. Overall, we do not think that taking apart an older staircase, replacing certain parts, and fixing some of its squeakiness and

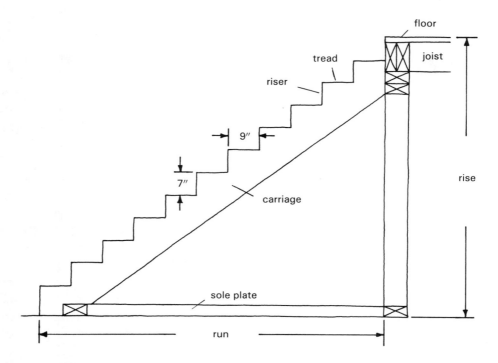

FIGURE 13–8. *When laying out stair stringers, you need to calculate the length of the carriage, the angle and width of the tread, and the height of the rise.*

groaning is that difficult. You simply must be willing to tackle the task and be extremely careful about taking it apart. It might be a good idea to keep a notebook about how things came apart and in what order. You might even number the parts. We do think that building a complete staircase requires woodworking tools that most do-it-yourselfers do not have, as well as a lot of experience. Thus, it does not make sense to try to build a staircase from scratch unless it is a simple one.

Building a New Staircase

Building a staircase is like putting together a stepladder. In a stepladder, the sides, technically called strings (which is where the word *stringer* comes from) hold flat treads in place. The attainment of the perfectly level tread depends on your finding the correct length of the strings and on your placing the treads in the strings at the correct angle. The same principle is used in stairs.

You must determine the length of the carriage, the angle of the tread, the height of the rise, and the width of the tread. To determine the rise, measure from the top of one floor to the top of the upper floor. Make sure the measurement is from finished surface to finished surface—that is, the height of the total rise. Divide that number by 8 inches and 7 inches. One answer will be closer to a whole number than the other. If you use the answer achieved by dividing by 7, ignore the fraction and use just the whole number. If you use the answer achieved by dividing by 8, round off to the next highest whole number. Using 7 results in more risers, with a smaller riser height and less incline. Using 8 results in a smaller number of risers, with a greater riser height and more incline. The former method usually produces a stair that is easier to ascend. Figure 13-8 contains an example.

Next, determine the unit rise by dividing the total rise by the number of risers. Carry the answer to the nearest hundredth of an inch. Then determine the unit run. A rule of thumb is that unit rise plus unit run should be between 17 and 18 inches, so subtract the unit rise from 17½ inches to get the unit run. Total run is determined by multiplying the unit run by the number of treads. There is always one less tread than there are risers.

You now can cut the carriage out of a 12- to 14-foot two-by-twelve. The tread will be 10⅛ inches, and the rise will be 7⅜ inches. You can cut

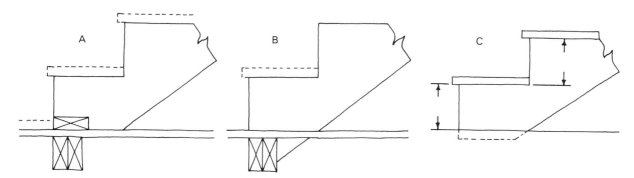

FIGURE 13-10. Dropping the carriage *ensures that the bottom step of the staircase will have a rise equal to the other stairs.*

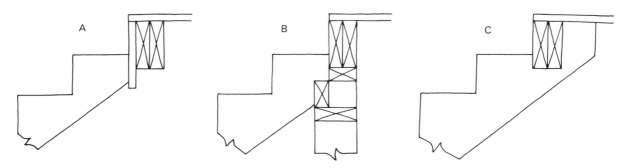

FIGURE 13-11. *In example B, the carriage is cut out to allow the top riser to rest on blocks, against the header joist. In A and C, the top of the carriage is cut to rest against the header, usually in joist hangers.*

a block of wood that size, or you can make marks on a framing square (see Figure 13-9). Most carpenters have little clamps called stair gauges that are attached to the framing square for this purpose.

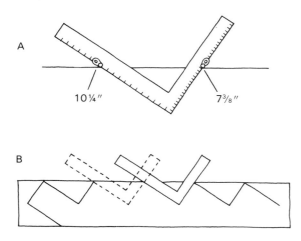

FIGURE 13-9. Stair gauges are little clamps attached to a framing square (A) that allow for accurate measurement when cutting out a stair carriage (B).

One side of the triangle is a tread, and one is a riser. You simply place the square or block of wood on the two-by-twelve and draw a line for the riser and one for the tread. When cutting out the triangles, finish the cut with a handsaw to leave the maximum amount of wood between the stair cutout and the bottom of the carriage.

You may encounter various conditions that will affect how the carriages are cut and attached at the upper floor line. The cutting of the lower end of the carriage is usually the same in all cases, so we will discuss it first.

Because the carriage is laid out to fit the space between finished floors, an allowance for the tread thickness must be made on the bottom step of the carriage. This process is called dropping the carriage. In Figure 13-10, the carriage is shown set in place, and the first steps have equal rise. When the treads are put in place without adjustment, the lower step rise increases by an amount equal to the tread thickness, while the remaining steps remain at the same height. To compensate for the additional height of the bottom step, the lower end of the carriage is laid out and cut as shown in Figures 13-9 and 13-10. The carriage drop is always equal to the thickness of the tread material.

Three fairly common conditions that you may encounter in installing the top of carriages are shown in Figure 13-11. Fitting carriages between two walls allows the carriages to be fastened to the walls, but when there are no side walls, the carriage must be fastened securely to the floor frame.

In Figure 13-11, a two-by-twelve carriage is cut out to allow the top riser to be placed on blocks or wedges against the header joist, and the others are cut to rest against the header, usually in joist hangers. You will need three carriages like this for most staircases. They will be installed using joist hangers at the top and nails. A common method is to nail a two-by-four to the floor, with the stair stringer slipping over the two-by-four. You also may use angle irons or other metal fittings. Keep in mind that the bottom of the stair stringer must fall on joists or solid bridging placed between the joists. The flooring and subflooring do not have enough strength to take the weight of the stairs.

Now it is time to install your risers and treads. If one or both sides of the stairs are exposed, apply any kind of finish that you wish. If you are a novice, we suggest that you build the staircase with the three stringers and then build a half wall on the outside of the stairs with some kind of plate and rail on top of the half wall rather than a rail and baluster with newels. The latter carpentry is very complex. If that is what you want, we recommend that you buy a manufactured staircase and install it according to the manufacturer's directions or hire an experienced staircase carpenter to build the staircase. Keep in mind that the staircase carpenter will probably build the staircase from premade parts anyway.

Look in back issues of *Old House Journal* and *Fine Homebuilding* for articles dealing with the more technical aspects of building stairs (see, for example, S. Eggert, "Installing Manufactured Stair Parts," *Fine Homebuilding*, April/May 1987). You also may write to Benchmark Stair & Wood Work Co., 182 Chesterfield Industrial Blvd., Chesterfield, MO 63005.

References

OLD

Dewell, Henry Dievendorf. *Timber Framing*. San Francisco: Dewey Publishing Company, 1917.

Hodgson, Frederick Thomas. *Stair Building Made Easy*. New York: Industrial Publication Company, 1900.

_____. *Light and Heavy Timber Framing Made Easy*. Chicago: F.J. Drake & Co., 1909.

Monckton, James H. *The National Stair-Builder*. New York: G.E. Woodward, 1873.

New System of Hand-Railing by an Old Stair-Builder. New York: The Industrial Publication Co., 1885.

Riddell, Robert. *The Scientific Stair Builder*. Philadelphia: W.S. Young, 1854.

_____. *The Carpenter and Joiner Modernized*. Philadelphia: Claxton, Remsen & Heffelfinger, 1880.

Williams, Morris. *Stair Builders' Guide*. New York: David Williams Company, 1914.

NEW

Baker, Glenn E. *Carpentry Fundamentals*. New York: McGraw-Hill, 1981.

DiDonno, Lupe and Phyllis Sperling. *How to Design & Build Your Own House*. New York: Alfred A. Knopf, 1987.

Gross, Marshall. *Roof Framing*. Carlsbad, California: Craftsman Book Co., 1984.

Mannes, Willibald. *Techniques of Staircase Construction*. New York: Van Nostrand Reinhold, 1986.

Merritt, Frederick S. (ed.). *Building Design and Construction Handbook*. New York: McGraw-Hill, 1982.

Syvanen, Bob. *Carpentry: Some Tricks of the Trade*. Charlotte, North Carolina: East Woods Press, 1982.

Wilson, John Douglas. *Simplified Stair Layout*. Albany, New York: Delmar Publishers, 1973.

Chapter 14

WINDOWS

The major decision regarding windows in a rehab is whether to keep the existing windows or replace them. There are two issues in this decision (1) the quality and condition of the existing windows, and (2) whether the building you have purchased is in a historic district. If the sash, frames, and sills are all rotten, you should probably replace the windows (see Figure 14-1 for parts of a window). If the

frames and sills are sound but the sash are rotten, you can either fix the sash yourself or go to a planing mill and have them replaced. The cheapest thing to replace is usually the sill. It will come out fairly easily, and you can replace it with treated two-by lumber. If there is rotten material in the frames, though, you will have to replace the windows.

In most historic districts, you are not allowed to replace the front windows with anything that is not an exact replica of the existing windows. This can be very expensive because the front windows are usually fairly intricate, often have curved tops, and are usually very large. In this case, you would probably choose to fix the windows or to replace the sash but use the old frames.

Some rehabbers dismantle, fix, reinstall, and caulk the entire window so that it cannot be opened. This is not a good idea, however, because you may want to be able to open the windows, especially if the building is long and narrow or is a row house with few side windows. Another thing rehabbers do is repair the front windows so that they are fairly sound and then buy aluminum storm windows (usually white) that they reverse and install from the inside on the front window frames. Most storm windows have a flat rear flange and are built out in three steps for triple-track sash. As you can see in Figure 14-2, you can have these storm windows measured so that the triple track goes inside, toward the existing window, and the flange is screwed to the window moldings, resulting in a flat surface. This is not the prettiest treatment for the inside of the house, and it means you have to open the storm

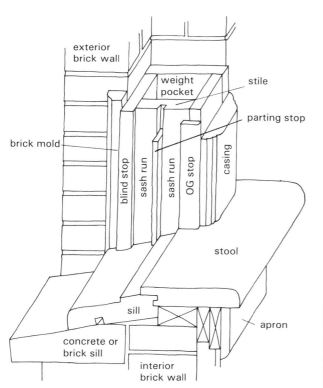

FIGURE 14-1. *The parts of a window frame.*

window to get to the exterior window. It does create a thermal space between the windows, though, and is somewhat airtight.

Our preferred strategy is to either repair the front windows or replace them. Obviously, this depends on how much money you have to spend. The cost of replacing large, curved-top, intricate windows, especially those with built-in shutters, is usually

is about 3½ to 4 feet wide across the top and 6 to 8 feet long on the bottom of the T. Take a piece of 2-inch (1¾ inches, assuming that the sash is 1¾ inches wide) poplar, cypress, or pine (or whatever you are using to build your window) that is 5 to 6 inches wider than the window and screw it to the top of the T.

Using the mathematical formula shown in

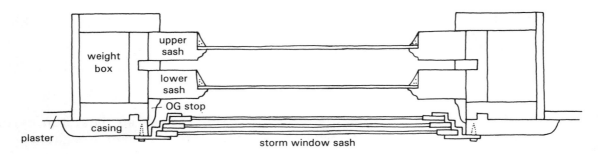

FIGURE 14.2 *An overhead section view of the triple-track storm window sash, reversed to fit inside the existing window.*

prohibitive. If you do choose to replace the windows, find a contractor or planing mill that has done a lot of this type of work.

If you have these windows made, it is easy to take the entire window (frame and all) right out of the brick wall and put the new one back in—providing the new window is made correctly. Be prepared for sticker shock when you get the bid.

The next section is written for experienced woodworkers who have the proper equipment to make windows. This means that you have a "cope and stick" cutter (on a router or shaper) so that you can turn sash pieces, and you have a band saw set up to cut curved tops.

CUTTING YOUR OWN CURVED WINDOW PARTS

The secret to cutting curved sash pieces is a mathematical formula. You need a good band saw with a table extending about 6 feet in front of the saw (in other words, 90 degrees out from the plane of the blade). The top should be wood so that you can drive drywall screws into it.

Cut a large piece of ¼-inch plywood into a T that

Figure 14-3, take the measurements off the window, plug the dimensions into the formula, and derive the radius from the edge of the blade to a point on your table. Make an X down the centerline that is lined up with the blade. Take the T with the sash material screwed to it, place it up against the saw, and drive a screw in the centerline at your mark. Proceed to swing the T through the saw blade to make the top of the curve. You will be cutting the 2-inch material and the ¼-inch plywood.

Measure the height of the sash piece and move

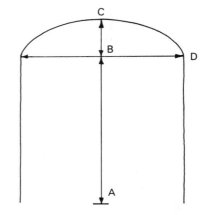

FIGURE 14-3. *To cut a curved sash top, follow this formula:*

$$AC = \frac{BC^2 + BD^2}{2BC}$$

the T that distance toward the saw blade. Redrive the screw into your table. Swing the material through the band saw again. The result is a piece of sash material exactly the height and width of the existing sash material at the proper curve. Rout or shape it to make a finished sash piece. You will have to cut the ends either flush or cope and stick to fit the top sash piece together with the side sash pieces.

If a planing mill makes your windows, it is not likely that it will know this formula. Some planing mills cut curved windows by making templates. If the mill uses templates, don't just give the mill this formula. Sell it to them.

REPAIRING EXISTING WINDOWS

If all the front windows in the building are fairly sound, but there are some rotten or loose sash or the sash are loose in the frames, it is easy to fix them. The job is time-consuming but not very costly.

The first thing is to make sure the frames and sills are good; forget the stops for now. If the sills are rotten, replace them with treated lumber, usually two-by-six or two-by-eight. If the stool (see Figure 14-1) is bad, replacing it depends on what you plan to do for trim inside the building. If you use dry-wall-returned windows (see Figure 15-3, p. 153), you don't need to replace the stool now.

The sill usually sits on a stone subsill, and the subsill is usually not very easy to remove if it needs replacing. The sill is nailed to the bottom of the weight box in the window (see Figure 14-1). If you push down on the inside and pull up on the outside, the sill will usually come loose. You can pull it out and cut a new piece to match. If it fits well, put it back in, glue it down, and nail through the bottom of the weight box into it. Do not nail down the weight doors. (A *weight door* is a little door at the bottom of the frame that allows you to get in and see the sash weights.) If you are studding out the exterior walls of the building, it may be easy (depending on how far in your stud wall is) to build a small frame wall to stick underneath the sill to hold the inside of it up (see Figure 14-4). You will need more than a two-by-eight to do so, however.

On the inside of the window, you will see a piece of molding called the *OG stop*. This holds the inside, or bottom, sash in. Pull the stop off. Save it for now. When you get the stop off, you can pull out the bottom sash. If the ropes or chains are still attached, cut them at the sash and let the weights fall to the bottom of the weight box, but do not allow the rope or chain to go through the window pulley.

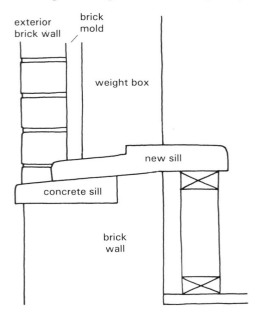

FIGURE 14-4. *When studding out the exterior walls of a building, you may be able to construct a frame wall to support the inside of the sill.*

You will find another piece of molding that fits in a slot, or dado, in the window frame. It separates the lower sash from the upper sash and is called the *parting stop* or *bead*. Pull it out, being extremely careful. Do not damage the dado in the wood frame. Pull the stop out by very carefully driving a chisel between it and the dado at one point and slowly prying it out. If the parting stop holds the weight doors in, they will fall out when you remove the stop. Pull the upper sash out and cut the cords or chains as you did before; set both sash aside.

You will have one outer piece of molding left. This is called the *blind stop* because you cannot see it when the sash are in. Leave the blind stop as it is.

If the corners of the sash are loose, you can reglue them and screw them back together with drywall screws. If they are very loose, put an L-bracket in each corner on the outside. Mark it and then chisel out a place where the bracket will fit flush with the sash. Screw it in so that the sash corner is tight, making sure that the sash is square. Caulk or putty over the whole L-bracket. When it is painted, you won't be able to see it. This is much cheaper than buying new sash.

Now you must choose whether you want to fix the upper sash in place or leave it so it can be opened. In most old houses, the windows are *double-hung* — that is, the upper sash comes down, and the lower sash goes up. Double-hung windows are designed so that you can open the upper sash to allow better circulation of air in the summer. If you plan to install central air-conditioning, you probably won't need to open the upper sash. If that is the case, you can save a lot of time and effort by driving 3-inch drywall screws into the bottom of the sash and into the frame at an angle, fixing it in place. Use one or two small finish nails at the top to hold the sash in, then caulk it completely from the outside. The upper sash will then be secure and airtight. The biggest potential drawback to this method is when you have to fix broken glass; it must be done with the window in place unless you remove the caulk and screws.

Now we are going to make the sash fit tighter and be airtight. This takes some work, but it is well worth the effort. If you want to be able to open the upper sash, cut a piece of material to the width of the blind stop and ½ inch thick. Glue and nail it on top of the existing blind stop. This can be very difficult if you have a full curved-top window. Back-cut the piece to get it to bend to the curve, nail it to the existing blind stop, and then caulk all the backcuts that are exposed.

Follow these steps to make the sash fit the window (and refer to Figure 14-5): Using a table saw, cut ¼ inch off each side of each sash (not the top and bottom). Then, make sure that the *check rails* (the top rail of the bottom sash and the bottom rail of the top sash) match when the windows are closed. This is particularly important if you replaced a sill. To do this, place the sash back in the window as they would sit and make sure the check rails meet. An angle piece may have to be added to them, or the sash pieces will have to be cut so that these rails slide together tightly. If they do not,

adjust one of the sash. It is usually easier to cut off or add to the bottom of the bottom sash. If the check rails are not smooth, replace them. Replace any glass that needs to be replaced (see the next section) and make sure that all the glazing is redone or repaired. If you reglaze the glass, let the window sit flat for a day before you replace the sash, or the glazing will sag.

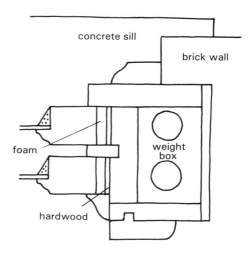

FIGURE 14-5. *When fitting sash to windows, you can make the windows airtight by cutting strips of ¹/₂″ automotive foam to the width of your sash. Affix the foam to the sides of the sash with spray glue made for foam. Glue thin strips of hardwood to the foam to butt up against the frame.*

In order to keep the window airtight, buy ½-inch-thick automotive foam cut to the width of your sash and long enough to cover both sides of all of them. Use special spray glue for foam, as it will work better than anything else, and stick the foam onto the sides of the window sash. Cover the slot and hole where the rope or chain used to come down the side.

When you slide the sash in the window frame, you want it to ride with the foam squeezed up. So, cut pieces of hardwood (preferably oak) ³/₃₂ or ⅛ inch thick by the width and height of your sash. Glue these pieces to the outside of the foam. Measure the width of the window, figure out what the foam will reduce to (probably ¼ inch on each side) and add the widths of the hardwood on each side of the window. All of this has to fit in the frame fairly tightly. Otherwise, you will have to cut more than the ¼ inch indicated earlier off the sash. Make sure that you measure everything correctly before you start. Also make sure that all the paint, glue, and crud is off the window frame so that the sash glides smoothly. The easiest way to do that is to sand the whole frame after you remove the stops. Also use your sander to round the ends of the hardwood pieces on the side of the sash so they don't hit the weight doors. Wax the inner edges of the window frame and the outer edges of the oak pieces.

Make sure the correct weights are in the window. If you have to weigh your sash, do so. Each weight should be equal to half the sash weight. This is particularly important if you replace the glass, as new glass may not weigh as much as old glass.

You can use the old chain or rope, but we suggest you don't. Instead, buy a rechaining kit. You can get sash chain at almost any hardware store, but if you are going to fix all your windows, go to a wholesaler. Push the chain through the pulley, making sure the pulley works. You can usually find pulleys at an architectural antique supplier if you have to replace them. Starting with the outside pulleys (those for the top sash), attach the chains to the weights. Run the weights to the bottom of the weight box and pull them up about 3 inches; put a nail through the chain to hold them there. You don't want to leave more slack because when you run the sash all the way up, the weights will hit the bottom of the weight box. For the interior pulleys (for the bottom sash), run the weights up to the top of the weight box and then lower them about 3 inches. Insert nails at the pulleys. Make sure your weight doors are installed and smooth. Using 3-inch drywall screws, screw the chains into the side of the top sash first. The screw should be about an inch below the top of the sash (above the foam) while the sash is where it will sit in the frame when closed. Make sure the drywall screw is 3 inches long and goes into solid wood. This is a tricky maneuver. It takes two people, one to hold the sash and the other to screw in the chain.

Very carefully slide the window sash into the opening. It should be very tight. If you are using double-hung windows, do the top first. If you have single-hung windows, fix the upper and then do the lower. Once the upper sash is in place (either fixed or movable) and before you do the bottom sash, put the parting stop in. If you have cut your sash down and used foam, you need to cut a new parting stop that is deeper than the old one. Most parting stops are ½ inch wide and ¾ inch deep. Use 1¼-inch stock and cut ½-inch-wide pieces as long as the height of the window. Install the new ½-inch by 1¼-inch parting stop. One thing you will have to do on both sash is cut back the check rails. You will find that the wedge piece on the check rails was cut back so that the sash would slide up and down the parting stop. Now that you have added ¼ inch to each side of the parting stop, you must cut ½ inch off that wedge on each side of the sash, or the windows won't fit into the frames. Install both sash, making sure that they run up and down and that the check rails meet.

Now install a new OG stop. The new OG stop has to be ½ inch wider on each side than the old stop. You can buy 1-inch quarter round molding to use as an OG stop or have something made to replicate the original. Put the OG stop up against the bottom sash with the window closed and nail the bottom of the stop. Before you nail the top of the stop, run the bottom sash up so that you make sure the stop isn't too far in. If the sills are not level, run the OG stop all the way around the window (top and bottom) to ensure a good seal.

REPLACING BROKEN GLASS

Removing and replacing windowpanes is not a difficult job, but it does require a certain amount of skill if it is to be done correctly. There is more to replacing glass than just inserting a new pane and adding a little putty. If the piece of glass to be replaced is large, you should remove the window sash and place it on a flat surface before attempting to remove the broken glass or install a new pane.

The first step is to remove all broken glass and putty. Wear gloves to do this and keep in mind that, in old windows, the putty is sometimes harder than the wood to which it is attached. It is relatively easy to break a *mullion*, which is the small piece of wood between the windowpanes. The best way to remove old putty from a window frame is to use a very sharp wood chisel or a stiff putty knife. Take your time and remove all the old putty. Do not try to remove too much at one time. If you do, you will split the frame or break another pane of glass. Also be sure to remove all the *glazier's points*, which are small metal triangles driven into the frame underneath the putty to hold the glass in place. If the old putty is very difficult to remove, you can use an electric soldering iron to soften it.

After you have removed the old putty and the glazier's points, use the point of the chisel to smooth out any rough spots in the frame. If you cannot get them all out, lay a very thin bead of clear silicone putty on the frame before you insert the glass. (You'll need to size the glass before you do this.) You also should coat the frame all around with linseed oil. This helps keep the oil in the putty from soaking into the wood, thus preventing the putty from drying out.

When you cut the glass or have it cut, make it slightly smaller than the size of the opening so that it is sure to fit. When you insert the new windowpane into the frame, press it firmly into the silicone. If you have too much silicone, you can cut out the excess later with a razor blade after it has dried. Hold the new pane in place with one hand and insert glazier's points on each side to keep it in place. Glazier's points can be inserted with a small amount of pressure or pushed slightly with a screwdriver.

Make sure that you putty the window with glazier's putty and that you knead it before you start to use it. The easiest way is to roll it into pencil-size strips and then place one of these rolls along the edge of the window glass and frame. When all the putty is in place, you can smooth it out with a putty knife or a very sharp chisel. The key is to use a clean putty knife or chisel and to oil it. Use long corner-to-corner strokes and do not let the putty get far enough out on the windowpane to make it visible from the other side. Use a razor blade to clean the excess putty off the glass and wait at least two days before painting the putty.

STEEL WINDOWS

Steel windows, and particularly steel casement windows, are usually very easy to remove from an old building. If they are in fairly good shape, however, it is probably better to leave them in place because removing them will detract from the building's appearance. In many cases, repairing these windows and then retrofitting storm windows is more economical than replacing them.

We cannot tell you to what extent steel windows define your building's historic character or are significant to its architectural design; you and your architect will have to make that decision. However, we can tell you how to evaluate the window's condition. Look for the presence and degree of corrosion; the condition of the paint; deterioration of hinges or other sections, including bowing or misalignment; and the condition of the glass and glazing. Corrosion is the controlling factor in window repair or replacement. If the corrosion is heavy, particularly in the working hardware, steel windows may not be worth keeping. Although major repairs can be made, they normally require removing the window unit to a workshop, and that is probably more than any do-it-yourselfer would want to do. Only if the window is an integral part of the house's architectural style should you consider such repairs or replacement with equivalent steel windows.

If the window is basically sound, remove all light rust, flaking, and excessive paint; prime the exposed metal with a rust-inhibiting primer; replace the glass as needed; and rehabilitate the hardware as needed with new screws, fasteners, cleaning, and lubrication. Never mix metals in replacing hardware. This may increase corrosion through galvanic interaction. Finally, caulk the window to the masonry and paint it. Wipe any bare metal with a cleaning solvent such as alcohol, then dry it in preparation for the application of an anticorrosive primer. Corrosion will recur very soon after metal has been exposed to the air, so it should be primed and painted immediately. Keep in mind that all metal primers are toxic, so be careful when you are using them.

Steel windows are generally not energy-efficient: This often leads to their wholesale replacement. They can be made energy-efficient in several ways, however. Caulking around the masonry openings and adding weather stripping are easy and important first steps in reducing air filtration through the windows. Other treatments include applying fixed layers of glazing over the old windows, adding operable storm windows, and installing thermal glass in place of the existing glass. In combination with caulking and weather stripping, these treatments can produce energy ratings rivaling those achieved by new windows. The best kind of weather stripping to buy for steel windows is vinyl that is folded into a V configuration with one side having glue on it. This weather stripping is glued to the frame in such a way that the window sash comes up against the V and squeezes it together when the window is closed. Compressible foam tape weather stripping is also used with this kind of window, but it tends not to stay in place as well as the V-configuration vinyl.

Most companies that make aluminum windows also make a product that can be used to double-glaze steel casement windows. It is called casement glazing or threshold glazing and is a single pane of glass in an aluminum frame, much like a storm window sash, where the sash has a rubber backing. The aluminum sash fits right over the steel sash and is screwed to it, with the rubber gasket between the two. The frame itself can still let in air, so some people prefer to add a storm window on the inside of the casement window. The window cannot be opened without removing the inside storm window, but since windows are not often opened in the winter, this may not be much of a problem.

We do not particularly like steel casement windows, but no other material can match their thin profile. Aluminum, for example, is three times weaker than steel and must be extruded in a box-like configuration that could not possibly match the distinctive thin profile of most steel windows. Wooden and vinyl replacement windows, too, are generally made to the same boxlike dimensions.

REPLACING FRONT WINDOWS

If you purchase a building that has fairly small windows (3 feet by 6 feet or less), you may be able to use premade wooden windows to replace the front windows. Marvin windows are usually the least

expensive, but there are many other options, including Pella and Andersen. Many developers use Marvins because they are inexpensive and come in 3-inch increments, allowing you to come very close to the dimensions of your brick opening.

If you choose this option, measure the brick opening (the full width from brick to brick and from the stone subsill to the top where the arch starts). Make sure to order replacement windows (with brick mold attached and preprimed) that are as close to but less than these dimensions. Try to get within about an inch or so. When the windows arrive, tear out the old window frames. You will find that the inner bricks are stepped back about 6 inches; that is where the window weight box sat. Don't worry about it. Find where the brick mold sits in the brick opening; there is usually an old paint line there. The brick mold is usually about 1½ to 2 inches from the edge of the brick toward the inside of the house. You should already have your exterior stud walls built on the inside (see Chapter 15), so measure the distance from where the brick mold falls to the inside of the stud wall. Then subtract the depth of the new brick mold (which is preattached to the new window) plus ½ inch or so. When you frame the window opening on the interior studded wall, you will have to know how

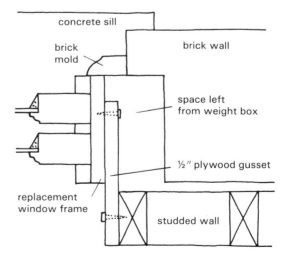

FIGURE 14-6. *When framing window openings in interior studded walls, allow for the width of the replacement window, plus an additional $^{1}/_{2}''$ on either side. Then cut and attach $^{1}/_{2}''$ plywood gussets to the studs on the inside window frame.*

wide your replacement windows are plus an additional ½ inch on each side. The studded opening is therefore 1 inch larger than the window (see Figure 14-6).

Buy ½-inch plywood and cut it into 6- to 8-inch strips as long as the measurement determined above. Screw 6 of these strips to the sides of the frame inside the brick mold (one on the top, one in the middle, and one on the bottom on each side). They will stick out from the window toward the inside. With a helper, set the window into the brick opening right where you want it. You may have to put the window in from the outside. The strips that you cut out of ½-inch plywood will go up against the stud on the inside frame wall. Center the window, making sure it is plumb and level. Push the window as high as it will go. If you have to put a double sill in, do it. Most historic districts require that the top of the replacement window be right at the top of the arch. Using a screw gun and drywall screws, screw the plywood strips to the studs at the window opening. Depending on how closely the window matches your brick opening, you will have to shim or caulk the gap between the replacement window brick mold and the brick opening. If the gap is less than ¼ inch, you can just caulk it, but if it is bigger, you will have to fill it with a new piece of molding and then caulk the whole thing. If you intend to apply for historical tax credits, you may wish to ask your local representative to approve your windows before you caulk them in and do final finish work.

There will be an open arch at the top of the window. Cut an arch to match the window opening out of a treated two-by-six or two-by-eight. Use a lot of construction adhesive and nail it as much as you can so that it is good and tight. You might have to build from the new stud framing on the inside of the house to support these arch pieces.

The exterior of the window is now done unless you want to put some fancy brick mold around to cover the caulking. Fill the gaps between the plywood strips that connect the window to the stud with ½-inch plywood so that when you drywall the whole affair, the corner is flush and you have something to which you can nail the drywall cornerbead.

The advantage of this method is that you can replace the old windows with new thermal-pane windows without having to buy custom-made replacements. However, repairing existing windows is still less expensive in most cases, particularly if the windows are 6 to 8 feet tall.

INSTALLING NEW WINDOWS (OR DOORS) IN NEW OPENINGS

The process of cutting and opening a brick wall and adding a new window, standard door, or sliding glass door is not very different from that of taking out an old window, frame and all, and replacing it with a new one. The difference is opening the brick wall so that the new window or door will fit in the hole. This is a very tricky, time-consuming, and costly operation. Unless you are changing the whole structure of your house and rearranging rooms, we suggest that you do not do this. In fact, in our experience, most rehabbers tend to close up windows rather than open new ones, unless they are putting apartments in a former single-family structure.

If you do cut new openings, you will have to size the opening properly. It is also critical that the rough opening be square and plumb. If it is not, the frame will not fit or the door may not slide or latch properly. Measure the opening diagonally to check the mason's work. Also make sure that he or she has put a steel (or some other kind of) lintel across the opening or has arched the top of it. When installing any kind of wood header, if there is any bow or crown through the material, make sure that the high side is up. Once the window is in, remember to insulate it well before it is totally flashed to the brick.

REPLACING SIDE AND BACK WINDOWS

You can either repair the side and back windows as already described, replace them with wood windows as already discussed, or replace them with aluminum or vinyl thermal-pane windows. The last option is always less expensive. Since you are prepared to buy wholesale, you need to find a local company in your town that makes aluminum or vinyl thermal-pane double-hung or single-hung windows. We recommend aluminum, since large vinyl windows can sag. The windows will usually be either white or dark bronze. Most historic districts will only accept white or bronze; some will only accept bronze.

Find a manufacturer that makes aluminum thermal-break windows (see Figure 14-7). A thermal break is a piece of plastic that separates the exterior from the interior of the aluminum frame and prevents the window from sweating in cold weather. Also make sure to get windows that have a $^7/_8$-inch rather than a $^3/_8$-inch thermal space. In some cases, you can get triple-pane glass, but that might not be economical. Have the manufacturer measure your windows. The company's representative will measure the width of the frame inside the blind stop and then subtract $^1/_4$ inch. The manufacturer will then make a window to fit in the frame up against the blind stop. These windows can be installed from the inside after removing the OG stop, the sash, and the parting stop.

Before you get the manufacturer to come out and measure your windows, check your frames and sills. If they are bad in any way, replace them. Make

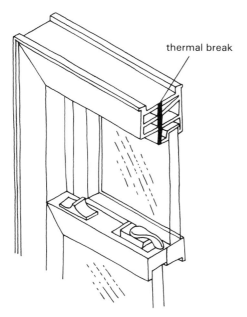

FIGURE 14-7. *An aluminum window frame with a plastic thermal break.*

thermal break

sure you do this before the manufacturer measures for the windows.

Cut the weight chain or rope. Let the weights fall to the bottom of the weight box and leave them. Use a screwdriver to remove the pulleys. If the manufacturer's workers come out to install the windows, they will probably take a hammer and smash the pulleys in.

Make sure the weight door is secure and leave it in place. Install the new window, sliding it in against the blind stop. Make sure it is centered and square and screw it in place (there will be six to twelve screw holes inside the window frame). Do not screw the middle screws in too far, as doing so will bow out the rails and the sash will be very loose in the middle. The lower sash may even fall out. Use some thin plywood or other material to shim the center of the windows before securing them. If you shim with shingles, the inside will be tight and the outside loose because a shingle is not the same dimension along its length. Some windows have adjusters in the middle that screw out against the window frame to keep the frame plumb. We shim these windows, too. If the window does not have an adjuster at the top, drive it all the way to the top of the window frame before you screw it in. After you install the stud wall, drywall-return the window. The new sill that goes in that opening will be $^3/_4$ to 1 inch thick and it will cover the gap left at the bottom of the window. Insulate the gap between the window and the sill and cover it outside.

Go outside and caulk the space between the window and the blind stop. If you retain the existing brick mold without any covering, scrape the blind stop off before you caulk so the painters won't scrape the window when they prepare it for painting. If you are not in a historic district, the window manufacturer's workers can flash the outside of your window to cover the brick mold with aluminum. They will caulk the flashing to the window and to the brick. The windows then become maintenance-free. In historic districts, you usually have to retain the brick mold, and the paint has to match the color of the windows. Make sure you buy high-quality, pliable caulk, because the aluminum flashing will move with the weather.

On the inside, make sure that your stud walls are flush with the window frame if you plan to drywall-return them. It is best to use J-channel, which is a plastic channel that goes on the edge of the drywall. Cut the drywall, put the J-channel on the edge, and put the drywall with the J-channel right up against the window. The only thing left to do is cut a sill to fit in the bottom of the window.

BASEMENT WINDOWS

You can use any of the options discussed previously when dealing with basement windows. You can replace them with aluminum or wood windows or repair existing ones. It is possible you will want to put bars on these windows to keep people from breaking into your house. That creates a problem if you are going to use the basement for living space because you will not be able to get out in case of a fire. If there is a rear entrance to the basement, that's okay. But if you have to go from the living area through the furnace room to the rear entrance, it is not okay. Usually the safest thing to do is not to bar the front windows but to bar the rest of them. You also can replace all the basement windows (except the front openings) with glass blocks. It looks okay and saves you the cost of buying new windows and bars. Many historic districts will not allow this, however.

ADDING A SKYLIGHT

In many areas of the country and with some kinds of houses, adding a skylight can have several benefits. The most obvious is an abundant supply of natural light to a central portion of the house. Skylights transmit up to five times more light per square foot than conventional wall windows.

Although some people build their own skylights using acrylic plastic sheets, it is difficult to achieve a permanent weather-tight seal because of expansion and contraction. It is better to buy a prefabricated skylight made out of acrylic or glass. Regardless of what you do, one of the biggest problems with skylights is leaks. Whether they are expensive or inexpensive, they tend to leak. Keep

that in mind if you are considering a skylight. If you want to use a glass skylight, many building codes specify wire mesh or tempered glass. Check your local building codes for any provisions relating to skylights.

Most skylights are sized to fit between standard rafter openings, ranging from 14½ to 48 inches. The existing rafter spacing in your house is a major factor in determining which size skylight you need. In addition, the ratio of the skylight opening to the floor space (assuming 8-foot ceilings) is approximately 1:20. This means that a 4-square-foot skylight provides adequate lighting for an 80-square-foot floor.

To prepare the rough opening, measure precisely where the skylight will go in relation to the rafters. One of the best ways is to drill through the roof next to the rafters. You may not be able to do this if you have a flat or slate roof. In fact, if you have a slate roof, we would argue against even thinking about installing a skylight. You must add 1½ inches to the top and bottom edges of the opening because new headers must be installed between the rafters. If you cut more than one rafter, we suggest (and your building code will probably require) doubling the rafters on each side, on the outside away from the skylight opening. Cut the rafter for the opening and then cut the subroof to the dimensions required. On the roof, double-check the dimensions and make sure that the opening is square. We recommend that you cut the shingles with a knife rather than try to saw through them and the roofing material because you will get tar all over your saw. Also try to avoid cutting through nails. Install the headers and any trimmers needed to double up rafters before cutting the roof opening. This is a good procedure when threatening weather reduces the time your roof can be open.

If the skylight requires a curb (we always put skylights on curbs), build it with two-by-fours or two-by-sixes on edge, with the inside frame, curb the size of the rough opening. Set the skylight over it to make sure it fits. Put the curb over the opening and nail or screw it down. When you install flashing, make sure it wraps around the top of the curb, goes down the outside to the curb, and comes out at least 6 inches across the roof (or more if you have a flat roof). Nail down the flashing, placing it under the shingles. Apply roofing cement around the top of the opening, regardless of whether the skylight requires a curb or flashing, and along the edges and any seams. You are now ready to install the skylight using the manufacturer's instructions. Make sure that everything is tight and waterproof.

At this point, unless you have a flat roof, you will need to build a light shaft, which is an enclosed space leading down to the ceiling. It can be straight, angled, or flared. The flared design maximizes the distribution of light but requires cutting at angles and making difficult attachments in tight spaces. To make a straight shaft, drop a plumb bob from the four corners of the skylight to the ceiling and mark the opening on the ceiling joists and ceiling material. Then drill holes down from the attic and into the house, marking the corners. Go down to the next floor and use a sawsall to cut the opening. If you are cutting out more than two ceiling joists, it is best to support the ceiling as you would when removing a bearing wall. Double the joists on each side if needed and install headers as in the roof. Frame in the opening all the way around and drywall the space up into the skylight. Insulate a light shaft as you would an exterior wall.

FURTHER READING

The Department of the Interior, National Park Service, has issued two short documents that are very useful in the repair of windows. *Preservation Brief Number 9* deals with the repair of historic wood windows, and *Preservation Brief Number 13* deals with the repair and thermal upgrading of historic steel windows. Both pamphlets are available from the Superintendent of Documents, U.S. Government Printing Office, Washington, DC 20402.

References

OLD

English Casement Windows and Leaded Glass. Jamestown, New York: International Casement Co., 1913.

NEW

Building Doors, Windows, and Skylights. Newtown, Connecticut: Taunton Press, 1989.

Burns, Al. *The Skylight Book: Capturing the Sun and the Moon. A Guide to Creating Natural Light.* Philadelphia: Running Press, 1976.

Jensen, Tom. *Skylights: The Definitive Guide to Planning, Installing, and Maintaining Skylights and Natural Light Systems.* Philadelphia: Running Press, 1983.

Ramsey, Dan. *Doors, Windows and Skylights.* Blue Ridge Summit, Pennsylvania: TAB Books, 1983.

Williams, T. Jeff. *How to Replace and Install Doors and Windows.* San Francisco, California: Ortho Books, 1984.

Wilson, H. Weber. *Great Glass in American Architecture: Decorative Windows and Doors before 1920.* New York: E.P. Dutton, 1986.

Windows and Doors. Alexandria, Virginia: Time-Life Books, 1987.

FRAMING

Now that you have the building gutted and cleaned, the floors are level, all structural problems are resolved, and the windows are installed, the next thing that you need to think about is framing. Except for shoveling plaster, framing a building is probably the heaviest work involved in rehabbing. Having the correct tools to do it makes it much easier (see Chapter 8).

To determine how many studs you need, a good rule of thumb is to figure one stud for every foot of wall that you will put up. In actuality, you need one stud and 32 inches of two-by-four for every 16 inches because walls are typically framed on 16-inch centers. By the time you cut things such as fire blocks, nailers, and corners, however, you are up to one stud for every foot of wall. Simply figure the running feet of total new wall in the rehab and order that to start. Add in any two-by-fours needed for lowering ceilings. These will typically be longer than studs and will have to be calculated from your plans. Don't forget the perimeter two-by-fours.

Distribute the lumber by floor when it is delivered; don't move it twice. Order studs in a length that corresponds to the height of the walls, unless the lumberyard charges a higher price per board foot for 10-foot or 12-foot two-by-fours. If so, try to be more precise about the number of studs and buy 8-footers for soleplates, headers, and nailers. You can use 8-footers even when lowering ceilings by running a double two-by-six beam across the room every 8 feet and hanging studs in joist hangers between the beams. Most established lumberyards charge a per-board-foot price for framing lumber regardless of length unless you get 20-footers or longer.

Set sawhorses up where you plan to work. When the lumber is delivered, stack 30 to 40 studs on the sawhorses and distribute the rest. Now you're ready to go to work.

LAYING OUT THE BUILDING

Let's discuss where to start framing. You can either start from the center of the building and work out (this is probably the most common method) or stud the exterior walls and work in. There are pros and cons to each approach. One of the reasons some builders stud the outside walls first and work in is because they can stud these walls very quickly. It is okay to stud the exterior first if you then go to the center and work out. Whether you have an architectural drawing, a sketch, or only a design in your head, you must make sure that things will fit where they are supposed to go. If you are not absolutely sure that this is the case, work from the center out, since you will typically run into structural problems more often in the center of the building.

Another issue is how to lay out the building. You can do that by nailing the soleplates down to the floors or by marking the walls on the floors with chalk or a grease pencil. Regardless of how you do it, make sure that the building is clean. The last thing you want to do is start framing a building with plaster and other debris still on the floors. Sweep and vacuum. Make sure that all the linoleum or old floor covering is pulled up. It is very difficult to lay things out and see the marks when the floors are dirty.

The problem with laying out the building with the soleplates is that you will either waste a length of two-by-four for every running foot of wall or you will have to *stick-build* your walls—that is, build them in place piece by piece rather than on the floor and then putting the entire assembly in place. In an open building, it is significantly more efficient to build walls on the floor and then stand them up in place and secure the assembly. This operation depends on having helpers, having fairly level floors, and on how tight the rooms are. If you have 11-foot-square rooms and 11-foot ceilings, you cannot build the wall on the floor and stand it up; you will have to stick-build it. In all houses, you will probably have to stick-build walls in bathrooms and other small rooms. In those areas, you can lay out the walls by cutting soleplates and nailing them down to the floor where they will go.

Two things can make laying out a house very easy. First, if you need a new subfloor or the floor is to be covered with plywood or particleboard, do it first. If the subflooring is ⅞ inch thick, if there are lots of holes in it, or if the tongues and grooves are coming apart, you might want to lay new flooring. It is easy to do this while you have the building totally cleared out, and you will have a nice new surface on which you can mark the walls. Second, after you sweep and vacuum, you can roll all the floors with some cheap white paint. Let it dry for a couple of days, then mark where the walls will go.

We like to lay out the building completely before starting to frame it. The only exception to this rule is when the existing interior walls are to be retained and the only framing to be done is along the exterior walls. The nice thing about having the building laid out before you start framing is that, where interior walls butt up against exterior walls, you will know where to place nailers. You can put the corner nailers into the exterior walls as you throw them up, which saves both time and effort (see Figure 15-1).

If a house is easy to lay out or few of the interior walls will be changed, it is probably a good idea to start studding out the exterior walls first. It also might be a good idea to start with the exterior walls if you are not familiar with carpentry. You can make more errors on the exterior walls and get away with them.

A major issue with exterior walls is how plumb they are. In a multistory building, the first-floor ceiling will not be in line with the floor. In other words, if you stand a two-by-four up against the wall, it might be touching the wall at the floor and

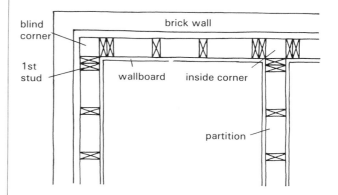

FIGURE 15-1. *A transverse section of a framed wall, showing studs placed as corner nailers on both blind and inside corners.*

be 3 to 4 inches away at the ceiling. The opposite is true of the second floor. The reason for this is that the exterior walls in brick buildings bulge out in the middle over time because of the weight they carry. How much bowing occurs depends on how well the second floor is tied to the walls. To try to prevent bowing, iron rods were often placed through the brick, with iron stars bolted outside. The rods were then nailed or bolted to the joists or floors. Never remove these items without replacing them. If you remove the floor, replace the old rods with new ones that run across the entire building. Without them the building might collapse.

Start in the front or rear corner of the house and plumb it—that is, use a plumb bob to determine which way the wall is leaning (either out at the top or in at the top) and mark where your header and soleplate will go on the floor and ceiling. If the wall bows out at the ceiling on the first floor, your mark at the floor will be about 3½ to 4 inches (the width of the two-by-four against the wall) out from the wall and your mark on the ceiling may be as much as 7 to 8 inches out from the brick. That is where the side of the two-by-four header and soleplate facing you will sit. If you place the wall inside those two marks, you will end up with a perfectly plumb wall (see Figure 15-2).

Go to the other end of the room or building and plumb the other corner. Then have your helper hold one end of the chalk line, stretch it from corner to corner, and snap a line. Do that on the floor and on the ceiling joists. You may have to mark each

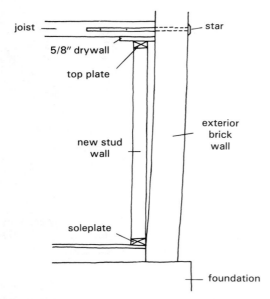

FIGURE 15-2. *Making the interior walls plumb ensures that they will be straight, despite the bowing over time of the outside brick wall.*

ceiling joist if they are not all the same height. (In the days of plastered walls, it was usually the plasterers who leveled and plumbed things, not the carpenters.) These lines mark the interior side of your wall, and when you put the wall up along them, it will be plumb. Do the same thing for each wall throughout the building.

If you are putting more than one dwelling unit in your building and have separate residential units on the first and second floors, most building codes require a complete "one-hour" wall or floor between units (a wall which theoretically should take one hour to burn through). A one-hour wall is either 1½ inches of wood or ⅝ inch of fireproof drywall. If units are separated by a wall, just install ⅝-inch drywall. Installing a one-hour floor is more complicated. When you frame walls, especially on the first floor, it is likely you will have a gap of 2, 3, or 4 inches at the top of the wall between the exterior of the studded wall and the interior of

the brick wall. If you stud the wall and then drywall the room on the inside, you have met the code requirements everywhere except that 2 or 3 inches between your new wall and the brick at the floor joists. There are two solutions: (1) Go back and fill in that space with two-by-fours or drywall, which is very difficult to do because you will have to rip two-by-fours to odd widths, or (2) before the stud wall goes up, cut ⅝-inch drywall into 6- or 8-inch-wide pieces that are 8 or 10 feet long and nail the drywall to the floor joists tight against the brick wall. Then put the wall up underneath the ⅝-inch drywall. When your drywallers are ready to drywall the room, they can simply cut off the excess drywall with a drywall knife at the edge of the new wall, then drywall inside the room. This results in a continuous one-hour wall between units.

FRAMING THE EXTERIOR WALLS

When studding out the exterior walls, it is much more efficient to start with the walls that are perpendicular to the ceiling joists where they are pocketed into the brick wall (see Figure 15-2). The reason for doing this is that the exterior stud walls that are parallel to the ceiling joists will need cross-nailers between the last joist and the exterior brick wall.

As we mentioned earlier, it is easier to build the walls on the floor, stand them up, and nail them in place than it is to stick-build them. In places where you have to stick-build the walls, start by nailing the soleplate and header at your marks. Nail a two-by-four soleplate right into the floor joists. Do that along the whole length of the wall. Then, using a tape measure and pencil, mark 24-inch centers all the way down both the header and the soleplate. Also, mark on which side the stud goes. (Most codes allow 24-inch centers on exterior walls in a brick building if the ceiling height is less than 12 feet but require 16-inch centers on interior walls.) Make sure you plumb the top and bottom where you start so the studs will be straight up and down. The easiest way to do that is to make a mark every

24 inches and put an X on the right side of the mark if you are working to the left, or vice versa, so that you know on which side of the mark the two-by-four goes. If you are working from left to right and marking every 24 inches, the two-by-four has to go on the right side of the mark for you to get 24-inch centers.

If you build the wall on the floor, measure from the floor to all the ceiling joists and find your lowest joist (the smallest measurement). Subtract $\frac{1}{8}$ inch from this to get the height of the wall. You have to build the wall so it goes up underneath the lowest joist. In old buildings, ceiling joists usually are not level. The joists were simply thrown in, close to level, and the plasterer put the lath across the joists and leveled them when he plastered the ceiling. In very old buildings, you often will find that the ceiling joists were hacked off to level them for lath. They will be very rough on the bottom and very irregular.

Our advice is to frame only the sections between windows. Do not try to build the entire wall on the floor with the window openings included. If you miss one window by $\frac{1}{4}$ inch, you will have to tear it all apart and do it over again. To save time, build the sections that go between windows and then stick-build the top and bottom of the windows.

Before we go any further, we need to discuss how to handle the windows. Are you going to "drywall return" your windows or reuse the old wood molding on the windows and exterior walls? *Drywall returning* means that you frame right up to the edge of the window opening, and the drywall (when it is finished) wraps around the wall corner right up to the window (that is, there is no molding). Most modern houses are built this way (see Figure 15-3). If you use metal windows, drywall returning is an easy way to handle a gut rehab. If you try to reuse all the old trim and baseboard, then you do not need to drywall return. If you drywall return your windows, the framing at the window has to be fairly precise. In other words, the two-by-four for the wall needs to be right at the edge of the window. If you reuse molding, the stud should line up with the outside of the window weight box. When you start to measure the wall sections, how you plan to handle your windows determines where the end two-by-four will go.

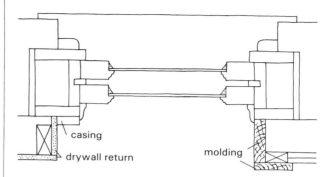

FIGURE 15–3. *An example, on the same window, of drywall returning (on the left side, requiring no molding) versus the traditional use of molding (right).*

Always double these studs or install the second stud perpendicular to the end stud.

Now you have the wall height (lowest joist to floor) and the marks on the floor and ceiling joists for where the wall is going to go. Find the straightest two-by-fours you can. If a two-by-four has a slight bow or crown, put it on the interior of the wall so that the crown faces you as you are putting up the wall. Use two-by-fours with extreme crowns for nailers. Cut your stud two-by-fours 3 inches less than the floor-to-ceiling measurement. That 3 inches represents the header and soleplate. Then measure from the corner to the first window and cut your header and soleplate to that length, or as long as the two-by-fours go. Put all of the two-by-fours on edge on the floor, mark the soleplate and header on 24-inch centers, line everything up on the floor, and nail them together. Put three nails in every junction where the studs are nailed to the soleplate or header. If you nail the wall together on the floor, you can nail from the bottom directly into the end of the stud rather than toenailing (see Figure 15-4).

When you build your first exterior wall, plumb the connecting side wall at the corner so you can determine where the walls will intersect. Start your first stud inside of the place where they will meet (see Figure 15-1) so that you do not waste a two-by-four by putting a stud in a blind corner.

When the frame is nailed together, it will wobble back and forth; don't worry about that. Just stand it up, line it up with your marks, and have your helper hold the wall while you put nails into the floor. Nail one corner of the wall in place. Check to see if it is plumb. Move your ladder to the other end, get the two-by-four on your marks, and nail that end. Recheck to make sure it is plumb and then nail two nails into every joist all the way across. If you do not know where the floor joists are, look

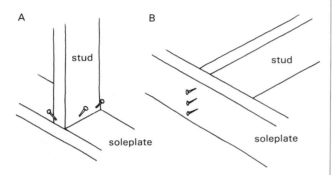

FIGURE 15–4. *If building walls in place, toenail the upright studs into the soleplate (A). If assembling the stud wall on the floor, nail from the bottom directly into the end of the stud (B).*

for the nails that are holding the flooring down or pound on the floor to find where it is solid. As a last resort, drill a hole. Make sure the wall is resting on joists or blocking (see Figure 15-5).

Once your wall sections are up, all you have to do is put your level on the sill and top of each window to mark your stud on each side. This will be the interior of the window. Then nail two-by-fours between the two studs above and below the marks to form the window opening (see Figure 15-6). Stud above and below the window headers on 16-inch centers. Make sure that you level the top and bottom of the window. This is critical.

After you have all your exterior walls in place, you need to install fire blocks. (Most building codes require fire blocks if your wall is 12 feet or higher and on all exterior walls.) A *fire block* is simply a block of wood placed between the studs halfway up the wall (see Figure 15-6). You also need to put back blocks in your walls. This is especially critical if they are 10 to 12 feet high. A *back block* is a short piece of two-by-four or two-by-six that is placed next to a stud, shoved all the way back tight against the brick, and then nailed to the stud. It keeps the wall from bowing out toward the brick.

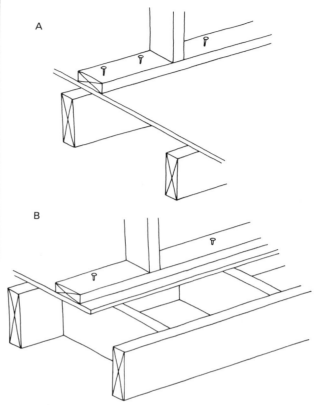

FIGURE 15–5. *Nailing the soleplate of stud walls into joists (A) and solid bridging (B).*

FRAMING THE INTERIOR WALLS

When you have all of the exterior walls framed and blocked, you are ready to start framing the interior walls. You can start just about anywhere, but it is best to work from the inside out, because things do not always fit as planned. Follow the same procedure in framing the inside walls as you did in framing the outside ones. The main consideration is to get the walls plumb and square. This is particularly true in bathrooms and kitchens where cabinets or countertops are to be installed. Where one wall meets another wall at a 90-degree angle, it is imperative that the corner be perfectly square. Your framing square is critical here. Double-check and triple-check those corners at all heights. Cutting countertops to fit corners that are not square isn't much fun and is unnecessary work.

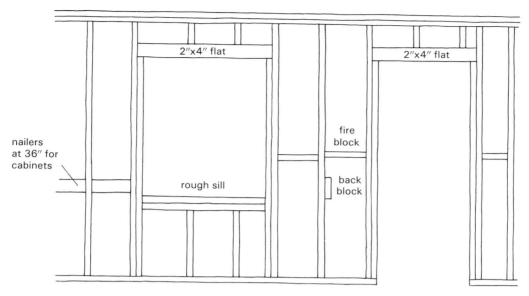

FIGURE 15-6. *An example of a framed stud wall, incorporating window and door openings, blocking, and nailers.*

Interior walls will be studded on 16-inch centers. You should have decided door sizes when you or an architect drew the plan for the house. Frame the door openings as shown in Figures 15-6 and 15-9. One set of two-by-fours goes floor to ceiling, and the other set goes inside it with the door headers sitting on top of the inside set. Put fire blocks on each side of the door whether or not they are required; they stiffen the frame.

If you are using new prehung doors, then the standard framed height is 6 feet 10 inches to 6 feet 10½ inches. The latter dimension is the safest to use, since it is easier to shim a prehung door than it is to cut out a frame that is too tight or slightly out of square. The doors should always be framed 2 to 2½ inches wider than the door specification. If you are installing a 30-inch door, the framing would be 32½ inches wide.

NAILERS

One of the critical aspects of framing a building is the nailers. Every corner needs a nailer on each side so you can nail the drywall to it. This is also true at the top of each wall (see Figure 15-7). As discussed previously, when you are framing a wall that runs parallel with the joists, you have to put cross-

blocks between those joists to have something to nail the wall to at the top. If you put those nailers in every 16 inches, then you do not need much else to nail the drywall to. Likewise, if you put a wall up in any area where you do not have a top corner for your drywall, you need to put a nailer in there. You will find many places where you will have to add nailers, particularly on the walls that run parallel to the floor or ceiling joists.

Whenever a wall comes to a door or a window,

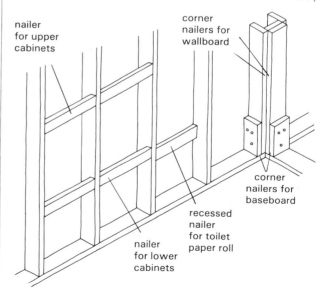

FIGURE 15-7. *A stud wall featuring various kinds of nailers.*

it should have a nailer set in like a fire block. Otherwise, you do not have to fire-block interior walls unless they are 12 feet or more high. You should block between the door or window and the first stud just to give it stability. This is also true in corners. The higher the wall, the more critical this becomes.

Other nailers are needed for kitchen cabinets, bathroom vanities, bathroom towel bars, toilet paper holders, and closet shelving. These are simply two-by-fours put in flat (see Figure 15-7). If you do not plan ahead for these things, you might not find a stud to nail them to. You will have a lot of short pieces of two-by-fours lying around. Use these for nailers. Figure out where you will put your towel bar in the bathroom and install a nailer for it. If you have a question about the bar's placement, install two or three nailers. Do the same for the toilet paper holder, unless you plan to have a recessed holder. If so, you must install the nailer on the back side of the wall (see Figure 15-7).

It is critical that you put nailers all the way around the perimeter where your kitchen cabinets will go (see Figure 15-7). Nailers for lower kitchen cabinets should be centered 35 inches from the floor. If you are using standard 30-inch upper cabinets, the nailers should be placed 7 feet from the floor

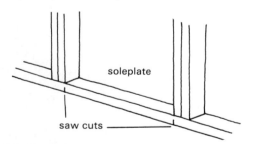

FIGURE 15-8. *Cutting up ¹/₂″ from the bottom of the soleplate to mark the door openings will enable you later, when the stud wall is up, just to saw down to the previous cuts.*

(add whatever extra is needed for taller wall cabinets). If your floors are not level, find the highest point in the floor and measure up 7 feet from there and keep the nailers level all the way across or around the kitchen so that they won't go downhill. As you install kitchen cabinets out each way on an angle, you will have to keep shimming them up higher and higher to keep them level (the cab-

inets must be level for the countertops to go on). When you do that, the cabinets become higher and higher while the blocking goes lower and lower. Make sure that you find the highest corner where you have a run of kitchen cabinets and measure 7 feet from there, then use a level out from that point to determine where your nailers go.

Other places for nailers are between ceiling joists for hanging ceiling fans or heavy light fixtures. The electrician can supply heavy boxes with brackets that nail between joists for hanging heavy fixtures, but if you are going to wire the house yourself or want to save some money, put nailers in there, and then all you have to do is screw metal boxes to the nailers. You must determine which thickness of drywall you will put on your ceiling (½ or ⁵/₈ inch) and put the nailer in accordingly so that the box sits ½ or ⁵/₈ inch below the joist.

If you are installing a "new construction" shower stall or tub (a tub/shower that is installed all in one piece, with the drywall butting up against it), then you will need nailers at the top rim of the enclosure. Some plumbers appreciate it if you throw in a few vertical nailers in the kitchen and bathroom where the pipes will go into the cabinets. This gives them something to attach their pipes to.

HEADERS

There are many inserts in load-bearing walls for things such as windows and doors in which you will have to install headers. In non-load-bearing walls, headers are not that important. When you stud out exterior brick walls, window openings can be framed in almost any way as long as they stay square and the windows can fit through them. However, with load-bearing walls, you need to construct headers. A header is basically a larger piece of timber put on posts at each end to carry a load. You will find that if you put two pieces of two-by lumber side by side, they make 3 inches, not 3½ inches, which is the width of your stud. To fix this, one of the easiest things to do is cut ½-inch plywood or drywall and put it between the two pieces that are going to become your header (see Figure 15-9) so that the resulting width is 3½ inches. We recommend using plywood; in fact, sandwiching two pieces of two-by lumber and ½-inch plywood together with glue is much stronger than using the two pieces of lumber alone.

Headers are critical, because any open space or window frame and glass is not strong enough to

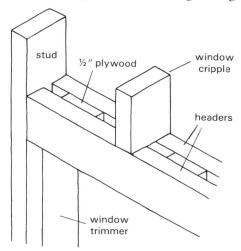

FIGURE 15–9. *The easiest way to construct headers over openings in load-bearing walls is to sandwich ¹/₂″ plywood gussets between pieces of 2-by material.*

support the load of a roof or a second floor. This fact becomes especially important over openings such as garage doors, bay windows, or major openings between rooms in bearing walls. The header, in fact, acts as a beam to transfer the load to the studs on each side. Headers can be made of two-by-sixes, two-by-eights, two-by-tens, or two-by-twelves, depending on the span (see Chapter 13). The header must sit on a stud post; it cannot run up against the stud and be nailed. As you can see in Figure 15–9, the header is actually sitting on a stud and sometimes several studs.

The recommended header size for anything over 3½ feet is a two-by-six; over 6 feet, a two-by-eight; over 8 feet, a two-by-twelve; and over 12 feet, triple two-by-twelves or a steel beam. Check with an architect or engineer to find out what you need.

FINAL POINTS

One point that is important in framing, especially

when you are stick framing or hand-nailing nailers, is that any nails that stick out are likely to break, bulge, or keep the drywall from going flat against the wall. Make sure all nail heads are flush with the wood.

Also remember that when you put down your soleplates, you can measure them for the doors and cut them as you put them down. But if you have a long run, it is a pain to be cutting two-by-fours where the doors go. Many carpenters lay the soleplates down and saw them out later for the door openings. One trick we have learned is that, before you put those soleplates down, you can simply run a saw blade about ½ inch deep across the bottom of the plate to mark where the door opening will be. These saw cuts make it a lot easier to cut out the plate for the door without cutting into the floor. You just have to cut down to the saw mark that is coming up from the bottom of the two-by-four (see Figure 15–8). If you are inexperienced, we suggest cutting each soleplate to fit.

References

OLD

Bell, William E. *Carpentry Made Easy, or, The Science and Art of Framing, on a New and Improved System.* Philadelphia: J. Challen & Sons, 1858.

Hodgson, Frederick Thomas. *Modern Carpentry: A Practical Manual.* Chicago: F.J. Drake and Co., 1917.

Tredgold, Thomas. *Elementary Principles of Carpentry.* Philadelphia: E.L. Carey and A. Hart, 1837.

NEW

Capotosto, John. *Residential Carpentry for the 1980's.* Reston, Virginia: Reston Publishing Co., 1983.

Clayton, Larry, and Jim Harrold, eds. *Better Homes and Gardens Step-by-Step Basic Carpentry.* Des Moines, Iowa: Meredith Corp., 1981.

Koel, Leonard. *Carpentry.* Alsip, Illinois: American Technical Publishers, Inc., 1985.

Tetrault, Jeanne, ed. *The Woman's Carpentry Book: Building Your Home from the Ground Up.* Garden City, New York: Anchor Press/Doubleday, 1980.

Williams, Benjamin. *Rafter Length Manual.* Carlsbad, California: Craftsman Book Co., 1986.

Chapter 16

PLUMBING

Modern materials make the process of plumbing a good deal easier than it was in the past. Instead of bulky cast-iron pipes, we have lightweight plastic pipes that can be joined together with glue in a matter of seconds. While the job is much easier, it is no less demanding in terms of doing a good job. A well-planned and well-executed plumbing job will provide many years of trouble-free service. In this chapter, we talk about some of the basics of plumbing and try to give you an understanding of how a plumbing system works, how a system is installed, and what types of materials are available. If you plan to do all your own plumbing and you don't have much experience in the field, we suggest that you spend some time examining other sources and your local building codes before attempting the task.

DOING IT YOURSELF VERSUS HIRING A SUBCONTRACTOR

Perhaps the most important decision to be made in approaching a plumbing rehab is to determine whether you have the skills needed to take on the job. If you don't have those skills, you must decide whether you have the time to learn them and whether you have the time to rip out parts of the system that you do not install properly. If you have some of the skills and have the time to learn the rest while doing the job, then you might want to do your own plumbing. If, however, you do not have the skills, do not particularly want to learn them,

and want to get the job done as quickly as possible, then you'd better go looking for a plumber to do the job for you. If you fall into the second category, you might still be able to save a good deal of money by doing some of the less difficult plumbing tasks yourself and leaving the rest for the subcontractor. Of course, you will have to find a plumber who is willing to work in this way. It is very important that you discuss this with the plumber before you start the job. Be sure that you agree on what each of you will do. In some areas of the country, ordinances require that all plumbing be done by a licensed plumber, so make sure to check your local building codes.

If you do decide to do your own plumbing, you should first hire a professional plumber to perform the initial inspection of your system. Then you should acquire some basic tools if you do not already have them. You also need to take the time to learn about your local plumbing codes. This is very important, because the codes in your area will specify exactly what types of installation are allowed, what types of materials must be used, and at what point during the project it must be inspected. Finally, it makes good sense to learn some of the vocabulary of plumbing. This makes it a good bit easier to talk with a plumber, plumbing inspector, or supply center.

BASIC PLUMBING TOOLS

Pipe wrenches. You need two of these to turn a pipe. Wrench sizes are expressed from the top of

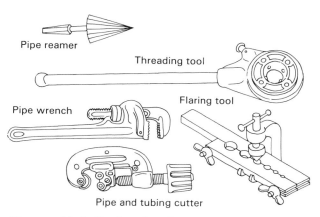

FIGURE 16-1. *Basic plumbing tools.*

the upper jaw to the bottom of the handle. If you will be working with a pipe up to 1 inch in diameter, then two 10-inch wrenches will do. If you will be working on a pipe up to 2 inches in diameter, then you will need two 18-inch wrenches. A pipe with a diameter of more than about 2½ inches will require two 24-inch wrenches.

Pipe and tubing cutter. You turn this device around the pipe or tubing to cut it. The size of the device will depend on the size and type of the pipe that you intend to cut.

Pipe reamer. This device removes the burrs that result when a pipe is cut with a pipe cutter and is often an integral part on tubing cutters.

Flaring tool. This device is used to make flare joints in copper tubing. In most areas, flared fittings are mandatory for gas line hookups. All other connections of copper pipes can be done with sweated or compression fittings.

Threading tool. If you will be working with steel pipes, you will need this tool to cut the threads in the pipe.

Miscellaneous tools. You probably ought to have the following tools: hacksaw, monkey wrench, pump-handled pliers, basin wrench, adjustable open-ended wrench, socket wrench, and spud wrench (for working with the large spud nuts on toilet tanks).

HOME PLUMBING SYSTEMS

Plumbing systems consist of three main sections (see Figure 16-2).

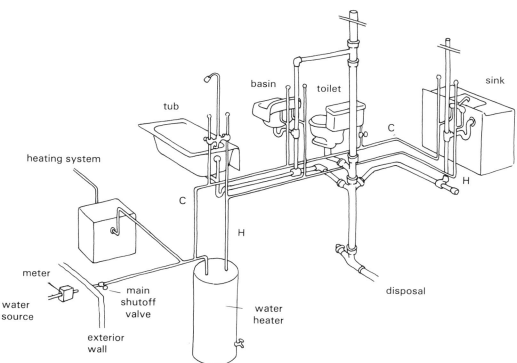

FIGURE 16-2. *A typical home plumbing system.*

First, a supply system brings the water in from the street. Normally the city water supply pipe is 2 to 3 feet underground to prevent freezing. It usually enters the house through the foundation. The city water meter is often outside of the foundation, and on the inside is the main shutoff valve for the house. The supply system splits into two pipes inside the house. The cold water pipe goes directly to the various fixtures in the house, and the hot water supply pipe goes to the hot water heater and then to the various fixtures. Remember that the water is carried under pressure to your house and the pressure varies with the area in which you live. Pressures of 100 to 120 pounds per square inch (psi) are common, so joints must be secure and leak-free.

Second, the home system consists of the waste or drainage system, which is totally separate from the supply system. A cross-connection between the systems occurs anytime an open supply source can be contaminated by the wastewater. This might be present if, for example, the water faucet opening extends below the water level in a bathroom sink. Drainage pipes are usually larger than supply pipes, varying from 1½ to 4 inches. You will notice that, at each fixture in your home, the drainage system passes through a P-shaped trap. This curved pipe holds an amount of water in it after a fixture has been drained, and this prevents gases, bacteria, and insects from coming up into the house through the drain. Every fixture and floor drain in the house, with the exception of the toilets, must be trapped. The toilet contains its own trap. Since the drainage system handles the drain water removal, the waste removal, and the venting that is necessary, it is sometimes referred to as the drainage-waste-removal (DWR) or the drainage-waste-vent (DWV) system.

The drainage system accomplishes drainage and waste removal through the force of gravity. The wastewater passes through a smaller pipe leading from the fixtures into larger, more central pipes that carry the water into the sewer outside the house. The vent pipe in the DWV system carries off the sewer gases and keeps the whole system at atmospheric pressure. This is needed to ensure that some water will stay in each trap. Without the vents, the trap water would drain away or the pressure from the accumulating gases would break the seal and send fumes into the house. Usually the vent pipes enter a larger pipe that goes out through the roof of the house. This pipe, called a vent stack or soil stack, can usually be seen exiting the roof over the bathroom area.

The third part of the home plumbing system is the fixtures themselves. This part of the system includes lavatories, kitchen sinks, basement utility sinks, washing machines, shower stalls, bidets, toilets, tubs, and any fixture with similar components. Most fixtures regulate the flow of water with a faucet or some other type of valve. The drain hole, which is connected to the DWV pipes, is found in the bottom of the fixture's water container.

EXAMINING THE PRESENT SYSTEM

The best time to examine the plumbing system is after the plaster walls have been removed. The process will be even easier if the ceilings also have been removed. If this is not the case, then the system will have to be inspected wherever it can be seen. If the spots you can see are in poor shape, it is usually safe to assume that the same conditions exist inside the walls and ceilings. Normally problems in a plumbing system exist in the supply side, not in the DWV system. You should, however, look at the drainage pipes to determine if they are badly rusted. If you can see the waste pipe beneath a toilet, have someone flush the toilet several times while you watch and listen for leaking. If leaking does occur, remember that it could be as serious as a leak in the waste pipe or as simple as a broken wax-ring seal around the toilet. Check the main drain trap in the basement. Look to see if it shows signs of repeated application of pipe wrench teeth. If so, you should suspect that it has been a problem in the past and will be in the future.

Through the years, the supply pipes and their connectors tend to collect rust and other deposits. Rust can eat away at the joints and cause a leak, and the deposits inside a pipe slowly narrow the inside diameter so that the water flow becomes very restricted. There is no way to remove this corrosion, and if pipes are found to be badly damaged, they must be replaced. The only way to determine the state of the pipe is to take it apart and look inside it. Look particularly at the threads. Since the threads are the thinnest part of the pipe, it usually fails there first. Chapter 15 of *Renovating the Victorian House* by Katherine Rusk (see the reference list at the end of this chapter) has a useful section on how to examine the supply pipe as well as the DWV pipes.

In our opinion, if your house is 50 to 100 years old and you find that it is plumbed with iron pipes, you should replace the system with newer materials. Replacing sections of iron pipes is a difficult process because, as you tighten one end of a section, you will be loosening the other end. In addition, the old iron pipe system is probably inadequate for your needs, and you will want to add a number of branch circuits to accommodate additional fixtures in your rehabbed house. Once the interior walls are removed, it makes sense to remove and replace the existing plumbing system. The additional expense of total replacement will be offset by the security of a leak-free system.

BASIC PLUMBING FACTS

Remember that pipe sizes are expressed as nominal values and those values may not be the same as the actual inside or outside diameter of the pipe. For the most part, these discrepancies are not important, and you may order and use the pipe on the basis of its nominal dimensions. The actual outside diameter of a piece of pipe may be important when it comes to cutting holes in studs for the pipe to pass through, but otherwise it is not crucial.

Types of Supply Pipe

Rigid Copper Pipe

Rigid copper pipe comes in various diameters and in 10- and 20-foot lengths. It also is sold as type M (thin-walled), type L (medium-walled), and type K (thick-walled). If your local codes permit the use of type M, it is adequate for most house plumbing.

Rigid copper may be cut using a tubing cutter or hacksaw. Try to avoid the hacksaw method, though, since it leaves burrs on the cut end that make attaching fittings difficult. These burrs will also catch any foreign material in the line and eventually clog it. If you must use a hacksaw, you will have to file down the burrs before you attach any fittings. Joints are made by sweating the fitting onto the end of the pipe. When measuring rigid copper, remember that you must allow for the distance that the pipe slips into the fitting, which is usually ³/₈ to ½ inch. Measure the pipe face to the fitting's face and then add twice the depth from the face to the inner shoulder of the fitting.

We have found that the best way to build a run of copper pipe is to cut and assemble everything dry, make any adjustments, and then clean and sweat the joints together. One very important thing to remember is that, once you turn on the water and find that you have a leak, it will be virtually impossible for you to get the joint apart if you cannot completely drain the pipe. If you have doubts about how well you are doing in producing tight joints, it's a good idea to sweat a cap on the end of the pipe every few joints, turn on the water, and look for leaks. Caps are very easy to get off when on the end of a run of pipe, even though the pipe may still contain water. Just turn off the water, drill a hole in the cap to drain the water from the pipe, and then heat the cap and remove it.

Flexible Copper Tubing

The major advantage of this type of material is that it can be bent. Often an entire run of pipe can be assembled with fittings only on the ends. This and the absence of tight right-angle bends greatly reduces the friction that slows down water delivery. Flexible pipe is sold in 15- to 100-foot rolls. It is made in type L for general-purpose usage and type K for hard usage. Flexible copper can be cut in the same manner as rigid copper and used with the same type of fittings, which are sweated on in the same fashion. You can also use compression fittings. These are quick to install, but they cannot be removed. Another option is to use flared fittings. Make sure you are familiar with the proper use of the flaring tool.

Rigid Steel Pipe

Most rigid pipe sold today is galvanized steel. To work with this type of pipe, you must have a pipe cutter and a pipe threader. Cutting threads takes some practice, so it is best to start on pieces of pipe that you are not going to use. Once again, there are literally dozens of books that show you how to cut threads in galvanized pipe. For example, consult chapter 12 of Litchfield's *Renovation* (see the reference list at the end of this chapter). For short runs, you can buy precut and prethreaded lengths of pipe at the local hardware store, which will also stock a substantial supply of fittings. One thing to keep in mind when using steel pipe is that the pipe turns into the fittings' threads. This means that, as you are tightening the pipe in a fitting on one end, you are loosening it in the fitting on the other end. Once the pipe is together, this can make it difficult to make repairs. To alleviate this problem, you can install unions, special fittings that allow you to take a pipe apart in the middle of a run and therefore give you enough play to be able to take apart one fitting without disturbing the other one.

PVC Pipe

Not all rigid plastic pipe is polyvinyl chloride (PVC) pipe, though that is what most codes require. Plastic pipe also is made of acrylo-mitrile butadiene-styrene (ABS) and chlorinated polyvinyl chloride (CPVC). Local codes sometimes prevent use of plastic pipe behind walls. In addition, some codes prevent its use in the supply system but permit them in the waste system. These restrictions are unfortunate because this type of pipe is easy to work with. You simply cut it with a hacksaw or a regular wood saw, taking care to allow enough length for the pipe to go into the fittings. Then you clean it, prime it, dress the end with solvent cement and push it into the fitting. Some solvents also contain the primer. The solvent actually melts the two pieces together to form a leakproof bond. Of course, the major disadvantage to this is that you cannot take the pipe apart. However, plastic pipe tends not to be very expensive; it comes in lengths of 10 and 20 feet, and is available in standard dimensions. You can even buy fittings that will join plastic pipe to copper or steel pipe.

Flexible Plastic Tubing

This material has all the advantages of flexible copper tubing, but it should never be used for the hot water supply. Connections are the friction-type, with clamps to ensure that the connection stays intact.

Types of Waste Pipe

Cast Iron

Most rehabbers run into cast-iron waste pipes. These have a rough, black appearance and are quite heavy. It is difficult to cut and work with cast iron, and you should probably turn the job over to a professional plumber. If you want to do repair jobs on your own, you can rent the appropriate tools and get advice from the rental outlet on their use. The traditional method of joining cast-iron pipe is with oakum and lead, a practice that no inexperienced rehabber ought to try. Fortunately, a joint also can be accomplished with a rubber and stainless steel sleeve. The sleeve fits around the joint and then tightens down on it with screw clamps, much like those found on a radiator hose.

ABS and PVC Pipe

Acrylo-mitrile butadiene-styrene (ABS) and polyvinyl chloride (PVC) pipe is lightweight and easy to handle, but, because it is bulky, it is easier if two people work on the job together. ABS pipe is cut and put together the same way as PVC and other types of plastic pipe. One note of caution: In gluing the pipe together, the setting time of the solvent is very short. Decide before fitting the ends together which way you want the pipe fitting to face. Cut the pipe squarely so you get a good fit. Once together, the ends are very difficult to twist. Some kinds of glues can be used with both ABS and PVC pipe, but most are made specifically for use with one or the other.

PLUMBING INSTALLATIONS

Sweated Fittings

The process of sweating fittings on copper pipe is the most common method used and the one that we recommend. You will need a bottled-gas torch, which is available at any hardware store. You just purchase the regulator/nozzle, and it attaches to the bottle of gas. Once the gas is used up, just discard the bottle and buy a new one. You will also need a roll of plumbing solder (buy 50/50 solder, not 60/40), a container of solder flux, a flux brush, and some steel wool. Once you have cut the pipe to the dimensions you need, scour the ends with steel wool until the copper is bright. Then paint the ends of the pipe with flux and place the fitting on the length of pipe. Heat the area around the pipe and fitting and then apply the solder. When the heat is correct, the solder will actually be pulled into the space between the pipe and fitting. It doesn't take much solder to create a good joint.

Roughing In

Putting in new plumbing for a house addition or replacing the existing plumbing usually involves a process called *roughing in*. This is simply the planning, carpentry, and installation of the supply and drainage systems. Always check the local building codes for information about what types of materials you can use and any special steps that you must take. Ventilation systems must be constructed according to code; be sure to check with a plumber. Otherwise, the steps for roughing in are pretty much the same for most projects. Always plan pipe layouts in advance to take advantage of the shortest routes to the points that the system has to serve. Pipes that will go in the floor can parallel the floor joists, and pipes that can go in the attic can run across the ceiling joists. Pipes that go under the first floor can be run under the floor joists in the basement. Pipes that will go in the walls will have to run through the wall studs, and holes will have to be made for these. Remember that when you notch out studs or joists, you should cut out as little as possible. Whenever possible, it is best to drill holes in these members instead of cutting notches.

Most experts on plumbing will tell you to install or replace the DWV system first. This is because the pipes are bigger than those in the supply system, and the latter can be run along the same route as the DWV pipes. Once you have decided where the DWV system will go, you can decide where the drains and the soil stack should go. Figure 16-3 shows the details of a typical DWV system.

The soil stack should be approximately centered in the middle of the fixtures it is to serve, so that

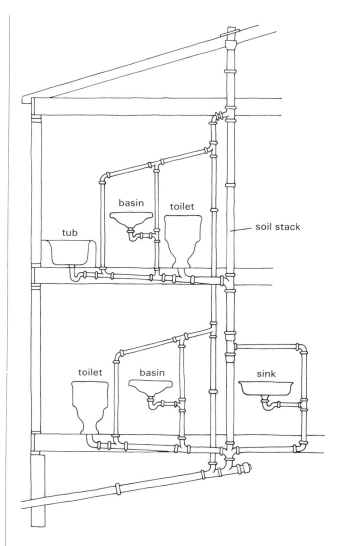

FIGURE 16-3. *A typical DWV system.*

branch drain lines to it can be made conveniently. When installing the stack, it is a good idea to start at the highest floor that will have fixtures and drill a small hole. Hang a plumb bob through the hole down to the floor below so that you can see where the next hole should be drilled. After doing this all the way to the basement, go back up to the first hole and plumb up to the roof to the point where the stack will exit. When you are satisfied that the holes are properly marked, enlarge them so that you can set the stack pipe. Then rough in the additional vent pipes, the closet bend for the toilet, and the branch drains. Your local building codes will detail which fixtures can be on the same stack, and it is critical that you find out these requirements. For exam-

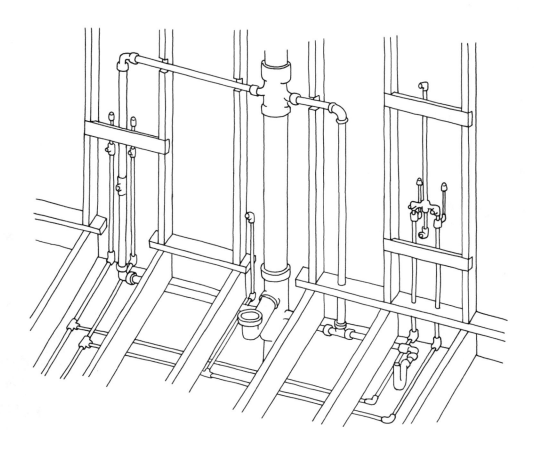

FIGURE 16-4. *A typical rough-in for a one-wall bathroom.*

ple, it is not proper to have a sink on a lower floor attached to the same stack as a toilet on an upper floor. The DWV system generally uses 4-inch sewer lines; 3- to 4-inch main drains, vents, and soil stacks; 3-to 4-inch toilet drains; 2-inch shower drains; and 1½-inch drains for sinks and tubs. Refer to the book *Bathroom* by Donald R. Brann (see the reference list at the end of this chapter) for a complete guide to roughing in and pipe setting. Figure 16-4 shows a typical rough-in for a bathroom wall. Your local chapter of the American Institute of Architects (AIA) can supply a copy of the plumbing code.

The water supply system usually consists of a ¾-or 1-inch service entrance (1½ inches if you have a pool), ¾-inch hot and cold mains, and ½-inch branches to sinks, tubs, showers, dishwashers, and the like. Toilets can be fit with ⅜-inch lines.

If you have town or city water, the connection to your house will have to be made by a licensed plumber. Check the local building codes for specific requirements. As you run the hot and cold water pipes to their respective sites, remember that they should never touch. It is also a good idea to insulate the hot water lines as you go, as this will save a good deal of energy later on. Install water shutoff valves at the site of each fixture and between each floor. This will make repairs much easier than if they were not there.

Installing the Toilet

If you are replacing the old toilet, keep in mind that the rough-in for the old one may not be correct for the new one. The rough-in dimension is the distance from the wall against which the toilet sits, out to the center of the floor flange to which it will attach. Most toilet rough-ins are 12 inches. If the 12-inch toilet will fall over a joist, you can purchase a 15-inch toilet. In addition, note that old toilets usually had four floor flange bolts and new ones normally have two. The extra bolts can simply be removed. Remember to install a water shutoff valve in the supply line to the toilet.

If you are doing new or replacement rough-in, the closet bend that connects to the toilet floor flange and the soil stack can present a problem. The closet bend should be run between two floor joists so that a support can be nailed under the bend and between the joists. The closet bend then attaches to the sanitary T or Y, which fits into the soil stack. The makeup of the sanitary T/closet bend installation is slightly different depending on whether the pipe is to be run parallel with the floor joists or under the joists. Figure 16-5 details both kinds of installation.

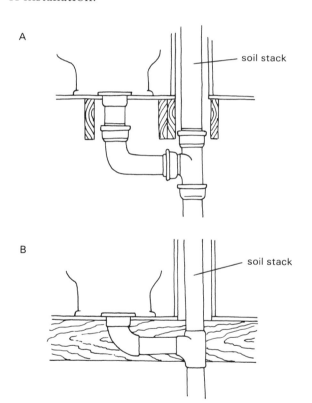

FIGURE 16-5. *Two methods of installing a sanitary T/closet bend under the toilet fixture: running under the joists (A), or parallel with the joists (B).*

Installing the Tub

The first thing you should do when installing a new tub is to make sure that you have enough room to do so. Most new tubs are at least 5 feet long and are designed to be closed in on three sides. The

supply pipes are usually brought up to 32 inches above the floor. The tub spout is centered at 22 inches above the floor. Make sure that you measure the opening on the tub for the spout before you run the pipe. If the tub that you removed was the freestanding type, you will have to box in some excess space. Try to do this at the head of the tub because the extra space there will be handy if later repairs are needed. A small trapdoor on the opposite side of the wall at the head of the tub will be necessary for access to the tub hookup components. Keep in mind that the old tub may be salvageable, as you might be able to redo the finish. This is especially important to consider if the tub has clawed feet, as it might be quite valuable.

Installing the Shower

Showers can be purchased as prefabricated enclosures that fit into roughed-in areas in the bathroom, or they can be built as custom units. If you choose to build a shower rather than buy a prefabricated one, it is important to remember that the shower floor must be waterproof. The easiest way to ensure this is to purchase a prefabricated shower pan. These come in standard dimensions, so be sure that your shower will accommodate the pan. The shower pan has a drain attached to it that easily hooks up to the floor drain. Also remember that a custom-built shower will have to be made of special waterproof drywall. Fixtures in a custom-made shower can be placed wherever they are most convenient, but 3 to 4 feet from the floor for faucets and 5 to 6 feet for shower heads is about right.

Installing the Sink

Sink installation is very easy with the use of plastic washers for the drain connection and compression fittings for the supply connections. If you are removing and reinstalling according to an existing rough-in, you can buy flexible tubing to make the supply connections with the walls. This will prevent having to reroute the wall supply. It is wise to replace all the drainage fittings, as they will probably be well worn and full of deposits. Use plastic washers between all the fittings for a tight seal.

The Laundry Room

Give careful consideration to including a well-planned laundry facility in your rehab. In addition to the drain for the washing machine, you should have a drain hookup for a laundry tub, which should have hot and cold faucets. A tub is invaluable when you have paintbrushes to wash or have been working on your car and need a place to clean up. Most laundry rooms are required by code to have a floor drain.

References

OLD

Bennett, Samuel Barlow. *A Manual of Technical Plumbing and Sanitary Science.* London: N.P., 1910.

Cosgrove, John Joseph. *Principles and Practices of Plumbing.* Pittsburgh: Standard Sanitary Mfg. Co., 1914.

Detrick Supply Co. Illustrated Catalogue of Plumbing and Sanitary Goods. St. Louis: Buxton and Skinner Stationary Co., 1896.

Dye, Frederick William. *Hot Water Supply.* 8th Ed. New York: Chemical Publishing Co., 1937.

Plumbing, Heating, Air Conditioning, Water Systems: Catalog. Chicago: Crane Co., 1935–36.

Porcelain-Lined Baths and Sanitary Plumbing Supplies. New Brighton, Pennsylvania: Dawes and Myler, 1894.

Sugg, William T. *The Domestic Use of Coal Gas as Applied to Lighting, Cooking, Heating and Ventilation.* London: W. King, 1884.

NEW

Alth, Max. *Do-It-Yourself Plumbing.* New York: Harper & Row, 1986.

Better Homes and Gardens Do-It-Yourself Plumbing. Des Moines, Iowa: Meredith Corp., 1989.

Brann, Donald R. *Bathroom.* Briarcliff Manor, New York: Directions Simplified, Inc., 1974.

Hicks, Tyler G. *Plumbing Design & Installation Reference Guide.* New York: McGraw-Hill, 1986.

Litchfield. Michael W. *Renovation: A Complete Guide.* New York: John Wiley & Sons, 1983.

Rusk, Katherine. *Renovating the Victorian House.* San Francisco: 101 Productions, 1982.

Sullivan, James A. *Plumbing: Installation and Design.* Englewood Cliffs, New Jersey: Prentice-Hall, 1980.

Traister, John E. *Planning & Designing Plumbing Systems.* Carlsbad, California: Craftsman Book Co., 1983.

Zim, Herbert S. *Pipes and Plumbing Systems.* New York: Morrow, 1974.

Chapter 17

ELECTRICAL SYSTEMS

You can do many types of electrical projects yourself. Some basic knowledge is required, however, because mistakes can be lethal. It is extremely important that all electrical work be done according to local and national electrical codes.

HOW ELECTRICITY WORKS

Electricity is such a common item that we rarely if ever think about where it comes from or what it is. Briefly, electricity is the flow of electrons through a conductor. Electrons have a negative charge, and because of this, they are attracted to a positive charge. The positive charge is provided by the power station. Since your house and the generating power station are connected by wires (conductors) the current flows between your house and the power station.

Most modern electrical wire consists of two conductors, one white and one black, and a third, uninsulated or green wire that acts as a ground. The black wire is the hot wire, and the white is the neutral wire. A convenient though oversimplified way of thinking about the flow of electricity is that it flows to your house through the black wire and returns to the power station through the white wire. The green wire does not conduct any electricity unless there is a failure in the circuit. If that happens, electricity is shunted through the ground wire to the earth.

Three terms are used most commonly when talking about electricity. They are voltage, amperage, and wattage. Think of the flow of electricity as if it were water flowing through a garden hose. The *voltage* is like the pressure of the water in the hose, the *amperage* is the speed at which the water flows, and the *wattage* is the total amount of water that flows past a certain point in the hose in a given time.

The electricity travels to your house over power lines that may carry as much as 10,000 volts. The voltage is stepped down to a value usable in your home by a transformer. Usually this transformer can be seen up on a pole in back of either your house or your neighbor's. The service to your house is through a two-line (one hot and one neutral) or a three-line (two hot and one neutral) system. The two-line system carries 120 volts and, the three-line system carries 240 volts. The former is usually found only in old homes and is usually inadequate for modern usage. The wires enter your house through the service head and go into the service box.

Inside the service box is the fuse box or circuit breaker panel. The hot wires attach to the main power lugs, and the neutral wires attach to the main neutral lugs. In addition, a grounding bus, which has a large copper wire running from it to a pipe (usually a water pipe), ultimately travels out into your yard. Running down inside the service box are the bus bars, containing fuses or circuit breakers for all the branch circuits in your house. In almost all 120-volt installations and hookups, it is important to attach the wires black to black and white to white. Never mix them. In 240-volt installations, such as those for electric ranges or some electric dryers, there will be two hot wires (one red and one black) and one neutral wire (white).

FUSES, BREAKERS, AND GROUNDS

Fuses come in two types, screw-in and cartridge. In both cases, the primary element is a metal strip that is made to handle the heat caused by a certain amperage rating. If the circuit overloads, the heat increases and the metal strip melts, which causes the circuit to be open. A circuit breaker has a thin strip of metal that bends when the circuit overloads and causes the breaker to trip and the circuit to open up. In both cases, the open circuit prevents the flow of current. Fuses and breakers should be installed with caution and should never be larger than the amperage rating of the circuit.

Another type of circuit breaker is the ground fault interrupter (GFI). Sometimes a fault will occur in a wiring circuit that is not great enough to trip a standard circuit breaker. Nevertheless, under certain circumstances, these small faults can cause great damage. For example, a very small current leakage that occurs in a bathroom where there is a good deal of water could cause someone to experience a life-threatening shock, whereas it may have been felt only as a tingle if it had occurred in a dry place. For this reason, most codes require that all circuits in bathrooms and outside the house be ground faulted. GFIs are easily installed by following the directions that come with the devices. We highly recommend their use.

The ground wire in the circuit is designed to shunt a short circuit to the earth. Electricity will take the path of least resistance, and if a circuit should short or if a person touches both the hot and neutral wires of a circuit, the path of least resistance may be through that person's body. The earth is such a large neutral body that a properly grounded circuit always provides the path of least resistance, thus preventing potentially life-threatening situations. Inside every modern service box you will find the grounding bus, and all circuits should have a grounding wire running to the bus. Never ignore this part of your circuit and never break off the round ground lug on an electrical plug.

DO YOU NEED AN ELECTRICIAN?

Wiring is basically an easy job, and hundreds of books on the subject are available (see the reference list at the end of this chapter). Despite these aids, you might think that it is not safe for you to do your own wiring. If you take a few precautions and learn some fundamental procedures, however, you can wire a house without incident. It is important to understand that many local building codes require that you at least consult with a licensed electrician before you begin any wiring job. Check this out. You will probably find that it is okay to do your own wiring if you have the proper permit. The catch might be that you will have to pass a very simple test of wiring before you receive the permit. Usually these one-page tests consist of questions about wiring switches, how many outlets to a circuit and how far apart they can be, how often you must secure the wires to the studs, what type of wire must be used, and other such questions. Since the test will be specific to the codes in your area, consult the building commission concerning the requirements for owner-occupied electrical installation.

Wiring in the United States must be installed according to the National Electrical Code. In most cases, this national standard has been incorporated into local municipal codes. The primary reason for the code is safety, and you should never attempt to do things that deviate from it. A copy of the electrical code can usually be purchased at your local building supply outlet. It is also published in various books on wiring.

A final word of caution: Never attempt to complete the outside wiring hookup to your box or to set up the box itself. These tasks should always be left to a licensed electrician.

SAFETY TIPS

At one time or another, most of us have come into contact with a live wire and received a shock. While this was probably an unpleasant experience, it by no means seems to warrant all the fuss that is made about working with electricity. Beware of this attitude: The same minor shock that you received in the past could kill you under the right conditions, and since it is difficult to predict what those conditions might be, it is extremely important that you respect the electrical current. If you follow these simple precautions, the chances of your having a life-threatening accident will be slim.

The first and most important safety tip is to make sure that, before you begin to work on a circuit, you turn off the power at the main supply box. After you have turned off the power, make sure that it is off at the point where you will be working. This check is most easily accomplished by making or buying a circuit tester. Taking this simple precaution might save your life.

Since water is a very good conductor of electricity, you should make sure that the place where you will stand while working is dry. In addition, you can decrease your chances of receiving a shock by wearing rubber-soled shoes and rubber-lined gloves and using tools that have rubber insulation on the handles.

Always make sure that you know where you are drilling or sawing when you perform these tasks. If you are not sure what is inside the wall that you will be cutting or drilling into, it is important that you turn off all electricity before proceeding. Also, do not hold on to any plumbing pipes while you are working with an electrical circuit.

BASIC ELECTRICAL TOOLS

Wire Stripper. This device has holes in it designed to strip the insulation cleanly off wire of various gauges. Wire stripping can be done with a knife, but a stripper makes the job go more quickly and helps you avoid the possibility of cutting a finger.

Pliers. You will need a pair of side cutters for cutting the wire, a pair of electrician's pliers for bending and twisting the wire, and a pair of needle-nose pliers for getting wire into and out of tight places.

Screwdriver. This will be used for tightening down the wire lugs on switches.

Circuit Tester. This is a very important safety tool, as well as a tool for determining if you have made the proper connections. You can either purchase one of these or make one yourself. Making it yourself is easy. Just purchase a light bulb socket from your local hardware store and attach wires to the terminals. Strip the insulation back about $1/8$ inch on both wires and screw in a light bulb. Now, when you wish to determine if a circuit is live, just touch the two wires to the two sides of the circuit and see if the bulb lights up. Be sure to check that the bulb is good before using it in a test.

Wire fishing tape. If you will be running wire through studs that are behind finished walls, this

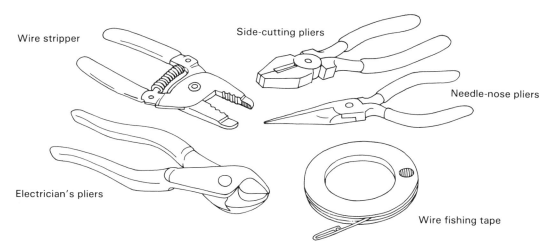

FIGURE 17-1. *Basic electrical tools.*

is an indispensable item. The tape allows you to pull the wire to the place where you want the light or switch outlet. Basically, this is just a roll of flat, springlike wire that can be pushed into holes in the walls and ceilings. The end of the tape has a hook on it for catching or attaching the wire that is to be pulled.

Miscellaneous tools. Electrician's tape, wire nuts, a wood saw, a drill, and drill bits.

ASSESSING YOUR WIRING NEEDS

In most cases, the wiring that came with your old house will not be sufficient for the electrical needs of many modern appliances. The first step in assessing your system is to find the electrical service box and look inside it. Do you see fuses? Are there lots of them or just a few? If you see just a few fuses, you probably ought to replace them with a multi-circuit circuit breaker box. It is much easier to add circuits to this type of box, as you just have to add circuit breakers when needed.

While you are looking into the service box, note whether there are two or three large wires entering the house from the street. If there are only two, then you have 120-volt service, and that will not be enough for an electric range, dryer, or air conditioner. Note the amperage of the service box. In most old boxes, the service rating will be 30 to 60 amps, which is not enough to power a newer home. You will need a box with a rating of at least 100 to 200 amps.

The next thing to observe is the type of wire that leads away from your service box. If your house is old, chances are that it will have nob and tube wiring, in which the wires run through ceramic tubes and around ceramic nob insulators. Notice the state of the insulation on the wire. Is it frayed? Does it crack when you bend it? If so, you should think about replacing the wiring. Also check the state of the wire insulation in the attic.

Before beginning to restructure your wiring and electrical service, take a few minutes to decide how much power you will need on each circuit and how many circuits you will need. For the most part, the electrical code will help you determine how many circuits and what rating you need. For example, the code indicates that you should have separate lighting and appliance circuits. Lighting circuits should be rated at 15 amps, and there should be one 15-amp circuit for about every 500 square feet of floor space. The small appliance circuits should be 20-amp, and no more than 1,500 watts should be connected to any one circuit. Most local codes require that there be a wall receptacle every 12 feet and that no space along the wall be more than six feet from a receptacle. The number of outlets per circuit is fixed by your local code but probably will be limited to about nine or ten outlets per 15-amp circuit and 12 per 20-amp circuit. Each stationary appliance should have its own circuit. The kitchen should have three circuits. Remember, the bathroom circuits, as well as those in other wet areas, should be ground-faulted.

To decide what the total capacity will be in your system, add up the wattage of (1) the lighting and general use circuits, (2) the small appliance circuits, (3) the laundry circuit, (4) the major appliance circuits, and (5) the heating and air-conditioning system. You can calculate the wattage of the general use circuits by estimating the total square footage of the house. Multiply the square footage by three watts. Next give each small appliance circuit and the laundry circuit 1,500 watts each. The wattage values of the major appliances will be listed on the nameplate of each. This will also be true of the air conditioner and furnace. Once you have totaled up this wattage, you can divide the sum by 240 volts to determine the size (in amps) of the service box you need. Convenient charts for calculating loads are given in many books on electrical systems.

INSTALLING NEW WORK

Types of Wire

Wire comes in various sizes and is constructed in various ways according to the way it will be used. The most common sizes of wire are, from smallest to largest, numbers 14, 12, and 10. These are used in circuits that have amperage ratings of 15, 20, and

30, respectively. Larger wire sizes, such as number 8 for 40-amp circuits and number 6 for 50-amp circuits, will be used for items such as stoves, ovens, and dryers. Plastic-sheathed solid wire is the most commonly used wire. There are three principal types: NM, used in most indoor installations; NMC, used indoors where moisture might exist; and UF, used in underground applications. Another type of wire is called BX. This wire is armor-wrapped cable with a flexible outer covering of galvanized steel and either two or three conductors on the inside wrapped in paper. BX has no ground wire, as the metal of the cable armor is connected to the metal of the outlet boxes to provide the continuity to ground. BX is usually used in dry indoor applications where it is important to protect the wire from nails and other carpentry projects. Finally, individual wire can be run in conduits for areas where the wire must be protected (for example, basement walls).

The term *new work* generally refers to work that is done when the walls are not in place. If you have gutted your dwelling and are redoing the wiring, you are doing new work. If the walls are still in place and you are doing wiring, then you are doing old work.

Running the Wire

Normally the work will be done with number 12 or 14 wire. This wire has two conductors (one white and one black) and also an uninsulated ground wire. Some of the work you do will involve three-way switches, which require three conductors, plus a ground wire, but most of the wiring can be done with two-conductor wire. Always use copper wire.

Assuming that there is no drywall or plaster to impede your progress, you should begin by locating the positions of all the outlet boxes and ceiling fixtures. Drill holes through all the studs and run the wire through the holes, starting at the outlet box that is farthest away from the service panel. Staple down the wire every 2 feet or so (check the code in your area). Usually the wire must be stapled within 12 inches of each box. Wire that will be run to the ceiling boxes can be run under the floor joists if a suspended ceiling will eventually be used. If the ceiling will be attached directly to the underside of the joists, the wire will have to be run through drilled holes. Pull about a foot of wire out of each junction box so that you will have plenty to work with when you begin to attach the receptacles and switches. Also, as you run the wire, it is a good idea to leave a surplus loop once in a while in case you have misjudged the distance.

Placing the Wall Boxes

Wall boxes are usually placed about 12 inches above the finished floor, and switch boxes are usually about 4 feet up the wall. When you place switch boxes near doors, be sure that they are on the side opposite from the hinges. Whether you place a switch for a room on the outside of the wall or the inside is a matter of preference, but it is sometimes easier if the switch is outside the room. You need special receptacles for 220-volt circuit outlets, and the wire size will be much larger than that used for typical 110-volt circuits.

Placing the Ceiling Boxes

Boxes for ceiling lights are usually placed in the center of the area to be lighted. If the area is large, you will want to install several fixtures, so you will have to divide the room evenly, with the boxes at equal distances from one another. If you do not have a ceiling fixture, tie one wall plug into a switch near the door.

The type of ceiling or wall box you should use is dictated in part by the local code. Boxes are made of metal or plastic. Most have a tab through which you can drive a nail to attach the box to a stud. Some even have nails preattached so that all you have to do is drive them into the stud. Some boxes have a mounting depth gauge etched onto the box so that you can see how far the box should stick out from the wall and thus can account for the finished thickness. If you intend to hang heavy light fixtures or fans from a ceiling box, you will have to purchase a special box that hangs across two ceiling joists. You also can hang these heavy fixtures from a standard metal box if it is secured with screws to a block nailed between two joists.

Attaching the Wire to the Switches and Receptacles

Attaching the wire is pretty straightforward. You

must first strip off about 6 to 8 inches of the outside insulation so that you have the individual wires exposed. Make sure that the outside insulation is still intact where the wire exits the box to prevent wearing or breaking of the individual inside wires. Then strip off about 1 to 1½ inches of insulation so that you can make a loop to go around the switch or receptacle attaching screws. You can stick ⅜ inch of stripped wire into the back of modern switches and receptacles, but we recommend taking the extra attaching time to fasten the wire to the screws. Splice the wires together with wire nuts, as these will provide a tight fit that can later be undone if something needs to be done to the system before it is finished. Wire nuts come in different sizes to fit the number of wires that are joined together. Ground wires should always be attached to the switches and to the grounding (green) screw on the receptacles.

Common Types of Connections

Figure 17-2 shows some of the more common types of connections. These diagrams should provide you with the information you need to wire many two-way switches, three-way switches, and other types of switches, lights, and outlets. Answers to less common wiring questions can be found in the references listed at the end of this chapter.

INSTALLING OLD WORK

Perhaps the easiest method to determine where an old circuit goes and how much power is on it is to throw all the circuit breakers or unscrew all the fuses except for the circuit in question. Then it is a simple matter of going around the house with a lamp, plugging it into each receptacle that you come across, and throwing each switch that you see. By doing this and keeping notes of watts and amperes, you can determine where the circuit goes and what it does.

Installation of additional wall outlets, switches, and lights is usually a matter of deciding where you want them to be and then figuring out where you are going to tap into the power supply to add onto the circuit. The most convenient place to tap into

the circuit is at a wall outlet. Sometimes this will not be possible, and you will have to go into the attic or the basement to find a circuit that you can use. The rest of the problem is figuring out how to run the wire for the addition and cause the least disturbance of existing wall structures. Any empty space in the wall is fair game when it comes to this activity. If the run of new wire is of any length, you will often have to "fish" the wire from one spot to another. This is done with wire fishing tape and a helper. One person feeds the tape through the space where the wire will run, and the other person looks for it to appear. Once he or she sees it, the wire can be pulled out of the space, the new wire can be attached to it, and it can be pulled back in the opposite direction with the wire attached. While this description sounds easy, it is often a very frustrating experience and requires great patience. Figure 17-3 illustrates this activity.

SPECIAL PURPOSE OUTLETS

Water heaters, electric stoves, air conditioners, clothes dryers, and other heavy users of electricity require 240-volt service and special wire and connectors. It is best to consult the wiring diagrams of the items that are to be hooked up for information about the type of wire that is required. In most cases, the 240-volt circuit will be run on number 8 or 10 three-conductor wire into special 240-volt outlets. A short three-wire cable with a special plug called a pigtail is usually attached between the 240-volt appliance and the outlet. (Hot water heaters, furnaces, and permanent air-conditioners are normally wired directly to the service.) Since the loads involved in a typical 240-volt system are large, it is important to pay close attention to details. Each should be on its own circuit. If you do not feel up to the task, it may be wise to call in a professional electrician.

If you have made a careful assessment of your potential electrical needs and have allowed for plenty of circuits and outlets, your finished wiring project should be a source of pride. If you have completed the project carefully and according to code, you should have years of trouble-free service.

FIGURE 17-2. *Common types of electrical connections.*

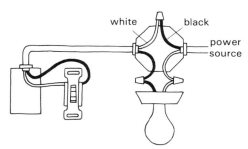

17-2A. *Wall switch controlling ceiling fixture at end of run.*

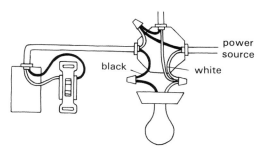

17-2B. *Wall switch controlling ceiling fixture in middle of run.*

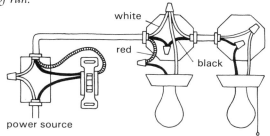

17-2C. *Two fixtures on same line controlled by different switches.*

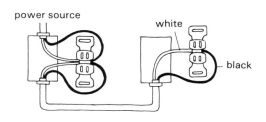

17-2D. *Adding a supplementary outlet.*

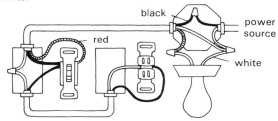

17-2E. *Adding a new switch and outlet to an existing fixture.*

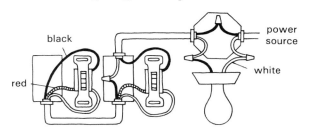

17-2F. *Same ceiling fixture controlled by two different switches.*

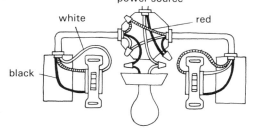

17-2G. *Ceiling fixture between two switches, controlled by either.*

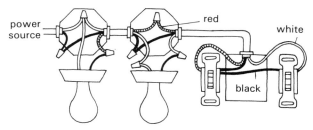

17-2H. *Two separate fixtures controlled by two switches.*

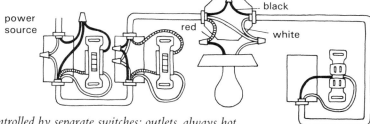

17-2I. *Fixture controlled by separate switches; outlets always hot.*

FIGURE 17–3. *Fishing an electrical wire using metal tape.*

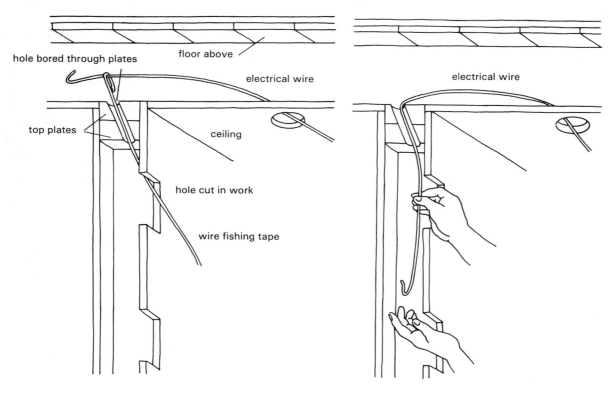

17–3A. *Fishing the wire.*

17–3B. *Pulling through the wire.*

References

OLD

Graham, Frank D. *Hawkins Electrical Guide.* 2nd Ed. New York: T. Audel & Co., 1925.

Horstmann, Henry Charles. *Modern Illumination: Theory and Practice.* Chicago: F.J. Drake and Co., 1912.

Wilcox, Edgar Andrew. *Electrical Heating.* San Francisco: Technical Publishing Co., 1916.

NEW

Complete Do-it-yourself Manual. Pleasantville, New York: Reader's Digest Books, 1981.

Guide to Electrical Installation and Repair. New York: McGraw-Hill, 1979.

Kittle, James L. *Mastering Household Electrical Wiring.* Blue Ridge Summit, Pennsylvania: TAB Books, 1983.

Mullin, Ray C. *Electrical Wiring Residential: Code, Theory, Plans, Specifications, Installation Methods.* New York: Van Nostrand Reinhold, 1979.

Richter, H.P. *Wiring Simplified.* St. Paul: Park Publishing Co., 1983.

Traister, John E. *Practical Electrical Installation, Repair & Rewiring.* Blue Ridge Summit, Pennsylvania: TAB Books, 1979.

Chapter 18

HEATING AND COOLING SYSTEMS

Heat moves around your house in three ways:

- By *conduction,* where the heat moves from a warmer position to a colder position. This is why heat is continually being lost to the outside through the walls and windows of your home.

- By *radiation,* where a warmer object gives off heat to the surrounding cooler air. The freestanding wood stove is a good example of this principle in action.

- By *convection,* where heated air rises to the ceiling, cools, and gradually falls back to floor level.

The heating capacity of a system is typically given in British thermal units (Btu's). A Btu is the amount of heat required to raise the temperature of one pound of water 1°F. If you calculate the heat loss in your house, you can then figure the Btu's per hour rating needed in the furnace. Obviously, you should select a furnace with a rating that matches the heat loss of the area being heated. Btu ratings are usually printed on the nameplate of the furnace.

The air-cooling capacity of the air-conditioning (AC) system is given in tons of refrigeration. A ton of refrigeration is the amount of heat required to melt a ton of ice in one day and is roughly equivalent to 12,000 Btu's per hour. Put slightly differently, one ton of refrigeration is comparable to the cooling effect of melting one ton of ice over a 24-hour period.

Heat load is the amount of heat lost in a building and is expressed in Btu's. Heat load can be calculated by taking into account the total volume of the space, the effects of humidity, the insulation, and the window and door area. There are several methods for determining the heat load of a dwelling (see, for example, *Central Heating and Air Conditioning Repair Guide* by Price and Price, listed in the references at the end of this chapter). Several books also contain information on calculating cooling loads. Anyone contemplating the purchase of a new heating or AC system should be familiar with these calculations.

TYPES OF HEATING SYSTEMS FOUND IN OLDER HOMES

Until the invention of the oil heating stove, the fireplace was the main source of heat in the home. Chances are that if your house is old, it will have one or more fireplaces. While fireplaces are nice to have and add a certain charm to any room, they are not particularly efficient sources of heat. In a poorly designed fireplace, most of the Btu's go right up the chimney and never reach the room. However, fireplaces can be made more efficient, as we discuss later in this chapter.

In general, old heating and cooling systems are not very energy-efficient. In this section, we discuss various types of heating systems and some of the advantages and disadvantages of each.

Hot Water and Steam Heat

Both of these systems depend on heating water in a boiler to circulate the heat through the house. The water is heated by running it through tubes that are exposed to the heat source. Old boilers tend to be quite inefficient, and if you decide to keep your hot water or steam system, you should purchase a newer, more efficient boiler.

can be somewhat noisy if there is air in the system.

Gravity Feed Furnaces

Developed in the 1930s, gravity feed furnaces were the first modern central heating systems. These furnaces were usually located in the basement and were

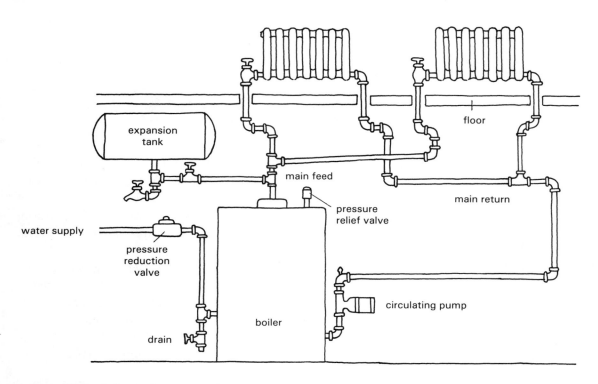

FIGURE 18-1. *A basic hot water heating system.*

In the hot water system, water is heated in a boiler and pumped through circulating pipes to the various rooms in the house. The heat is exchanged with the surrounding air by means of radiators. The water circulates through the radiators and, as it loses its heat, it drains back down to the boiler, where it is reheated and recirculated. Figure 18-1 shows the basic design of the hot water system.

In the steam system, water is heated in the boiler until it becomes steam. It then rises under its own pressure to the radiators. As the heat in the steam is exchanged with the cooler air, it returns to its liquid state and flows back to the boiler, where it is reheated and recirculated. Figure 18-2 shows the design of a typical steam system. These systems are relatively clean, but do not provide for cooling and

connected to cold air returns. As the cold air settled into the returns, it was heated by the furnace. As the air was heated, it expanded and rose through the floor registers to heat the house. Since these furnaces were convection heaters, and since heated air moving by convection doesn't go far before it cools, these furnaces heated only the rooms directly above them.

Forced Air Systems

These systems have been used since just after World War II. In the beginning, they were usually fed by modified gravity feed furnaces. The blowers that were added were able to force the hot air to distant parts of the house, thus providing a more even heat throughout the house. Several types of forced air heating systems are discussed later in this chapter.

TYPES OF MODERN HEATING SYSTEMS

Most experts agree that if your present heating system is ten or more years old, you will probably save money by replacing it with a newer, more energy-efficient system. If the system in your house is one of the type described in the previous paragraphs, you will realize an even more substantial savings by replacing it. If you live in the northern part of the United States and are heating with hot water or steam, you may be spending a great deal of money. Chances are that a replacement boiler will pay for itself in just a few heating seasons. In this section, we discuss some of the pros and cons of several modern systems.

Gas and Oil Forced Air

These systems work in approximately the same way. The choice of whether to install oil or gas depends largely on the cost of each in your area. One advantage of gas heat is that it can be contained in a smaller package. If you have severe space limitations, you probably should install gas rather than oil. In either case, a burner mixes the fuel and air together and heats a surface called a heat exchanger. A fan in the furnace forces the air over the heat exchanger and into the house through the duct work. The primary disadvantages of both gas and oil, are that they use an open flame and they tend to be dirty.

A relatively new product, the high-efficiency gas furnace, lends itself well to rehabs. In one such system, the energy transfer occurs between an enclosed gas flame and an enclosed system of antifreeze and water. This heated solution is sent to the existing duct work via PVC pipe, where it is circulated in a standard heat exchanger that has air blown over it. The combustion gases are somewhat cooler than in a standard forced air system and can be routed to the outside through PVC. The energy savings with a system like this can be substantial. We recommend a high-efficiency gas forced air system over all others.

Electric

Some electric heat works on the principle of forced air, but the heat exchanger is an electric coil. The rest of the operation is the same as with gas or oil. In other electric systems, the heat is provided by strip heaters that run along the base of the walls. Electric heat also can be provided by installing heating elements in the ceiling, floor, or walls. This is called *radiant heat*. You can run radiant heating cables in the walls of a new construction, or you can buy wall and ceiling panels that contain the heating elements. One of the advantages of this type of electric heat is that it is decentralized, which means you can have zone heating, or individual thermostats in each room. When you do not want to heat a particular part of the house, you simply turn off the thermostat. For successful use of electric heat, the house must be well insulated, as electricity is expensive. In many areas of the country, the cost of electricity may be too high to consider it as a heat source.

Heat Pumps

A heat pump is sort of an air conditioner in reverse. In the winter, it extracts heat from the outside air (yes, there is heat in cold winter air) and transfers it indoors. In the summer, it works in reverse to draw heat from the house and transfer it to the outside. Once the thermostat is set to the temperature you desire, the heat pump automatically reverses itself to maintain that temperature. A heat pump consists of an outdoor coil, an indoor coil, and a compressor. The coils contain a refrigerant that picks up the heat from either the outside or the inside and transfers it to a compressor, where it is dispersed. Indoor air is forced through duct work in the same fashion as with gas or oil furnaces.

If you live in an exceptionally cold climate, where the temperature drops to below 15°F. on a regular basis, a heat pump is not a good choice. Under those circumstances, you need a supplementary heating system. In addition, good insulation is needed to make the heat pump option workable. It is best to have 9 inches of insulation in the attic and 4 to 6 inches in the walls. Storm windows and doors also are a must. Even then, you must remember that the heat pump will work 12 months out of the year instead of just six, so it may not be cost-efficient over its total life. Heat pumps also provide rather lukewarm air, which may not be desirable for those accustomed to gas forced air heat.

OTHER TYPES OF HEATING SYSTEMS

Wood

Nothing smells as wonderful as a burning fireplace on a cool autumn morning, and nothing is as relaxing as looking into the dancing flames of a fire in a stove or fireplace. At one time in this century, wood was the principal method of heating, but it fell out of favor when more efficient and less demanding methods came into use. Wood has made a comeback in recent years, however, and it could be considered as a primary or supplemental heating method.

Like electric heat, wood heat is radiant—that is, as the stove warms up, it heats all the surrounding surfaces in the house, and they in turn give off heat. This type of heat is far more even and constant than that provided by a forced air system, where the heat rises and falls depending on where you are in the thermostat's cycle.

When contemplating wood heat, most people think of the potential fire hazard that an open flame presents, but wood heat is as safe as any other if you take a few common-sense precautions. Your local building codes will have something to say about the installation of wood stoves, and you should follow these rules to the letter. In addition, you must clean the chimney about once a month during the heating season, depending upon the type of wood you burn. As wood burns, it deposits a layer of creosote in the chimney. This is extremely flammable if it is allowed to build up. Cleaning the chimney is not a difficult task and takes only about an hour once a month. In addition, the wood stove must be thoroughly cleaned and inspected each year before the heating season. You can either hire a professional chimney sweep to do this or do it yourself.

Many types of stoves and fireplace inserts are available for burning wood. Some stoves are more efficient than others. A reputable dealer should be able to help you make the right choice. Many books about heating with wood also are available (see the reference list at the end of this chapter).

Solar

Many people want to use the sun's energy to heat their homes. Whether you can use solar heat and to what extent you can use it depends largely on where you live and the number of sunny days that you have during the year.

Solar systems are generally classified into two types—*passive*, or those requiring no additional energy to make the system work, and *active*, or those that require additional energy. Usually the additional energy is electricity, which is used to help circulate the solar-heated water from the solar panels to the living areas.

One of the most popular and cost-effective applications of solar technology is in solar water heaters. These can be a very good buy and can pay back your original investment in as little as five years. Solar space-heating systems, however, are very costly, and the payback period can extend over 20 years or more. If you are interested in solar heating systems, consult *Solar Age* and *New Shelter* magazines.

Even if you choose not to install an active or passive solar water-heating system or a solar space-heating system, you can do a number of things to heat your house with sunlight. Since the south side of your house faces the sun, you can give thought to adding additional windows along that wall. If you do, you also will have to give some thought to reducing heat loss through the windows. In addition, you can install one or more greenhouses in your house. If these greenhouses have heavy slate or brick floors, or they are attached to a brick wall, they will trap heat during the day and slowly release it during the evening and night. Actually, you can add a thermal mass wherever the sun will fall on it. Thermal masses can be brick walls or tubes of water. An easy way to take advantage of the greenhouse effect and the thermal mass effect is to add a greenhouse along an existing south-facing masonry wall. The wall collects the radiant heat, and the greenhouse traps it for later release after the sun has gone down.

CALCULATING HEAT AND COOLING LOADS

Before you get to the point of purchasing a heating and/or cooling system, you need to calculate your heat and/or cooling load. There are a number of ways to calculate the heat load, or the amount of heat that is escaping while the furnace is running. One method is to apply the k-factors of the materials from which your house is constructed and then calculate the U-factor. The U-factor is the sum of all of the k-factors, or the heat transfer through the entire wall, not just the component parts. Lists of k-factors, such as the one in Table 18-1, are available at your local building supply outlet.

The first step in such a calculation is to find the k-factors for each of the materials used in the walls

TABLE 18-1
CONDUCTIVITIES (K-FACTORS) FOR VARIOUS MATERIALS

Material	Thickness (inches)	k-factor
Corkboard	1	0.27
Glassfoam	1	0.40
Glass fiber	1	0.27
Mineral wool	1	0.29
Polystyrene foam	1	0.25
Wood fiber	1	0.33
Cork (granulated)	1	0.31
Sawdust	1	0.41
Pine	1	0.86
Fir	1	0.67
Brick wall	8	0.50
Brick wall	12	0.30
Brick wall	12 (½" plaster)	0.25
Stone wall	8	0.70
Stone wall	12	0.50
Poured concrete	8	0.70
Poured concrete	12	0.50
Concrete block	8 (air space)	0.55
Concrete block	12	0.45
Cinder block	8	0.50
Cinder block	12	0.35

and ceilings of your home. Then use the following formula to obtain the U-factor:

To find the U-factor, you will first have to find the k-factors of the materials used. The U-factor equals

$$\cfrac{1}{\cfrac{\text{thickness of A}}{\text{k-factor of A}} + \cfrac{\text{thickness of B}}{\text{k-factor of B}} + \cfrac{\text{thickness of C}}{\text{k-factor of C}}}$$

where A, B and C are the different materials in the wall.

The U-factor is a measure of the number of Btu's that will escape from the house each hour. Your furnace will have to be large enough to keep up with this loss. If heating is the concern, the U-factor indicates how much heat is escaping from the inside. If cooling is the consideration, the U-factor is a measure of how much heat is coming in through the walls. If this sounds like a complicated method of finding the heat or cooling load, you can use charts developed by the Air Conditioning and Refrigeration Institute and the Central Heating and Air Conditioning Institute. The use of these charts is beyond the scope of this book, but *Central Heating and Air Conditioning Repair Guide* by Price and Price is a good source of information (see the reference list at the end of this chapter). We recommend getting bids from different HVAC contractors who can design your entire system. Compare these bids to a total do-it-yourself installation.

CONVERTING YOUR HEATING AND COOLING SYSTEM

If you have an old house, the chances are that you also have a hot water or steam heating system. If so, you may have decided to install a new heating system during your rehab work. Your choice of energy will be dictated by your own preferences and by the price of fuel in your area. A popular choice is a forced hot air system. This requires that you run duct work in your walls or ceilings to get the heat to the desired locations. Running the duct work can be challenging and costly, especially if you are not gutting the entire house. The added cost will have to be weighed against any efficiency gained by converting to forced hot air. Most people

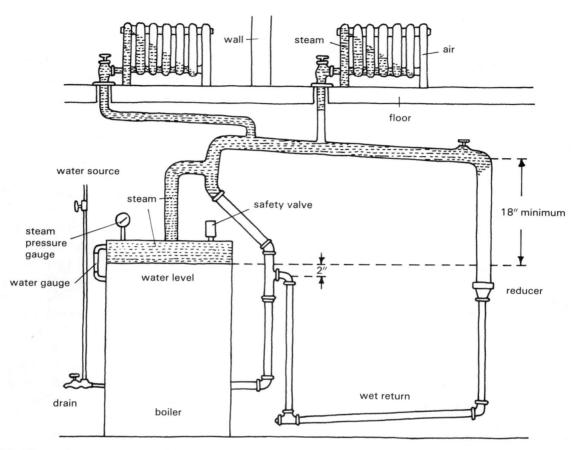

FIGURE 18-2. *A basic steam heating system.*

think that they have to get rid of the hot water or steam system to have central air-conditioning. If that is your only concern, keep in mind that some AC systems can be installed in your attic with duct work running across the attic floor and down to lower floors through stacked closets. One can also install a new high-pressure system in flexible 2-inch ducts. These systems are designed for existing walls, but they tend to "whistle" a bit.

Running Duct Work

Once the walls have been opened up and the existing plaster removed, running the new duct work is fairly easy. If this is not the case, the job will be a good deal more difficult. Getting the ducts to the second floor requires some ingenuity. Often the duct work can be run between floors through existing closets if they are stacked on top of each other. Once into the attic, the duct work can be distributed across the attic space, and registers can be cut into the ceilings of the second-floor rooms. For the

first floor, the duct work can be run underneath the floor, and registers can be cut in the lower walls of the rooms. Sometimes you can build a boxed-in chase between the floor and the ceiling in a corner of a room and then run the duct work inside this chase. Another method of hiding the duct work is to lower the ceilings in hallways and run the ducts above the false ceilings. Creativity is the key.

Types of Ducting Systems

There are basically four types of ducting systems: the graduated system, the extended plenum system, the radial system, and the loop system.

Graduated Duct System

This system is useful in a long house, such as a row house. Figure 18-3 shows the design of the system. As you can see, it is basically one long duct with several branches. As each branch goes off, the size of the main duct is reduced to maintain the static pressure. If this were not done, the pressure would

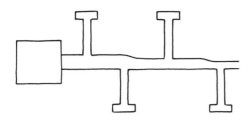

FIGURE 18-3. *A graduated duct system.*

not be great enough to push the hot air into the most distant rooms.

Extended Plenum System

This system is shown in Figure 18-4. As you can see, the furnace is located in the middle of the system, and the main duct runs in either direction. In this system, as in the graduated duct system, the size of the main ducts must be reduced as they get farther away from the furnace.

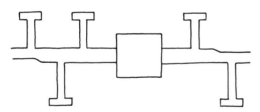

FIGURE 18-4. *An extended plenum system.*

Radial Duct System

This system, shown in Figure 18-5, has several individual ducts taking off from a centrally located furnace. Each duct goes to a separate room and usually remains the same size throughout its run. While this type of system is easy to install, it has the drawback that long runs do not heat as well as short runs. If the run has elbows and turns, rooms that are farther away will probably be colder than closer rooms. It is sometimes a good idea to make the size of the long duct larger than the others to compensate for the increased resistance.

Loop Duct System

This type of system is often used in single-level dwellings, and the duct work is often laid in the foundation. Once again, as Figure 18-6 shows, the duct work is reduced in size as it gets farther from the furnace.

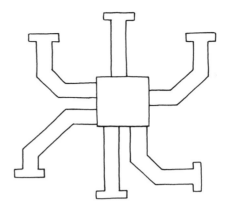

FIGURE 18-5. *A radial duct system.*

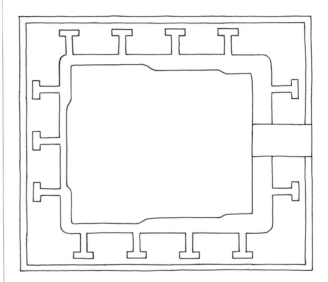

FIGURE 18-6. *A loop duct system.*

Sizing the Runs

As we have said, the size of the duct work is important in maintaining the static pressure, so that all the rooms in the system will be heated. The major issues relating to duct size are air flow, or pressure, and friction loss. Air pressure is created by the fan on the furnace that blows the warm air. The pressure rating of the system will be indicated on the furnace or can be obtained from the manufacturer. The proper duct size must be used to ensure that this pressure is maintained throughout the system. Friction loss is the loss of pressure as the moving air travels through the system. The sides of the ducts offer resistance to the flow of air. A fine balance must be maintained between large ducts with low resistance and ducts that are so large that there is a loss of static pressure. Charts for calculating the friction loss of certain duct diameters and shapes are given in several books.

Normally the runs to the rooms will be done with 6-inch round pipes. The major consideration is that the pressure at the registers in the rooms be as uniform as possible and as close to the cubic feet per minute (cfm) designated by the manufacturer as possible. Once again, you should consult one or more books on this specific subject.

Return Air Systems

Because the return air system is the route for the cold air to get back to the furnace, it is just as important as the delivery system. The usual method for creating a return air system is to use the spaces between floor joists as boxes in which the air travels. The return air duct usually spans the width or length of the house, and cold air return grills are placed at either end of the dwelling. Since the cold air will naturally fall to the first floor, it is not always necessary to have cold air returns on the upper floors of the house if you have large open staircases.

Where to Put Registers

Normally the registers on the first floor of a house are put along the outside walls, as this is where the greatest heat loss occurs. Often these are placed at the windows. On the second floor of the house, it is sometimes necessary to put the registers along the inside walls. Generally a room that is larger than 12′ × 12′ should have more than one register. If you have large expanses of glass, such as a sliding glass door or a floor-to-ceiling window, registers should be installed in front of these. In addition, the registers ought to be of the heating/cooling type, since these will have a larger opening than the heating-only type. This is to allow the free flow of cool air, which is denser than hot air.

OTHER COOLING METHODS

In addition to the heating/air conditioning furnace combination, there are other ways that you can cool your house in the summer.

Attic Ventilation and Fans

If you have ever gone into your attic on a hot summer day, you know that the temperature can rise to well over 100°F. It doesn't take long for that heat to begin to seep down through the insulation and ceilings and heat up the house, particularly the upper floor. Several methods are available to prevent this heat buildup from taking place.

The simplest method is to cut holes in the attic wall at the roof peak and put in louvers. When the wind blows across the louvers, it draws the hot air out of the attic. Of course, you must make sure that there will be a free flow of cool air into the attic. This is most easily accomplished by placing vents in the soffits of the house. Cool air is drawn into the lower part of the roof and exits near the peak.

Another method is to use wind turbines. These are metal stacks topped with a finned turbine that revolves in the wind. The revolving of the turbine draws the hot air out of the attic.

The most active method is to use an attic ventilator fan that runs off power to your house. It is controlled by a thermostat that monitors the temperature in the attic. When it gets too hot, the fan turns on automatically and removes the hot air.

Whole House Fans

Whole house fans have become very popular in climates where the outside temperature goes down in the evening and the humidity at night is not very high. These large-bladed fans pull 7,000 to 10,000 cfm. They are placed in the ceiling at the top of a stairway in a two-story house and anyplace in a single-story dwelling. When the fan is turned on and the windows are opened, cool air is pulled into the house from the outside and the hot air is exhausted into the attic. For these fans to work properly, there must be a good deal of free vent area (FVA) for the exhausted air to escape from the attic. This can be accomplished by placing vents in the roof or by putting louvers into the gable ends of the house. A general rule of thumb is that there should be about 1 foot of free vent area for every 750 cfm of the fan's rating. For example, if the whole house fan is rated at 10,000 cfm, you will need to provide about 14 feet of FVA. Before you purchase such a fan give careful thought to this need, because 14 feet is a large amount of open space in the roof of a house.

References

OLD

Allen, John Robins. *Notes on Heating and Ventilation.* Chicago: Domestic Engineering Co., 1911.

Baldwin, William James St. John. *Steam Heating for Buildings: Hints to Steam Fitters.* New York: John Wiley & Sons, 1885.

Hasluck, Paul Nooncree. *Practical Gas-Fitting.* Philadelphia: David McKay Co., 1909.

The Ideal Fitter: American Radiators and Ideal Boilers. Chicago: American Radiator Co., 1913.

King, Alfred Grant. *Progressive Heating.* New York: Sheet Metal Publication Co., 1914.

Whitelaw, Norman. *How to Heat the Home.* New York: N.P., 1926.

NEW

Flagler, Gordon. *The North American Wood Heat Handbook.* New York: Scribner, 1982.

Gilman, Stanley F., ed. *Solar Energy Heat Pump Systems for Heating & Cooling Buildings.* University Park, Pennsylvania: Pennsylvania State University Press, 1966.

Khashab, A. M. *Heating, Ventilating & Air-Conditioning Systems Estimating Manual.* 2d Ed. New York: McGraw-Hill, 1983.

Kipp, Jerry. *Firefacts: The Consumer's Guide to Wood Heat.* Woodstock, Vermont: Countryman Press, 1980.

Price, B., and J. Price. *Central Heating and Air Conditioning Repair Guide.* Blue Ridge Summit, Pennsylvania: TAB Books, 1983.

Price, Billy L. *The Master Handbook of All Home Heating Systems: Tune-Up, Repair, Installation & Maintenance.* Blue Ridge Summit, Pennsylvania: TAB Books, 1979.

Shelton, Jay W. *Wood Heat Safety.* Pownal, Vermont: Garden Way Publishing, 1979.

Stanford, Herbert W. III. *Analysis & Design of Heating, Ventilating, & Air-Conditioning Systems.* Englewood Cliffs, New Jersey: Prentice-Hall, 1988.

Swenson, Allan A. *Wood Heat.* New York: Fawcett, 1980.

Traister, John E. *Do-It-Yourselfer's Guide to Modern Energy-Efficient Heating & Cooling Systems.* Blue Ridge Summit, Pennsylvania: TAB Books, 1978.

Chapter 19

WHAT ELSE GOES IN THE WALLS?

Once the plaster has been removed from all the inside walls, you should consider all the things that will go back into the walls before you resurface them. You have probably already thought about systems such as plumbing, electrical wiring, and heating duct-work, but other things also go in the walls.

Now is the time to stop and think about all those other systems that run through the walls of the average home. If you install the cables for these systems now, a contractor will not have to tear out a portion of a wall later on to run, for example, lines for an intercom system.

Certainly you will want a telephone system in your house, a doorbell, and maybe an intercom system. You also may want to have speaker wires, a central vacuum cleaning system or a burglar alarm, which will require additional wiring. In this chapter, we look at a few of these systems and also discuss insulation.

TELEPHONE CABLE

The telephone company will bring the service to your home, but the choice of where to put the outlets and how many you want is yours. It is a good idea to overestimate the number of places that you might want to have a phone. As your family increases in size, the demand for phone outlets will change. Phone cable is inexpensive and should be run through the wall studs to any rooms where you might eventually want a phone. We recommend wiring every room. Cable for the phone can be run through the studs in the same fashion as the wiring for the electrical system. It also can be run down near the floor at the edge of the wall. Later it can be covered by the base molding.

TELEVISION CABLE

It is also often difficult to decide where you will want television sets. These frequently end up in places that you never even considered. For this reason, it is a good idea to run the cable to most rooms where people live (for example, living rooms and bedrooms). Like telephone cable, the coaxial cable used for TV transmission is inexpensive and easy to run when the walls are exposed.

SPEAKER WIRE

Whether you intend to have fixed speakers or plan to move a pair of speakers around from room to room as you need them, you will need outlets. While the best fidelity comes from large-gauge wire, it is fairly common to see zip cord used for speakers. *Zip cord* is the type of double wire that is used to wire lamps. Once again, it is a good idea to wire any room that might eventually be an area for listening to music. Telephone wire can be used for this purpose, since it is four-conductor wire.

THERMOSTAT WIRE

Your heating system will need a thermostat, so you will have to run four- to six-conductor wire for that. The thermostat will likely be placed on an inside wall away from drafts. It is a simple matter to drill a hole for the wire through the floor and into the basement. Once into the basement, the wire can be run along the floor joists to the furnace room.

DOORBELL

Don't forget the doorbell. The wire for the door-bell can be run alongside that for the thermostat. Usually the bell, chime, or buzzer is placed in the back of the house, so the wire will run down to the basement and then back up through the floor to the position of the bell. The doorbell wire will be connected to a stepdown transformer. Refer to the instructions that came with the door chime.

INTERCOM SYSTEM

An intercom system is a nice addition for several reasons. First, if your house is a multistory dwelling, having an intercom can save you a good deal of legwork going up and down stairs. Second, certain intercom systems allow you to play a radio over them. If you enjoy music and listening to the radio, this will allow you to have music all over your house. Intercoms may be installed in the bedrooms and in any other place where family members are likely to gather. Some newer systems are wireless, and, if you choose one of these, you won't have to worry about running wire in the exposed wall space.

BURGLAR ALARM

Burglar alarms range from very simple systems that are activated by a movement-sensing device and emit a loud warning signal to very sophisticated types that are connected to a remote security site. Some of these systems will not only monitor your home for break-ins but also watch for fires and notify the fire department if necessary. In addition, some systems will monitor your furnace and air conditioner, and if they shut down while you are gone and the temperature drops below freezing or rises above 100°F, the appropriate call for help is made.

Since the more sophisticated systems are generally connected by a small monitor to an external computer, installation is best left to the pros. Some of these systems cannot be guaranteed to perform correctly unless they are installed by the manufacturer or its local representative. Be sure to have the wiring installed before you seal up the walls.

VACUUM CLEANER SYSTEM

Perhaps you would like to have the convenience of a central vacuum cleaning system. Now is the time to plan the layout. Where you put the valves for the system will depend on the length of the hose in the system you are going to purchase. Let's assume that the hose will be about 30 feet long. This means that you will need an outlet about every 30 feet and that several rooms will be able to be serviced from a single outlet. The easiest method to determine where you will need outlets is to use a piece of rope about the same length as the hose. Make sure that every square foot of space can be reached, keeping in mind that when the house is done, the hose will probably have to stretch around large pieces of furniture. The best locations for the valves are in hallways and closet walls that are near doorways.

The tube system that connects the valves to the central vacuum unit are generally made of PVC pipe. You will need to consider the runs for this while the inside of the walls are exposed, keeping in mind that the best suction will come from a tube system with a minimum number of bends. More detailed installation details can be obtained from manufacturers of central vacuum cleaner systems.

Often, these systems cost no more than a top-quality portable vacuum cleaner.

INSULATION

Perhaps nothing that goes in the walls is as important as the insulation, which reduces the flow of heat to and from the outdoors. It can be used in the walls, ceilings, and floors. If you are rehabbing a brick house, insulation in the walls is especially important. Brick tends to convect heat and cold with relative ease, and the insulation that you put in the walls will help counteract this characteristic.

How Much Insulation and What Type?

The amount of insulation that you need depends on the heating and cooling requirements of your area of the country. Many home repair and do-it-yourself books list the R values of the insulation that you will need in various parts of the country. The R value is a standard specification of the insulation value per inch of insulation.

Insulation comes in many forms. It can be blown in as pea-size granules, glued in place as large sheets of polyfoam, rolled out in large blankets of fiberglass, or pumped in as a liquid. The type of material you choose depends on where you are going to put it and how easy it will be to gain access to that space.

Assuming that you have opened up your walls, the best type of insulation to use is foil-backed fiberglass batts. They do the best job of reflecting the heat, and the fiberglass will not get all over when you install it. The batts are placed between the studs in the walls. They have tabs that overlap the studs and are stapled to them, resulting in a continuous vapor barrier. Still, once the insulation is in place, a polyethylene vapor barrier should be placed over it—a step recommended by almost every expert in the area of heat transfer in houses.

If sections of the walls have not been opened up, you can have insulation blown in through small holes cut into them. Once this is done, the vapor barrier should be applied to the existing wall surface and a new layer of drywall placed over that. If you are thinking about replacing the wiring outlets and switches and changing all the baseboard and door trim, it is probably easier to tear down the original walls and use the first method.

Insulation Materials

Fiberglass

Fiberglass batts and blankets account for the bulk of the insulation sold today. The batts are available in thicknesses of 3½ to about 12 inches and in widths of 11, 15, and 23 inches. These widths allow the batts to be pushed in between framing. Typically this type of insulation comes with a paper backing that contains foil to act as a vapor barrier. Despite this, it is still a good idea to install plastic film as a vapor barrier. The amount of surface area that a roll will cover is usually marked on the outside of the roll. Remember that the paper covering and any plastic barrier should always face the inside of the dwelling. This prevents the moisture inside the house from penetrating the walls and getting the insulation wet.

Cellulose

This material is usually available as a loose fill that can be poured or blown into the walls or attic. Normally cellulose is made of recycled newspaper and is treated to increase its insulation value. Keep in mind that paper is flammable—even though cellulose insulation has been treated with a fire retardant, it is potentially combustible.

Vermiculite and Perlite

These materials are lightweight granules of minerals that are usually blown into walls. They tend to be resistant to rot and mildew and are also fire-resistant. Their primary drawback is that they are expensive.

Polystyrene

This material is usually fashioned in sheets of varying widths and thicknesses. The widths are standard so that the sheets fit between the studs. Because the material is water-resistant, you do not need to use a vapor barrier. Another advantage of this material is that it is quite light and can be easily cut with a utility knife.

Polyurethane and Urea-Formaldehyde

Both of these materials are plastics that can be

obtained in sheets but are more often used as a foam. The foam, which is forced into the walls, hardens into a solid block. These materials may be hazardous to your health, so you should check your local building codes to determine if you can (or want to) use them. There is also a possibility of bulging your walls with these materials.

Insulating the Walls

After you have determined where all the wiring and piping will go in your walls and have installed it, you can put the insulation in place. For the purposes of this discussion we are assuming that you are using foil-backed fiberglass batts, which have advantages over most other forms of insulation for most do-it-yourself rehabbers. Walls are typically rated R–13 to R–19. Cut the insulation a bit long and push it into place, stapling the tabs as you go. When the next piece of insulation is placed between the next set of studs, its tabs should overlap those of the previous piece. This produces a tight seal against moisture. Remember that the side of the insulation with the paper backing must face the inside of the house.

Insulating the Attic

Since heat rises, most heat during the winter is lost through the ceiling and into the attic. In the summer, the attic gets very hot, and heat begins to infiltrate the living space. Thus, it is very important that the attic be treated with enough insulation to give it the appropriate R value, usually R–30. The chances are quite good that your attic already has some insulation. Most likely it is blown-in cellulose. It is a relatively simple matter to use roll insulation over the existing insulation. As you do this, be careful not to cover any soffit vents, because the attic must be free to take in fresh air. Beyond that, there is very little to the job except cutting the batts to the proper lengths. Blown-in fiberglass is also an easy way to insulate an attic, but it is not typically a do-it-yourself job. An effective means of cutting down on the heat that builds up in the attic during hot summer days is to staple aluminum foil across the attic side of the roof joists, with the reflective side facing the roof. A good deal of the heat that comes through the roof will then be reflected back so that it does not heat up the attic.

Insulating the First Floor

If you live in a house that has an unfinished basement, just a crawl space, or no basement at all, you should insulate the floors with roll batts like those used in the walls. When you install this material, the paper backing must face up into the living space. Even if the insulation has stapling tabs, you should support it by using lath strips or chicken wire across the floor joists. Another reason for insulating the floors is to reduce noise that might come up from the basement if it is finished and used by members of the family as a recreation area.

Insulating the Basement Walls

If you want to finish the basement or if you just want to increase the insulation in your home, you can insulate the basement walls. If the walls are unfinished, then you can simply glue rigid foam, foil-faced, fire-resistant insulation to the masonry. If the walls are to be finished, wait until you have to put up the studs or furring and then either use rigid foam or fiberglass batts. It is critical to finish the job with a layer of polyethylene sheeting as a vapor barrier.

References

OLD

Hoffman, James David. *Insulation for House Construction.* Lafayette, Indiana: Purdue University, 1933.

NEW

Albright, Roger. *547 Easy Ways to Save Energy in Your Home.* Pownal, Vermont: Garden Way Publishing, 1978.

Cole, Richard B. *The Application of Security Systems and Hardware.* Springfield, Illinois: C.P. Thomas, 1970.

Do-It-Yourself Insulation and Weatherstripping. Menlo Park, California: Lane Publishing Co., 1978.

Duncan, S. Blackwell. *The Home Insulation Bible.* Blue Ridge Summit, Pennsylvania: TAB Books, 1982.

Sherwood, Gerald E. *Energy Efficiency in Light Frame Wood Construction.* Madison, Wisconsin: Department of Agriculture, Forest Service, Forest Products Lab, 1979.

Chapter 20

DRYWALL AND PAINTING

Painting is probably the first job that a typical rehabber considers to be within his or her capabilities. You might have done a good deal of painting up to this point in your life and feel that you are fairly good at it. But we may be able to teach you some tricks that you don't already know. If you have not worked with drywall before, you may not want to tackle the job. Putting up drywall is not much more difficult than painting, however, and we will start with a discussion of this process.

DRYWALL

Chances are that your house had plaster walls and that you have removed most of them in the initial stages of your rehab. Redoing the walls in plaster is unthinkable in this day and age, when a good drywall job is impossible to tell from a plaster wall, at least from a distance. Drywall, sometimes called plasterboard, gypsum board, or Sheetrock, is composed of gypsum pressed between two layers of heavy paper. Drywall comes in standard widths of $3/8$, $1/2$, $5/8$, and $3/4$ inch and in standard dimensions of 4' x 8', 4' x 10', 4' x 12', and 4' x 16'. Most drywall panels are tapered on the face side along the outer 3 inches or so and all along the length to allow for the application of drywall joint compound and the tape that spans the joint between two panels. For most drywall applications, $3/8$- or $1/2$-inch material is best because thicker drywall is too heavy to handle alone. Most construction codes require the use of $5/8$-inch drywall for fire walls, such as between units in a duplex. Green drywall, often

called *greenboard*, is moistureproof and is used in kitchens and bathrooms near sinks, tubs, and showers.

A new kind of drywall has recently appeared on the U.S. market — one which promises to be more popular and available in the future. Unlike regular paper-covered gypsum board, this new kind of fiberboard combines gypsum, cellulose, and perlite into a solid sheet that resembles particleboard and that has certain advantages over conventional drywall.

On one hand, the new fiberboard is sturdier and easier to install than standard drywall; it holds nails better, has greater insulating value, and doesn't need taping — just a two-coat application of a special joint compound. On the other hand, the new board is heavier and more expensive than regular drywall, and its surface is not quite as smooth.

Cutting Drywall

You should cut drywall with a sharp utility knife along the face surface. Score the surface along a premeasured line and then bend the panel carefully away from the face side until it breaks. After that, you can finish the cut with the knife from the unfinished side. If any edges do not break smoothly, you can smooth them down with a coarse file or utility knife. The main thing is to be careful that you do not tear the paper facing or backing, as that will lead to damage of the gypsum center. Change the blade in your utility knife often. When you cut the drywall, be sure that you do not cut it exactly to the dimension of the floor-to-ceiling measurement, as you will want some room to position the panel as you install it. Your baseboard will cover any gap, so remember to always put the factory edge up and shove it tightly to the ceiling drywall.

Installing Drywall

The drywall is attached to the studs, which have been previously spaced on 16-inch centers. You may use drywall nails or screws to attach the material. We prefer screws for at least two reasons. First, the process goes much faster with screws and an electric drill or screw gun than it does with nails and a hammer. Secondly, if you make a mistake and do not like the way you cut or hang the panel, you can always unscrew it and take it down or reposition it. Besides, nailing drywall requires a special rounded-face hammer. Don't use your regular claw hammer, as it will break the paper face of the drywall quite often.

Use a small level to help position the drywall. Just put a two-by-four on the floor next to the panel and put a piece of two-by-six over that and under the panel. You can then use a free foot to raise and lower the panel as you adjust it in place and set a few screws. Any gap that remains after the panel is in place will be covered by the base molding, so don't worry if you have a gap of 1 to 1½ inches. Drywall panels can be put up vertically or horizontally. The choice depends on which way will result in fewer joints. This usually means you will install it running horizontally, especially with the longer sheets.

Taping the Joints

After all the drywall is in place, the joints must be taped so that you have a smooth surface to paint or wallpaper. The tape also prevents the joints from cracking open. Taping is by far the most important part of the job because, if you are not careful to get a smooth surface, you will see every mistake after it is painted.

Taping is accomplished with joint compound and either paper or fiberglass tape. Resist the temptation to use the less expensive paper tape. Fiberglass tape costs a bit more, but you can skip at least one step in the process and the job will proceed much more quickly. For comparison's sake we will describe both methods, and you can be the judge.

Paper Tape Method

Cut the tape to fit the length of the joint. Place the cut tape into a bucket of water to soak. Apply a coat of joint compound in the indentation in the panel on either side of the joint. Press the tape into the joint compound and, using a 6-inch drywall knife (never try this with a putty knife), begin to smooth the tape along the joint. Once this is done, you must wait until the joint compound is dry. The length of the wait will depend on the humidity and how thickly you applied the compound, but figure on four to five hours under normal conditions.

When the compound is dry, apply more compound over the tape. This time use a 12-inch drywall knife. Wait for this layer to dry. The tape should now be buried in dry joint compound.

Place another layer of compound on the joint. Try to feather the compound so that it blends smoothly into the drywall on either side of the joint. You do not want a lump or bulge that you will have to sand for hours.

After that coat has dried, you must sand the joint smooth. Purchase a drywall sanding tool with drywall sandpaper, since regular sandpaper will clog the tool and become useless in short order. Drywall sandpaper will not clog the tool and will cut quickly through the dry joint compound. Resist the temptation to use an electric sander to correct your mistakes—if it eats into the paper face, you may have to drywall all over again.

Inspect the wall carefully for indentations and bumps. If you find any bumps, sand them down, for they will surely show after you paint. Fill in indentations with another thin layer of well-feathered joint compound and then resand.

When you are satisfied that the joint is smooth and well tapered, apply drywall primer to the wall as a first paint coat. Be aware that any imperfections in the drywall will show through after painting and in strong light, especially if you plan to use a high-gloss paint. A trick that will help you find these flaws is to light up the wall with a fluorescent light and then mark the bad spots with a pencil.

Fiberglass Tape Method

Fiberglass tape is thinner than paper tape and so blends into the panel much better. In addition, fiberglass tape is covered with adhesive on one side, so you can attach it to the joint without applying an underlayer of joint compound. Thus, you have already saved considerable time in not having to wait for the first layer of compound to dry. Since the tape is thinner and composed of a mesh screen, you will not need to apply as thick a layer of joint compound over the tape. This means that the first coat will dry faster, and you will be ready for the next and usually last coat much sooner.

Taping the Corners

Taping the joints between two pieces of drywall is time-consuming, but it is not that difficult. Taping the inside and outside corners, however, takes a bit more practice, patience, and care.

The Inside Corners

If you are using fiberglass tape, you can simply bend the tape into a 90-degree angle and stick it to the corner. Run your 6-inch knife gently down each side to make sure it is tight. Then apply the joint compound with the same 6-inch trowel that you used on the wall itself or with a special inside corner trowel. This latter special trowel will make it easier to get a smooth application, but it is not essential. The remainder of the job is the same as for the main section of the wall.

The Outside Corners

Outside corners can be finished with tape if they are cut very square, but a better method, and one that will keep them looking nice much longer, is to use a drywall angle or corner bead. This is a piece of sheet metal that is full of holes and bent at a right angle, much like angle iron. You just cut the metal to fit the corner and then nail it on the corner. After the compound dries, continue to add joint compound until you have an edge that you feel will dress up nicely when it is sanded. Drywall angle provides a metal corner which, when bumped, may yield paint chips but will not allow damage to the drywall.

Finishing Nail and Screw Holes

Cover the heads of nails and screws with several coats of joint compound. This is where a drywall hammer comes in handy. It indents the nail heads enough to do this. Build up the layers so that, when they are dry, you can sand them down level with the surface of the drywall.

Drywall on the Ceiling

In some situations, it might be appropriate to drywall the ceiling. While this does not present any special problems in the finishing process, you do have to figure out a way to hold the panels while you screw them in place. If you are working with someone, the problem is simplified. But, if you are going it alone, fashion a tee out of two-by-twos to hold the drywall. Simply cut a two-by-two long enough so that it reaches almost all the way (within 2 inches) to the ceiling and then place a short two-by-two cross-member on the end. Now you can rest one end of the drywall panel on the tee while you attend to the other end.

After the drywall is attached to the ceiling, it must be taped. The quickest and best method to finish the ceiling after that is to rent a texture blower and blow on a textured ceiling. This will hide the taped joints and finish the ceiling at the same time.

PAINTING

Tools

Painting tools fall into two broad categories, brushes and rollers. Each has its place in the job, and you will find that, after you have painted for a while, you will have a preference for what you use where. When you purchase a brush, don't skimp on the price, because you get what you pay for. Less expensive brushes are made of synthetic bristles and usually are stiff. This stiffness will prevent the brush from holding a good load of paint, and it will result in streaks. Spend the extra money and buy a natural bristle brush. The bristles in this type of brush are usually made of hog or badger hair. Some experts will tell you that a natural bristle brush will not work well with latex paint and should be used only with oil-based paint. We have not found that to be true, but you should experiment and form your own opinion.

In addition to brushes of several sizes, you will need a roller for large expanses of wall. You can even purchase special rollers that are made to do the corners, although these are optional. Roller covers have various types of nap for jobs ranging from simple wall painting to texturing to painting over

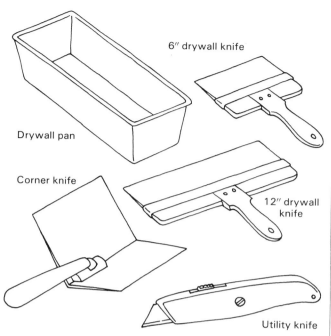

6″ drywall knife

Drywall pan

Corner knife

12″ drywall knife

Utility knife

FIGURE 20-1. *Basic drywall tools.*

rough concrete. If you choose the right roller cover, the job will be much easier. You can rent or purchase a paint roller with a continuous-supply paint pump attached to it. This is a good idea for large expanses of wall because it saves you from dipping the roller repeatedly into a tray.

Another type of paint applicator is the flat applicator. You dip this into the paint like a roller, but it spreads the paint on the wall as if it were a brush. This type of applicator is also available in a shape that allows you to get close to woodwork, floors, and ceilings without putting paint anywhere but where you want it.

Finally, if you have a large job (such as priming all the new drywall in a total gut rehab), you might consider using a spray-painting system. Give careful thought to this decision, however, as these are difficult to use. If you have to be very careful about where you put the paint and you have not used a sprayer inside before, it is probably not a good idea to use one now.

You can find more information about painting tools and techniques in a number of the references listed at the end of this chapter.

Paint Types

The major consideration when you buy paint is whether it is interior or exterior paint. We assume that you will be painting inside and therefore will be purchasing interior paint. Paint is usually divided into five types: alkyd, latex, clear finish, stain, and specialty. There are interior and exterior counterparts of each.

Alkyds are usually referred to as oil-based paints. They have to be thinned with petroleum products, and they do not wash off with water. They are tougher and last longer once on the surface. Drying time usually runs 12 to 24 hours depending on the humidity, and they may have a strong paint smell while drying.

Latex paint usually dries in two to four hours and has little smell. These paints can be cleaned up with water, which can shorten the task considerably. In addition, if you think that you may spill or paint things that you do not wish to, this type of paint is much more forgiving than oil-based paint. Latex paint usually does not stand up to repeated scrubbings as well as oil-based paint, but we have found that the ease of use more than makes up for this shortcoming.

Latex and alkyd paints are also classed according to the gloss of the surface that is left after the paint dries. The paint that leaves the highest gloss finish is usually referred to as enamel, and the one that leaves the lowest gloss finish is referred to as flat. Enamels are good to use on surfaces that you feel will have to be washed frequently, such as kitchens, stairwells, and bathrooms. A paint in between enamel and flat is semigloss. This paint is also common in kitchens and baths. They also tend to be more waterproof than lower gloss paints. Flat paints are used on walls and other surfaces where the subtle imperfections in the surface are to be hidden. For instance, flat paints can hide most of the minor imperfections in your drywall job. The major drawback is that they are difficult to wash and are not water-repellent.

Clear finishes are things such as varnishes, polyurethanes, lacquers, and shellacs. Each of these must be thinned with a special solvent—for example, shellac must be thinned with alcohol, and lacquer must be thinned with acetone. Usually these paints are used in situations that call for a clear, protective coating. For instance, you may wish to protect a floor but not want to cover up the grain. Polyurethane is perfect for such a job. Finally, there is a special class of products that are used to paint metal and masonry. Some are used to texture walls and ceilings, and others are used to waterproof or to acoustically deaden the surfaces to which they are applied. You should contact your local dealer for more information on any such specialty paints.

Preparation

Time taken to prepare the surfaces to be painted is time well spent. If a surface is not prepared properly, you may find that you are painting the same surface again after only a short time. Adhesion of the paint depends on the quality of the first coat's contact with the substrate, or surface to be painted. The substrate must be clean. It must not have wax, grease, oil, soot, or anything else on it that will form a barrier between the paint and the surface. Experts say the preparation should take 90 percent of the total time spent painting.

You may find that the existing surface paint is peeling, flaking, checking, or alligatoring. In all these cases, painting over this paint will trap moisture or allow moisture to get in and lead to further paint failure. Walls that are peeling or checking need to be well sanded and primed. Places where you cannot get off all the old paint will have to be feathered into the remainder of the wall, or they will stand out when the job is done.

The primer will help the finish coat remain smooth and prevent the surface from soaking up too much paint. Priming an unfinished surface such as new drywall is an absolute necessity. If you do not prime the surface, the paint will go on unevenly, and the finish over the joints will be duller than on the remainder of the wall. In addition, if you intend to wallpaper the drywall, you must apply a good primer coat first. Before painting a surface that has been previously painted and then prepared to receive new paint, you should wash the surface thoroughly with trisodium phosphate (TSP) mixed in a solution of about ½ cup TSP to one gallon water.

Application of Alkyd and Latex Paints

Once the surface is prepared, you are ready to paint. Whether you are using a brush or a roller, keep in mind that two thin coats will probably look better than one thick coat. If you attempt to put the paint on too thickly, it might run, and you will not be satisfied with the job. As you put the paint on the surface, it will appear as if it is not going on smoothly. Normally any rough appearance during the application smoothes out as the paint dries. Try to do the best job you can of blending the brush or roller strokes, and the paint will take care of itself. When painting walls, we paint all the corners, the space at the top of the wall, and the bottom of the wall next to the floor with a brush, as it is difficult to work close to right angles with a roller. Once we have done all these areas, we paint the rest with a roller. When using the roller, go slowly because if you roll too fast, paint will fly off the roller and get on surfaces where you do not want it to go. Some rollers come with a splash protector.

Application of Stains and Varnishes

Stains are usually oil-based and are meant to be applied to bare wood. They can be applied with a rag or with a brush. If you apply the stain with a brush, you will have to wipe off the excess shortly after you apply it. The depth of the stain is usually a function of how long you allow the stain to soak into the wood before you wipe it off. If the stain does not have a sealer in it, you will have to finish it with a sealer such as varnish or polyurethane. For a stain to penetrate into the wood in a uniform manner, you must remove all the old paint and sealer before you begin. If you are not sure that you have removed these completely and that the stain will penetrate evenly, you can try a partial sealing of the wood before you use the stain. We have found that a very weak solution of varnish (varnish mixed with alcohol) rubbed into the wood and allowed to dry before applying the stain will sometimes help in a uniform uptake of the stain. Be careful, though, as nothing can take the place of careful surface preparation.

Stripping Wood

If you are planning to restain wood trim in your home, you will have to strip all the old finish off the wood. If this old finish is varnish, you can soften it or even rub it off with the application of alcohol or acetone. The same is true of lacquer. If this does not work, or if the finish is paint, you will have to resort to paint stripper. Paint stripper is a caustic chemical solution that should be applied in an open room. Make sure that you protect your eyes while you are working and that you always wear gloves. Carefully follow the directions for using the remover.

Another way to remove paint is with a heat gun. This is similar to a hair dryer, as it directs hot air against the surface. As the paint softens, you can scrape it off with a putty knife. Be careful, however, because you might burn the wood if you hold the heat on one spot for too long. Some people have used a blowtorch with a special paint-removing tip, but the chances of burning the surface (and, indeed, the whole house) are such that we do not recommend this approach. Heat guns should not be used around windows, as the heat will crack the glass. Stripping of fine detail work will usually have to be done with chemicals and fine wire brushes, picks, and dental tools. If the wood is burned or remains heavily stained, wood bleach can be used to achieve an even, restainable surface.

Stenciling

Stenciling is a process whereby paint is applied to a surface through a shape that is cut from a material that is impervious to the paint. If you are remodeling a Victorian home, the chances are good that some surfaces in the house will have stencils, and you may wish to preserve some or all of these.

Stenciling is not difficult to do, and if you are interested in learning how, you might consult *The Art of Decorative Stenciling* by Bishop and Lord (see references below), which describes every aspect of the art, from cutting the stencils to laying out the patterns. Make sure that you prepare the underlying paint very well so that you will not have to repaint for a long time. It is best to use oil-based paint on a surface that you intend to stencil. Other sources for stencil design are also given in the following references.

References

OLD

Arrowsmith, James. *The Paper Hanger's Companion.* Philadelphia: Henry Carey Baird, 1856.

Desaint, A. *Three Hundred Shades and How to Mix Them.* London: Scott Greenwood and Sons, 1907.

Hodgson, Frederick Thomas. *The Up-to-Date Hardwood Finisher.* Chicago: F.J. Drake and Co., 1915.

Kelly, Albanis Ashmun. *The Expert Paper Hanger.* Malvern, Pennsylvania: Master Painter Publishing Co., 1912.

_____. *The Expert Wood Finisher.* Philadelphia: David McKay Co., 1927.

Lowndes, William S. *Plastering and Stucco Work.* Scranton, Pennsylvania: International Textbook Press, 1924.

Pearce, Walter John. *Painting and Decorating.* London: C. Griffin, 1907.

Waring, J. *Early American Stencils on Walls and Furniture.* New York: Dover Publications, 1937.

Whittock, N. *The Decorative Painters and Glaziers Guide.* London: I.T. Hinton, 1828.

NEW

Bishop, Adele, and Cile Lord. *The Art of Decorative Stenciling.* New York: Penguin Books, 1978.

Frane, James T. *Drywall Contracting.* Carlsbad, California: Craftsman Book Co., 1987.

Geary, Don. *Interior and Exterior Painting.* Reston, Virginia: Reston Publishing Co., 1979.

Gillon, Edmund. *Victorian Stencils for Design and Decoration.* New York: Dover Publications, 1968.

Grafton, Carol. *Victorian Cut and Use Stencils.* New York: Dover Publications, 1977.

Harris, William Robert. *Drywall: Installation and Application.* Chicago: American Technical Society, 1979.

Koziozki, A.J. *Do Your Own Drywall: An Illustrated Guide.* Blue Ridge Summit, Pennsylvania: TAB Books, 1985.

Moss, Roger W. *Victorian Exterior Decoration.* New York: Henry Holt, 1987.

Paint and Wallpapering. Alexandria, Virginia: Time-Life Books, 1980.

Pegg, Brian F. *Plastering: A Craftman's Encyclopedia.* New York: Crown Publishers, 1976.

Chapter 21

DOORS

Cabinets, doors, trim, and shelves are installed after the walls have been framed and the plumbing, electrical system, heating and cooling system, insulation, and drywall are in place. In a renovation, the rehabber often gets a second wind at this time, for the rehab is beginning to look like a real house. In many renovations, however, rehabbers also experience a tremendous amount of frustration because they have run out of money and cannot afford the quality items they desire. Regardless of the state of your pocketbook or mind, the installation of doors, as well as trim and cabinets (discussed in the next two chapters), will make or break your renovation. In this chapter, we examine the different doors found in a house and their installation.

REPAIR OR REPLACEMENT?

The factors that determine whether you repair or replace a door, particularly an exterior door, are similar to those concerning windows: Is the door a standard size? Is the frame sound? Are the door-jambs parallel, and are the head and sill of the door square to the jambs? (See Figure 21-1 for the parts of a door.) Keep in mind that it is considerably easier to build door frames than window frames and that, if you have removed the plaster and the lath and replaced it with one thickness of drywall, the door frame will be too large. Are the doors themselves worth saving? They may not be if they are simple unpaneled doors, if the frames are too wide because of the thickness differential between the plaster and drywall, if the doors are pine or fir, or if they have a lot of problems such as holes or inoperable hardware. Remember that you may be able to sell the doors to an architectural salvage firm and replace them with new paneled doors (prehung and pre-painted) for about the same price as having the old doors repaired. The only constraint is the door's height, but if you have tall openings you can always use modern stock doors and install transoms over them. (We often install stained glass in the transoms.)

If the existing doors are hardwood, are double paneled (pre-1900), and are in fairly good shape, we suggest saving them, even if you have to take every door frame in the house apart and cut it down or build new frames. If you have quality doors, leave the lath on the wall when you redrywall the house. The thickness of the rehabbed wall then approximates that of the original, and the original trim and door frames can be used or duplicated. Probably the only handwork that you will have to do is strip the door frame in place.

With exterior doors, the same questions apply, as well as the energy efficiency of the doorway. Sixty to 80 percent of the heat loss through a doorway escapes around the door rather than through it. Weatherstripping is crucial whether the door is new or old. If the door is sound, it can be fixed and weather-stripped. If, however, the door or door frame is warped, it is difficult to seal. To determine whether a door frame is plumb, hold a level against the inside of a jamb. If the jamb is skewed, you can pull off the interior trim and replumb the jambs by adding or removing shims and using drywall screws to attach the jamb to the studs behind it. Use galvanized drywall screws for this purpose. Before

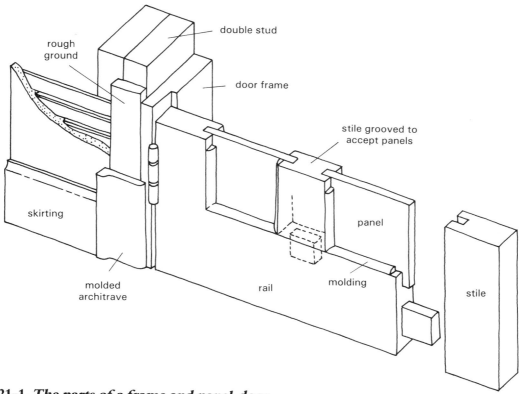

FIGURE 21-1. *The parts of a frame and panel door.*

you replace the trim, make sure to insulate between the rough opening and the frame, and caulk everything when you are finished. If an exterior door is out of square, you can take it to a woodworking shop and have it fixed, or you can use bar clamps to square it up while you redowel and reglue the joints.

SOLVING COMMON DOOR PROBLEMS

One of the most common problems with exterior doors is rotted sills. You have two choices when repairing sills. You can cut them out and put in new ones, or you can scrape off as much of the rot as possible and replace the missing material with something else (such as automotive body putty). In either case, you must treat the surrounding materials with a preservative.

To begin any repair on a sill, you need to brace the doorjambs so they do not move while you remove the rotted sill. Jambs usually rest on the sill,

so the easiest way to do this is with some kind of bracing to the floor and porch on each side. The easiest way to remove a sill is to cut it in half in the center and pry up the pieces with a pry bar. Try to remove the sill in one or two pieces so that you can use it as a pattern to build a new one. When the old sill is removed, inspect the adjacent areas for rot. If you find any, remove the exterior trim for a closer look at the jambs. If the rot goes higher than an inch or two, you will need to epoxy the rot or replace the jamb.

Make your new sill out of pressure-treated wood. If you smear a little petroleum jelly on the two ends of the new sill, you should be able to knock it into place with a mallet or a hammer and block. If the sill is hardwood, predrill the nail or screw holes. Nail the jambs to the sill and the sill to the structure beneath it.

Another problem that commonly occurs with an interior door is that it does not fit the frame correctly. This is particularly true when you reuse an old door in its previous jamb or in a new jamb that you have constructed. First, determine whether you have swollen wood. A wood door may not fit during a wet or humid period (in summer, for instance) because the moisture makes it swell. Cutting it down to fit in wet weather often means it will be loose during the dry season when it shrinks back to normal. You have to judge whether the sticking is bad enough to justify that. Be particularly leery when you are trying to install a door that has been stored in the basement or garage into a frame made out of new, dry lumber. Make sure your tolerances are very tight because the door will shrink and the frame will not.

Once a door is installed, the first area to check when it sticks is the hinges. Open the door and make sure all the screws are tight. If a screw is not tight or does not go all the way into the hole, remove it, coat a wooden match with glue, and push it into the hole. When the glue is dry, drive the screw into the hole. If you are reinstalling doors in existing frames and you suspect that you will have a number of instances where the screws will not fit in the old holes, you can either try new, larger screws or install the doors with toggle bolts that go all the way through the frame. If the jamb is close to the stud behind it, you could use 2½- or 3-inch drywall screws and screw all the way through the jamb and into the studs.

If a door sticks and the hinges are tight, stand back and study the closed door, particularly as someone opens and closes it. You should see variations in the gaps around the door. Wherever the gap is wider, at the top or bottom, shim that hinge out to straighten the door. You can do that by loosening the leaf of the hinge on the jamb and cutting a piece of cardboard to go behind it. Be reluctant to remove material from underneath the hinges, because the door may bind and not close. If you have hinge problems with heavy doors, particularly heavy exterior doors, that allow the door to sag, examine the hinges carefully. If they seem to be loose, install thrust bearing hinges. These hinges are generally quite expensive.

A sticking door or a door that does not fit its opening can often be fixed with a little sanding or planing. Sanding is slower but more precise when only a little wood must be removed. When sanding, wrap the sandpaper around a block of wood to keep it flat on the door edge. The first problem is finding where the door sticks. If you cannot see

it, slip a piece of paper in the closed door around the suspect area. Wherever the paper cannot be pulled out, the door is binding.

To work on a door, always remove it from its hinges. When planing the edges, work with the grain, or you will gouge the wood. When planing the top or bottom of a door, work from the outer edges toward the center. Planing from the center to the edges will almost certainly result in your splitting a large chunk off the stile edge.

When a door must be cut to fit in an opening or to clear a new threshold, remember the following points:

1. The cut must be perfectly straight and must not leave a ragged saw edge.

2. Hollow-core doors cannot be trimmed more than about 1 inch without major work to rebuild the door.

3. It is always easier to cut off the hinge side of a door than the knob side.

4. If you are cutting down a panel door, keep in mind the width of the rails. They should remain matched as closely as possible.

When you cut the edge of a door, you must use a straight board or straightedge to guide your saw because cutting freehand is not accurate. For smooth cuts, use a carbide-tipped plywood blade, especially if you are cutting veneered doors. It is very difficult to keep veneered doors from splintering, so if you do not have to remove too much material, you should use a power plane or a belt sander rather than a saw.

Fixing a Warped Door

A perfectly good door can become nearly unserviceable because it is warped or bowed. If that door is an expensive exterior door or a beautiful paneled interior door, it should be straightened rather than thrown away.

If a door is bowed in the middle, it can be straightened with weights. Put it on a pair of sawhorses with the bulge up, wet it, and place weights in the center until the door is straight. Leave the weights in place until the door doesn't bulge when they are removed. This usually takes about a week.

If a door is twisted, it must be pulled back into line. This is done with heavy wire and a turnbuckle. First, put two screw hooks at diagonal corners of the warp. Attach the wires and turnbuckle to the screw hooks and tighten them. The wires should stretch over a short two-by-four laid on edge in the center of the door to provide more leverage. If it is a paneled door, lay the two-by-four across the cross formed by the rails and the stiles. Increase tension daily over a period of three or four days. If the door begins to come apart, you can reglue and redowel it while it is being pulled back into shape. When you have a door in this position, the warp or the bow should be removed within a week.

When a door is just slightly out of line and you do not want to try straightening it, you may simply wish to move the doorstop to conform with the door.

Fixing a Hole in a Hollow-Core Door

Hollow-core doors are easily damaged, but they are also easy to repair. The first step is to pull away any splintered wood around the break and lightly sand the hole to remove any rough edges. Then ball up a sheet of newspaper, stick the back of it in glue, and push it into the hole. Using a wide putty knife, cover the paper with a layer of Spackle and allow it to dry. Then sand the edges and apply a second coat of Spackle, bringing it out flush with the door surface. If you try to fill the hole with just one thick layer, the Spackle will shrink too much as it dries. When the Spackle is completely dry, sand it smooth and repaint the door.

Replacing a Panel

Cracked or broken panels can be fixed relatively easily. If a paneled door is simply cracked, you may be able to fill it with flexible filler such as good quality caulking compound and repaint it. If the panel is missing or broken beyond repair, it will need to be replaced. If it is a molded door, you may be able to replace the panel by removing the molding on one side of it and pulling it out, much like a piece of glass. Typically, however, the molding that you see is actually part of the stile or rail of a door. In that case, you will have to take the door apart.

To do this, remove the door, lay it on two-by-fours or on a flat work surface, and carefully pry off the stile or side rail of the door, working down along the stile at the points where it meets the rails. You will pull tenons or dowels out as you do this. Remove the damaged panel carefully. You will probably have to remove the paint from around the edges to do this. In fact, we have found that the best way to do this is to have the door dipped and stripped before you attempt to take it apart, as this will loosen the glue. You can take the damaged panel to a woodworking shop to have it duplicated or to a salvage yard to see if you can find an identical panel. If the panel is flat, ¼-inch plywood may do as a replacement. Once the panel is replaced, clean the dowels and tenons and apply a thin coating of wood glue to the stile and tenons. Reassemble the door, clamp it with bar clamps, and allow it to dry before hanging it. Make sure you square it. Remove any excess glue with a wet rag.

Other Repairs

A common repair on wood doors, particularly veneer hollow-core doors, is a splintered edge, especially where it fits too tightly in a door frame. You can fix this by squirting some glue under the splintered area and pushing the veneer back in where it belongs. You may have to hold it in place with a C-clamp until the glue sets. If you do clamp the door, put a piece of waxed paper and then a block of wood over the repaired area and a block of wood on the other side to protect the door. If a piece of wood is missing from a door, you can fill it with wood putty and then sand it.

Another repair may involve fixing a dent in a metal exterior door. One way to fix a dent is to sand the area down to the bare metal and then use a putty knife to smooth in plastic automobile body filler. After this has dried, sand the filler down and repaint the door.

Sliding glass doors often do not work properly because of a bent rail. Simply bend the rail back into line with a pair of pliers or by placing a two-by-four against the bowed-out section and tapping it with a hammer until the door slides smoothly. Spraying the area with silicone will facilitate movement of the door.

If a screen door is sagging, it may be coming apart at the joints. The proper way to fix it is to pry the joints apart, fill them with glue, and reclamp them while squaring the door. You also can drill through the edge of the stile into the end of the rail and tighten the screws. If the door still sags after these repairs, attach T-braces to the inside top corner and the outside bottom corner and connect them with a light galvanized steel cable, using a turnbuckle near one corner to pull the wire tight and keep it that way.

REPAIRING POCKET DOORS

Freeing a sticky or inoperative pocket door is one of the most vexing problems in a renovation or restoration project. Pocket doors come in two basic varieties: (1) those that ride on grooved metal wheels along a raised metal track that sits on the floor and (2) those that ride on a track above the door (see Figure 21-2). The simplest way to tell what kind of door you have is to look for the track on the floor and look in the slot in the overhead to see if there is a trolley track.

Most problems with pocket doors occur because the floor or the header on which the door rides is not level. This can be a severe problem for either type of door because it is so difficult to get at the track behind the walls. We have had to break through the walls to fix a problem on more than one occasion. Don't be afraid to do this, however, because restoring the beauty of an operating pocket door is worth the effort of fixing the holes in the walls.

Inside the walls, these doors fit into pockets framed by studs installed on their flat side. Each door's top fits between stop moldings, and, in some cases, wooden pegs fit in a grooved track to hold the door in line. Double pocket doors have a stop screwed to the middle of the door frame to keep the doors from sliding beyond the middle of the opening. Sometimes in older houses, the studs in the pockets warp, particularly when the pocket door is in a bearing wall. To detect such studs, you must first remove the door from its pocket. To remove a double door, unscrew the center stop and slide the door to the opposite side of the doorway. To remove a single door, you must remove the door's trim. Probe inside the pocket with a piece of scrap wood as wide as the door and notice where the scrap binds. The studs at the edge of the opening can be planed easily, but you may have to remove part of the plaster wall covering to reach the studs deep within a pocket.

Also, bits of plaster often pile up in pockets. This debris should be swept or vacuumed out when the doors are removed. If a door track is dented or crushed, bend it back into place with pliers. If the floor has settled in the door pocket, you will probably have to remove the molding and some of the wall behind it to get into the pocket, then reinforce the area below the track with a piece of wood cut to match the sagging floor so that the door sits level.

To remove a jammed door, screw metal eye

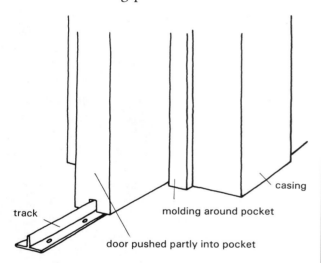

FIGURE 21-2A. *A pocket door with a bottom track.*

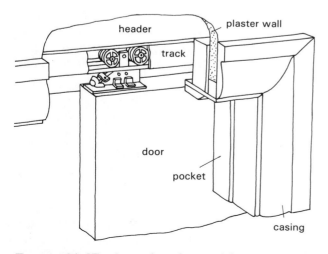

FIGURE 21-2B. *A pocket door with a top track.*

screws into the edge of the door approximately halfway between the floor and the head of the door and about a foot apart. Run a loop of heavy wire between them and use the wire as a handle to drag the door out of its pocket, placing your foot against the doorstop and casing. If you have to remove the door from its frame, unscrew the center stop on the double door and slide the door to the center of the opening. Pry off one of the stop moldings from the top jamb. If the door has wheels on the bottom, simply lift it off the track and pull it out of the opening. If the door rides on a trolley above, pull the door out on the opposite side of the wheel carriage, lifting the wheels off the track and pulling the door down and out. For a single door, you must remove the casing jamb and stop at one end to remove the door.

If the door's rollers are broken, you may find replacements in salvage shops or make new wheels from large window pulleys. If you have to, you can even make them out of hardwood. One way to make replacements for rollers is to cut a block of wood as thick as the deep mortise in the bottom of the door, wide enough to fit snugly between two large window pulleys set within this mortise, and long enough to reach the top of the deep mortise and line up with the shallow faceplate mortises at each side. In other words, you are replacing one large wheel with one wheel on each side of the block of wood. Cover the block with glue, tap it into the center of the mortise, and fasten it with 4d finish nails. As the glue sets, fasten the window pulleys to the door bottom on each side of the block using 1½-inch wood screws.

If your doors hang on a track and the track is level, the doors may simply need adjustment. If the track is not level, you will have to level it. About the only way to do that is to cut a hole in the wall and reattach the track to the header. For instance, sometimes the hanging track is nailed to the header, and those nails have pulled out at the back of the track in the pocket. If the track is level and in good condition, you have to find the adjustment screw on the wheel trolley and adjust the door. The best way to do this is to move the door to the center of the opening and tap shims beneath it to lift it ¼ inch off the floor. Then tighten the adjustment screws on the rollers on each trolley until the wheels come

down tight against the track. If the adjustment screws are not visible at the ends or if the door has a third roller between the outer ones, remove one of the top casings that conceal the metal track so that you can get at the screws. You also must remove the casing before you adjust a door that has a hexagonal adjustment bolt rather than screws.

INSTALLING PREHUNG DOORS

Installing a door used to require a highly skilled carpenter, but interior and exterior prehung doors are now fairly easy to install. A prehung door is factory-assembled with a door hinged and mounted on the side jamb and a hole drilled for the doorknob. In selecting prehung doors, you will need to know which way the door will open and its size. Whether a door is right-handed or left-handed is always determined by the side on which the handle is located when viewed from inside the room into which the door opens. A door is right-handed when the door opens toward you on the inside of the room and the knob is on the right.

There are three basic types of prehung doors:

1. The door is mounted inside a fully assembled jamb.

2. The door is mounted to the hinge jamb only, and you must nail together the head jamb and the other side jamb included in the unit.

3. The jambs are made out of tongue-and-groove pieces that fit together from opposite sides of a rough opening. This is called a *split jamb*. The door is hung from one side of the jamb, and the other side fits into that. One advantage of a split jamb is that you can adjust the width of the jamb to match a slightly irregular wall, but split-jamb doors are slightly more difficult to install. They are designed so that you can install the door with all of the casing preinstalled.

Once a prehung door is placed in a rough opening, it must be shimmed to make it square, since the opening itself may be slightly out of square and will be larger than the door frame. Shims such as shingles or precut wedges should be placed from both sides. If they are not, they will cause the jamb to twist. You can control the spacing between the frame and studs by pushing the shims in farther or withdrawing them. If you cannot shim an exterior door from the outside because of the brick mold, you should use flat stock of varying widths rather than shingles. A prehung door will be installed approximately 2 inches from the bottom of the frame to accommodate the threshold or the carpet and pad. If the space between the door and the floor is not appropriate, you may have to remove some material from the bottom of the jambs.

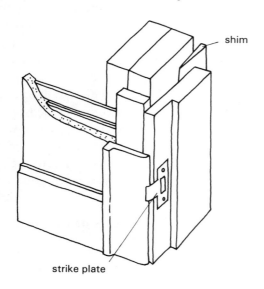

FIGURE 21-3. *Shimming a prehung door.*

Center the frame in the opening and hold it in place by driving 12d casing nails through the shims and into the trimmer stud near the top of the hinge-side jamb. Close the door, then place a steel framing square against the jamb corners to check squareness. Adjust the shims until the door is square and nail the head jamb to the header. Since the head jamb keeps the top of the unit rigid, the trick is to get the bottoms of the side jambs properly spaced so the door fits evenly and tightly. One trick that we use is to drive a drywall screw through the jamb and into the trimmer stud, then tighten or back off the screw until the jambs are exactly spaced. Installing wedges as you go, nail the hinge side and then the other side as you keep double-checking for

squareness. Score the shingles with a utility knife next to the jamb and snap them off. The final steps of the operation are to install the casing if the prehung door does not come with it (split-jamb doors often do), then install the doorknob and strike plates (see Figure 21-3).

HANGING YOUR OWN DOOR

If hanging your own door, it is best to buy premade door jambs. They will already be routed for the head jamb and cut to size. If you make your own, use stock that is at least a full 1 inch thick and rip it to the width of the finished wall. At the top of the side jamb, rout a ½-inch-deep dado the thickness of the jamb material so the head jamb fits flush with the tops of the side jambs. The rough door opening should be as wide as the door plus the thickness of the two side jambs plus 1 to 2 inches for shimming.

Put the jambs together with glue and nails, then install them in the opening, shimming each so that the opening is square. Make sure to shim behind each hinge location, check that the frame is plumb and square, and then nail the top of the hinge-side jamb in place. When the jamb is square, plumb, and installed, again check that it is square by placing your steel framing square in the corners. Also use a level to check that the head jamb is level.

When everything is squared, double-check that the door fits evenly. The door should be trimmed ¼ inch less than the jamb width to get a ⅛-inch clearance on each side. On exterior doors, you may wish to trim it for weather stripping. Do all the trimming for width on the hinge stile if possible so you will not have to deepen the lock mortise. Bevel the inner edge of the lock stile ⅛ inch with a jack plane so that it will clear the weather stripping as it closes.

On doors up to 7 feet high, use three 4-inch butt hinges. On doors over 7 feet high, use four hinges. Exterior doors should use ball bearing or thrust bearing hinges. The door and the jamb must be mortised so the hinges will be flush with the surface. Set the door on edge and brace it. Exact hinge locations vary, but a common practice is to place the top of the top hinge 7 inches from the top of the door and the bottom of the lower hinge 11 inches from the bottom of the door. Place the other hinges evenly. Trace the hinge outline on the stile edge, allowing the leaf to extend ¼ inch beyond the stile edge so that the knuckle will not bind against the casing when the door is fully open. On exterior doors, remember that the knuckle is inside, not outside, the house.

Hinge mortises can be cut with a router and template, a hinge marker, or a hammer and chisel. A router and template and a butt hinge marker not only speed the work but also are much more precise than a hammer and chisel. To use a hinge marker, you just place it over the hinge area, hammer it down to the depth required, and chisel it out.

After the mortises are cut, put the hinges in place and punch the center of each screw hole with a nail or an awl and then screw in the hinge. Make sure that the screws go in straight because, if a screw is crooked, it will pull the hinge out of alignment when the door is closed. When the door hinges are installed, put the door in the jamb and mark where the hinges will fit, allowing the knuckles to extend ¼ inch beyond the edge. This is easier said than done, so you should have a helper. Put shims or blocks under the door to raise it to ⅛ inch from the top. Mark the outline of the hinges with a sharp pencil or a hinge marker. A good trick is to mark, cut, and install the top hinge first, then put the door up and mark the other hinges. If the hinges do not line up, loosen the screws on both leaves, while a helper supports the door, and tap the leaves together. When the door is up, check that it closes without binding and that it has approximately a ⅛-inch clearance on all sides. Then tighten the screws.

The final step is installing doorstops made of ½″ x 1½″ material. While you hold the door closed at the proper position, have a helper trace the outside edge of the door along the jamb with a sharp pencil. Measure and cut the stops to length, nailing in the head stop first and then the two legs. For greater security, stops for exterior doors are often milled as an integral part of the jamb so they cannot be pried off. If you are working with an exterior door, the last item to install is the threshold. If it is hard-wood, drill holes and nail it to the floor. If it is aluminum, drive screws through the predrilled holes. Now measure the height of the threshold and cut the door to clear it and any weather stripping. Finally, install the trim, if needed.

INSTALLING A MODERN POCKET DOOR

Modern pocket doors are sold in two varieties: (1) a ready-made unit complete with a door and (2) just the hardware, to which you add the door of your choice and build your own frame. If you have saved doors from the building and want to use one as a pocket door, you would buy the hardware and build your own frame. Regardless of the type of installation, the first step is to prepare the opening.

The easiest type of pocket door to install is the ready-made unit. It is sold with a hollow-core door installed in the frame, with all the jambs and the overhead track packed separately. It usually comes unassembled with instructions. When the opening is ready, remove the door jambs and track and put the unit together according to the manufacturer's instructions. Put the frame in the opening and then mount the wheels on top of the door about 1 inch from each end. Put the side jamb in place against the trimmer stud on the latch side of the opening and install the head jamb. Place shims between the head jamb and the header to level it and stiffen it, then nail the head jamb through the shims to the header. Screw the overhead track to the head jamb, being careful to keep the track centered and level. Lift the door and hook the wheels on track. After adjusting the wheels and trimming the door if needed, fasten the bottom of the ready-made pocket frame to the floor. Now it is ready to be drywalled and then trimmed.

If installing your own unit, the first step is to put the overhead track in the opening and open it if it is adjustable until both ends are flush against the trimmer studs. Check that it is centered and level, then screw it in. Draw a chalk line on the floor between the outer edges of the trimmer studs to be used as guides for positioning the split jambs (jambs on each side of the door at the pocket) and the studs in the pocket. Then install the studs and a split jamb. Hang the door and slip it halfway into the pocket. Install door guides at the base of the split jamb, one on each side of the door, and the rubber door bumper on the trimmer studs inside the pocket. Then push the door against the bumper and make sure that it works properly. Install the frame slats between the split jamb and the trimmer studs so that the opening can be drywalled. Install the side and head jambs and a doorstop on the side jamb. To cover the metal track, nail a standard doorstop in front of the rail, making sure that the door will go past it. After you drywall, trim the doorway with the door casing.

INSTALLING BIFOLD DOORS AND SLIDING CLOSET DOORS

In places where a conventional door would be in the way, bifold and sliding doors come to the rescue. These are usually used in closets and pantries. They can be plain, paneled, or louvered. Besides the advantage of opening so there is little obstruction, they are easy to install. Sliding doors come in pairs for each standard door width. Bifold doors come in hinged pairs for each standard door width. Single units consist of two doors hinged together. For larger openings, two bifold units that meet in the center are used. If you cannot find doors that fit the opening exactly, you can trim the doors down, but rough openings should be framed for a particular door width.

The hardware for bifold doors includes an overhead track, top and bottom pivots for the doors, and an adjusting bracket and guide for the bottom of the doors to rest in. If you purchase antique doors from a salvage dealer, you can buy just the hardware for bifolds.

The first step in installing bifolds is to measure the dimension of the opening and trim the doors to fit if needed. Then install a track in the center of the head jamb with screws and insert the rubber bumper on the door-closing side of the track. For a pair of doors that close in the middle, the bumper would be in the center of the track. Install the pivot

brackets in the top and bottom of each door according to the manufacturer's instructions. (The outside door will only have a top pivot.) Drop a plumb bob from each end of the rail to position the bottom pivot brackets directly under the top ones. Screw them to the wall and to the floor. If carpeting is to be installed, cut a strip of plywood to fit under each bottom bracket and thick enough to raise it slightly above the carpet pad. Now attach the doors one at a time. First set the bottom pivot into the bottom socket, tilting the door toward the center of the top rail, then slide the top pivot bracket into the rail. The top pivot should slip into its socket at the end of the rail. The top socket can be adjusted. Tighten down the socket so that it stays in its proper place in the rail. If it's a double bifold, install the other side in exactly the same way. Open and close the doors and adjust the sockets and bottom pivots as needed. Install trim around the door if it is not a drywall-returned opening and a doorstop to cover the rail.

Installing sliding doors is easier than installing bifold doors, although the hardware is similar. The basic hardware for sliding doors consists of a double overhead track, a pair of wheels that attaches to the top of each door, and a door guide that is fastened to the floor. Some better-quality sliding doors include a floor track with rollers built into it to guide the doors. Again, if you have antique doors, you can buy the hardware kit separately.

The height of the doors should be 1½ inches less than that of the opening. This allows room for the track at the top and some clearance above the floor or carpet. Each door should be ½ inch wider than half the opening so that the doors overlap by one inch when closed.

Screw the overhead track into the center of the jamb. Mount the wheels on the top edge of the doors about 2 inches in from the sides. Hang the inside door on the inside channel of the track, then hang the outside door and push the doors back against the door jambs. See if they hang straight by comparing them to the jambs. If the doors are not hanging properly, loosen or tighten the adjusting screw to raise or lower one side until they hang evenly with the jambs. Once this is done, slide both doors in one direction and insert the track guide underneath them; mark where it goes. Remove the doors and place the track guide in the center of the opening. Replace the doors. Finally, install the trim, if needed, and a one-by-two stop to cover the track.

EXTERIOR STEEL DOORS

Approximately 40 percent of all entry doors sold and installed today are made of steel. Steel doors are competitively priced and energy-efficient, and they provide more security and ease of maintenance than other types of doors, particularly in the back of a house or for a basement entry door. Steel doors typically have a dense core of polyurethane foam and have R values as high as 15. They are installed just like any other door, either as a prehung unit or as a separate door. You must be careful not to dent the door, and remember that the door cannot be changed in size. The jambs must come to meet the door. The best way to install a steel door is to install it as a prehung unit. We prefer them for all basement installations.

EXTERIOR TRANSOM DOORS

Entry doors in old brick buildings are typically 9 feet tall with a transom and often a curved top. If the frame and jambs in a door like this are rotted or unusable for some other reason, we tend to tear out the entire unit and rebuild it. This means creating a very extensive prehung unit to go back in that space. It sounds difficult but it isn't. Usually a door like this will be 14 to 16 inches deep. We construct new jambs out of ¾- or 1-inch plywood. Nail the two sides, top, and transom bottom together. Attach brick mold to the edge of the jambs after they are put together. The frame must be up to 4 inches smaller than the opening so the brick mold will be close to flush to the brick opening. The top brick mold would be constructed of two-by-six material by the method described for the top brick mold of curved-top windows (see Chapter 14). At this point, the entire component is laid on its back (inside or houseside), and the threshold is installed.

If the transom bottom is plywood, use molding to cover the edge.

Then measure the transom. It is best to have a hermetically sealed double-paned glass made for it. Do not install the glass until the door is attached and the unit is installed. Measure and cut stop material for both sides of the glass all the way around the transom and install one side. The entire glass unit should be sealed with silicone when installed. Purchase or construct the door to fit in the opening. Prehang it and install a doorstop. We usually install the stop and then the door.

Set the entire unit into the opening after removing the old threshold. Using 3- to 5-inch galvanized drywall screws, screw through the frame and into the trimmer studs, using shims to square the door. Caulk the outside brick mold to the brick with construction adhesive. The inside of the door frame should be ½ inch beyond the interior stud wall of the building when installed. Finally, install the last stud in your interior wall up against the jamb (leaving ½ inch for the drywall). Install the drywall and case the inside of the jamb. Weatherstrip the door and install the hardware and the glass transom.

DOORKNOBS AND LOCKS

A visit to a hardware store or specialty door store will give you an idea of the wide variety of locks, doorknobs, and door latches that are available. Going through an architectural antique shop and looking at the parts it stocks will give you an idea of the types of hardware used in early houses. We tend to keep the existing door hardware if it is workable and unique and install dead bolts in addition to that.

The purpose of this section is to give you a basic idea of how to install a cylinder lock, a dead bolt, and a mortise lock, which are the three basic items that you may encounter. You may also have rim locks, in which the lock case and the strike plate are exterior to the door. Unless these are antiques, they probably aren't worth saving. Whatever kind of lock you have, you should make sure you can exit the house quickly in case of a fire but still deny

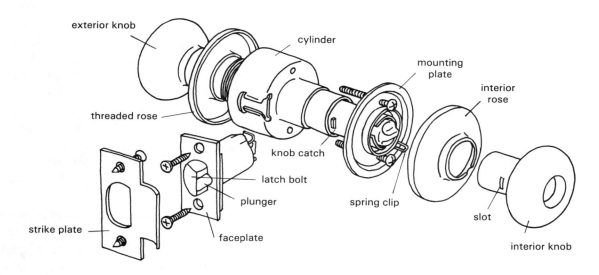

FIGURE 21-4. *An exploded drawing of a typical cylinder lock assembly and doorknob.*

access to an intruder, especially one who may break a window to gain access to a lock on the inside.

Installing a Cylinder Lock and Interior Doorknob

The cylinder lock is made in many different styles. Some have twist knobs, some have button locks, and some have no locks. Those with key locks are usually found on exterior doors. The standard cylinder lock consists of two handles, two plates to cover the hole in the door, a central cylinder to retract the bolt, the bolt mechanism, the strike plate, and the faceplate (see Figure 21-4). Cylinder locks are always installed after the door is hung. One of the nice things about prehung doors is that the doorknob and bolt holes are already drilled. One of the reasons that we put a $2\frac{1}{8}$-inch hole saw in our tool list (see Chapter 8) is that you need it to drill the holes for cylinder locks.

If you drill your own holes, the knobs should be located at the same height as other knobs in the house (which is usually 36 inches from the floor). The manufacturer will give you instructions regarding what holes to drill for the given thickness of a door and the setback (how far the cylinder is from the edge of the door). The manufacturer will usually supply a template that shows where to drill. Always put a wedge in the door or have a helper hold it while you are drilling. To prevent splinter-

ing, drill part way through the door with the hole saw; when the drill bit emerges on the other side, use that as a guide to complete the job from the opposite side of the door. Drill the bolt hole with a spade bit of the size specified on the template (usually 1 inch). Make sure that this hole is perfectly horizontal and straight. Locate the positions for the strike plate and faceplate and install those next. In most cylinder locks, the faceplate comes preinstalled to the bolt. Test the door to make sure that it operates correctly with the faceplate and bolt installed. Then install the cylinder according to the manufacturer's instructions.

Installing a Dead Bolt

A dead bolt assembly requires a key on the outside and either a key or a turning knob on the inside. To prevent break-ins, especially break-ins where an intruder may break a door window to get access to the inside of a lock, you should have a double-keyed dead bolt—that is, you need a key to open the dead bolt on the inside. But if you do not leave the key in it, it may be very difficult to find the key when you are in a panic situation such as a fire. Even so, we usually install double-keyed dead bolts in most houses unless there is no glass near the door. Just make sure you have a well-rehearsed fire plan.

A dead bolt is a shaft of hardened steel that enters

a hole drilled through the door jamb and sometimes into the trimmer stud behind it. A dead bolt lock is installed much like a cylinder lock, except that you drill a deeper hole and the strike plate is installed more securely. Dead bolts are usually installed 6 to 18 inches above the doorknob.

Installing a Mortise Lock

Mortise locks are found in most Victorian homes. These locks, mounted in a thin steel case, must be set in doors at least 1⅜ inches thick. In addition, they are set deeply into the end of the door. You must be careful that the mortise you install is less than the width of the stile. Be particularly careful if you have a glass panel in the door because the panel will extend into the stile and you may shatter the glass by drilling for the mortise lock. Mortise locks generally include a dead bolt in addition to the latch and offer good security in one package, but they are very difficult to install unless you have the proper tools.

The first step is to mark the outside of the door both on the side and the end (where the holes will be needed for keys and where the lock case will be set in the door). There are two ways to mortise for the lock case. Most rehabbers drill a series of holes within the outline, making sure that the drill bit is ¹/₁₆ inch wider than the actual lock case, then remove the wood between the bore holes with a straight chisel or a mortise chisel. The difficult part is cleaning out the back part of the mortise. This can be done only with a lock mortise chisel. You then insert the lock case, with the faceplate up against the door edge, and mark an outline of the faceplate. Mortise the door so that the faceplate is flush with the door edge. You can use a routerlike tool, called a power lock mortiser, to mortise doors, but this tool is very expensive to buy or rent. After you install the lock case, install the strike plate and any faceplates on the side of the door to cover the holes for the dead bolt and knob spindles. The strike plates are fairly difficult to install because they must be aligned not only for the dead bolt but also the latch. Remember that there is only so much wood to screw into when installing faceplates, so you must be careful.

In most large cities, architectural antique stores carry a very large supply of mortise locks, strike plates, and side plates. Most stores will offer these items cleaned and polished or uncleaned. They also will stock a wide variety of knobs. The hardest thing to come by in door hardware is the screws used to hold the knobs to the spindles. Some hardware stores do stock these screws, however.

SOME FINAL TIPS ON DOORS

We do not suggest that you attempt to make your own doors unless you are an established woodworker and have the tools required for the task. Making virtually any kind of door is a very complex process, and doors are readily available at salvage yards and lumberyards. Since you have so many things to do, you do not need to spend time making doors.

If you plan to gut your building totally, buy all new prehung doors. You will have new walls, and 4⅝-inch-deep prehung doors will be quite easy to install. If you are restoring or rehabbing with old material, replace missing doors with those found in salvage yards. If you live in a small community, do not be afraid to call salvage yards in large cities that are a reasonable distance away. As you get ready to trim your house, it may be worthwhile spending a weekend in the city while the drywallers are working. Search through all the salvage yards and large retailers for the items that you need to finish your rehab.

We suggest that you do not try to have doors made new at a planing mill or a woodworking shop as we suggested for windows. Duplicating a window not only is important for historical and aesthetic reasons, but may also be cost-effective. In contrast, you can furnish your entire house with prehung doors for the price of building one or two from scratch at a planing mill.

References

OLD

Late Victorian Architectural Details. Watkins Glen, New York: American Life Foundation Study Institute, 1978.

Radford, William A. *Radford's Portfolio of Details of Building Construction.* Chicago: Radford Architectural Company, 1911.

NEW

Johnson, Edwin. *Old House Woodwork Restoration.* Englewood Cliffs, New Jersey: Prentice-Hall, 1983.

Talbot, Antony, ed. *Handbook of Doormaking, Windowmaking, and Staircasing.* New York: Sterling Publishing Co., 1980.

Williams, T. Jeff. *How to Replace and Install Doors and Windows.* San Francisco: Ortho Books, 1984.

Chapter 22

TRIM AND FINISH CARPENTRY

ow you trim your house will depend to a large extent on how much you have done to the structure. If you have totally gutted the building, you may decide to use modern trim. If you kept some or all of the building intact and restored it, you will probably reinstall or fix the existing trim. If you gutted the building but want to use period material, you may buy it new or used or have it recreated. We tend to let the house speak to us in this regard.

To some extent, using old trim is a cost-benefit decision. Dealing with old trim can be quite expensive, as you must pay to have it stripped, buy it from someone who has stripped it, or strip it yourself. Then you have to repair all the nicks, dents, and nail holes in it. This is a very time-consuming task. Trim is, however, extremely important to the aesthetic and resale value of the house, so decisions about how to handle it are quite important.

The Victorian penchant for detail and ornamentation led to the widespread use of moldings in late nineteenth-century houses. In most cases, moldings were either painted or heavily stained or grained. Some white pine was used in the West and some yellow pine in the Midwest, but fir is harder and thus was a better candidate for structural moldings.

The words *trim* and *molding* were often used interchangeably because trim is made of more than one piece of molding. Andrea Palladio, a sixteenth-century Italian architect, measured Greek and Roman ruins and published the proportions and sizes of eight classic molding shapes. These form the basis for molding design today (see Figures 22-1 and 22-2). In many Victorian houses, molding

became the personal signature of the carpenter who built the house, and by 1880 standardized molding was being milled commercially.

If you plan to save your molding, you must remove it very carefully. If the molding is painted,

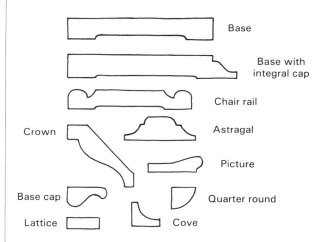

FIGURE 22-1. *Some basic molding shapes.*

you can sand the surface lightly to locate the nail heads. Then work a putty knife or a flat pry bar behind the molding to remove it or use a punch to push the nail all the way through the back of the molding. If you are prying the molding base, pry it just far enough away from the wall to allow you to insert another pry bar by the next nail. If you are leaving the plaster intact, put a small block of plywood between the pry bar and the wall. Work from nail to nail, increasing the gap; after two or three passes, the molding should come loose.

You can usually find replacement molding in an

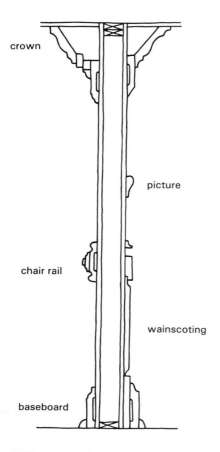

crown

picture

chair rail

wainscoting

baseboard

FIGURE 22–2. *A sectional view of different kinds and placements of trim.*

architectural antique store. If not, you can have it remilled. Sometimes you can replace the original molding with a precise reproduction made from standard shapes. The standard shapes can be combined in many different ways to duplicate more complex moldings. In 1957, the WP/S system was introduced to categorize a vast number of stock moldings and styles. This classification replaced a numbering system developed in the 1880s.

A catalog illustrating high-volume stock molding designs and sizes with WP numbers is available for $2.50 from the Western Wood Molding and Millwood Producers (P.O. Box 25278, Portland, OR 97225). Also, authentic copies of Victorian moldings are available from a number of manufacturers and local planing mills. A full line of oak-veneered doorjambs and moldings, which are less expensive than solid oak materials, is available from Contact Lumber (275 Duniway Center, 2525 Southwest First, Portland, OR 97201). Finally,

Abitibi-Price Corporation (Building Products Division, Troy, MI 48084) produces the Canterbury molding line. We suggest using this line, because the moldings are built around a collection of corner pieces designed to fit every application, so the only way you have to cut a molding is straight and to length (no mitering). You just butt these pieces up to the corner accessories.

RESCUING THE OLD WOOD TRIM

In many old houses, the moldings were painstakingly shaped by the builder and were made of fine hardwoods (mahogany, walnut, ash, cherry, and oak) that would be very expensive to replace today. This trim is often in poor condition, with surfaces dulled or shapes concealed under layers of paint. The obvious solution, if you plan to restore or reuse this molding, is to refinish the wood.

The amount of work involved in stripping old finishes depends on the nature of the finish and the number of layers. If woodwork is stained or varnished and the finish has darkened with age, you need only clean the finish thoroughly to reveal the wood grain pattern. You can do this with turpentine to remove wax and grime and then strong cleansers such as trisodium phosphate (TSP) or ammonia. If part of the finish needs to be removed, lacquer thinner will remove varnish and denatured alcohol will remove shellac. Always wear gloves and goggles when you do this, especially on vertical surfaces.

Probably the most difficult aspect of retaining old trim is stripping painted woodwork. We usually check to see what kind of wood we have. If we find pine or fir and the painted finish is not too bad, we repaint the woodwork. If we find some hardwood, we strip it. There are two ways to strip wood. One is to get all the molding out of the house and take it to an architectural salvage house or paint-stripping operation. Have the people there dip the wood to remove all the paint. This is an easy way to handle the problem, but using it depends on your budget, whether you are going to leave the molding in place, and the amount of molding to be done.

The second way to strip wood is to leave it in place and strip it as is. Most do-it-yourselfers opt to strip the wood in place if they do not have to remove it for any other reason.

There are several ways to remove paint from woodwork. It can be loosened with a chemical stripper and then scraped off with paint knives and molding scrapers, or it can be softened with a heat gun and then scraped. Keep in mind that a chemical strong enough to remove several layers of paint is very hazardous. The best stripper for inside work is methylene chloride because it is nonflammable. It is, however, very expensive. Methylene chloride is very effective on oil-based paint but less effective on latex paint. To remove latex paint, you need a stripper that contains methylal toluol and acetone. These chemicals are flammable, so you should never smoke while using them, and you should keep some doors and windows open to vent the fumes.

Strippers are sold in both liquid and paste form. We recommend a semipaste version that contains a compound to help it adhere to vertical surfaces. Keep in mind that strippers contain active solvents that must be chemically neutralized on the wood after the stripper has done its work. Most solvents in strippers can be neutralized with trisodium phosphate and hot water.

Before you strip large sections of trim, we suggest that you use some stripper and a scraping tool to clean a small piece of trim and consider both the difficulty of the job and the quality of the wood you expose. Only a fine-grain hardwood warrants the labor of full-fledged stripping down to the bare wood. In many old houses, softwood moldings were intended to be painted or heavily stained and are best repainted. We often repaint these moldings white because white hides irregularities better than other colors. If details have been obscured by many coats of paint, you may have to do some stripping but not all the way down to the bare wood.

A stripped piece of molding must be finished with hand sanding or steel wool to smooth and clean the surface. Sanding smoothes out grain that is raised above the surface by the stripping chemicals. It also removes dark patches of wood and stains. Many stains will run deep into the grain and these can be lightened with oxalic acid, common laundry bleach, or wood-bleaching products normally used to refinish wooden boats. Spot bleaching may suffice, but generally you will have to bleach an entire piece of wood.

When you complete your stripping job, you may be surprised at the appearance of the wood you end up with. Raw walnut is not dark brown but grayish. Mahogany is not deep red but ranges from brown to tan, and cherry tends to be a very light tan. Only the application of shellac, polyurethane, varnish, or wax will bring out the deep tones in these woods. Thus, in most cases, refinishing with shellac or varnish, and possibly staining, is in order. You can buy a wide range of wood fillers designed for different hardwoods to fill nail holes and other irregularities.

CREATING A MATCHING MOLDING

When a section of wood trim is damaged beyond repair or missing altogether, you will often be able to find matching molding as new stock in a good lumberyard, in architectural antique stores, or in salvage yards. In some cases, however, your trim will have to be duplicated from scrap. You can reconstruct some wide moldings by gluing or nailing together several simple stock pieces, as most old moldings break down into a limited number of classic shapes that can be found in modern moldings.

It is possible to cut many molding shapes with a planer, a router, or with shaped blades that can be fitted to a power plane. The most practical and safest approach is to use a table saw with a molding cutter head. Molding cutters are special tools that mount three identical blades onto a saw arbor and can be purchased in most tool outlet stores. Sears sells a kit that comes with about a dozen different cutting blades.

You select the proper blades by physically matching them to a sample piece of your molding. If it is absolutely necessary, you can buy three blank blades for the cutter head, trace the profile of the molding onto a cardboard template, transfer that to the cutters, and grind your own blades. If you have to do this, it may be better to take the entire project to a woodworking shop and have the molding duplicated there.

Cutting moldings on a table saw demands the utmost caution because many of the tool's normal safety features cannot be used with the molding cutter. Since the cutter head will probably have to come right up to the edge of the fence and most fences are made of metal, you will have to face your rip fence on both sides with 1″ x 3″ hardwood by screwing straight through it to make an auxiliary fence. Lower the cutter head below the table and slide the wood fence over it. Raise the cutter head slowly to cut a semicircular notch in the wood fence no more than 1 inch high. We use pieces of wood to hold the molding in place on the top and side. We lay a piece of the molding stock against the rip fence with the blades in the correct position, then place a wood block on top of the wood molding and clamp that block snugly to the fence. This will keep the molding thrust firmly to the blades and keep it from coming up out of the saw. We also use a piece of wood to keep the molding aligned while it is being cut. We place a second board on the table flush against the edge of the molding and clamp it to the table. Finally, we use a stick to push the lumber through the saw so that our hands never get near the blade.

If the work begins to chatter or vibrate, you should slow the rate of feed and also check whether your guide blocks on the top and side are loose. Be extremely careful. Never cut short pieces. If you are making long molding pieces, you might want to have a helper pick up the wood as it comes out of the table saw. Never pull it through the table saw, however. If you have no experience with a table saw or with woodworking, it is better to pay a woodworking shop to create your molding than to risk losing a finger or an eye because of an accident with a table saw.

TIPS ON WORKING WITH MOLDING

Working with molding is not difficult, but it does take patience because every mistake you make will show up, especially if you are not going to paint the molding but will stain or varnish it. Use the right tools. The accuracy of your miter box will determine how your trim job looks. You need to use a miter box with a backsaw to cut moldings. You cannot expect to do it with a circular or hand saw. We suggest that you buy a medium- to high-quality chop box. In nailing, make sure that you predrill holes in hardwood and semihardwood stock and use nail sets. Do not be afraid to use construction adhesive where nails are hard to drive. Mistakes can be remedied by using a drywall knife to cut the drywall paper along the top of the molding and then carefully removing the molding, paper and all. Finally, you should prepare the surface to which you are going to nail the molding thoroughly, making sure that it is as flat as possible.

Store trim out of the way and bring it into the house only when the exterior work has been completed, the finished walls are completely dry, and the house is cleaned up. Trim that is installed on a damp surface will absorb water and swell, causing joints to separate. If you intend to paint trim, prime it as soon as possible and install it preprimed. You can save a tremendous amount of time by painting and staining trim before it is installed. This is particularly true of hardwoods on which you will use an oil-based varnish. Only the cut ends and nail holes will have to be touched up later, and you will avoid the frustration of getting trim paint or varnish on the walls.

Use the longest, best-looking links of trim where they will be most visible. Do not combine a lot of short pieces. Also try to match wood grains. Poor-quality wood and short lengths can be patched together in inconspicuous spots, such as closets. When a wall is too long for a piece of wood, join the trim sections by mitering the ends rather than butt-joining them, as shrinkage will be much less noticeable. We lay the pieces of molding around the room to see what they will look like before we do any cutting so that we can match the grain and use the long pieces in the most appropriate places.

Because trim is usually fragile, avoid nailing it too close to the edges. Always use the correct size nails. Four-penny finish or casing nails are required for the inside of door and window casings, and 6d and 8d nails can be used for the outside and most baseboard trim. If you are applying pine trim and planning to paint it, you can use caulking compound to fill nail holes and cover any irregularities at miter cuts. If you are using hardwood, you should use the appropriate wood filler, as filler is more noticeable in work that is varnished. Nail holes should be precise, and you should nail only where there is a stud. Also, if carpet will be laid, baseboards should be installed ½ inch above the floor. Set the baseboard on small pieces of drywall when installing.

Mitering is probably the most common and the most difficult method of joining molding on inside and outside corners. It can take a lot of time to learn how to cut a piece of molding, especially because you must take the molding away from the wall to cut it. To avoid this problem, on the back of the molding mark which way the angle is cut or work out some other system. It is often easier to miter the corner before you cut the length of the molding. This allows you to adjust the miter cuts if necessary so they fit better. On outside corners, always nail the corner together or clamp and glue it.

In a coped joint, the end of one piece is cut flush to the wall and the other piece is shaped to match its face. This is a relatively easy procedure with some moldings and is an acceptable way of joining moldings on inside corners, especially if the walls are not perfectly square and you can caulk and paint the joint. If you have a high-quality miter box, it is easier to miter the corner than to cope it.

You can also use *plinth blocks,* which are square or oblong blocks commonly found in corners and at the bottom of doors and windows in Victorian houses. They are especially useful when two different kinds of molding meet, such as a base molding and a door casing. The moldings butt up against these blocks, so you don't have to worry about mitering joints. Plinth blocks can be made or purchased at lumberyards and planing mills.

INSTALLING BASEBOARD TRIM AND SIMILAR MOLDING

Baseboards should be nailed into each stud. Pieces of baseboard should be joined over a stud so that you have something solid to nail the pieces to.

Otherwise, they should be glued with construction adhesive. If quarter-round molding is used at the bottom of the baseboard, it should be nailed at an angle to the edge of the flooring rather than to the bottom of the baseboard so that it will stay in place and will cover any gap if the baseboard shrinks.

Outside corners should always be mitered. If you miter each piece slightly less than 45 degrees, you will get a better grip on most square corners. You can trim each miter cut slightly with a plane until the fit is perfect. When nailing baseboard trim, always drive the nails at an angle to inhibit warping. On outside corners, nail each piece to the other with 4d finishing nails. Inside corners often need no nailing at all because the pieces will hold each other in place, particularly if they are mitered.

WAINSCOTING

A *wainscot* is a wooden lining on an interior wall. Although modern paneling is technically a wainscot, it is set flush to the wall and usually covers the entire wall. Most wainscoting in old homes projects out from the wall about ½ inch and is decorated with trim or molding at the top and bottom. Most wainscoting was constructed of tongue-and-groove planks. When used in kitchens, pantries, and bathrooms, wainscoting not only protects the walls from grease, dirt, and water but is also very beautiful. Most early wainscoting was varnished so that it could be scrubbed.

In more expensive houses, wainscoting was created from panels with rails, in much the same way that doors were constructed. We have seen at least one instance in which a rehabber took several eight-panel doors, laid them on their sides, topped them with a chair rail, and created a ready-made wainscot. A wainscot made of panels and rails is more difficult to build than a wainscot constructed of vertical tongue-and-groove planks, although the former can be constructed of paneling fairly easily. We have built such wainscots by using a 31″ x 8′ piece of ¼-inch paneling as the backing and putting doubled 6-inch pieces of paneling on its face for the rails. We then covered the edges of each panel with picture-frame molding to conceal the edges of the plywood used as rails. We topped the entire affair with chair-rail molding.

You can use tongue-and-groove flooring to replicate a partial wall wainscot. Some lumberyards carry flooring with a V groove at each edge, which is more authentic to the original detail. We are fond of using ¼-inch tongue-and-groove cedar or redwood paneling, which makes a very nice wainscot in a bathroom.

One note of caution about wainscoting: Too much wood in a small room can make the room seem even smaller, so plan carefully when you think about using dark woods in small rooms.

References

OLD

Maginnis, Owen B. *How to Join Mouldings, or, The Arts of Mitring and Coping for Carpenters, Joiners, and Cabinet Makers, Picture Frame Makers and Woodworkers*. New York: N.P., 1882.

Riddell, Robert. *The Carpenter and Joiner Modernized*. Philadelphia: Claxton, Remsen & Haffelfinger, 1880.

Ross, George Alexander. *Elementary Course Work*. Chicago: A. Flanagan Company, 1901.

NEW

Ball, John E. *Millwork, Power Tools, and Painting*. Indianapolis: T. Audel, 1982.

Bergquist, Craig. *Finish Carpentry Techniques*. San Francisco: Ortho Books, 1983.

From Tree to Trim: A Guide to Wood Mouldings and Jambs. Portland, Oregon: Western Wood Moulding and Millwork Producers, 1975.

Chapter 23

KITCHENS AND BATHS

When people buy a house, they most often want to remodel the bathrooms and kitchen, since those rooms were usually tailored to the previous owners and therefore never quite fit the new occupants. The kitchen and bathrooms are the most complex rooms in a house, however, and designing them is not simply a matter of building a larger room but of using the space correctly. Renovating kitchens and bathrooms is really a three-step process: Step one is planning and designing the space; step two is purchasing the materials; and step three is installing the materials. We discuss these steps in order.

DESIGNING KITCHENS AND BATHS

Design Constraints

A number of factors constrain the design of a kitchen or bathroom. The most important consideration is the size and shape of the room. This is not as much of a concern in designing a bathroom, as long as it is a minimum of 5' x 8', but it may be a significant concern in designing a kitchen. The placement of windows, doors, and other projections such as chimneys and closets will affect the entire layout of your kitchen. Whether you end up with a one-wall, shotgun, or open kitchen will depend on the room you start with.

Keep in mind that long runs of plumbing cost money and take up space. Putting in supply lines is rarely a problem, but waste and vent pipes, because of the larger dimensions, can be troublesome. Four-inch vent pipes require 6-inch walls. Waste pipes running horizontally will have traps and must be pitched at least ¼ inch per running foot, so a main line running 10 feet will need a total height of 8 to 11 inches. Clustering fixtures near a single plumbing wall is, therefore, advantageous.

Because a water heater uses a large share of the energy in a house, it should be located as near as possible to the bathrooms, washer and dryer, and kitchen—ideally, it should be centered in the house. Also, the hot water heater and hot water pipes should be insulated. If bathroom or kitchen walls containing plumbing are located near the exterior brick, the walls must be carefully insulated.

Ventilation carries off undesirable odors, and a fan capable of 12 changes of air in a room per hour should be installed in both kitchens and baths. Kitchen fans are commonly located in a hood above the stove, although countertop models are also available. Bathroom fans are usually in the ceiling near the shower. Ventilation duct work must be planned for kitchens and baths, and it makes sense to minimize the length of the run. It also makes sense to place stoves along outside walls for the same reason. Circulating vent hoods are available for stoves, but they are not very effective.

Because a high percentage of household accidents take place in kitchens and baths, you need to give some thought to safety in these rooms. Anything that will prevent falls, such as increased lighting, is important, as is installing electrical service to wet areas in accordance with local building codes. That means installing ground fault interruption (GFI) circuits in most situations.

Adequate lighting is 3 to 4 watts of incandescent light, or 1 to 2 watts of fluorescent light, per square foot of bathroom space. Light is usually concentrated around the bathroom mirror. Kitchens require 2 to 3 watts of incandescent light, or 1 to 1½ watts of fluorescent light, per square foot. No receptacle should be within 5 feet of a tub, and no heating unit should be capable of shocking or burning anyone in the kitchen or bathroom. Also, electrical codes typically require a minimum of two 20-amp circuits in kitchens to handle appliance loads, with receptacles every 3 to 4 feet of countertop. We recommend putting in three or four 20-amp circuits, with the refrigerator and microwave on individual circuits, because electrical loads in the kitchen will probably continue to increase as they have in the past 50 years.

Planning Your Kitchen

The first order of business in designing a kitchen is to measure the space in the room. You need to do this approximately six weeks before you plan to install the kitchen if you are ordering cabinets. If you can purchase your cabinets in stock from a local supplier, though, you may need no more than a week. There is no room for error in measuring a kitchen for cabinets and appliances. You must measure the available space completely and accurately, record your measurements on paper, and, using those measurements and other drawings, plan how the different elements will fit into the kitchen. If you plan your kitchen early because of the constraint of ordering cabinets, you must wait until the kitchen is framed, although you do not need to wait until it is drywalled. You will know whether you will use ½- or ⅝-inch drywall and where you will use the different types of drywall. You can measure the framing and simply add the dimension of the drywall as needed.

The best thing to use to measure a kitchen for cabinets is a 6-foot folding carpenter's rule. Never use a yardstick. A steel tape measure is acceptable if you are careful not to let it sag or slip. Also, never rely on the measurements you took when you inspected the building or when you or the architect drew plans for the building commission, as they will not be accurate enough.

Measure all room dimensions to within ¹⁄₁₆ inch or less and record them in a drawing as accurately and neatly as possible. Even the slightest error may mean that you have to return a cabinet or remove drywall to install the last cabinet. When you measure the dimensions of the kitchen, try to measure all of them at a height of 34 inches from the floor, which is where the top of the base cabinets will be, and at the floor. Make sure to note all obstacles such as chimney offsets and radiators on your sheet. Also measure the height of the ceiling and any obstructions that are within 7 to 8 feet of the floor. If you have not gutted the room, indicate the location of all existing electrical outlets, light switches, and lighting fixtures on your sketch. When you do a wall, measure each increment, add all the measurements together, and then go back and take an overall measurement to check yourself.

While you are measuring the room, use your framing square to check the squareness of every wall on the floor, 34 inches up from the floor, and 7 feet up from the floor. Another way to check for squareness is to measure 36 or 48 inches out from each corner or to a stud along each wall. If you measure 36 inches on one wall, measure 48 inches on the other wall and vice versa. Then measure the distance between those two points, which is the hypotenuse of that triangle. It should be 5 feet if the wall is square. It is essential that you check the squareness of the corners at 34 inches and 7 feet. Corners are seldom perfectly square, but you must allow for discrepancies in squareness when designing the kitchen, or your cabinets will not fit. Transfer your original drawing to grid paper and make several photocopies so that you can work out a kitchen design.

Probably the best place to start designing the kitchen is a window where you think you might want to put a sink. Another possible starting point is an existing plumbing stack. If you have left a stack intact, it is probably very close to the old location of the sink, which was probably in front of a window. If you have only one window, you may wish to reserve it for an eating area and put the sink elsewhere.

You must deal with two basic issues at this point. The first is kitchen use, and the second is the work triangle. Determine whether you use your kitchen

FIGURE 23-1. *Basic kitchen designs.*

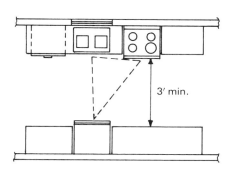

23-1A. *Galley*

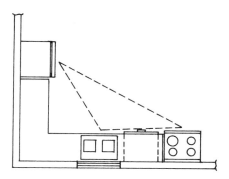

23-1B. *L-shaped*

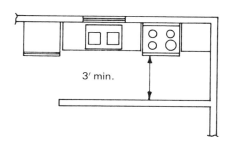

23-1C. *Single line*

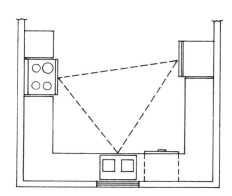

23-1D. *U-shaped*

for cooking, dining, and/or family entertainment. If you use it primarily for cooking, you should be extremely concerned about the work triangle. If, however, you use it more for dining or as a family entertainment or craft area, the work triangle may be less important than allowing extra space for these activities.

The three most important appliances in a kitchen are the sink, the stove, and the refrigerator. The cook will spend most of his or her time at or moving between these three points, and the lines that connect them make up the so-called "work triangle." Designers have theorized that a kitchen is used most effectively if these items are arranged in a tight triangle and if the distance between them is less than 20 feet. Some basic kitchen designs are shown in Figure 23-1. Three of these kitchens have the basic triangle. The shotgun, or single-line, kitchen does not. This type of kitchen is more likely to be seen in apartments than in large houses. One variant of a kitchen that is not shown is one including an

island. Islands are common in multiuse kitchens because they provide a buffer between the cooking and the entertainment or dining areas. In some cases, a sink or stove is placed in the island.

One item that many kitchen designers neglect is counter space. Meal preparation consists of a number of functions, including preparing the food, cooking it, and cleaning up, and there should be separate counter space for each function. There should be at least 2 feet of clear counter space to one side of the stove. The sink should have counter space on both sides—at least 3 feet on one side and 2 to 3 feet on the other. Dishwashers, which are usually placed next to a sink, are 2 feet wide, so you will typically have 2 feet of counter space on one side of the sink. The area that is most often neglected is the food preparation area, which is best placed near the refrigerator or between the refrigerator and sink. You also should consider the storage of small appliances in this area.

Given these basic considerations and the dimensions of your kitchen, you can attempt to lay out counter space and appliances in the most expedient way. Think about storage, including drawer bases (cabinets of drawers) and other storage cabinets such as lazy Susans (corner cabinets with round rotating storage shelves). Stoves are typically 30 inches wide unless you buy a large stove. Refrigerators vary, but you should allow at least 36 inches in width for them. Measure the refrigerator that you own or intend to buy for the house.

The first thing is to establish the placement of the sink and the countertop around it. Then work over to the stove and refrigerator, filling in cabinets as needed. Most kitchens are L-shaped, which makes for an efficient work triangle and allows for other activities. U-shaped kitchens also are common and efficient, as they provide the most storage area, but they may be more difficult to change later.

Most cabinets are made in 3-inch increments. Three-inch fillers also are available. Those can be cut narrower so that you can use them to fit your cabinets together. Keep in mind that it is less expensive to plan for fewer large cabinets than more small ones. Doing so will save time and money. Lazy Susan corner cabinets, both upper and lower, are very expensive, so it may be better to buy a return cabinet — that is, a cabinet that fits all the way back into a corner, with the other cabinet fitting flush against it. Return cabinets do not have a door for the section that fits back into the corner and are a bit inconvenient to use, but they provide more storage space than lazy Susans and are less expensive. If you must put a sink in a corner, we suggest that you use a diagonal front with a regular sink. This will slightly increase the cost of your countertop, but it will be significantly more convenient than a corner sink. Do not forget to include drawer bases, and keep in mind that you can order large pullout drawers in standard bases.

If you are planning a *peninsula* (a counter that sticks out into the center of the kitchen for a bar or divider to separate activities in the kitchen), you have several options. A divider peninsula top need be only 18 inches deep if you buy wall cabinets (only 12 inches deep) to put underneath it. Most island countertops tend to be 26 inches wide unless they are increased to 36 inches for eating or because a sink or range is incorporated into the island. If you

design an island, make sure you have enough room between the island and the other countertops. You may think that 3½ feet is a lot of space until you get that island in there. We suggest that you find a place where you can draw all the elements in chalk on the floor (or use cardboard boxes) and see what you think.

Dreaming about your ideal kitchen is not a waste of time. It is an important part of planning. Look at photos of kitchens in every book you can find. Also walk through as many different kitchens as you can. Each family has special problems and requirements that call for imaginative solutions, but you can get some great ideas examining other people's solutions.

Many contractors specialize in remodeling kitchens and bathrooms. The National Kitchen and Bath Association (NKBA) is a trade group dedicated to the design and construction of kitchens and baths. This group has established a qualification program for kitchen designers, and you will find individuals who call themselves certified kitchen designers based on the fact that they have passed the NKBA's designer qualification program. We suggest, however, that you buy kitchen cabinets, bath vanities, countertops, and appliances from a wholesaler or directly from a manufacturer (see Table 23-1 for some suggestions). If you find a large operator that deals only in kitchen cabinets, you will probably get your design work done for free. Home centers frequently offer some design service. Large hardware stores and home centers often have computerized kitchen design programs that will help you design your kitchen. Keep in mind, however, that you will pay for those services in the higher prices charged for the cabinets.

When buying kitchen cabinets, it pays to buy the best materials you can afford. Plastic laminate or particleboard boxes are durable, but wood is still the most popular material. Do not be fooled by the label "solid wood." There is no such thing anymore. What the manufacturer is trying to say is that the cabinet is made of plywood rather than particleboard. Doors and door fronts sometimes are made of glued-up pieces and sometimes are solid. Do not be afraid of particleboard. New, high-density particleboard is very stable, sometimes even more stable than solid wood, but heavy loads left in place

TABLE 23-1

TABLE 23-1

Allmilmo Corporation, 70 Clinton Rd., P.O. Box 629, Fairfield, NJ 07007

Capri Kitchens, Inc., Armstrong Rd., Plymouth, MA 02360

Chabert Duval USA, Ltd., 221-227 North St., Elkton, MD 21921

Corsi Cabinet Company, 611 Churchman Bypass, Indianapolis, IN 46203

Crystal Cabinet Works, Inc., 1100 Crystal Drive, Princeton, MN 55371

Fieldstone Cabinetry, Inc., P.O. Box 109, Highway 105 East, Northwood, IA 50459

Haas Cabinet Co., Inc., 625 W. Utica St., Sellersburg, IN 47172

Helena USA, Inc., 7705 La Cosa Drive, Dallas, TX 75248

Interlit USA, Inc., 7705 La Cosa Drive, Dallas, TX 75248

Lager Kitchens, 35 Agnes St., East Providence, RI 02914

Medallion Kitchens, 180 Industrial Blvd., Waconia, MN 55387

Mid-Continent Cabinetry, 30 East Plato Blvd., St. Paul, MN 55107

Plato Woodwork, Plato, MN 55370

Poggenpohl USA Corp., 6 Pearl Court, Allendale, NJ 07401

Quaker Maid, WCI Cabinet Group, Route 61, Leesport, PA 19533

Rutt Custom Kitchens, Route 23, Goodville, PA 17528

SieMatic Corporation, One Neshaminy Interplex, Suite 207, Trevose, PA 19047

Wood-Mode Cabinetry, Wood-Metal Industries, Inc., Kreamer, PA 17833

for a long time can permanently deform particleboard shelves. Pay particular attention to the fronts. If you are buying wood cabinets, make sure the entire front is solid wood, including the door. Also pay attention to the hinges. These play the biggest part in determining price differences among some cabinets. Make sure you buy quality hinges. The last thing to look for is drawer slides. The main reason people replace cabinets is because the drawer slides wear out. This is a shame, because drawer slides are one of the easiest things to replace once a cabinet is installed.

The do-it-yourselfer can probably save more money in the kitchen than in any other part of a rehab. We highly recommend a thorough investigation of how to do kitchens, where to buy the materials, and how to install them. If you buy the cabinets, countertops, and appliances wholesale and install them yourself, you may save tens of thousands of dollars.

Planning Your Bathroom

The biggest decisions about bathrooms involve not what goes in them, but where to locate them and how many to have. Obviously, rehabbers with large budgets and large houses would prefer a bathroom with each bedroom, but others may be content with a centrally located bathroom that is easily accessible from all rooms. If the main bathroom will receive heavy use, a half bath off the master bedroom may serve the adults well. There also should be a half bath downstairs for guests. As with designing kitchens, you must think about the secondary activities that take place in the bathroom — such as reading, exercising, tanning, tending plants, soaking and doing the laundry — and plan your space accordingly.

The most important item in designing bathrooms is knowing that some minimum distances are required by local plumbing codes. The toilet centerline can be no closer than 15 inches to any wall. Thus, if the toilet fits between two walls, the walls must be 30 inches apart. The face of the bowl can be no less than 18 inches from the wall it faces; the same goes for the vanity. All fixtures must be at least 2 inches away from the tub.

In addition to these dimensions, the number of wet walls in a bathroom is an important consideration. Keep in mind that every wall that includes a supply line to a fixture will probably also require a vent and therefore have to be a 6-inch wall. Therefore, the more wet walls you have, the higher the cost. Also keep in mind the direction of the joists underneath the tub or shower. Try to position tubs or showers so that the waste pipes run between the joists; otherwise, you will have to cut holes in these joists to run a pipe across them or lower ceilings beneath them.

Vertical dimensions are important in bathrooms, because fixtures and accessories should reflect the height of the people living in the house. Shower heads are usually set at 5½ feet, with shower curtains being 6½ feet. Tops of mirrors should be set at about 6 feet. These dimensions should be adjusted for the individuals inhabiting the house.

When you plan a bathroom, you also must consider its maintenance. Waste pipes and water supply lines for the lavatory and toilet are usually accessible, but those for the tub usually are not. A removable panel in the tub's head wall will make it easy to get at the plumbing pipes behind the wall.

As with a kitchen, choosing fixtures is important. Again, you should buy the best fixtures you can afford. In rehabbing, there is a trend toward keeping the older fixtures in bathrooms while updating the kitchen. For instance, there has been a resurgence of salvaging claw-footed tubs and pedestal sinks. These also are available new (see Table 23-2 for manufacturers of period fixtures). If your bathroom has its original fixtures and they are discolored, chipped, or scratched, you may want to have them resurfaced. In most cases, this process involves repainting the surface with a liquid synthetic porcelain acrylic, epoxy, or urethane. As with any paint job, resurfacing is only as good as the fixture's preparation, so make sure you find a reputable dealer to do it.

Toilets vary in size, shape, and flushing mechanism. One aspect that may be important is the method of mounting. Most toilets are floor-mounted, although you can buy wall-mounted ones, which look nice and are easy to clean underneath. Most builders think that these are not a good investment because supporting them is problematic and they clog easily. You usually see wall-mounted toilets only in commercial applications. You may wish to install a bidet, which should be placed in the same amount of space as a toilet.

Showers and tubs are made out of many different materials. Fiberglass and plastic are probably the easiest to install and maintain, although other options include marble and tile. One thing to consider is whether you will have a tub/shower combination or a separate shower and tub. In our opinion, tub/shower combinations are not a good idea because the tub is not big enough to soak in

and a 30-inch-wide space is not enough room to shower in. We recommend a 36-inch-square shower plus a separate tub. Finally, you must con-

---

TABLE 23-2

A Ball Plumbing Supply, 1703 W. Burnside St., Portland, OR 97209

Antique Baths and Kitchens, 2220 Carlton Way, Santa Barbara, CA 93109

Barclay Products Limited, 424 N. Oakley Blvd., Chicago, IL 60612

Bathroom Machineries, Domestic Environmental Alternatives, 495 Main St., P.O. Box 1020, Murphys, CA 95247

Besco Plumbing, 729 Atlantic Ave., Boston, MA 02111

The Brass Finial, 2408 Riverton Rd., Cinnaminson, NJ 08077

Cumberland General Store, Route 3, Crossville, TN 38555

Decorum Hardware Specialties, 235 Commercial St., Rt. 1A, Portland, ME 04101

Heads Up, A Division of Sonoma Woodworks, Inc., 133 Copeland St., Petaluma, CA 94952

Kohler Co., Kohler, WI 53044

Mac the Antique Plumber, Inc., 885 57th St., Sacramento, CA 95819

Remodelers & Renovators: Supplies for Vintage Houses, 1920 N. Liberty, Boise, ID 83704

The Renovator's Supply, Inc., Millers Falls, MA 01349

Restoration Works, Inc., P.O. Box 486, Buffalo, NY 14205

Roy Electric Co., Inc., 1054 Coney Island Ave., Brooklyn, NY 11230

The Sink Factory, 2140 San Pablo Ave., Berkeley, CA 94702

Sunrise Specialty, 2204 San Pablo Ave., Berkeley, CA 94702

Tennessee Tub, Inc., 6682 Charlotte Pike, Nashville, TN 37209

Victorian Warehouse, 190 Grace St., Auburn, CA 95603

Walker Mercantile Co., P.O. Box 210129, Bellevue, TN 37221

FIGURE 23-2. *Basic bathroom designs.*

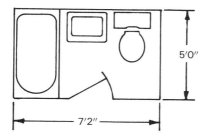

23-2A. *Pipes in one wall*

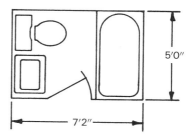

23-2B. *Pipes in two walls*

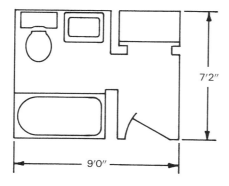

23-2C. *Pipes in two walls*

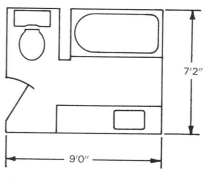

23-2D. *Pipes in 3 walls*

sider whether you wish to install a whirlpool-type tub or hot tub in your bathroom. Figure 23-2 shows some different bathroom designs.

INSTALLING KITCHENS AND BATHS

Kitchen Cabinet Make-Overs

If you find yourself in a situation where (1) you have no money, (2) you have a reasonable kitchen in which you cannot justify the cost of replacing all the cabinets and/or appliances, or (3) you buy a house that needs to be totally rehabbed except for the kitchen (because that happens to be the one room on which the previous owners worked—but you hate it), what should you do? You can refinish and/or reface the cabinets. If the hinges and the basic boxes are sound, resurfacing may be appropriate. The simplest thing to do is to paint the cabinets and replace the hardware. Painted cabinets must be

treated a bit more carefully to avoid chipping, but you can't beat the price.

If you are happy with the basic cabinets, and particularly the color or finish, but don't like the style, you can get a whole new look by changing the doors and drawer fronts. This is a simple do-it-yourself job that requires no skill beyond patience. Make sure that you double-check all your measurements before you order the materials or have the supplier order them. Many of the large companies that manufacture drawer and face fronts do not want to sell to individual home owners, but you may be able to talk a refacing contractor into selling you just the parts. If not, the manager of your local lumberyard or home center should be able to order the parts for you.

You can change entire cabinets by gluing wood veneer or plastic laminate over face frames and cabinet sides. In fact, you can redo virtually every part of the cabinet as long as you have the basic box. One of the advantages of having your cabinets refaced instead of buying new ones is that you can use the money saved to hire someone to do the work.

Installing Kitchen Cabinets

Kitchen cabinets must be installed with painstaking care, and doing so is not always easy. The floor must be prepared so that it is level, or the cabinets must be shimmed. The walls on which the cabinets will be mounted must be made so that they are close to plumb. Any higher or unshimmed low spot on the wall or floor will cause racking of the cabinets, which will force the drawers and doors to move out of line. No cabinet can compensate for improper installation, unplumb walls, and especially corners that are out of square. Even the best cabinets will be ruined if they are poorly installed.

Before you start, you need the following:

- One or two helpers
- Strips of wood for shims
- Long one-by-twos to use as cleats to help support wall cabinets
- An electric drill with a $1/8$-inch bit or a combination screw bit
- A level, screw gun, and framing square
- Drywall screws ($1^5/8$ and $2^1/2$ inches)
- A small bar of soap (to lubricate drywall screws)
- Several C-clamps
- A box of toggle or molly bolts (for those times in securing the cabinets when you miss the blocking that you installed when you framed the house or if there is no blocking)

Unpack the cabinets, removing all the staples that hold the cardboard protecting them, and arrange them in some other area of the house that is close by and spacious enough to let you lay out all of the cabinets in the order that you will probably need them. Start at the corners and work out, or start at the highest point in the room if your floors are not level.

We assume that all electrical and plumbing rough-in is complete and that you have sanded obvious high spots on walls and corrected any unevenness in the floor. Mark the locations of the studs on the walls. One trick that builders use, particularly in new construction, is not to paint approximately 24 to 30 inches up from the floor where the base cabinets will go, thus leaving the drywall and tape to indicate the positions of studs. You need to mark the location of every stud 35 inches above the floor so that you can see the mark above the base cabinets.

Always start with the wall cabinets; otherwise, you will have to crawl over the base cabinets. You can use a one-by-two as a cleat on which the bottom of the wall cabinets will rest when they are against the wall. For standard 30-inch wall cabinets, the top of the cleat should be 54 inches above the floor at its highest point.

A common carpentry trick is to find the high point in the room and measure up 34 and 54 inches. Then, using a chalk line and a level, draw a line all the way around the room at these distances. If your wall cabinets are taller than 30 inches, we assume that the extra dimension will go toward the ceiling and that the top of your cabinets will be above 7 feet. Securely nail or screw the cleat to the studs, double-checking to make sure it is level. Then set the back edge of the cabinet on top of the cleat, having your helper hold it up so you can screw it to the studs. Use $2^1/2$-inch drywall screws for this purpose.

If several cabinets go on one wall, you can either screw them together on the floor and set them up as a unit or put them up one at a time and screw them together once they are attached to the wall. We suggest that you screw them together once they are up or that you compromise and put two cabinets at a time together on the floor. It is very difficult to work with a whole wall of cabinets sitting on a one-by-two cleat. The problem with screwing one cabinet up at a time is trying to align them, although you can do this by loosening and tightening the screws in the wall studs. Use a C-clamp with protective blocks to clamp the face of two cabinets together so they are perfectly aligned. Then drill a $1/8$-inch pilot hole into the outside stiles of each adjacent pair and install $1^5/8$-inch screws to keep the two cabinets aligned and fastened together.

With most modern wall cabinets, make sure you screw them to the wall both at the bottom underneath the floor of the cabinet and at the top, through the mounting rails of the cabinet, not just through the backing material. A minimum of four screws should be used for small cabinets, two at the top and two at the bottom; place screws every foot for larger cabinets, at both the top and bottom. If a screw does not hit the blocking in the wall, make sure that you use a toggle bolt, but never use more than one toggle bolt at the top because more solid support is needed there.

Base cabinets are installed in much the same way, usually starting in the highest corner. It is extremely important to keep base cabinets level so that the countertop fits on them without racking. In old houses, the floor typically settles as it moves out from the wall, so the face of the cabinet may have to be shimmed. If significant shimming is needed, the best way to hide it is to run commercial rubber shoe molding around the kick plate of all your cabinets after your flooring has been installed. Like wall cabinets, base cabinets should be screwed together through the stiles or mounting plates. They need to be screwed only through the top back rail to the studs. The base can be left as it is. There will be enough weight in the base cabinets so that they will not move once they are tightly screwed to the wall and to each other.

Depending on your measurements, you may have to install spacers in wall and base cabinets. It is best to do this either next to a dishwasher or where a cabinet meets a wall. The manufacturer will usually supply a one-by-three spacer with a kick plate added to it. There is no particular way to attach this spacer to the cabinet. The best thing to do is to glue or screw a two-by-two to the side of the cabinet so that one side of the two-by-two is against the cabinet side and rides up against the edge of the faceplate that sticks out beyond the side. After it dries, use glue to attach the spacer to the two-by-two. (You may need a table saw to cut the spacer to the exact dimension you need.) With the correct size screws, back-screw through the two-by-two and into the back of the spacer. The major reason for putting the spacer against the wall is that it is not as noticeable there.

If you have a house where the plumbing for the kitchen sink comes up through the floor, you may have to cut your cabinet, as most sink bases are made with open backs. Be very careful to cut holes only as large as are needed to slip the cabinet over the roughed-in plumbing. In most cases, if you have replumbed the house, your pipes will come out of the back wall as is required by code, so no modifications are required. If your floor is fairly level, install the cabinets over the new flooring. This makes installing the new flooring much easier, since you do not have to worry about making precise cuts around the cabinets.

Installing Countertops

If you are reusing old cabinets, you may wish to apply new laminate to old countertops or to make your own countertops. We do not recommend the latter because countertops are fairly inexpensive and making them yourself is not worth the effort unless you use ceramic tile.

If you wish to resurface existing countertops or build new ones, the following tips are in order. The surface to which the plastic laminate is applied should be thoroughly sanded and cleaned. If you are making your own countertops, you can use plywood or particleboard as a base for plastic laminate. Most countertops today are made with high-density particleboard. (Do not use low-density particleboard.) You can cut plastic laminate with a circular saw or saber saw. The circular saw will make straighter cuts, but you must use a very fine tooth blade, and the sharpness of the saw will determine the quality of your cuts. Unless you are doing a large job, it is usually best to cut plastic laminate with a fine-tooth backsaw or a utility knife used with a straightedge or framing square. Always cut it on the decorated side and always make it slightly oversized to allow for trimming.

Since laminated plastics are applied with contact cement, you should roughen the surface of the base with coarse sandpaper. When you brush the contact cement onto the base, also apply it to the back of the laminate. Let both surfaces dry for 15 minutes, then lay the laminate on the base. Be very careful when doing this because up to 75 percent of the bonding power of contact cement is in the first contact. You'll need a helper for this task. Once they are aligned and bonded, use a roller to apply pressure to the sheets to eliminate any air pockets.

If any overlapping seams are required, you can make a clean joint by overlapping the two sheets approximately 1 inch and then using a sharp knife to cut through both sheets at the point of overlap. Lift and remove the waste strip underneath the cut, and the sheets should align perfectly. A block and mallet can be used to ensure good adhesion at the joint.

If you use the same laminate for the edging, apply two coats of contact cement to the edges, attach it, and let it dry thoroughly. Edges can usually be finished with a very small sanding block or with special router blades that are made especially for this purpose. Contact cement can be removed with a special solvent or with nail polish remover.

Countertops are either self-edged or post-formed. Self-edged tops have a square front and are faced with a separate strip of the same material or hardwood. The back splash is a separate piece joined at right angles to the top. A postformed countertop is rounded over the front edge with a raised no-drip edge and wraps over the back splash in one continuous piece. Postformed tops are usually less expensive.

Countertops are available in varying lengths (18 inches to 20 feet) and are usually priced by the foot. If you have to join two lengths to form an L, you must use a 45-degree miter. Ask the dealer to cut the miter for you. Some companies will even put it together for you and deliver it like that. If you can.get it into your kitchen put together, do so. If not, you will have to put the pieces together yourself. Also order the countertop with the proper outside edges and the sink installed.

You will need the following to install a countertop:
- A helper
- A screw gun and $1\frac{5}{8}$-inch drywall screws
- A small bar of soap (to lubricate the drywall screws)
- An adjustable wrench to tighten bolts

Check the base cabinets to make sure they are all level, shimmed at the floor if necessary, and tightly screwed together. Always place the countertop in position to make sure it fits in every direction before you do anything. Make sure it is tight against the back wall all around. Some countertops have riser blocks, which are pieces of wood that double the thickness, making it $1\frac{1}{2}$ inches thick. These are installed so that when the countertop sits on the base, it is 36 inches above the floor. Many manufacturers of inexpensive countertops do not add riser blocks, so you may want to consider adding them yourself. The main reason for adding them is to raise the countertop up ¾ inch so that there

is more room between the tops of the drawers and the countertop. Also, with these risers, the gap between the lower cabinet door and the drawer will be the same as the gap between the drawer and the countertop. To add risers, turn the top over and glue and/or screw ¾-inch-thick blocks along the front and back, spacing them about every 8 inches. Never use nails or screws longer than $1\frac{1}{8}$ inches for this.

Assemble any miter joints by placing the sections together, bottom side up, on a soft surface that will not damage the countertop. You need at least one helper to do this. Apply adhesive caulking compound to the surfaces to be joined, then join them using the bolts that should come with the top and fit into the special slots made to hold the sections together. Turn the fasteners so that they are snug but not tight, then check the alignment on the front and top surfaces. Keep checking the alignment as you tighten the fasteners. When all the fasteners are tightened, turn the top over and remove any excess caulk. Then place the countertop on the cabinets and double-check for problems such as bulges in the wall. If you see a bulge, push the countertop against the wall and mark the top with a pencil. Then sand away a little of the drywall so that the entire back splash fits against the wall.

Fasten down the top with wood or drywall screws through the triangular gusset plates in the corners of the base cabinets. If your cabinets do not have these gussets, you should find wood blocks in those corners through which you can drill holes for screws to hold down the top. Make sure that the blocks will accommodate $1\frac{5}{8}$-inch drywall screws, because you do not want to ruin a new countertop by putting a screw up through it. One of the nice things about having a countertop with preinstalled riser blocks is that the extra $1\frac{1}{2}$ inches allows you more leeway with your screws. Do not glue down the countertop; someone may want to remove it someday.

If you purchased your countertop and sink from a large dealer, the sink will probably be installed in the countertop. If not, you will have to cut a hole and install it yourself. Position the sink upside down exactly where you want it on the countertop, aligning it with a window or the plumbing, whichever is appropriate. Mark the circumference of the sink with a pencil. Reduce this by about an inch all the way around and redraw the rectangle to the actual roughed-in dimension. Drill a large pilot hole in the center of the cutout. You may not have enough room along the back splash to cut the hole with a large saber saw, so use a keyhole saw or some other type of saw to do that. To avoid chipping the laminate, put transparent tape over your cut line or masking tape along the outside of it. Do not saw too fast.

To install the sink, lay a very thick ribbon of caulk or plumber's putty around the edge of the cutout where the sink rim fits and set the sink in place. Tighten it down with the sink fasteners and wipe away any excess caulk.

Installing a Ceramic Tile Countertop

One approach to countertops, and an easy one for some do-it-yourselfers, is to use ceramic tile. This is probably one of the messiest approaches to installing a countertop, but many people believe that it is the most durable.

You will need the following tools:
- A notched trowel
- A tile cutter
- Tile nippers
- A rubber trowel
- Measuring tools

You can rent tile cutters and nippers from the place where you buy the tile (unless you buy it wholesale) or from a rental center. Make sure that your cabinets are level and your countertop is clean, level, and firmly attached. The base for the tile is usually one ¾-inch sheet of exterior plywood, although many rehabbers use two sheets. Make sure that these are securely attached to the cabinets.

Make the sink cutout and any other cutouts in the plywood before you start. You can lay the tile wet (in mortar), or you can fasten it down with epoxy or some other adhesive. The tile manufacturer will usually recommend a specific kind of adhesive for installation. The adhesive method is much easier and faster than the wet method, as it is very difficult to get tile perfectly level in mortar. Spread the adhesive evenly on the base with a notched trowel. Do only one portion of the work at a time. Lay the tile just a couple of rows or sheets at a time. Put each tile into the adhesive but avoid sliding it, as doing so thins the adhesive. You will probably have to cut some of the tiles to fit the pattern. If so, use a tile cutter to score the tile and then break it.

One thing you must determine is the width of the grout line. If you have sheets of tile, the width of this line is already determined. With some large tiles, a small tab attached to the tile provides the correct spacing. You can also buy small crosses that fit between the tiles at the corners to provide the correct spacing. Knowing the width of the grout line also helps you calculate how much tile and grout to buy. When buying tile, make sure that you buy bull-nose, cap, and cove pieces to use on the back splash, the edge of the sink, and the front edge of the countertop.

Let the adhesive dry overnight before applying any grouting. Mix the grout to the manufacturer's specifications and apply it with a rubber trowel. Hold the trowel at an angle and keep forcing the grout down between the tiles. When the grout begins to dry, run the wet rubber trowel across the job or run the eraser end of a pencil down the grout line to get an even depth. Wipe off as much excess as you can with a damp rag. When the grout is completely dry, wipe it thoroughly and either spray or soak it with a silicone sealer to prevent oil and dirt from discoloring it.

Installing Bath Vanities

Most bath vanities are installed in exactly the same way as kitchen cabinets and counters. If you are using a single-piece top, such as a cultured marble sink top, you simply lay it on top of the vanity with a few dabs of silicone. (We suggest that you install the faucet and drain spud/pop up before you install the sink.) Most of the other operations involved in installing a bathroom are covered in other chapters (see, for example, Chapter 16 on plumbing). We do have one tip, however: Install the vanity and the toilet over the flooring material.

NOISE CONTROL IN KITCHENS

Noise control is particularly important in kitchens,

especially if your washer and dryer are located in the kitchen. Try adjusting your television to a comfortable hearing level, then turn on the dishwasher, the disposal, the vent hood, and the washer and dryer and try to watch television. Appliance manufacturers are doing something about this problem: Disposals now come with rubber mounts and rubber hose sections and dishwashers are insulated, but the kitchen can still be a very noisy place.

Here are some things you can do to cut down on kitchen noise:

1. Mount the dishwasher, garbage disposal, and other appliances on rubber pads to prevent vibrations from being transmitted through the floor or countertop.

2. Make sure that when you install the dishwasher, you cover it thoroughly (top, sides, and back) with insulation.

3. Make sure that the rubber insulation gasket at the mouth of the disposal is installed.

4. Buy a deep sink that is insulated.

5. Make sure that the refrigerator is balanced by adjusting the set screws.

6. Place sound-absorbent mountings on the exhaust fan and make sure that the fan is large enough to operate efficiently at low speeds.

7. Install flexible pipes (where building codes permit) between the drain from a disposal and the trap to keep vibrations from being transmitted to other plumbing and into the walls.

8. Make sure that air chambers are placed in water lines to prevent water hammer.

9. If your washer and dryer are installed in a laundry room near the kitchen, make sure that the walls around the laundry are insulated with fiberglass. The same is true for an interior wall behind the dishwasher.

References

OLD

The Bathroom: A New Interior. Pittsburgh: Standard Sanitary Manufacturing Co., 1931.

NEW

Bianchina, Paul. *Bathroom Remodeling: A Do-It-Yourselfer's Guide.* Blue Ridge Summit, Pennsylvania: TAB Books, 1988.

Cavendish, M. *Kitchens: A Complete Guide for Creative Designs and Projects.* New York: Beekman House, 1977.

Conran, T. *The Kitchen Book.* New York: Crown Publishers, 1977.

Galvin, P.J. *Kitchen Planning Guide for Builders and Architects.* Farmington, Michigan: Structures Publishing Co., 1972.
_____. *Book of Successful Kitchens.* Farmington, Michigan: Structures Publishing Co., 1974.

Guide to Bathroom and Kitchen Remodeling. New York: McGraw-Hill, 1980.

Henkin, William A. *How To Design and Remodel Bathrooms.* San Francisco: Ortho Books, 1982.

Kitchens and Bathrooms, Alexandria, Virginia: Time-Life Books, 1977.

Niles, Bo. *Planning the Perfect Kitchen.* New York: Simon & Schuster, 1988.

Olson, Wanda. *Kitchen Planning: New and Remodeled.* St. Paul: Agricultural Extension Service, University of Minnesota, 1980.

Schram, J.F. *Book of Successful Bathrooms.* Farmington, Michigan: Structures Publishing Co., 1976.
_____. *Successful Bathrooms.* Farmington, Michigan: Structures Publishing Co., 1980.

Stanforth, D., and M. Stamm. *Buying and Renovating a House in the City.* New York: Alfred A. Knopf, 1972.

Sunset Kitchens & Bathrooms: Planning & Remodeling. Menlo Park, California: Lane Publishing Co., 1988.

Walker, Jenepher. *How to Design and Remodel Kitchens.* San Francisco: Ortho Books, 1982.

Chapter 24

FLOORS

Most older homes have wood floors that are difficult to reproduce today. Restoration should be your first thought if the floors are made of unusual wood such as maple or quartersawed red oak or if the wood is laid in a parquet pattern. Chances are good that sanding and other cosmetic work will restore the luster to your wood floors. If your floors are beyond repair, you may wish to recover them with wood or choose some other type of covering.

It is important to point out that no amount of finish work will make up for a sound underlay and good floor joists. If the joists are sagging, whatever you do to the floors will not last. In addition, sagging joists can cause squeaky floors. Therefore, before you do anything to the floors themselves, make sure that the joists and the underlay are in good shape (see Chapter 13).

TYPES OF FLOORING

Wood Flooring

Wood flooring materials fall into two broad categories, softwood and hardwood. Many varieties of each are available. Hardwood is usually preferable to softwood because it resists marring better than softwood.

The two hardwoods most often used are oak and maple, although beech, birch, and hickory also are used. Hardwood flooring is usually finished and sealed with varnish or some other sealer such as urethane or wax. The floor is constructed by nailing the flooring to the subflooring. The flooring usually comes in long, uneven length strips about 1½ to 3¼ inches wide and ⅜ to ¾ inch thick. The strips are designed for tongue-and-groove construction so that they fit firmly together and hold each other down. Prefinished strip or square wood flooring also is available. It is laid over the subflooring or over the old hardwood floor and can be used immediately. Prefinished wood flooring comes in a variety of designs and finishes, and some is made of exotic woods such as cherry, mahogany, teak, and walnut. Some is made of plywood, which we don't recommend because it can never be refinished.

Softwood flooring is usually made of yellow pine or Douglas fir, but redwood, cedar, and cypress also are used. It comes in the same thicknesses as hardwood but is generally wider, ranging from 3½ to 4½ inches.

Nonresilient Flooring

This category includes items such as brick; ceramic, marble, and slate tile; and terrazzo. These materials last a long time but are more difficult than wood to install. If the material is glazed, it will resist staining. If it is unglazed, it will need to be sealed with a commercial sealer. All these materials are set in some sort of adhesive or cement, and the spaces between them are filled with grout.

Resilient Flooring

This category includes materials such as vinyl sheets or tiles, as well as asphalt and cork tiles. By far the most common resilient flooring is vinyl sheets or tile, which are made of PVC and provide a strong, wear-resistant surface. The decorative upper surface is bonded to the backing. Some types of vinyl floor covering can be purchased with a soft, spongy backing, which makes walking on it much more comfortable. This type is more difficult to lay because tight corners cannot be cut as precisely as with the thinner vinyl. The sheets are usually manufactured in 12-foot wide rolls and the tiles usually come in 9- or 12-inch squares.

REPAIRING FLOORS

Inspecting the Underlay

Looking up at the floor joists in the basement gives you a good idea of how the floors on the first floor shape up. Does the subflooring meet the top of the joists all the way across, or do the joists sag away from the floor in places? If you find a sagging joist, you should jack it up level with the others and attach a new joist that fits flush against the floor from foundation wall to foundation wall (see Chapter 13). If you can see places where the floor moves when someone walks around upstairs, you can probably insert screws, wedges, or nails to prevent any movement. If the subfloor is rotten, pull up that section of floor and redo the subflooring.

The second floor is a bit more difficult to inspect unless you have removed the ceiling on the first floor. Fortunately, the second floor does not take the same punishment as the first, so it is usually in much better shape. Nevertheless, you must make sure that it is smooth and flat before you think about further restoration.

When you are satisfied that the floors are secure and level, you can get on with the task of restoring or replacing the flooring.

Fixing Squeaks

Squeaks can be a terrible nuisance, but with a little effort, you can usually get rid of them. They are almost always caused by two pieces of wood rubbing together. To eliminate the squeak, you have to eliminate the rubbing. Repairs to squeaking floors can be made from above (or from below, if the underside of the floor is exposed). If working from above, you can stop most squeaks by nailing in 6d or 8d flooring nails every 8 to 10 inches. Flooring nails are spiral-shaped and made so that they will not come out when the floor is walked on. Do not nail directly into the wood. Drill a pilot hole first and then drive the nail into the wood and subflooring. If you would rather not drill holes and pound nails, you can try using powdered graphite or liquid silicone (ceramic tile sealer, for instance). You can also buy graphite in tubes; to apply it, squeeze the powder between the two boards. This will not tighten the boards, but it will lubricate the surface between them and probably eliminate the squeak. Sooner or later, however, the squeak will return.

If the underside of the floor is exposed, as it may be in your basement, you can use several methods to eliminate squeaks. If the squeak is over a joist, try putting a shim between the floor and the joist. Use a tapered piece of wood such as a shingle and drive it in just tight enough so that the squeak stops. Sometimes it is a good idea to put glue on the shim before you drive it in. The squeak may be between joists, in which case you might have to put a screw up through the subfloor, thus pulling the finish flooring down onto the subfloor. Another cause of squeaking is loose joists. To test this, have someone walk around on the floor above while you watch from below. If the joists move up and down, you will have to install a new joist alongside the old one or use bridging between several joists on both sides of the squeak (see Chapter 13).

Replacing Damaged Floorboards

If a small section of the floor is damaged, it is easy to remove that section and replace it. First, drill several holes in the board across its width. Try not to drill too far into the subflooring. Then, using a sharp chisel, cut off the tongue of the board to be removed and pry it out. Alternatively, you can use the chisel to split the section to be removed and then take it out in pieces. After you have removed the board, square up the end of the remaining piece. Measure the opening and cut a replacement board. Try to match the grain and the color of the wood as closely as possible. Some salvage dealers will allow you to sort through their supply of old flooring to find the piece that you need. Once you have the replacement board cut, cut off the bottom side of the groove so that the board will fit down over the tongue of the board next to it. Coat the replacement piece tongue and groove with wood glue or construction adhesive and gently tap it into place. You can finish the job with several well-placed flooring nails if needed.

If you are replacing large sections of flooring, it is a good idea to rent a nailing machine, which will facilitate the process of driving nails at the proper angle into the tongue. It is also a good idea to keep the replacement flooring in the house for a day or two before you install it. This will allow for a humidity change and ensure that the linear dimensions of the wood do not change after you put them down. Usually lengths of new flooring will be random, so the seams will not be in a straight line. If you purchase secondhand flooring to do the patching job, make sure to saw them into uneven lengths so you don't get a line of seams. Do not take out even squares. Several good books on laying hardwood flooring are available. In addition, back issues of the *Old House Journal* have articles on flooring.

Filling Cracks

Small holes and indentations can be filled with wood putty, which can be stained to match the floor. Furniture scratch-repair sticks, which come in various colors, also can be used on floors. Any cracks or splits in the flooring should be filled and sealed. If there are large cracks and you think you might have trouble matching the finished color, you can fix them as follows. Find a floorboard with the same grain and color (use one that you may have replaced). Saw it and save the sawdust. Mix the sawdust with wood glue and use that to fill the crack. You may have to use several applications, but when you are done and have sanded it smooth, you should not be able to tell where the patch is.

Sanding and Finishing

Sanding a hardwood floor is necessary if it is stained or heavily pitted or if you want to restore the natural wood grain and seal it with a modern-day sealer. The sanding process is not difficult, and you can do it yourself, or you may wish to hire an expert and have him or her do it for you. If you decide to do it yourself, you will need to rent two sanding machines, one for the main part of the floor and a smaller one, called an edger, for close to the walls. Before you begin, consider how many times the floors have been sanded in the past. The wood is

only so thick, and if you sand through the top of the groove, you will tear it out and end up with long strips of wood missing between boards. One method of determining how much wood is left is to pull up a floor register or take off the shoe molding and look at the wood. If you are in doubt about the floor's ability to withstand another sanding, consult an expert before you start.

When using the large sander, you should start in a corner. Turn on the sander and hold the paper up off of the floor until the rotating drum reaches full speed, then lower the drum to the floor. On strip flooring, you should move with the grain of the wood; start with fine paper until you get used to the process, then use coarse paper. If the floor is parquet or some other pattern, you should use medium paper and move on a diagonal across the floor. Remember to keep the sander in constant motion, or you will end up with waves in the floor. Let the sander pull you forward at a constant pace. When you get to the far wall, tilt up the drum and pull the sander back over the area that you just sanded. When you get back to the starting point, start a new strip, making sure that you overlap the one you just did. From time to time, stop the sander and empty the dust bag. Be sure to protect your eyes and ears while you are working.

After you have finished with the main part of the floor, you can do the edges. Hold the edger any way that is comfortable, but make sure that you sand all the areas you missed with the larger sander. After you have done this, you may still find places that you were unable to finish. This calls for hand sanding or bleaching.

You may finish the sanded floor in several ways. If you want to stain it before you seal it, use an oil-based stain, as this type soaks into the wood very well and dries quickly. Apply the stain with a rag, making sure that you keep stirring the pigment and wipe any excess stain off the floor. When the stain is dry, you may apply a penetrating sealer such as linseed oil or tung oil or a surface finish such as shellac, varnish, or polyurethane. The decision of which type of sealer to use depends on how you want the final finish to look and how much routine maintenance you are willing to put into the floors. A penetrating sealer will produce a low-luster finish that can be enhanced through the use of paste wax and a floor buffer. Once the wax is applied, you will have to buff the floor once in a while to maintain the luster. A surface finish will produce a lustrous shine that will dull somewhat with age. Water-based polyurethane is the most common finish. You can use a liquid floor wax on this type of finish, which results in somewhat less demanding routine maintenance. A penetrating sealer is nice in high-traffic areas, whereas a surface finish is better in places that have less traffic.

Replacing Baseboards and Moldings

Once the floor has been refinished, replace the baseboards and shoe molding. If you are doing a restoration, you probably began this job by salvaging as much of the molding as you could. If you numbered or otherwise coded the position of each piece, then replacing it is simply a matter of putting it back down. If the molding was painted, you must refinish it first. When you pulled the molding off the walls, most of the nails probably came with it. To remove the nails from the molding, you will have to pound them back through the wood. If you will not be refinishing but only repainting, just cut the nails off flush with the wood and paint over them.

If the molding was damaged, you will need to purchase new molding or make your own. In many cases, the old molding will no longer be commercially available, so you will need to copy it using a contour gauge. This device looks a bit like a comb, except that the teeth push in, so that, when you push it against the old molding, the tool assumes the shape of the molding. You can transfer this pattern to another piece of wood, then use a router to duplicate the design. If you do not feel up to this job, most cabinetmakers can do it for you. Cutting the baseboards and shoe moldings is discussed in Chapter 22.

INSTALLING NONWOOD FLOORING

Sheet Vinyl

Sheet vinyl is not the easiest type of floor covering to install. In fact, we don't recommend that the average rehabber attempt it. Sheet vinyl is expensive, and the chances of making a major mistake are quite high. It is probably a good idea to call in the experts, especially if the vinyl requires adhesive or seams. Bathrooms are good do-it-yourself areas, though. If you want to do it yourself, the following steps should be of some help to you.

Make sure that the vinyl has been at room temperature for at least a day so that it won't crack when you bend it. Since most sheet vinyl is 6, 9, or 12 feet wide, you probably will not have to join sheets except in very large rooms. Roll the vinyl out in an adjoining room and transfer the measurements of the installation room to the vinyl. Try to mark as many angles and cuts as you can before you lay it in the final position. Then roll it up and transfer it to the room where it will be installed.

Begin to unroll the vinyl from one wall, making the cuts that you need as you go. Do not cut to the final dimension until you are sure it is correct. If you need a seam, overlap the two sheets, making sure to match the pattern, then cut down through both layers. Remove the top and bottom cut portions and lay the vinyl back down. You should put a coating of adhesive under the seam to prevent the edges from coming up. Leave a little space between the vinyl and the wall to allow for expansion. The base molding will cover any small gap that remains.

Vinyl Tile

Before beginning to install any type of tile, snap a chalk line across the middle of the room. Begin by laying tiles over half the room. Apply them in a growing pyramid fashion. When you come to the wall and find that there is not enough room for a full tile, you will have to cut the last one to fit. Leave a little room between the tile and the wall. Now go back to the center of the room and finish the other side. If you started in the center and the room is square, the cut border tiles should all have the same dimension. Thin tile can be cut with scissors, and thicker tile can be scored with a utility knife and broken along the line.

Vinyl tile can be purchased with a self-stick backing, and all you have to do is peel off the backing paper and place the tile where you want it. All other types of tile require the use of an adhesive. If you choose the self-stick type, make very sure that the floor to which it is applied is clean, dry, and flat. Once these tiles are down and then are pulled up, it is very difficult to make them adhere a second time. If you use tiles that require an adhesive, ask your supplier which type of adhesive you should use. Apply the adhesive with a trowel that has a notched edge, with the notches being about ⅛ to ¼ inch deep. This allows for the application of the proper amount of adhesive. Put down only as much adhesive as you can cover before it begins to dry.

Ceramic and Marble Tile

Ceramic tile usually comes in 4- or 6-inch squares and may be glazed or unglazed. Marble comes in 6-, 12-, and 18-inch squares, both natural and synthetic. In either case, it is necessary to seal all tile, although it is doubly important to seal unglazed tile. Most floor tiles do not have the spacers that ceramic wall tiles have, so you must be careful to maintain consistent spacing.

Often floors are not level enough for tile. You can buy various products to help you achieve a flat finish. You pour these substances onto the floor in thicknesses of from ¾ to 3 inches; they are self-leveling and can withstand a good deal of pressure. In the thicker applications, the substance must be pumped into the room, and some surface preparation is required, so it is a good idea to hire a professional to perform this task. The cost associated with this type of floor preparation depends on the square footage to be treated and the depth of the topping. It is usually less than a dollar per foot, so if you have a very uneven floor, the benefits are worth the cost.

Once the surface is level, you are ready to lay the tile. The first step is to find the exact center of the room. The easiest way to do this is to locate the center of each wall and mark that spot on the floor. Have your helper hold one end of a chalk line on that spot while you walk to the opposite wall and snap a line on the floor. Repeat this process to mark the centerline between the other two walls. An X marks the center of the room. You can check to make sure your walls are square by measuring 3 feet along one line and 4 feet along another line, then measuring the top (hypotenuse) of the triangle. It should measure exactly 5 feet. If it does not, your walls are not square, and you will have to adjust

your lines until the hypotenuse equals 5 feet.

The next step is to lay the tiles end to end across one dimension of the room and then along the other dimension. It is unlikely that you will end up with full pieces of tile along the walls. Ideally, you should not use pieces that are less than 2 inches wide. If you find that this is going to be the case, you may be able to reduce or expand the size of grout joints or move the column over against one wall. It's a good idea to open all the cartons of tile to make sure that they are all the same color. It is even a good idea to dry-lay all the tile in the room except for the last row against the wall (the row that will probably have to be cut).

Now you are ready to apply the adhesive. Use a trowel with teeth to do this. Do not do more than about an arm's reach at a time. Some slate tiles will be a bit uneven, and you may have to apply cement to the back of them before setting them. Put the tiles down into the adhesive with a slight twisting motion and some pressure. Do not twist too much, or adhesive will well up between the joints.

After the tiles have set, apply sealer. This is very important, especially if you are using unglazed tiles, because, if they are not sealed, the grout will stain them. Force the grout down into the joints with a rubber grout float. Do not use metal, or you will scratch the tiles. Clean each section as you go so that the grout does not set up on the surface of the tile. After you have applied the grout, wait about 36 hours before you attempt to walk on the tiles and wipe up any excess grout. Apply sealer again for the grout.

CARPETS

Carpet is made of many different materials. To a great extent, the type of material (wool versus synthetic) and the thickness of the weave will determine the cost of the carpet. The carpet will either be jute-backed or kanga- (foam-) backed. Jute-backed carpet requires a carpet pad, which softens the walking surface and protects the carpet from excessive wear. Kanga-backed carpet can be laid without any padding. Because the foam backing is usually waterproof, this type of carpet is ideal for below-grade applications such as in a basement. Kanga-backed carpet is generally less expensive than jute-backed carpet.

Laying Wall-to-Wall Carpet

Quality carpet is expensive, so it is probably a good idea to have it professionally installed. If, however, the room is square with few jigs or jogs and you will be laying kanga-backed carpet, you might be able to do it yourself if you take your time. If you have a larger room where you can lay out the carpet, make the appropriate measurements and cuts before you put the carpet in the intended space. Jute-backed carpet, which requires an underlying pad, requires some special installation techniques and a few special tools.

Before beginning this type of carpet installation, surround the room with carpet tacking strips, which can be purchased in 4 to 6 foot lengths and look like the material that lumberyard yardsticks are made of, except that they are full of sharp tacks. Nail these to the subflooring, then lay down the carpet pad. Roll out the pad between the tacking strips but not over them. Apply carpet tape or duct tape over any seams in the pad and staple it to hold it down. Cut the carpet to a size that is slightly larger than the dimensions of the room. Then use carpet-stretching tools to stretch it down over the tacking strips. The edges of the carpet at entrances or inside closets will have to be finished with metal edging. Use carpet seam tape for any seams that are required. Some seam tapes need to be applied using a special heating iron. (For more information, consult the books listed in the reference section below.)

Carpeting Stairs

If carpeting a room is difficult, carpeting stairs is even more so. Carpet can be purchased in special 27- to 36-inch runners, but chances are you will add enough carpet to your initial room estimate to allow enough leftover material for the stairs. That means that you will have to cut your own carpet runner to the dimension of the stairs.

If the stairway is straight, you can calculate the amount of carpet needed by measuring the depth of one tread and the height of one riser. Add these two measurements together, multiply by the number of stairs, and divide by 36 to determine how many linear yards you need. If the stairs are not straight, you will need to estimate the total length for all the straight steps, then add to that the dimensions of all the curved steps. Measure each curved step at its widest point and add that measurement to the total.

Stair carpeting can be laid in a number of different ways. You can tack it down or use stair rods, tacking strips, or double-faced tape. We recommend that you consult a book that has specific instructions on laying stairway carpet and study it carefully before you begin.

Laying Carpet Tiles

Manufacturers have recently begun to make a wide variety of carpet tiles. These tiles have a kanga backing and usually some type of self-stick material. Once these tiles are laid, it is difficult to tell that they are not a continuous piece of wall-to-wall carpet. The installation process for carpet tiles is basically the same as for any other type of tile. The major thing to be aware of is that the floor must be very clean and smooth, or the tiles will not stick and you may have to trowel on a layer of mastic before you put them down.

References

OLD

How to Finish Wood Floors, Old or New. Buffalo: Pierce & Stevens Chemical Corporation, 1956.

Vanderwalker, Fred Norman. *Modern Floor Finishing.* Racine, Wisconsin: S.C. Johnson & Son, Inc., 1931.

NEW

Brann, Donald R. *How to Lay Ceramic Tile.* Briarcliff Manor, New York: Directions Simplified, 1974.

Building Floors, Walls & Stairs. Newtown, Connecticut: Taunton Press, 1989.

Busch, Akiko. *Floorworks: Bringing Rooms to Life with Surface Design and Decoration.* New York: Bantam Books, 1988.

Byrne, Michael. *Setting Ceramic Tile.* Newtown, Connecticut: Taunton Press, 1987.

Floors & Flooring. New York: Random House, 1986.

Geary, Don. *The How-To Book of Floors and Ceilings.* Blue Ridge Summit, Pennsylvania: TAB Books, 1978.

Gray, Jerry E. *Floor Covering: The Only Complete Installation Guide.* Belgrade, Montana: Cameo Publishing Co., 1983.

Ramsey, Dan. *Hardwood Floors: Installing, Maintaining & Repairing.* Blue Ridge Summit, Pennsylvania: TAB Books, 1985.

Revere, Glenn. *All About Carpets: A Consumer Guide.* Blue Ridge Summit, Pennsylvania: TAB Books, 1988.

Salter, W.L. *Floors & Floor Maintenance.* New York: Elsevier Science Publishing Co., 1974.

Schansberg, David. *Homeowner's Guide to Floors & Floor Coverings.* Nashville: Ideals Publishing Corp., 1983.

von Rosenstiel, Helene. *Floor Coverings for Historic Buildings.* Washington, D.C.: Preservation Press, 1988.

Your Floors & Stairs. Des Moines, Iowa: Meredith Corp., 1985.

Chapter 25

AND YOU THOUGHT YOU WERE DONE...

Once the groundwork of renovation has been laid, the cleanup and cosmetic phase can be fun and rewarding. The results come fast and tend to be dramatic. After having poured thousands of dollars into much less visible improvements such as utilities, insulation, and walls, you can direct your efforts toward beautifying the house. In decorating and cleanup, you can become a true do-it-yourselfer if much of the earlier work has been done by professionals.

CLEANING UP

After the walls have been painted and the trim applied, you should clean the house thoroughly before you do the final finishing touches. Scrape any excess paint or drywall mud off the windows and wash them. Thoroughly clean the floors, and remove all the debris from the house. Clean the bathroom so that drain openings sparkle. Clean the fireplaces; polish and seal all the tile and metal surfaces; clean all the surfaces in the kitchen, whether they are chrome, stainless steel, or tile; clean mirrors; polish any brass fixtures. Check all high places and corners for sawdust and cobwebs, and clean every place where dust settles — mantels, windowsills, moldings, light fixtures, and doors.

Depending on the time of year, this cleanup should occur outside as well. Trim bushes and hedges, cut away broken and dead limbs, edge sidewalks and driveways, weed borders and flower beds, and mow the lawn. Clean the outside windows, wipe off the doors and exterior windowsills, and sweep porches.

Once you have attended to these matters, you can turn your attention to the electrical fixtures and plates, fans, closets, and fireplaces.

LIGHT FIXTURES AND FANS

If the original light fixtures (or the remnants) are in place, they can be made serviceable if you choose to do so. This is often just a matter of installing new standard electrical parts, which is an inexpensive task. If you do not know enough about electricity to do this yourself, an electrical repair shop can do it for you. If you choose to replace old fixtures in kind, seek originals or legitimate reproductions at salvage yards and historic specialty shops. Also, check the different supply houses for historic items. To satisfy most electrical codes, replacement light fixtures must be UL listed. Typically, this disqualifies used fixtures, but it may not be a problem if you retain the fixtures already in the house. When buying new light fixtures, go directly to a wholesale outlet or manufacturers' catalogs.

The biggest mistake people make in lighting is buying the fixture because it looks nice without first evaluating where it will go and what it is supposed to do. Your first step should be to create a lighting scheme for your house. Analyze your lighting needs room by room. All parts of a room should have enough light so that you can move about without stumbling. Places where you focus your attention need good task lighting so you can work without straining your eyes. Also consider the color of the walls and molding. A room with white molding and light-colored walls will need less light than one with dark molding and walls.

Monotony results when all the lighting in a room is the same brightness. But beware of too much contrast. The eye should not have to adjust to sudden changes in light. You may need to create buffer zones of transitional lighting, such as brightening up a hallway next to a sunlit room so that the eye can adjust gradually.

Basically, in fluorescent light, the wavelengths at the blue end of the spectrum predominate. In incandescent light, the wavelengths at the red and yellow end of the spectrum prevail. Thus, incandescent light is warmer than fluorescent light. It also seems more natural because sunlight has a yellow glow in early morning and mid-afternoon, but it never seems blue. Incandescent light casts a shadow because the light is more focused, like the sun. Fluorescent light does not because it is more easily diffused, as on a foggy day. As a general rule, you should use incandescent light. Reserve fluorescent light for work areas such as your shop or kitchen and for indirect lighting. Although fluorescent lights are normally used in kitchens, they make food look unappetizing and wear on your eyes. Thus, if you can use incandescent light in the kitchen, do so.

Select simple fixtures. Plain fixtures made of expensive materials add style. Or replace the fixtures with period reproductions. Choose a fixture that is in harmony with the room and wall. If there is a high ceiling, use a pipe or extension fixture to bring the chandelier down to a practical level. If the room is small, use a wall fixture that minimizes intrusion into usable space. Do not use a gigantic lamp in a small room. Also, install the fixture high enough to cast light down on the people and objects in the room. Immobile wall fixtures should be above eye level but below the cornice molding. Glare occurs when light is reflected or shines directly into the eye. To avoid glare, install a diffuser on the troublesome light source, reduce its intensity, or remove it.

The opposite of glare is shadow. Make sure you have adequate lighting on stairs and in work areas. A central ceiling light is convenient because it illuminates a dark room by flicking a switch at the door, but it is relatively useless in providing good light for specific activities. One outlet in the room also can be wired to a switch. A combination of wall lights and floor or table lamps is much more effective in illuminating areas for work and leisure. It is also more flexible in accommodating the different uses of a room.

If there is a ceiling socket in place, think about using track lighting or a fan/light combination. Track lighting provides several direct and adjustable light sources and is visually appealing. Fans tend to have a period look and have practical uses as well in rooms with high ceilings. Also consider installing dimmers, which let you create different atmospheres for different occasions. Keep in mind that high light levels create a sense of activity and low light levels encourage relaxation.

When mixing artificial light with daylight, use bulbs that produce light resembling the spectrum of daylight. If you need fluorescent bulbs, buy the warm white type. All the lamp shades in a room should be at the same height. Right-handed people should have light coming over the left shoulder. Left-handers should have light coming over the right shoulder. Never place lights where they can be splashed by water, particularly in kitchens, garages, bathrooms, shops, and outdoors. Install a ground fault interruption circuit (GFI) to protect against electric shock in those cases. Always light stairs with two-way switches. Keep in mind that lighting requirements change with age. Thirty- to 40-year-old people need 17 percent more light contrast to see an object than 20- to 30-year-olds. Older people require even more light contrast and tend to benefit from soft, diffused lighting that minimizes shadows.

Bulbs

You have four basic choices when it comes to light bulbs: incandescent, fluorescent, halogen, and full-spectrum. The high-intensity HID bulbs (high-pressure sodium, mercury vapor, and so on) are primarily used for outdoor lighting.

As mentioned earlier, incandescent bulbs are preferred in the home because they give pleasant, warm light similar to that of the sun. Fluorescent bulbs provide good room lighting and excellent task lighting but produce cooler white light. Halogen bulbs are the newest addition to the home lighting scene. The bright white light that they produce is closer to daylight than light from any other source. Although halogen lights are more expensive to buy and run than incandescents, they last longer. The disadvantages of halogen lights are the intense heat they give off and the need for special fixtures. Also, halogen lights create glare unless they are shaded. The full-spectrum bulb is designed to provide the full spectrum of daylight as well as bright, efficient diffuse light. Full-spectrum bulbs fit into normal fluorescent sockets and are sold in hardware stores, but they can be very expensive. Studies have shown that full-spectrum bulbs can relieve symptoms of seasonal affective disorder, which is believed to result from the shorter daylight hours during fall and early winter.

Fixtures

A mind-boggling array of fixtures is available. Chandeliers provide good background light, but they are not intended to light the whole room. They tend to be used in formal settings such as above the dinner table or in an entryway. Chandeliers hanging from the ceiling should not be used as the only light source in the room.

"Down" or "can" lights are unobtrusive fixtures that are located in or on the ceiling and send a beam of light into a room or onto a particular object. Some are fitted with baffles or louvers to reduce glare. "Up" lights rest on the floor and point a beam of light upward, producing an unusual and dramatic effect. They provide good background lighting, but they are not used very often.

Wall lights come in many shapes and sizes and can create various effects. Table and floor lamps create a feeling of warmth and lend a sense of scale to the room. Make sure that table and floor lamps are proportional to the room and to each other. With current building codes requiring electrical sockets every 12 feet and at least one socket tied to a wall switch if there is no overhead light, a room can be effectively lighted with table and floor lamps. Track lights are good for background and spot

lighting. Track spotlights are available in many different shapes that fit into an electrified track, which is installed on a ceiling or wall.

The amount of light needed depends on the size of the room and the type of fixtures. A small room (under 150 square feet) should have three to five incandescent lamps for a total of at least 150 watts for pendants and ceiling lights. If the lights are recessed, the room should have four 75-watt incandescent lamps. If the lights are wall fixtures, there should be four 50-watt lamps. A medium-size room (150 to 250 square feet) requires at least 200 to 300 watts of ceiling light, 400 watts of incandescent light, or 120 watts of recessed light. Medium-size rooms require 600 watts of incandescent wall light or 160 watts of fluorescent light. A large room (over 250 square feet) requires at least 250 to 350 watts of incandescent light or 100 watts of fluorescent light in pendants and ceiling lamps. Large rooms also require 750 watts of incandescent light or 160 to 200 watts of fluorescent light in recessed fixtures.

Sockets and Switches

Sockets are required to be placed so that you never have to use an extension cord over 6 feet long. The sockets in an older house that is being preserved should be installed on the baseboard horizontally (or vertically, if possible), so that the sockets and any cords are unobtrusive. If you are keeping the plaster in the house, it is often easy to remove the baseboard and run the wire behind it to accomplish this. If you are using modern materials, the socket should be placed vertically and approximately 12 inches above the floor (or 10 inches above the base molding).

Switches should be located 3 to 4 inches away from the door casing on the doorknob side at 48 inches. Avoid putting a switch on or against the door casing or having a switch on the wrong side of the door swing.

Fans

Using a fan in conjunction with your central air-conditioning and heating unit can result in a tremendous savings. Even in the hottest climates, you can often turn down your air-conditioning system and let a fan cool you and the house.

Ceiling fans can be used in any room, and they require virtually no electrical work over and above that for a light. They do, however, require a heavier box and bar designed to carry the weight of the fan. We screw a metal box onto a two-by-four, which we then nail between the joists to hold the weight of the fan. That can be done only if you are taking out the lath and plaster. Otherwise, you must buy a box and bar designed to be installed in an enclosed ceiling or knock out a larger hole, which you can then cover with a plastic rosette. Old houses often have plaster rosettes attached to the ceiling with wire ties. These circular decorations were used for gas light fixtures. Wood and plastic imitations are now available to conceal the large hole made to install a fan.

Fans come in a wide variety of styles and prices. Cheaper fans are built much like more expensive ones. Fans are available in 36-, 42-, 52-, and sometimes 56-inch sweeps. Typically fans have four blades, but some have five. They are easily assembled by following manufacturer's directions. The only thing you need to be concerned about is making sure that the electrical box will hold the weight of the fan or that the box is close enough to a joist so that the fan can be attached to the joist. As mentioned earlier, you can use a rosette to cover the electrical box, but we have found that plastic rosettes tend to make some noise when the fan is in operation.

CLOSETS AND STORAGE SPACE

One of the most challenging tasks in rehabbing is creating storage space. Some possibilities are forgotten areas in the basement, spaces under staircases or beds, corners in the attic, or dead space anywhere in the house. If a house is very tight on storage space, we suggest that you build bed frames out of plywood and install drawers on both sides under the mattress. You also can purchase beds made like this.

Most older homes lack closet space. One of the most important things to look for in a house is where you can create closets. Also, closets are often not arranged for optimum usage. In the past few years, some carpenters have begun specializing in redesigning closet space. You can do this yourself by analyzing what kinds of things you will put into a closet. If all your clothes are short, you probably can install two rods and double the amount of clothes you can store, or you can install a divider using ¾-inch plywood with two rods on one side and one rod on the other side, creating a much more efficient space.

One of the things you can do to improve closets is to replace small doors with full front openings. Do not be afraid to remove the wall finish and studs to a width required for a standard paneled or louvered bifold door. Another option is to install a standard double door if you can match the existing closet door. If the closet wall is load-bearing, you will have to install a header.

Plastic-coated wire shelving has become very common in new construction. If you are gutting your house and wish to install this, make sure that you install nailers or studs at the depth of the shelves so that you have something to screw them to besides the drywall. This shelving may not be cost-efficient, since you will probably have plenty of plywood or wood scraps left over for shelving. Also, shelves can be installed in a closet at any time to fit a particular need. We sometimes build an entire box of shelves and set it in the closet rather than hanging the shelves on the wall. The problem with hanging shelves on the wall is that there probably are not enough studs or nailers behind the drywall to which you can nail them.

When designing closets, don't forget to design a space for the vacuum cleaner, your golf bag, or any other large pieces of equipment. Plot out the space each item requires and build storage space to accommodate those items. This will open up the basement area for other uses.

Before you start taking room space to build closets, consider wardrobes, which require significantly less space because the wall is single-layer material (without framing) and will not go all the way to the ceiling. You can build wardrobes or purchase them in various styles. We have found that wardrobes can be fairly inexpensive if purchased at an antique or used furniture outlet. People even put televisions and VCRs inside of wardrobes to maintain the historic flavor of the room.

If you must construct a new closet in an existing room, construction entails standard framing and drywalling, as well as the installation of trim. The only hint we have is not to square off the corner in such a closet. Rather, build the wall of the closet parallel to the existing wall and then angle into the existing wall at the corner or 10 to 12 inches away from a door. This makes the closet less noticeable. You can put a bifold door in the long wall of a closet only 24 inches deep, or you can put a single door on the sloping end for a walk-in closet.

FIREPLACES AND STOVES

If you add a fireplace to your renovation, it is important to have some way of bringing exterior air into the fireplace for combustion. Otherwise, it will simply suck warm air out of the house. A bewildering variety of fireplace and stove designs in a wide price range is available.

You must consider several things when determining where to install a fireplace or stove. If a stove

engineer. In most brick houses, you can either use an existing fireplace, install an insert, or place a stove in front of a fireplace. Rarely do rehabbers place a stove in the center of a room because of the difficulty of constructing a flue chase up through the house. Also, rehabbers rarely create an outside air supply for a fireplace, when all it really requires is the removal of a few bricks. Usually, the total duct length for outside air is limited to 20 feet, and the vertical height must be at least 3 feet below the flue termination.

The most difficult aspect of installing a new fireplace, insert, or stove is deciding where and how to run the chimney system. If you are installing an insert or stove in front of an old fireplace, then the flue will be the existing flue or will be inside the existing flue. Many old coal inserts were not lined. If the chimney is a straight drop, you can buy a new stainless steel single-wall flue pipe, connect it on the roof, and drop it down the old flue to connect to your insert.

Most chimney flues have bends, such as a first-floor flue bending around a fireplace on the second floor. Commonly, the existing unlined flue is 8

FIGURE 25-1. *The 10-foot rule.*

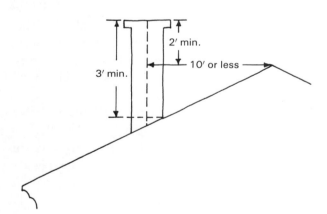

FIGURE 25-1A. *When the horizontal distance from the center of the chimney to the peak of the rook is 10 feet or less.*

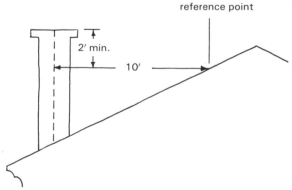

FIGURE 25-1B. *When the horizontal distance from the center of the chimney to the peak of the roof is greater than 10 feet.*

is installed in a room with carpet or vinyl flooring, a fireproof surface is needed around the stove. If it is placed in a corner or on a wall, the wall must be protected with fireproof material. If it is installed outside the wall, you should consult an architect or

inches square. This means the largest pipe you can get down it is 6 inches, which is not acceptable for most inserts or stoves. If you have a crooked flue, you can either construct another flue chase or reline the existing one. Discuss the possibilities with a mason or investigate the various methods of lining the flue with clay.

We suggest that you calculate the cost of heating your house with and without a fireplace. In most areas, you can use a gas log in an existing opening from which a coal or gas insert was removed. Even if you cannot use a gas log in an unlined flue, you can insert the thinner flexible stainless steel flue pipe (which is too thin for burning wood) into most flues, even if they are not straight. Make sure that you seal the pipe at the bottom before installing a gas log.

Never install a fireplace in a slipshod or illegal manner. We have seen more than one rehab go up in flames because of poorly installed fireplaces or unlined flues. If you use an unlined flue, creosote builds up in it and catches on fire. The pressure of that fire can send flames through any cracks or missing mortar in the chimney and start a fire in your attic. It may burn fiercely for some time before you know you have a fire. In many areas, you have to have a permit to install a fireplace. Most fire inspectors will not approve an installed fireplace without looking at the flue or flue chase before it is covered up.

Follow the manufacturer's instructions when installing a fireplace insert or stove. Make sure you get it level and construct the flue correctly. Keep in mind our recommendation for an exterior air supply. In many cases, you may install a new "zero clearance" fireplace system directly against an exterior brick wall (or a stud wall) and construct a flue chase. We have worked on row houses where we simply knocked out the old flues and built in modern zero clearance fireplaces with new flues and chases. The most complicated part of this process is deciding where and how to run the chimney system. Accurately figuring out where you want the chimney to penetrate the upper floors and the roof, and whether the flue will be straight or offset, will determine whether you have extensive work ahead of you and how much material is needed. Straight installations are usually the most economical option.

You cannot use existing chimneys to install zero clearance fireplaces, because all the components of this type of fireplace must usually be made and approved by the manufacturer and installed as one

unit. Also, zero clearance fireplaces usually require an 8-, 10-, or 12-inch flue, which will not fit in an existing chimney.

A critical issue in installing a chimney system is that the chimney must be enclosed in what is called a *chimney chase,* which is a fireproof vertical box-like structure. Most building codes require that the chase be drywalled on the inside with ⅝-inch fire-resistant drywall and that it not be broken or interrupted by any joists.

To determine the materials required, start by measuring the height of your roof above the bottom of the fireplace and the pitch of the roof. If you know the distance from the peak to the fireplace plus any curve or offset pieces, you can determine the number of pieces needed to create the chimney. The pitch is needed to determine which type of roof cap (the piece that fits on your roof and holds the pipe vertically) you need. Find out what your local building codes specify for minimum chimney height above the roof. Most major building codes in the United States are based on the 10-foot rule — that is, if the horizontal distance from the center of the chimney to the peak of the roof is 10 feet or less, the top of the chimney must be at least 2 feet above the peak of the roof and not less than 3 feet above the highest point where it passes through the roof (see Figure 25-1). If the horizontal distance from the center of the chimney to the peak of the roof is more than 10 feet, a chimney height reference point is established on the surface of the roof 10 feet from the center of the chimney in a horizontal plane. The top of the chimney must be at least 2 feet above this reference point but never less than 3 feet above the highest point where it passes through the roof.

A zero clearance fireplace can be installed right up against any wall; if this is a brick wall, you do not need to drywall the brick side of the flue chase, which makes for a slightly easier installation in brick rehabs. This also reduces the distance that the fireplace sticks out into the room. We commonly build bookshelves on each side of the fireplace if it is installed in the narrow end of the room or put the fireplace between two windows so that it is not an obvious intrusion into the middle of the room. Most zero clearance fireplaces come with double-wall pipe; you need to find out if this is acceptable in your location. You also must build a hearth in front of the fireplace. Typically, the hearth must be 18 inches out from the fireplace and 6 inches to each side of the firebox. Most zero clearance fireplaces include a hearth extension, which is required to protect the floor directly in front of the fireplace.

Bette Wahlfeldt's *Home Remodeling* (TAB Books, 1984) includes a very detailed chapter on how to install zero clearance fireplaces. Manufacturers also supply complete instructions on installing these fireplaces.

FINISHING YOUR PROPERTY FOR SALE

If you are renovating your property for sale, you will be on the lookout for prospective buyers throughout the renovation process and will probably contract with a real estate agent long before the project is done. Naturally, renovators tend to be anxious about the sale of a property as they renovate, and they are usually anxious to impress others with the progress being made. It is tempting to invite potential clients in for a sneak preview, but unless a buyer appears with a check in hand and is on a one- or two-day layover en route to Tokyo, it is advisable to wait until the structure has been completely renovated and cleaned before opening the door.

This does not mean that you cannot bring people in before everything in the house is done. But keep in mind that asking a client to visualize what a certain room will look like when the remaining strips of wallpaper are hung may result in a much lower purchase offer than would be made if he or she saw the room when the wallpapering was done.

Two books might be helpful if you are rehabbing for resale: Jones, Cury, and Cury's *Restore Your Future: A Profit Guide to Renovation* (Cury-Jones Publishers, 1980) and Sam and Mary Weir's *How We Made a Million Dollars Recycling Great Old Homes* (Contemporary Books, 1979).

One thing to avoid is decorating too extensively. You should select those decorating projects that will have the maximum upgrade effect and bring the largest profit at resale but cost the least. This also goes for the general rehab of a building. We assume you will bring the building up to some standard with new plumbing, electrical, and heating equipment. Keeping within a budget while making high-quality improvements in the home will beat an inexpensive cover-up anytime.

The repair, replacement, and refinishing of floors is one of the most important parts of house renovation for resale. This should be done last to prevent the floors from getting scratched during renovation. Generally, carpet and old floor coverings in kitchens and bathrooms should be replaced. Even if wood floors have been overlaid with carpet or tile and are in good shape, the old coverings should be removed and the floors refinished. A potential purchaser can usually visualize how the rooms will look carpeted, or with area rugs, if that is his or her preference.

If the house has hardwood parquet floors in the entryway, ceramic or marble tile floors in the kitchen, or slate or marble floors in the entryway or bathroom, you should investigate the cost of repair and restoration before you tear out these items. Repairing, cleaning, and refinishing any of these floors probably requires a craftsman, but the cost entailed should, in the end, be recouped in a higher house purchase price.

Kitchens and bathrooms are a problem because of cabinets, floors, and wallpaper. You need to balance what the purchaser may want against the cost to you and what you can do with the amount of money you have to finish the building. Many builders tend to finish kitchens in very traditional patterns and colors and use wood cabinets (such as lightly stained oak). European laminate cabinets have been popular because they are inexpensive, but be aware that this may be a fad. Others tend to leave the kitchen decoration until last and hope they can get a buyer who will specify the wallpaper and type of cabinets he or she wants. For the most part, though, the cabinets will have to go in before the house goes on the market. How far you go in selecting paint, wallpaper, floor covering, appliances, and lighting fixtures can be a difficult question.

In some older homes, there may be a fireplace in almost every room, so you will have to decide which ones to restore to working order and which to close up and use only as decorative appointments. Repairs to existing chimneys and fireplaces can be costly, and a fireplace in every room can seriously detract from the building's energy efficiency. Fireplaces in living rooms, dining rooms, dens, and master bedrooms probably should be left as, or restored to be, working fireplaces. If you put a gas log in a fireplace with a flue damper, nothing prevents you from turning that fireplace into a wood-burning one at a later date. If we have a home with a large number of beautiful fireplaces and mantels with none of the flues lined, we turn them into gas log fireplaces so that we will not have to deal with fixing the flues. We make sure that the potential buyer understands that he or she is buying unlined flues and cannot turn the fireplaces into wood-burning ones without lining the flues and getting a fire permit.

Any fireplace left as a nonfunctional fireplace should be sealed off to prevent it from being used and to help retain heat in the building. Fireplaces should be sealed off in the chimney rather than at the fireplace opening. Placing andirons and logs inside any fireplace, whether it works or not, can give an aesthetic lift to any room. Chimneys that are lined and working should be swept by a chimney sweep, and the cleaning certificate should be presented to prospective buyers. Wooden mantels should be stripped and repainted or refinished to the natural wood grain.

If you completely gut the building, the basement will be a showcase for prospective buyers because of the new plumbing, wiring, and heating and air-conditioning systems. They also can see repairs to joists and beams. In a nongut rehab, you should make the basement look as much like a total gut rehab as possible, with all new utilities and systems. Make sure that you add adequate lighting and safe stairs to the basement. The same goes for the attic.

Your rehab should include a separate laundry room and as much storage as you can get into the house. Each of these areas should be well lighted and have easy access. Laundry rooms are usually small, but even if the laundry room is in the basement, the following rules should apply:

1. Make it as large as possible.

2. Clean it thoroughly, repairing the windows, floor, and walls.

3. Cover the floor with a light, serviceable linoleum.

4. Paint the walls white or cover them with bright wallpaper.

5. Install a functional, inexpensive light fixture, making sure that there are sufficient electrical outlets available.

6. Install a shelf over the washer and dryer space and other shelves for extra supplies.

Remember that a clean, bright laundry room is an asset that will help sell the building.

High ceilings are an impressive aspect of a house and should be retained. Adequate lighting and attractive fixtures should be included. We particularly like 52-inch five-bladed fans with fancy light kits because they usually cost less than very fancy light fixtures. You should install a fancy light fixture in the entryway or in a formal dining room.

Entryways and foyers are usually small but very important features in any house restoration or renovation. Unless you are dealing with an old home with an impressive hall-like foyer, renovation must be simple but attractive. It is important to create a good first impression for prospective buyers who are entering the home. We tend to follow a fairly standard procedure in dealing with the entryway or foyer. If it can be restored, we restore it. Otherwise, we renovate it in some way that complements the shape of the space and the home itself. We also tend to splurge on the wallpaper in the foyer and first-floor bathroom because they tend to be the first things prospective buyers look at. Distinctive lighting in the foyer is important for the same reason. If there is any stained glass in the foyer or along the stairs, you should retain it or replace it with new stained glass.

An important consideration in any project is determining what to remove and what to add. Many rehabs include poorly constructed bookshelves or storage spaces that detract from the house. Any additions to the house should complement the original design. If they do not, they are better removed or left undone.

You may discover many hidden treasures in a structure that you are renovating. Sometimes houses are full of antiques such as stained-glass windows and old doors, tools, and furniture. If you are modernizing a house, you may wish to sell all of these things. Antique dealers will be glad to take most of them off your hands. But we urge you to hold on to as many as you can until you have finished the rehab. You will find that some of them, if refinished and repaired, will fit right back into the house. Underneath dozens of coats of varnish, dirt, and dust, you might find furniture made of rosewood, teak, or some other valuable wood. Or you may find boxes of door hardware or lock mechanisms that will be invaluable once you start your rehab.

References

NEW

Coen, Patricia. *Closets: Designing and Organizing the Personalized Closet.* New York: Weidenfeld & Nicholson, 1988.

Coleman, Peter. *Wood Stove Know-How: How and Why to Use One.* Pownal, Vermont: Garden Way Publishing, 1974.

Fireplaces and Wood Stoves. Alexandria, Virginia: Time-Life Books, 1981.

Flagler, Gordon. *The North American Wood Heat Handbook.* New York: Scribners, 1982.

Harrington, Geri. *Fireplace Stoves, Hearths, and Inserts: A Coal and Wood-Burner's Guide and Catalog.* New York: Harper & Row, 1980.

Jones, Robert. *Fireplaces: Adding, Improving, Heat Saving Systems, Wood Stoves.* Passaic, New Jersey: Creative Homeowner Press, 1980.

Kauffman, Henry J. *Early American Andirons and Other Fireplace Accessories.* Nashville: Thomas Nelson, 1974.

Self, Charles R. *Wood Heating Handbook.* Blue Ridge Summit, Pennsylvania: TAB Books, 1977.

Chapter 26

RESTORATION AND REHABILITATION OF THE GROUNDS

Once you have repaired, replaced, or restored all the internal and external components of the house, it is time to turn your attention to the grounds. Outdoor activities have become a very important part of American life, and most home owners want to provide space for such activities. Your home probably has at least one covered porch. You may wish to restore or enlarge this structure. Porches are frequently on the front of the house, and you may wish to build a deck or a patio on the back. You also will probably need to have some landscaping done. If you did a fairly extensive renovation, it is likely that the grounds were torn up by trucks and other heavy equipment. In this chapter, we discuss what you can do to make the outside of your house more useful and attractive.

PORCHES

Sometimes porches extend all along the front of the house and there is a good deal of room for sitting and visiting. Most porches have at least some wooden parts and might even be constructed entirely of wood. Over the years, parts of the structure may have rotted or come loose and will need to be repaired.

The first thing to do is to make a careful inspection of the porch. Look for signs of settling or cracking in the foundation. Old houses may not have had a very good support structure, and you may have to reinforce the foundation. Go under the porch and look at the wooden members. Are there signs of rot or termites? If things seem to be in good shape, you may just have to treat the wood with a preservative. If, however, structural members are rotten, you will have to replace them. When replacing supports, remember that untreated wood should never come into contact with the ground. The support posts should rest on concrete footings, and their ends should be treated with a preservative designed to prevent rot. The same is true for the bottom step if the steps to your porch are made of wood. We use only treated lumber in porch and deck construction.

Inspect the skirting that hides the area beneath the porch. If it is made of wood, it may be rotten near the ground. If this is the case, you should probably remove the rotten pieces and replace them. Any wood that will come into contact with the ground must be treated with a preservative and should have plastic sheeting beneath it. Inspect the columns, railings, balusters, and stairs for dry rot and termites. You can replace the rotten wood or try to fix it with epoxy wood fillers. All open joints should be treated with a preservative, caulked, and painted.

If the porch deck is made of wood, at least some pieces of the flooring are probably loose, cracked, or in need of replacement. The porch's flooring is much like that in the house. The boards will usually be tongue-and-groove and will need to be replaced using the same techniques discussed in Chapter 24. Once you have repaired the deck, paint it with a good-quality deck paint. This will prevent moisture problems and will last longer under traffic than regular paint. If the deck is a concrete slab and is in good shape, you can paint it with a quality deck paint or a wax paint. If there are tiles on the slab, you may need to replace them or cement them in place if they are loose. The techniques you learned in Chapter 24 will serve you well here.

Inspect the ceiling of the porch. Older porch ceilings are frequently made of narrow tongue-and-groove lumber that may need to be replaced. Paint the ceiling with outdoor house paint. The roof also requires careful inspection. Repair the porch roof as you would the roof on the rest of the house. Porch roofs often have a low pitch and are covered with roll roofing. You can combine repairs to the porch roof with any repairs that are required on the rest of the roof.

If you have to replace the porch entirely, you may be able to salvage many of the important structural and ornamental pieces for later use. If you have any thoughts about altering the design of the porch, check the local covenants, as the new porch might have to match the structural styling of the rest of the house.

DECKS

Decks are usually built off the back of the house and level with the interior floors on that wall. Sometimes they are placed at the second-floor level, on a third-floor flat roof, or built out over a hill. Decks on roofs should not use the existing roof for support; they should rest on brick walls or posts going to the foundation. Low-level decks are usually supported on concrete piers or on posts that are embedded in concrete footings. Extra steps must be taken to ensure proper drainage.

The first step in planning a deck is to check the local ordinances and building codes. You may find that there are limitations on size, visibility, and materials, and on how close to the property line the deck can be built.

Situate the deck so that you have easy access to it. This may mean opening up another door to the outside or planning some other method of access. Most decks are placed on the back of the house, which is more private, but that doesn't have to be the case unless your local building codes say so. If your house has a back door and steps down to the ground, this might be the perfect place for the deck. Consider enlarging the door opening to accommodate a large patio-type sliding door. Once your deck is done, the increase in the glass area will allow you to gaze out onto your creation.

Materials

Decks are usually constructed of wood, but you must also consider fasteners, other fittings, and the structures on which the deck will rest.

Several types of wood are appropriate for decks. A good deal of useful information is available from the Western Wood Products Association in Portland, Oregon, and in the publication *How to Build a Deck* from the Wolman chemical preservatives company (which should be available from any Wolman dealer). In general, wood must be purchased with an eye to its primary function in the total construction project. For example, the wood that you use for structural members must be high in bending strength or stiffness. The wood that you use for the surface of the deck must not warp, and the wood for the supports must not be subject to pests or rot. In general, western red cedar and redwood are recommended for the surface and for railings because they resist warping, rotting, and shrinking. Ash, Douglas fir, and southern pine are good for structural members because they have good longitudinal strength. We recommend treated southern pine as being most cost-effective. Using the same type of wood for all parts of the deck is okay if it is a good all-around outside wood such as western red cedar or redwood. In fact, lumber supply outlets frequently sell deck kits that are made up of these types of wood.

Deck kits contain all the wood that is needed to make a deck of specified dimensions. Some deck wood is called treated, CCA, or Wolmanized wood. This wood has been pressure-treated with a chemical preservative. It is often less expensive than redwood or red cedar, but it does not have the same look as these other woods, especially soon after construction. All wood ages and changes color over time. Wolmanized lumber frequently has a peculiar light green color that usually fades with time. Pressure-treated lumber also shrinks and cracks more than cedar and redwood. On large decks requiring six-by-six posts we typically use cedar to avoid the twisting and cracking.

Construction

Once you have decided on the deck design and have checked it out with the local building commission, you are ready to begin. The first step is the preparation of the site. All large rocks, trees, and shrubs must be removed, and the ground must be prepared so that there is good drainage away from the house.

The next step is to mark off the area to be covered by the deck with string and batterboards. Batterboards are made of scrap lumber and are driven into the ground at the corners of the deck area. When the string is connected between the batterboards and the house, it will give you a good idea of what the deck will look like when it is finished. The strings also will help you establish where excavation for posts will have to be done. You can use the triangle method for determining if you have squared up the string. Measure down the house wall 4 feet from the place where the string is attached, then measure down the string 3 feet from that point. If the measurements are square, then the length of the remaining side of the triangle should be 5 feet. If this doesn't measure 5 feet, the string is not square and needs to be adjusted.

Prepare the site by removing all the sod and covering this area with polyethylene to prevent weeds from growing up through the deck when it is finished. After you have dug the post holes, cover the sheet with gravel or landscaping bark to hold it in place.

Locate and dig the holes for the footings. Some type of footing is required to transfer the load of the deck to the ground. Most posts are set back from the front edge of the deck by 18 to 24 inches so that they are not visible when the deck is finished. The size and number of footings will be determined by the size of the deck and the load it is expected to carry. For most decks, footings are placed on 4- or 5-foot centers all around the perimeter. The holes for the footings should be at least 30 inches deep; make sure they extend below the

frost line. If you live in the far north, this may mean going down as far as 4 feet. Your local agricultural extension agent or the National Weather Service can be of help to you here. The building codes in your area will be quite specific about the dimensions of the footings, so you need to check them.

There are a number of ways to create footings. The post can be put down into the hole and the concrete poured around it, or the footing can be poured and the post set on top of it. Pouring the footing around the post is not recommended because eventually the post will rot at the level of the concrete and the whole thing will have to be replaced. It is also difficult to set forms so the pier extends 6 inches above ground. It is better to dig the hole, make a square box with the same dimensions as the hole and at least 6 inches above the ground level, and then pour in the concrete. Allow the concrete to cure for at least five days before attempting to install the posts. The posts can be attached to a pin, corner angle, or post anchor previously set into the concrete. It is important that the ends of the post be thoroughly treated with a preservative before being set in place.

Another method we often use is to wait to do the footings until after you have built the deck's structural members. This will ensure that the footings will be placed exactly where they are supposed to go. Of course, if the deck is large, it will be difficult to support it all in a level position until the posts are in.

Once the posts are in place, find the desired height of the deck and attach the beams to the inside and outside of the posts. The best method is to start at the house and tack the beams to the posts. After you have an entire beam run up, check it for levelness. When you are satisfied that the beam run is level, attach the beam to the post using three or four lag screws at each post. All the remaining beams are attached in this manner. Beams can also be set on the post or on notches cut into the post.

Attach the joists to the posts, beginning with the skirt joist closest to the house. Set the joists 16 inches on center, or as specified by code. Where the joists cannot be attached to the posts or if you have cut the posts off level with the bottom of the deck floor, you will have to use joist hangers or toenail the joists to the top of the beams if they sit on them.

If you did cut off the posts, this is the time to install the posts for the railings. These can be bolted to the outside of the beams or to the joists. Then add the rails, and end with a suitable top rail.

Now it is time to add the deck surface. You can make a number of different designs depending on how you lay the boards. The easiest method is to lay the boards perpendicular to the joists. Attach them with 16d hot-dipped galvanized nails. Make sure that you separate the decking by ¼ inch to allow for shrinkage and, in some cases, expansion. This can be done with the use of a spacer board. Be very careful when setting the decking to keep the A side up on every board (review the lumber grading section in Chapter 8) and keep an eye on the wetness of the lumber. Deck lumber is stored outside, and the boards on the outside of the stack will be wetter than those on the inside. They will therefore shrink more: Adjust your spacing accordingly.

Stairs are usually easy to construct, because you can purchase precut stringers and attach them to the deck. Then attach the treads to the stringers. Remember that the stringers should rest on a concrete footing.

When your deck is finished and before it gets much use, treat it with a good grade of water-repellent preservative. This is especially important if the deck is made of CCA-treated lumber. Even redwood and cedar will last much longer if you treat them. Repeat the treatment about every five years. For more detailed information, see the reference list at the end of this chapter.

PATIOS

If you do not like the idea of a wooden deck, you may prefer a patio instead. A patio can be made of all sorts of materials, but concrete, brick, and flagstone are the usual choices. Whichever you choose, you will have to start by preparing a bed for the patio surface.

Begin by digging out the area to be covered to a depth of about 4 inches. If you are going to pour a concrete slab, make sure that the area is smooth and that there is a gentle slope of about ¼ inch per foot of patio. If the patio is not attached to the house, the slope should be from the middle of the area outward in all directions. This will ensure that water will run off the surface.

If you are going to use brick for the patio, it is a good idea to set the bricks on a layer of sand. You can establish the border by setting the bricks on edge in trenches that are about 5¾ inches deep. The remainder of the bricks can be set in whatever pattern you wish, as long as you leave a uniform space between them. After all the bricks are down, set them in place by sweeping sand over them until all the cracks are filled. You can mix mortar in with the sand for a slightly stronger structure. A good rain will take care of the rest.

Flagstones can be set down in much the same way, except that the depth of the cut in the ground needs to be only about 2 inches, or the thickness of the stone. After the stone is set where you want it, wet it down with a hose. Then mix 1 part portland cement with 3 parts sand and sweep that over the stone, filling all the cracks. Wet down the surface again to clean off the stone and let the cement set. If you have large stones, you might consider setting the entire patio or walkway in cement.

GARAGES

Older homes often do not have a garage, and, if they do, the garage is usually small and not very deep. If you have a one-car garage and you want to have a two-car garage, you will have to tear down the existing structure or add to it. If the garage is made of wood, it will probably be much easier to tear it down and start over. If it is brick and matches the house, you will probably want to leave it as is and park one of your cars outside. The door opening in older garages often is not square; in fact, you may not be able to close the door because of this. If you wish to keep the garage and perhaps add a new door with an automatic opener, you will have to square up the building and add braces to prevent further sagging. If an older garage is too small, or if you wish to tear it down and build a new one, investigate some of the kits sold by some lumber dealers. These contain all the materials you need to build a one- or two-car garage.

SIDEWALKS AND DRIVEWAYS

As you walk around your house, you may discover that the walks or driveway have cracked or that age has caused them to deteriorate so badly that they must be replaced. Be aware that the city probably owns the land on which your sidewalk rests, and it has a strong interest in what you do to it. Check the local building codes to make sure that you can make repairs yourself and what the specifications of those repairs are. If repair or replacement is okay, the following advice might be of some help.

If a sidewalk or driveway is badly broken, it is probably a good idea to replace it. You can usually break the large pieces into smaller ones using a 16-pound sledgehammer. Once that is done, you will have to prepare the ground before you pour new concrete. If the soil where you plan to lay the walk is already compact and free of excess moisture, you can pour the concrete directly onto it. If that is not the case, you must put down a 4- to 6-inch layer of gravel or crushed rock.

Use two-by-fours to make your forms for sidewalks and two-by-sixes for driveways. Most walks are made up to 4 inches thick and drives up to 6 inches. Support the forms about every 3 feet with two-by-four stakes driven into the ground beside them. Put linseed oil on the forms so that they will not stick to the concrete when you are done.

Make sure that you allow for drainage by building in a slope of ½ inch per foot of width. The slope should be away from the buildings. This is particularly important for a driveway, especially if it butts up against the foundation of the house. To allow for expansion of a driveway or walkway, place joints every several feet. Make these with a fiber divider board placed between the forms about every 10 feet for a driveway and every 5 feet for a sidewalk. Your city codes may have some specific instructions for this process.

FENCES

People build fences for many reasons, such as land-scaping, making a windbreak, or keeping the kids in or the neighbor's dog out. Whatever your reasons, though, building a fence is a good do-it-yourself project.

Fences can be constructed of many different materials, and the work required is related to the type of material used. For example, a fence made of brick will require a good deal more skill and effort than one made of wood or wire. In this section, we assume that you will be using wood for your fence. If you choose to use some other material or you wish to use a technique not described here, consult the references at the end of this chapter for assistance.

Components

A traditional fence consists of posts, rails, and slats. The posts hold the fence up, the rails extend between the posts, and the slats fill in the space between the rails. Fences can be made of the same types of wood as decks, and the same considerations of structural strength and weathering qualities are important in the decision of what type of wood to use. Building supply stores often sell premade fences, which are usually constructed in sections of rails and slats. All that is left for you to do is to set the posts and attach the sections to them.

A word of caution: The old saying "Good fences make good neighbors" may not always be true. Should you misjudge the boundaries of your property and put your fence in your neighbor's yard, you could cause a lot of problems. It is a good idea and common courtesy to consult your neighbor before you begin the project. The two of you can discuss where the fence should go and what materials are acceptable to both of you. Remember that fence ethics call for the finished side of the fence to face your neighbor, not you. That's why many people spend the extra money on an alternating slat fence, so that both sides are identical. Before beginning construction, it is also important to check the local building codes. Some areas have specific rules about fence building.

Setting the Posts

If you use prefab fencing, the spacing of the posts will be determined by the length of the sections. If you are building your fence from scratch, other considerations are the height of the fence, the weight of the material, and the strength of the posts. In most board fences, posts are set at 8 feet on center. Chain-link fence posts are often set 10 feet apart, and picket fences typically have posts 4 feet apart.

The basic techniques for setting fence posts are the same as those for installing posts used to support a deck, except the fence post is usually embedded in the cement footing. A cement footing surrounding the post is not necessary, but if the post is not set in concrete, it will rot and need to be replaced sooner than if it was set in concrete. In either case, it is wise to use posts that have been pressure-treated to prevent rot. If you use redwood or cedar posts, this may not be necessary, but it is still a good idea to treat the wood with a waterproofer before setting the posts in the ground. Many people mistakenly believe that cedar doesn't rot. It does; it just takes longer to do it than other kinds of wood.

Assembling the Fence

Attaching the rails to the posts and the slats to the rails is a straightforward task requiring only simple carpentry skills. Remember to use galvanized nails to prevent rusting and rust stains. When the fence is finished, you can either paint it, stain it, or allow it to weather naturally.

References

OLD

Wall, James C. *Porches and Fonts.* London: W. Gardner, Darton & Co., 1912.

NEW

Anderson, L. O. *Wood Decks: Construction & Maintenance.* New York, Sterling Publishing Co., 1977.

Beckstrom, Bob. *Deck Plans.* San Francisco: Ortho Books, 1985.

Better Homes & Gardens Deck & Patio Projects You Can Build. Des Moines, Iowa: Meredith Corp., 1977.

Day, Richard. *How to Build Patios & Decks.* New York: Harper & Row, 1976.

Decks: How to Build. Menlo Park, California: Lane Publishing, 1973.

Decks: How to Plan and Build. Menlo Park, California: Lane Publishing, 1980.

Decks & Patios. New York: Bantam Books, 1976.

Do-It-Yourself Decks, Patios, Fences, Walks. Des Moines, Iowa: Meredith Corp., 1989.

Hamilton, Geoff. *Design & Build a Patio or Terrace.* Newton Abbot, England: David & Charles, 1985.

How to Design & Build Decks & Patios. San Francisco: Ortho Books, 1950.

Meyers, L. Donald. *Expanding the Living Space in Your Home: A Guide to Remodeling Basements, Attics, Garages & Porches.* Englewood Cliffs, New Jersey: Prentice-Hall, 1976.
_____. *The Complete Backyard Planner.* New York: Scribners, 1985.
_____. *Designing & Building a Deck.* Englewood Cliffs, New Jersey: Prentice-Hall, 1988.

Nulsen, David R. *How to Build Patios, Porches, Carports and Storage Sheds for Mobile Homes.* Beverly Hills: Trail-R-Club of America, 1973.

Porches, Decks & Fences. Alexandria, Virginia: Time-Life Books, 1988.

Porches & Patios. Alexandria, Virginia: Time-Life Books, 1981.

Ramsey, Dan. *The Complete Book of Fences.* Blue Ridge Summit, Pennsylvania: TAB Books, 1983.
_____. *Fences, Decks & Other Backyard Projects.* Blue Ridge Summit, Pennsylvania: TAB Books, 1988.

Schuler, Stanley. *The Complete Terrace Book.* New York: Macmillan, 1974.

Sunset's Patios & Decks. Menlo Park, California: Lane Publishing, 1979.

The Workbench Treasury of Decks, Patios, Gazebos & More. Kansas City: Modern Handcraft, Inc., 1984.

Glossary

ATTIC VENTILATORS. In houses, screen openings provided to ventilate an attic space. They are located in the soffit area as inlet ventilators and in the gable end or along the ridge as outlet ventilators. They can also consist of power-driven fans used as an exhaust system. See also *Louver*.

BACKFILL. To replace excavated earth into a trench around and against a basement foundation.

BASE OR BASEBOARD. A board placed against the wall around a room next to the floor to finish properly between floor and plaster.

BASE MOLDING. Molding used to trim the upper edge of interior baseboard.

BASE SHOE. Molding used next to the floor on interior baseboard. Sometimes called a carpet strip.

BATTEN. Narrow strips of wood used to cover joints or as decorative vertical members over plywood or wide boards.

BEAM. A structural member transversely supporting a load.

BEARING WALL. A partition that supports any vertical load in addition to its own weight.

BLIND-NAILING. Nailing in such a way that the nail heads are not visible on the face of the work—usually at the tongue of matched boards.

BRACE. An inclined piece of framing lumber applied to a wall or floor to stiffen the structure. Often used on walls as temporary bracing until framing has been completed.

BRICK VENEER. A facing of brick laid against and fastened to sheathing of a frame wall or tile wall construction.

BUILT-UP ROOF. A roofing composed of three to five layers of asphalt felt laminated with coal tar, pitch, or asphalt. The top is finished with crushed slag or gravel. Generally used on flat or low-pitched roofs.

BUTT JOINT. The junction where the ends of two timbers or other members meet in a square-cut joint.

CASEMENT FRAMES AND SASH. Frames of wood or metal enclosing part or all of the sash, which may be opened by means of hinges affixed to the vertical edges.

CASING. Molding of various widths and thicknesses used to trim door and window openings at the jambs.

CHECKING. Fissures that appear with age in many exterior paint coatings; at first superficial, but in time may penetrate entirely through the coating.

COLLAR BEAM. Nominal 1- or 2-inch-thick members connecting opposite roof rafters. They serve to stiffen the roof structure.

COLUMN. In architecture: A perpendicular supporting member, circular or rectangular in section, usually consisting of a base, shaft, and capital. In engineering: A vertical structural compression member that supports loads acting in the direction of its longitudinal axis.

CONDENSATION. Beads or drops of water (and frequently frost in extremely cold weather) that accumulate on the inside of the exterior covering of a building when warm, moisture-laden air from the interior reaches a point where the temperature no longer permits the air to sustain the moisture it holds. Use of louvers or attic ventilators will reduce moisture condensation in attics. A vapor barrier under the gypsum lath or drywall on exposed walls will reduce condensation.

CONSTRUCTION, DRYWALL. A type of construction in which the interior wall finish is applied in a dry condition, generally in the form of sheet materials or wood paneling, as contrasted to plaster.

CONSTRUCTION, FRAME. A type of construction

in which the structural parts are wood or depend on a wood frame for support. In codes, if masonry veneer is applied to the exterior walls, the classification of this type of construction is usually unchanged.

COPED JOINT. See *Scribing*.

CORNER BEAD. A strip of formed sheet metal, sometimes combined with a strip of metal lath, placed on corners before plastering to reinforce them. Also, a strip of wood finish three-quarters-round or angular placed over a plastered corner for protection.

CORNER BRACES. Diagonal braces at the corners of a frame structure to stiffen and strengthen the wall.

CORNICE. Overhang of a pitched roof at the eave line, usually consisting of a fascia board, a soffit for a closed cornice, and appropriate moldings.

CORNICE RETURN. That portion of the cornice that returns on the gable end of a house.

COUNTERFLASHING. Flashing usually used on chimneys at the roof line to cover shingle flashing and to prevent moisture entry.

CRAWL SPACE. A shallow space below the living quarters of a house without a basement, normally enclosed by the foundation wall.

CRIPPLE STUD. A stud that does not extend full height.

DADO. A rectangular groove across the width of a board or plank. In interior decoration, a special type of wall treatment.

DECK PAINT. An enamel with a high degree of resistance to mechanical wear; designed for use on surfaces such as porch floors.

DIRECT NAILING. To nail perpendicular to the initial surface or to the junction of the pieces joined. Also termed *face nailing*.

DOORJAMB, INTERIOR. The surrounding case into which and out of which a door closes and opens. It consists of two upright pieces, called side jambs, and a horizontal head jamb.

DORMER. An opening in a sloping roof, the framing of which projects out to form a vertical wall suitable for windows or other openings.

DOWNSPOUT. A pipe, usually of metal, for carrying rainwater from roof gutters.

DRIP. (a) A member of a cornice or other horizontal exterior-finish course that has a projection beyond the other parts for throwing off water. (b) A groove in the underside of a sill or drip cap to cause water to drop off on the outer edge instead of drawing back and running down the face of the building.

DRIP CAP. A molding placed on the exterior top side of a door or window frame to cause water to drip beyond the outside of the frame.

DRYWALL. Interior covering material, such as gypsum board or plywood, which is applied in large sheets or panels.

DUCTS. In a house, usually round or rectangular metal pipes for distributing warm air from the heating plant to rooms, or air from a conditioning device or as cold air returns. Ducts are also made of asbestos and composition materials.

EAVES. The margin or lower part of a roof projecting over the wall.

FASCIA OR FACIA. A flat board, band, or face, used sometimes by itself but usually in combination with moldings, often located at the outer face of the cornice.

FIRE-STOP. A solid, tight closure of a concealed space placed to prevent the spread of fire and smoke through such a space. In a frame wall, this will usually consist of two-by-four cross-blocking between studs.

FISHPLATE. A metal or plywood piece used to fasten the ends of two members together at a butt joint with nails or bolts. Sometimes used at the junction of opposite rafters near the ridge line.

FLASHING. Sheet metal or other material used in roof and wall construction to protect a building from water seepage.

FLUE. The space or passage in a chimney through which smoke, gas, or fumes ascend. Each passage is called a flue, which together with any others and the surrounding masonry make up the chimney.

FLUE LINING. Fire clay or terra-cotta pipe, round or square, usually made in all ordinary flue sizes and in 2-foot lengths, used for the inner lining of a chimney, with the brick or masonry work around the outside. The flue lining in a chimney runs from about a foot below the flue connection to the top of the chimney.

FLY RAFTERS. End rafters of the gable overhang supported by roof sheathing and lookouts.

FOOTING. A masonry section, usually concrete, in a rectangular form wider than the bottom of the foundation wall or pier it supports.

FOUNDATION. The supporting portion of a structure below the first- floor construction, or below grade, including the footings.

FRAMING, BALLOON. A system of framing a building in which all vertical structural elements of the bearing walls and partitions consist of single pieces extending from the top of the foundation sill plate to the roof plate and to which all floor joists are fastened.

FRAMING, PLATFORM. A system of framing a building in which floor joists of each story rest on top plates of the story below or on the foundation sill for the first story, and the bearing walls and partitions rest on the subfloor of each story.

FRIEZE. In house construction, a horizontal member connecting the top of the siding with the soffit of the cornice.

FROST LINE. The depth of frost penetration in soil. This depth varies in different parts of the country. Footings should be placed below this depth to prevent movement.

FURRING. Strips of wood or metal applied to a wall or other surface to even it and, normally, to serve as a fastening base for finish material.

GABLE. In house construction, the portion of the roof above the eave line of a double-sloped roof.

GABLE END. An end wall having a gable.

GIRDER. A large or principal beam of wood or steel used to support concentrated loads at isolated points along its length.

GRAIN. The direction, size, arrangement, appearance, or quality of the fibers in wood.

GRAIN, EDGE (vertical). Edge-grain lumber has been sawed parallel to the pith of the log and approximately at right angles to the growth rings—i.e., the rings form an angle of 45 degrees or more with the surface of the piece.

GRAIN, FLAT. Flat-grain lumber has been sawed parallel to the pitch of the log and approximately tangent to the growth rings—i.e., the rings form an angle of less than 45 degrees with the surface of the piece.

GRAIN, QUARTERSAWED. Another term for edge grain.

GROUT. Mortar made of such consistency (by adding water) that it will flow into the joints and cavities of the masonry work and fill them solid.

GUSSET. A flat wood, plywood, or similar type member used to provide a connection at the intersection of wood members. Most commonly used at joints of wood trusses. They are fastened by nails, screws, bolts, or adhesives.

GUTTER OR EAVE TROUGH. A shallow channel or conduit of metal or wood set below and along the eaves of a house to catch and carry off rainwater from the roof.

HEADER. (a) A beam placed perpendicular to joists and to which joists are nailed in framing for a chimney, stairway, or other opening. (b) A wood lintel.

HEARTWOOD. The wood extending from the pith to the sapwood, the cells of which no longer participate in the life processes of the tree.

HIP. The external angle formed by the meeting of two sloping sides of a roof.

HIP ROOF. A roof that rises by inclined planes from all four sides of a building.

INSULATION, THERMAL. Any material high in resistance to heat transmission that, when placed in the walls, ceilings, or floors of a structure, will reduce the rate of heat flow.

JACK POST. A hollow metal post with a jackscrew in one end so it can be adjusted to the desired height.

JAMB. The side and head lining of a doorway, window, or other opening.

JOINT COMPOUND. A powder that is usually mixed with water and used for joint treatment in drywall finishing. Often called Spackle.

JOIST. One of a series of parallel beams, usually 2 inches thick, used to support floor and ceiling loads, and supported in turn by larger beams, girders, or bearing walls.

LANDING. A platform between flights of stairs or at the termination of a flight of stairs.

LATH. A building material of wood, metal, gypsum, or insulating board that is fastened to the frame of a building to act as a plaster base.

LINTEL. A horizontal structural member that supports the load over an opening such as a door or window.

LOOKOUT. A short wood bracket or cantilever to support an overhang portion of a roof or the like;

usually concealed from view.

LOUVER. An opening with a series of horizontal slats so arranged as to permit ventilation but to exclude rain, sunlight, or vision. See also *Attic ventilators.*

LUMBER, BOARDS. Yard lumber less than 2 inches thick and 2 or more inches wide.

LUMBER, DIMENSION. Yard lumber from 2 inches to, but not including, 5 inches thick and 2 or more inches wide. Includes joists, rafters, studs, planks, and small timbers.

LUMBER, DRESSED SIZE. The dimension of lumber after shrinking from green dimension and after machining to size or pattern.

LUMBER, TIMBERS. Yard lumber 5 or more inches in least dimension. Includes beams, stringers, posts, caps, sills, girders, and purlins.

MANTEL. The shelf above a fireplace. Also used in reference to the decorative trim around a fireplace opening.

MASONRY. Stone, brick, concrete, hollow tile, concrete block, gypsum block, or other similar building units or materials or a combination of the same bonded together with mortar to form a wall, pier, buttress, or similar mass.

MASTIC. A pasty material used as a cement (as for setting tile) or a protective coating (as for thermal insulation or waterproofing).

MILLWORK. Generally all building materials made of finished wood and manufactured in millwork plants and planing mills. It includes items such as inside and outside doors, window and door frames, blinds, porch work, mantels, panel work, stairways, moldings, and interior trim. It normally does not include flooring, ceilings, or siding.

MITER JOINT. The joint of two pieces at an angle that bisects the joining angle. For example, the miter joint at the side and head casing of a door opening is made at a 45-degree angle.

MOLDING. A wood strip having a curved or projecting surface used for decorative purposes.

MULLION. A vertical bar or divider in the frame between windows, doors, or other openings.

MUNTIN. A small member that divides the glass or openings of sash or doors.

NONBEARING WALL. A wall supporting no load other than its own weight.

NOSING. The projecting edge of a molding or drip. Usually applied to the projecting molding on the edge of a stair tread.

OC (ON CENTER). The measurement of spacing for studs, rafters, joists, and the like in a building from the center of one member to the center of the next.

OUTRIGGER. An extension of a rafter beyond the wall line. Usually a smaller member nailed to a larger rafter to form a cornice or roof overhang.

PANEL. In house construction, a thin, flat piece of wood, plywood, or similar material framed by stiles and rails, as in a door, or fitted into grooves of thicker material with molded edges for decorative wall treatment.

PARTING STOP OR STRIP. A small wood piece used in the side and head jambs of double-hung windows to separate the upper and lower sash.

PARTITION. A wall that subdivides spaces within any story of a building.

PENNY. As applied to nails, it originally indicated the price per hundred. The term now serves as a measure of nail length and is abbreviated by the letter d.

PIER. A column of masonry, usually rectangular in horizontal cross section, used to support other structural members.

PITCH. The incline slope of a roof or the ratio of the total rise to the total width of a house—e.g., an 8-foot rise and 24-foot width is a one-third pitch roof. Roof slope is expressed in the inches of rise per foot of run.

PLATE. Sill plate: A horizontal member anchored to a masonry wall. Soleplate: Bottom horizontal member of a frame wall. Top plate: Top horizontal member of a frame wall supporting ceiling joists, rafters, or other members.

PLUMB. Exactly perpendicular; vertical.

PLY. A term to denote the number of thicknesses or layers of roofing felt, veneer in plywood, or layers in built-up materials in any finished piece of such material.

PLYWOOD. A piece of wood made of three or more layers of veneer joined with glue and usually laid with the grain of adjoining plies at right angles. Almost always an odd number of plies are used to provide balanced construction.

QUARTER ROUND. A small molding that has the

cross section of a quarter circle.

RABBET. A rectangular longitudinal groove cut in the corner edge of a board or plank.

RAFTER. One of a series of structural members of a roof designed to support roof loads. The rafters of a flat roof are sometimes called roof joists.

RAIL. Cross-members of panel doors or of a sash. Also, the upper and lower members of a balustrade or staircase extending from one vertical support, such as a post, to another.

RAKE. Trim members that run parallel to the roof slope and form the finish between the wall and a gable roof extension.

REINFORCING. Steel rods or metal fabric placed in concrete slabs, beams, or columns to increase their strength.

RIDGE. The horizontal line at the junction of the top edges of two sloping roof surfaces.

RIDGE BOARD. The board placed on edge at the ridge of the roof into which the upper ends of the rafters are fastened.

RISE. In stairs, the vertical height of a step or flight of stairs.

RISER. Each of the vertical boards closing the spaces between the treads of stairways.

ROLL ROOFING. Roofing material, composed of fiber and saturated with asphalt, supplied in 36-inch-wide rolls with 108 square feet of material. It generally weighs 45 to 90 pounds per roll.

ROOF SHEATHING. The boards or sheet material fastened to the roof rafters on which the shingle or other roof covering is laid.

ROUT. The removal of material, by cutting, milling, or gouging, to form a groove.

RUN. In stairs, the net width of a step or the horizontal distance covered by a flight of stairs.

SAPWOOD. The outer zone of wood, next to the bark. In the living tree, it contains some living cells (the heartwood contains none), as well as dead and dying cells. In most species, it is lighter colored than the heartwood. In all species, it is lacking in decay resistance.

SASH. A single light frame containing one or more panes of glass.

SCRIBING. Fitting woodwork to an irregular surface. In moldings, cutting the end of one piece to fit the molded face of the other at an interior

angle to replace a miter joint.

SHAKE. A thick hand-split shingle is resawed to form two shakes; usually edge-grained.

SHEATHING. The structural covering, usually wood boards or plywood, used over studs or rafters of a structure. Structural building board is normally used only as wall sheathing.

SHEET METAL WORK. All components of a house employing sheet metal, such as flashing, gutters and downspouts.

SHINGLES. Roof covering of asphalt, asbestos, wood, tile, slate, or other material cut to stock lengths, widths, and thicknesses.

SHUTTER. Usually lightweight louvered or flush wood or nonwood frames in the form of doors located at each side of a window. Some are made to close over the window for protection; others are fastened to the wall as a decorative device.

SILL. The lowest member of the frame of a structure resting on the foundation and supporting the floor joists or the uprights of the wall. The member forming the lower side of an opening, as a doorsill, windowsill, etc.

SLEEPER. Usually, a wood member embedded in concrete, as in a floor, that serves to support and to fasten the subfloor or flooring.

SOFFIT. Usually, the underside of an overhanging cornice.

SOIL COVER (GROUND COVER). A light covering of plastic film, roll roofing, or similar material used over the soil in crawl spaces of buildings to minimize moisture permeation of the area.

SOIL STACK. A general term for the vertical main of a system of soil, waste, or vent piping.

SOLE OR SOLEPLATE. See *Plate*.

SOLID BRIDGING. A solid member placed between adjacent floor joists near the center of the span to prevent joists from twisting.

SPAN. The distance between structural supports such as walls, columns, piers, beams, girders, and trusses.

SPLASH BLOCK. A small masonry block laid with the top close to the ground surface to receive roof drainage from downspouts and to carry it away from the building.

SQUARE. A unit of measure—100 square feet—usually applied to roofing material. Sidewall coverings are sometimes packed to cover 100 square feet and are sold on that basis.

STAIR CARRIAGE. Supporting member for stair treads. Usually a 2-inch plank notched to receive the treads; sometimes called a rough horse.

STILE. An upright framing member in a panel door.

STOOL. A flat molding fitted over the windowsill between jambs and contacting the bottom rail of the lower sash.

STORM SASH OR STORM WINDOW. An extra window usually placed on the outside of an existing one as additional protection against cold weather.

STORY. That part of a building between any floor and the floor or roof above.

STRIKE PLATE. A metal plate mortised into or fastened to the face of a door frame side jamb to receive the latch or bolt when the door is closed.

STRING, STRINGER. A timber or other support for cross-members in floors or ceilings. In stairs, the support on which the stair treads rest; also stringboard.

STRIP FLOORING. Wood flooring consisting of narrow, matched strips.

STUD. One of a series of slender wood or metal vertical structural members placed as supporting elements in walls and partitions.

SUBFLOOR. Boards or plywood laid on joists over which a finish floor is to be laid.

SUSPENDED CEILING. A ceiling system that is supported by hanging it from the overhead structural framing.

THRESHOLD. A strip of wood or metal with beveled edges used over the finish floor and the sill of exterior doors.

TOENAIL. To drive a nail at a slant with the initial surface in order to permit it to penetrate into a second member.

TONGUE-AND-GROOVED BOARDS. Boards or planks machined in such a manner that there is a groove on one edge and a corresponding tongue on the other.

TREAD. The horizontal board in a stairway on which the foot is placed.

TRIM. The finish materials in a building, such as moldings, applied around openings (window trim, door trim) or at the floor and ceiling of rooms (baseboard, cornice, and other moldings).

TRIMMER. A beam or joist to which a header is nailed in framing for a chimney, stairway, or other opening.

TRUSS. A frame or jointed structure designed to act as a beam of long span, while each member is usually subjected to longitudinal stress only, either tension or compression.

UNDERCOAT. A coating applied prior to the finishing or top coats of a paint job. It may be the first of two or the second of three coats. In some instances, it may be synonymous with the priming coat.

UNDERLAY. A material placed under finish coverings, such as flooring or shingles to provide a smooth, even surface for applying the finish.

VAPOR BARRIER. Material used to retard the movement of water vapor into walls and prevent condensation in them. Usually considered as having a perm value of less than 1.0. Applied separately over the warm side of exposed walls or as a part of batt or blanket insulation.

VENEER. Thin sheets of wood made by the rotary cutting or slicing of a log.

VENT. A pipe or duct that allows flow of air as an inlet or outlet.

WEATHER STRIPPING. Narrow or jamb-width sections of thin metal or other material to prevent infiltration of air and moisture around windows and doors.

Adapted from *New Life for Old Buildings: Appraisal and Rehabilitation,* by G.E. Sherwood (Washington, D.C.: U.S. Department of Agriculture, Forest Service, Agriculture Handbook No. 481, 1975), pp. 88-94.

Index